MODERN

ARCHITECTURE

KUWAIT

The Deutsche Nationalbibliothek lists this publication in the Deutsche Nationalbibliografie; detailed bibliographic data are available on the Internet at http://dnb.dnb.de

The research and publication of *Modern Architecture Kuwait* was proudly supported by a grant from the Kuwait Foundation for the Advancement of Sciences, and Dar al-Athar al-Islamiyyah in Kuwait.

© 2018 Niggli, imprint of Braun Publishing AG, Salenstein, Switzerland
www.niggli.ch

ISBN 978-3-7212-0958-7

First edition 2018

EDITORS:
Ricardo Camacho, Sara Saragoça Soares, Roberto Fabbri

CONTRIBUTORS:
Abdulaziz Sultan, Adel Albloushi, Ala Hason, Asseel Al-Ragam, Charles Haddad, Claudia Cagneschi, Dalal AlSayer, Edward Nilsson, Enrico Mambelli, Hisham Munir, Ismail Rifaat, Łukasz Stanek, Maath Alousi, Manar Moursi, Marisa Baptista, Michael Kubo, Naji Moujaes, Ricardo Camacho, Roberto Fabbri, Saad Al-Zubaidi, Sabah Abi-Hanna, Sabah Al-Rayes, Sara Saragoça Soares, Stig Egnell, Thorsten Botz-Bornstein, Yannis Kitanis.

ENGLISH TEXT EDITING:
Mada Media LLC, with Laura Gribbon and Lina Atalha
Reem Al-Ali
Wujdan writing + editing – Noura Alsager

PROOFREADING:
Wujdan writing + editing – Noura Alsager

BOOK DESIGN: 79ers – metadisciplinary design

Cover Image: Al-Hassawi Residential Complex, Kuwait.
Photography by Nelson Garrido © 2015
Layout by 79ers

ESSAYS, ARGUMENTS & INTERVIEWS
ON *MODERN ARCHITECTURE KUWAIT*

EDITED BY **RICARDO CAMACHO** • **SARA SARAGOÇA** • **ROBERTO FABBRI**

With generous support from

KFAS
مؤسسة الكويت للتقدم العلمي
Kuwait Foundation for the Advancement of Sciences

دار الآثار الإسلامية

Dar al-Athar al-Islamiyyah

Acknowledgements

The *Modern Architecture Kuwait* project and publication could not have been possible without the help and support of several individuals and institutions. First of all, a special thank-you must go to the Kuwait Fund for the Advancement of Sciences and to Dar al-Athar al-Islamiyyah – two Kuwaiti institutions that believed strongly in the project and supported the idea from the very beginning.

Moreover, we specially thank Sheikha Hussah Al-Salem Al-Sabah, who is ever-curious and supportive of any project that explores the realm of art.

In addition, the editors would like to express their sincerest gratitude to the following institutions, organisations, and firms for their help and support, in alphabetical order:

Al-Babtain Library, Aga Khan Trust for Culture, Aga Khan Visual Archive at MIT Libraries, Archivio di Stato di Roma, American University in Cairo, American University of Kuwait, American University of Beirut, Arab Centre for Architecture, Archives of American Art, Chadirji Foundation, CAT Group, Centre for Research Studies on Kuwait, Centro Archivi Fondazione MAXXI, Center for Gulf Studies, Cité del'Architecture et du Patrimoine, Constantinos A. Doxiadis Archives at Benaki Museum, Croatian Academy of Arts and Sciences, Dissing+Weitling, ETH gta archiv, Fondazione Franco Albini, Frances Loeb Library, GSD at Harvard University, Gulf Bank, Fundação Calouste Gulbenkian, McGill University, Montois Partners Architects, KEO International Consultants, Kuwait National Cinema Company, Kuwait Municipal Archives, Kuwait National Library, Kuwait Oil Company, National Council for Culture, Arts and Letters, Pace, Royal Institute of British Architecture, Saudi Aramco World/SAWDIA, SSH International Consultants, Swedish Centre for Architecture and Design, The British Library, University of Guelph, United Real Estate Company, RIBA Collections at V&A, Vastu Shilpa Foundation – Sangath.

The editors would also like to thank the following people for their interest and cooperation, in alphabetical order:

Ali Hussain Al-Youha (NCCAL), Adnan A. Shihab-El-Din (KFAS), Abdullah Y. Al-Ghunaim (CSRK), Abdullah Al-Bishi (NCCAL), Abdulaziz Al-Kandari, Ala'a Ali Reda (URC), Alexandre Ragois (Cité de l'Architecture et du Patrimoine), Andrea Schuler (AKAA), Angelo Bucci (Universidade de São Paulo), Annika Tengstrand (ARKDES), Amena Elezaby (Pace), Blagoja Kolev, Brad Batcheller (KEO), Caecilia Pieri (IFPO), Carla Zhara Buda (Fondazione MAXXI), Catty Wilson, Claudine Abdelmassih (ACA), Dana Aljouder, Daniel Weiss (ETH – gta), Deema Al-Ghunaim (Madeenah), Elena Albricci (Fondazione Albini), Farah Al-Nakib (AUK – CGS), Filine Wagner (ETH – gta), François Pradal, Fahed Ben Salamah, Fajer Al-Hendi, Françoise Archambeau (MPA), Giota Pavlidou, Helena Njiric (University of Zagreb), Hugo Ferreira, Ines Zalduendo (GSD, Loeb Library), Ioanna Theocharopoulou (SCE-Parsons), Ivan Rupnik (Northeastern University), Ivana Nikšic Olujić (HAZU), Jad Cortas (Notre Dame University), Lobna Montasser (AKTC), Kata Gašpar (DAZ), Khalid Al-Qamlas, Khushnu Panthaki Hoof (Sangath), Kurt Helfrich (RIBA), Paola Albini (Fondazione Albini), Par Lindstrom, Peter Mandl, Mafalda Aguiar (Fundação Calouste Gulbenkian), Marco Albini (Fondazione Albini), Marinella Celli (Università di Bologna), Martin Buxtorf, Michael Toler (AKAA), Noorah Al-Sabah, Nuno Barreiras, Rania Ghosn (MIT), Rashid Binshabib (University of Oxford), Samir Alnimr, Samer Mohammed, Sarah Behbehani, Sara Machado, Saša Begović (FGAG), Seng Kuan (Washington University in St. Louis), Shehab A. H. Shehab (NCCAL), Sue Lowry (RIBA), Takis Candilis, Tarek Shuaib (Pace), Valeria Carullo (RIBA), Vladimir Deskov, Yousef Abdulaal.

Also, we would like to thank the Dar al-Athar al-Islamiyyah team for their invaluable help and support: Abdulkareem Al-Ghadban, Osama Al-Balhan, Katherine Baker, Zeinab Tarhini, Madoura Rao, Ahmed Al-Najadah, Harvey Pinces, Ali Akashah, Fahad Al-Najadah, Syed Hashim Ali, Mustafa Rabeea, and Susan Day.

Finally, we thank our diverse contributors and interviewees on their enthusiasm and readiness to participate in our research, as well as their generosity in giving us their time, opinions, and resources.

Kuwait City aerial view, 1960s.

FOREWORD

Ricardo Camacho
Sara Saragoça Soares
Roberto Fabbri

Although our research on modern building culture in Kuwait is still ongoing, we present the essence of the debate through our carefully selected essays, arguments, interviews, and other pieces of supporting evidence. These contents offer contexts for the buildings surveyed in the previous volume. The variety of contributions from scholars, commentators, and architects attempt to give an overall impression of the diversity of interests that lie beyond the common interpretation of modernity – centred in the social imaginary and the formal idea of urbanism.

These contributions are the direct result of multiple research collaborations that took place during the process of the building selection and survey. The texts and interviews have been edited to preserve consistency of facts and references, and where necessary, the flow of the argument. All interviews have been edited for length and clarity.

Some of the stories published here in essay or interview format do not correspond to buildings or design practices referenced in the first volume of this research, assuming that the interests of many of those show the larger framework in which the specific buildings and practices are situated, and the way they were ultimately determined. These do not aim at reaching a specific level of explanation of a particular building, design process, or the local practice in general. In contrast, these essays, arguments, and interviews remain self-constrained – they expose the energy, enthusiasm, conditions, and context experienced. Moreover, they illustrate how design proposals and ideas assume a concrete reality.

KUWAIT ARCHITECTURE IMPORTS 1949–1989

The diversity of production sources that travelled to Kuwait between 1949 and 1989 generated (and continues to generate) a series of remarkable architectural-urban models. The studies, buildings, and plans produced by architects, planners, land-owners, and developers introduced substantive content to the debates on Arab town development in particular, and urbanism and architecture in the region in general.

ARTHUR ERICKSON ARCHITECTS
PROJECT PLANNING ASSOCIATES LTD. PPAL
MACKLIN L. HANCOCK
SASAKI ASSOCIATES
THE ARCHITECTS COLLABORATIVE
EDWARD NILSSON
LOUIS A. MCMILLAN
BOB BRONZE
SOUZA & TRUE
SHOOSHANIAN ENGINEERING ASSOCIATES
PHILIP JOHNSON
MARCEL BREUER ASSOCIATES
PERKINS & WILL PARTNERSHIP
GEOTECHNICAL ENGINEERS INC.
NORMANDEAU ASSOCIATES INC.
RESEARCH PLANNING INSTITUTE
SKIDMORE, OWINGS & MERRILL
FULLER & SADAO INC.
I.M. PEI & PARTNERS
LLOYD, MORGAN & JONES
WEILINGER ASSOCIATES
JOSEPH W. STICHTER
CHARLES F. BREUEL

FELIX CANDELA

AFFONSO REIDY

CANDILIS, JOSIC, WOODS
EULALIA MARQUES G. & JORGE GARCES B.
BASIL SPENCE & PARTNERS
JOHN S. BONNINGTON PARTNERSHIP
BARTLETT & GRAY ARCHITECTS
FITZROY ROBINSON PARTNERSHIP
BRIAN COLQUHOUN AND PARTNERS
FREDERICK SNOW & PARTNERS
COLIN BUCHANAN AND PARTNERS
DENYS LASDUN & PARTNERS
HOARE, LEA AND PARTNERS
COODE & PARTNERS
PETER AND ALISON SMITHSON
L.G. MOUCHEL AND PARTNERS
LESLIE MARTIN
OVE ARUP & PARTNERS
RAGLAN SQUIRE & PARTNERS
JOHN R. HARRIS ARCHITECTS
EWBANK & PARTNERS LTD.
NEWTON WATSON
MAXWELL FRY & JANE DREW
MICHAEL CARAPETIAN ASSOCIATES
FARMER & DARK ARCHITECTS
JOHN TAYLOR & SONS
SCOTT & WILSON, KIRKPATRICK & PARTNERS
WS ATKINS & PARTNERS (WSA&P)
RENDEL, PALMER & TRITTON (RP&T)
SAM JAMPEL & PARTNERS
WILSON, MASON AND PARTNERS
WHITE YOUNG PARTNERS
TRIPE AND WAKEHAM PARTNERSHIP
DEREK LOVEJOY AND PARTNERS
BUREAU D'ETUDES CORDONNIER
JEAN-ROBERT DELB
REMI LOPEZ & ASSOCIATES
GUY MÉLICOURT
JACQUES SUTOUR
BUREAU D'ARCHITECTURE HENRI MONTIOIS
MICHEL ÉCOCHARD

BRIAN BROUGHTON
DOXIADIS ASSOCIATES (DA)
DINO GEORGIOU & PARTNERS
TECHNICAL STUDIES BUREAU (TEST)
GEORGE STAMATOS
ABDUL RAOUF
AHMED MANSOUR
SAID ABDEL MONEIM
ARAB CONSULTANTS BUREAU
GEORGE HABIB EL-HAG
MICHEL HABIB EL-HAG
MAHMOUD RIAD
HASSAN FATHY

AART (ATELIER D'ARCHITECTURE, RECHERCHE, TECHNOLOGIE)
ATEA (ATELIER D'ÉTUDES ARCHITECTURALES)
LLEWELLYN-DAVIES WEEKS ASSOCIATES
ICO PARISI
FRANCO ALBINI
ALFRED ROTH
FRANCO ALBINI
IGNAZIO GARDELLA
LUIGI MORETTI
BBPR
STUDIO NERVI
RAMBALD VON STEINBÜCHEL-RHEINWALL
DORSCH CONSULT INGENIEURGESELLSCHAFT MBH
FREI OTTO
ARNE JACOBSEN
DISSING+WEITLING
JØRN UTZON
ZDRAVKO BREGOVAC
STOJAN MAKSIMOVIĆ
ENERGOPROJEKT ENGENEERING AND CONTRACTING
BLAGOJA KOLEV
MILICA ŠTERIĆ
Z. JOVANOVIĆ
JANKO KONSTANTINOV
VÁCLAV BAŠTA
RADIM BOHACEK
MICHAL HRON
KRZYSZTOF WIŚNIOWSKI
ANDRZEJ BOHDANOWICZ
RYSZARD DACZKOWSKI
EDWARD LACH
HANS ASPLUND
SUNE LINDSTROM
VBB (VATTENBYGGNADSBYRÅN/ SWECO)
BJØRN & BJØRN DESIGN MALENE BJØRN
STIG EGNELL
THURF-JELL CONSULT
REIMA AND RAILI PIETILÄ
DEVECON ARKITEKTER
NICOLAE N. ENISTEANU

PACIFIC CONSULTANTS INTERNATIONAL
KENZO TANGE (URTEC)
ASABUKI ARCHITECTS
TOSHIKAGAKU INSTITUTE

SOHEIR FARID
RAMI AL-DAHAN
MEDHAT EL-ABD
ISMAIL RIFFAT
MOHAMED RAMZY OMAR
SAYYED KARIM
OMAR AZZAM
RAYMOND GHOSN
SABA GEORGE SHIBER
SABAH ABI-HANNA
SAMI ABDUL BAKI ARCHITECTS
VICTOR SHIBER
ELIAS DANIEL
DESIGN CONSTRUCTION GROUP
ALBERT MANASSAH
MOUNIR KHATIB
FOUAD ABDUL BAKI
VAROUJ AZADIAN
ABDEL MOHSIN AL-QATTAN
FAWZI GERMANUS
SOUHAYL BATHISH
AYMAN TAJI
HASIB J. SABBAGH
GEORGE AYOUB
SAID TAWFIQ KHOURY
KHALIL MAALOUF
SAMIR THABET
VICTOR ANDRAOS
NAZIH TALEB
NABIH MAJDALANI
ROBERT WAKIM
GHASSAN KLINK
SAMI KHOURY
SAID BREIK
MARWAN KALO
CHARLES TOUFIC HADDAD
JAFAR TUKAN
BASEL HASSAN
IRAQ CONSULT
HISHAM MUNIR AND ASSOCIATES
ALA HASON
SAAD AL-ZUBAIDI
MONCEF EL-HARDI
JAMIL JADALLAH
AKRAM OGAILY
SABAH AFAS
MAKIYA ASSOCIATES CONSULTANTS
MAATH AL-ALOUSI
BALKRISHNA V. DOSHI

INTRODUCTION
Ricardo Camacho
Sara Saragoça Soares

After the first *Modern Architecture Kuwait 1949–1989*, which brought together a selection and chronology of buildings and builders, this new volume propagates debate and investigates the modes of production behind these buildings. As of the 1960s, there has been ample and growing attention on the Middle East's urbanisation, due to the seminal work of Saba George Shiber in Kuwait in 1964.[1] Most of the recently published literature on Kuwait's modernisation has sought to situate the debate in the context of urban transformation, nostalgia, social segregation, and the 'right to the city.' The debate recognises that after the discovery of oil, the country invested largely in economic and urban development, yet failed in promoting the social transformations announced by its rulers.

The debate also explores the acknowledgement of modern urbanism with the idea of the *tabula rasa*, or clean slate – the *indifference* to history. Such indifference was promptly noted by Shiber in the early 1960s, "[…] the old city was considered not to exist […] judged by the planning standards in existence then."[2] However, Shiber was very clear in finding the implications of such an approach and the motivations for urbanisation. Contradicting the discourse of authors such as Stephen Gardiner,[3] who situates the first Master Plan in the context of modernist city planning, Shiber emphasises the (little) attention given to climate, which he claims to be "the number one determinant"[4] as well as the "undue importance given to the street"[5] and the "density of population."[6] Shiber's argument becomes clear in the words of planner Charles Anthony Minoprio, who blames the lack of information available at the time, such as missing climatic, cartographic, topographic, and demographic surveys, admitting that "All we could give them was what we knew."[7]

Moreover, Minoprio takes credit for the demolition of the old town:

The first thing I saw when we got to the old town was this wall, fourteen feet high, to keep invaders out. I can't believe it would have done the job – it was only made of mud-brick. […] It was always my intention to keep things of value […] you can't drive limousines through a gateway made for carts and goats. So we had to dismiss that idea and regard the wall as demolished. But we didn't forget it. Our Green belt followed its semi-circular form […], in memory of it, and as a boundary for the new town […].[8]

Nevertheless, even without the support of prior research or design processes, Jane Drew and Ove Arup foresaw all these considerations during their first visit to Kuwait in December 1946, when they accepted the invitation to evaluate the feasibility of erecting a new town. In his report on the desert sites at Ahmadi and Fahaheel, after two weeks Ove Arup describes the local craft and knowhow in detail:

Stones of various sizes are collected from the surface of the desert by hand […] With the temperature range from 36° to 118° [°F] in the shade, and sun temperature up to 170°, precautions must be taken against the effects of hear expansion of materials.[9]

Five years later in 1952, the Building Research Station headed by George Atkinson began to collect data on Kuwait,[10] and John R. Harris accepted his commission for the Building Research Laboratories in Kaifan (1952–54).[11] By 1953, as David Oakley started to work in Kuwait, principles for environmental considerations in building design had become available. At the same time, the plans of Ahmadi and Kuwait City were drawn away from such modern considerations, retaining only the obvious fascination for the car and the rigid geometric grid of the highway. Nonetheless, Shiber brings to the centre of this debate the main urbanisation purpose of the first Master Plan: the distribution of the oil revenue to the citizens – which, according to him, led to "the largest land bonanza in history," an "epic land-trade."[12] In addition, Shiber reveals that the "lack of architectural research"[13] and the commissioning of practitioners of "inferior, instead of intelligent and skillful"[14] quality led to a city that is "unnecessarily extended in spread,"[15] and where its constituents are "set in a disproportionate building lot in relation to building bulk."[16]

However, the nature of Kuwait's urban development extends far beyond the sphere of demolition and reconstruction, and modern planning dominant ideologies of post-war Europe.[17] The necessary questions remain: Did the free Kuwaiti citizens like the reorganisation of their lives in this way? Did they ever see the experience as paternalistic? Was it a top-down decision that drastically affected their lives, one that they had become increasingly unhappy with? The importance of research and practice skills in architecture drove the attention away from planners and contractors in the search for building qualities that can resolve the "damaging results"[18] of urbanisation. During an interview, Pace co-founder Sabah Al-Rayes introduces the relevance of design process in this debate:

1. Mubarak Al-Kabeer Hospital, Kuwait, 1980. © Kuwait Oil Company Archive.

For a city that used to be completely pedestrianised, it became completely the opposite. There was no room for pedestrians. We had to shout and really raise our voices. Where is our city? Where is our city? Where did the concept of malls and all of this come from? Kuwait was already malls. If you look at the old souqs, they were all connected to each other. They were all shaded. Yes, of course, it was primitive, but all of them were integrated.[19]

Shiber also concludes his discourse on the "Growth of the Town" identifying three categories of "damaging results"; the "convenience, aesthetic and economic," claiming that "if buildings and building-groupments are too far apart, the elements of civic design depending on scale, spatial relationship, and townscape are lost."[20]

Made of Buildings

Once desert, Kuwait's bareness was gradually replaced by a modern urban landscape made of buildings and highways disseminated across the territory. Nevertheless, both buildings and highways, apart from the flatness and "indifference", remain always responsive to varied conditions of site and program in distinctive moments. In the context of Europe's post-war, Greek architect Aris Konstantinidis suggests that "there are old buildings that seem contemporary" as well as "contemporary buildings that could have been built in the past."[21] Looking at these buildings, such proposals bring architecture back to the centre of the debate on Kuwait's urbanisation, planning aside. Although the argument acknowledges the ability of buildings and infrastructure to adapt and transform conditions such as site, program, and density – the debate must also include the important contribution to form and city from the non-planners, the non-architects.

2. Interior view of Port Authority Headquarters in Shuwaikh, 2015. © Dar al-Athar al-Islamiyyah, Nelson Garrido, 2015.

3. Overview of Kuwait City from Ministries Complex in Mirqab, 2015. © Dar al-Athar al-Islamiyyah, Nelson Garrido, 2015.

The Omnipresence

The role of planning was determinant in defining a set of conditions regarding site and program over which buildings were designed and built, such as the large modern souqs built during the 1970s in the city centre.

> It's [a] very rational way of doing the city because you get parking out of the way [...] The zoning plan had multiple layers of use [per level] including [a] residential component. The top of the building has the views and the lights, so that's where you put the offices [initially residences] and so forth. People on the ground floor, that's where the arcade [was]. The first sketches for these buildings were basically just taking the program and putting it in different layers. The second set was on a larger scale and there was a concern that the buildings needed to have some traditional form [...] This is the one thing that I think the principal Louis McMillan [The Architects Collaborative] said, see if you can add something to give it more local character.[22]

However, in the case of Souq Al-Wataniya, the local consultant undermined the intentions of the planner BBPR and the architect TAC, as after value engineering, the use of the building changed.

> Unfortunately, everything was against pedestrians, against people living in the city. And I see it, as someone very proud. We did value engineering for the Mirqab project [Souq Al-Wataniya] and decided it should be a commercial building rather than for housing.[23]

Throughout similar adjustments, planning premises were misplaced and the city was left with the building and its primary motivations such as the views on the top and the arcade on the ground. These are some of the qualities that Konstantinidis evoked in his writings from 1946 when referring to modern buildings from the past. The opportunity to look at and into these buildings in such way is a contribution to the building preservation debate in Kuwait.

Saba George Shiber: A Leading Model

Between 1964 and 1990, thousands of copies of *The Kuwait Urbanization* and *Recent Arab City Growth* were distributed, and an entire generation of architects, from inside and outside the country, turned to Shiber's work for guidance and stimulation. These books recommended for, or by, the readers included all kinds of practical debate, ranging from essays, newspaper articles, and arguments, to drawings, maps, transcripts, pictures, and conference communications. In fact, the work remains a relevant contribution to understand the motivations behind the modern production of the urban landscape. Its remarkable continuity and coherence as well as its extraordinary freedom offered a direct platform for critique and debate shared between architects and urban planners that brought a full circle of compartmentalised production/knowledge in the respective fields. Following the recently published first volume of *Modern Architecture Kuwait 1949–1989*, this volume further familiarises the reader with the intellectual world to which Shiber's work had opened a door. Published in 1969, Shiber described *Recent Arab City Growth* as "[...] an arranged selection of the writer's articles appearing in the Kuwaiti and Lebanese press during 1959–1967."[24] This collection of material was meticulously prepared; even if its contents and language of publication resemble that of so-called 'little magazines,' the book has retained broad appeal.

The Contribution

The second volume of *Modern Architecture Kuwait* opens up the debate to other research interests, mostly to those who designed and built in the country between 1949 and 1989. The volume combines a selection of essays and arguments intertwined with interviews and transcripts. This collection of testimonies uncovers not only the building initiatives, but also the platform of ideas and facts that revolve around the phenomenon and that were decisive in the production and practice of architecture during this period, and critical for the present discussion. Arguments across the local conservation practices and its importance for the coming generations are developed in Adel Albloushi's essay, while Sara Saragoça Soares explores in detail the relevance of preserving the 'old new souqs.' Marisa Baptista's piece crosses into the threshold of architectural theory, postcolonial critique, and visual culture studies in the Middle East. The sources behind the production of architecture across the region are investigated in the essays of Asseel Al-Ragam and Dalal AlSayer, with the latter more focused on specific transformations that occurred in Kuwait. However, in both there is a persistency to pursue an idealised version of being modern among a newly emancipated Arab post-oil community. The spirit of Arab solidarity gained special energy following the Suez Crisis and fueled the diaspora of architects and engineers who left the Levant for the young Gulf States. This movement, which can only be compared with the Palestinian diaspora and the Eastern European migration to the region after WWII, reveal a complex interaction of influences and practices that are explored in Ricardo Camacho's piece. In parallel moments Yannis Kitanis investigates Doxiadis Associates' 'evolutionary identity' that developed through their practice, including a specific proposal for Mina Al-Ahmadi in 1975, and the multiple correspondence exchanges between Doxiadis and Shiber during the 1960s. Thorsten Botz-Bornstein revisits Reima and Raili Pietilä's work in Kuwait, specifically the Ministry of Foreign Affairs that resulted from the Seif Palace extension completed in 1983. The Atlas presented together with the chronology, buildings' survey, and biographical records exposed in the previous volume are now relevant to situate in time and place many of the exchanges and opportunities for production and innovation between the West and the Middle East. These interactions are explored within the investigations of Ricardo Camacho and Manar Moursi on the practice and interests of local architects but also through the essays of Łukasz Stanek, Michael Kubo, and Roberto Fabbri. Stanek and Kubo explore the initiative speculation and the back and forth movement from socialist Poland and the United States to the region, while Fabbri pursues pedagogy, school planning, standardisation, and prefabrication as a way to modernity.

These contributions, together with the live testimonies in the form of interviews of Maath Alousi, Charles Haddad, Ismail Rifaat, Edward Nilsson, Sabah Abi-Hanna, Hisham Munir, Ala Hason, Stig Egnell, Saad Al-Zubaidi, and Sabah Al-Rayes reveal the diverse architectural production and influences one needs to consider prior to further investigate the experience of Kuwait. •

1. Saba George Shiber, *The Kuwait Urbanization* (Kuwait: Government Printing Press, Kuwait, 1964).

2. Saba George Shiber, "Kuwait the Growth of a Town," *Middle East Forum* (1962): 57.

3. Stephen Gardiner, *Kuwait, The Making of a City* (Harlow: Longman, 1983).

4. Shiber, *Kuwait Urbanization*, 115–121 (Chapter V: The Saga of Kuwait Planning: A Critique).

5. Shiber, "Kuwait the Growth of a Town," 57–8.

6. Ibid.

7. Gardiner, *Kuwait, The Making of a City*, 35.

8. Ibid.

9. Ove Arup, "Report on Kuwait," Arup Papers, 7/45.

10. George A. Atkinson, "West Indian Houses," *Architectural Association Journal* (February 1952): 194–199.

11. J. Morris, *John R. Harris Architects* (Westerham: Hurtwood, 1984), 8.

12. Ibid.

13. Ibid.

14. Ibid.

15. Shiber, "Kuwait the Growth of a Town," 59.

16. Ibid.

17. cf. Farah Al-Nakib, *Kuwait Transformed: A History of Oil and Urban Life* (Stanford: Stanford University Press, 2016), 5–6.

18. Shiber, *Kuwait Urbanization*, 285–294 (Chapter XIII: Architecture and Urban Aesthetics in Kuwait: Significance or Superficiality).

19. Sabah Al-Rayes interview, 64–70.

20. Shiber, "Kuwait the Growth of a Town," 59.

21. Aris Konstantinidis, autobiographic notes. Muriel Emanuel, ed., *Contemporary Architects* (London: The Macmillan Press Ltd., 1980), 436–37.

22. Edward Nilsson interview, 176–180.

23. Sabah Al-Rayes interview, 64–70.

24. Saba George Shiber, *Recent Arab City Growth* (Kuwait: Government Printing Press, 1969), 1.

Old Walls and New Streets:
Modernity, Global Capital and Orientalism in Kuwait's Urbanisation History

MARISA BAPTISTA

1. Sketch of the 'New Street' Abdullah Al-Salem Street by Saba George Shiber, Kuwait City, 1964.
© *The Kuwait Urbanization*.

1. Kuwait Airways advertisement, *Architectural Review* (May 1976): 40.

Let us start with an *image*. The image is the blurred face of a gold and leather wristwatch placed on an anonymous and aseptic surface. It is the year 1976 and this image figures on a Kuwait Airways ad that reads: "At the heart of the Arab business world." The watch suggests status and wealth, but the blurred watch face, alluding to the pressing instability of time, leaves an impression somewhat confusing. Who is being addressed by this ad? "Six times a week we leave London for Kuwait. And on this flight, we take more businessmen than any other airline."[1] This *image* is an expressive trace of the urbanisation boom that initiated with the development of Kuwait as a modern state, and of the complex cultural entanglements that this territory has since ever hosted, infused in the fluid times of Modernity. In this essay, we revisit this urban development story addressing the ways in which natural and built landscape and cultural representations affect and reflect each other.

The research undertaken to support this essay has resulted in an archive of collected writings ranging from architectural reviews, opinion and research based articles, and academic writings emanating from different periods of the twentieth century and from diverse cultural locales. It stands at the threshold of architectural theory, postcolonial critique, and visual culture studies. Rather than concentrating mainly on the formal specificity of Kuwait's urban landscape, in this approach we choose to focus on the *discursive gestures* that can be gathered around Kuwait's recent production of space and urban development, including texts from theoretical critique, formal approaches in architectural projects, and cultural practices inscribed in the panorama of postmodern displacement and global capital. In this effort, this research emphasises *what has been written* about the process of urban renovation and not *what was actually built*.

At stake in the traces of the discourses imprinted on the research material are not only the voices (objectives, desires, etc.) of 'active' participants in the urbanisation of Kuwait, but also the marginal voices of those who might have felt left aside, who upheld a critical wall against what was proposed and the ways in which it would be put into practice, or who could not be or were not recruited to actively intervene in the project. In the same sense that this research is not bounded to material form, it is also not bounded to time of conception, it constitutes its discourse *a posteriori*, interested in recognising the role of physical construction in causal and consequential events in the constitution of a cultural common, instead of concentrating in actual misconceptions and disadvantages that these projects might have contained.

This project of research is as much informed by Saba George Shiber's documental masterpiece *The Kuwait Urbanization*, dating from 1964, as it is by cultural studies and postcolonial theory, i.e. the writings on Modernity and the "discourse of the West and the Rest" by Stuart Hall, and Edward Said's critical approach in *Orientalism*. These three theoretical points orchestrate a triangle that defines a strategy to approach the development of social, visual, and material cultures in Kuwait.

Not of a lesser importance are the contributions of the writings of many theorists and practitioners in the field of architecture which focus on the urban development of Kuwait spread out through time, ranging from the early 1960s to the present decade. The voices expressed in these multiple articles represent the formation of a discourse around questions that link cultural identity and the cultural and social production of the environment for everyday life. Above all this, a continuous thread of contributions marks the strengthening of a network of people dedicated to constituting a body of knowledge centred around Kuwait in a dialogue that thrives to establish a local source of cultural critique. Shiber's seminal work roots this movement of cultural affirmation. It accomplishes it's author's aims: to create a document that is able to preserve the traces that link tradition to future generations, able to resist the velocity of change and displacement in global time, to build a solid milestone that can resist cultural colonisation and homogenisation.

> An important reason that induced me to undertake this study is the provision of a record – a documentation – of the many plans, photographs, aerials and schemes which often, no sooner are they realised (or cancelled), would cease to have a trace. Considering the liberal amounts of money Kuwait expended for the preparation of all types of studies and projects, I felt it was a loss not to have a partial record of it and, therefore, a strong justification for such a compilation existed, especially as a reference to the Kuwaiti students attending universities abroad and who should, on returning to Kuwait, be able to find background material about their fast-evolved city.[2]

Through a close reading of the many voices gathered around the project of constituting Kuwait as a modern nation, what can be read throughout, is in fact the different concepts of 'project' that have driven the various interventions in the process of modernising and urbanising the old Kuwait town. A project, be it a house, a system of communication, or a whole energetic infrastructure, involves various parties; it presupposes an action that is planned and orchestrated between a body of professionals providing a service, and a pre-existing structure providing a context (e.g. rules, recommendations, parameters, licensing), a commissioning client, being a public or private entity, and finally a group or community whose lives will be affected by the action. More than analysing who the participant parties are, one must understand the relationships they establish across and with each other. The project is in itself a matter of involvement, it ushers from an affective connection to a cultural geography and territory, a matter of belonging,[3] a push of the imagination across spans of time to be able to create an *image* of this territory, an image of a past and of a future that meet in the project.

The Project of Urbanisation and Modernity

This specific project is born at the heart of Modernity, it frames the Kuwaiti landscape in the history of industrialisation and the implementation of global capital. The discovery, exploration, and commerce of oil acts as a powerful springboard to urban development. While Kuwait held, around the 1950s, a peripheral position in the advances of architectural and urban planning in the light of new technologies and everyday life-driving concepts

2. Kuwait Airways advertisement in *Architectural Review, 1976.*
© Kuwait Airways Archive.

2. Saba George Shiber, *The Kuwait Urbanization* (Kuwait: Government Printing Press, 1964), 1.

3. Belonging is here referred to as an overarching concept that explores the role played by affect and physicality in establishing the connection between cultural identification and built environment, for more see, Neil Leach, "Belonging," *London: Postcolonial City, AA Files,* v. 49 (2003): 76–82.

4. Stephen Gardiner, *Kuwait, The Making of a City* (Harlow: Longman, 1983), 15.

5. Stuart Hall, et al., eds., *Modernity: An Introduction to Modern Societies* (Cambridge MA and Oxford UK: Blackwell, 1996), 599. Quoting a definition of modernity from David Harvey, *The Condition of Postmodernity, an Enquiry into the Origins of Cultural Change* (Cambridge MA and Oxford UK: Blackwell, 1990), 12.

6. Keller Easterling, "IIRS," *e-flux*, n. 64 (April 2015): 4.

7. Hall, *Modernity*, 186.

8. Easterling, "IIRS," 3. "Technocrats of the 1920s in several competing factions sought to replace political leaders with a 'technate' of engineers who could be better suited to comprehensively collect data with which to rationalise the world's production."

9. Hamid Shuaib, "Urban Development in Kuwait," *Alam al-Bina*, n. 98 (1989): 4.

10. Raglan Squire, ed., "Architecture in the Middle East," *Architectural Design* (March 1957): 74. "This issue is concerned with new buildings in this part of the world. Because there are so few technically-trained nationals in the countries concerned, there has been a great call on technicians from the West." This is the one of the main reasons given for the great number of Western, mainly British companies at work in the Middle East. Nevertheless, this sort of repeated assertion on the incapability of the local work force is a clear trace of Orientalist discourse, as will be approached further ahead.

11. The existence of a cultural elite in formation abroad is referred to in several articles. It is very clear in Shiber's introduction of his project that it will become a central question in the agreements between foreign architectural firms and Kuwait Municipality which demanded, from 1973 onwards, the collaboration of foreign firms with a counterpart Kuwaiti team which would provide information about the local culture and, in return, receive training in the new planning technologies and methods. Education is an issue to be visited further ahead.

centred in the Western industrialised world and its culture, the country quickly assumed the promise of becoming a centre in the global flows of capital, ignited by its fuels: oil, money, tar, and concrete. This traditional society, bounded in territory by the desert and the Arabian Gulf, constituted itself in that place through centuries of nomad movements and several disputes and negotiations of influences and protectorates, by harvesting the seas for pearls and fish, and by mastering its trade routes. After centuries of hardship in an untameable territory, these "hardy, ingenious and resourceful people"[4] saw themselves at the centre of a movement of "ruthless break with any or all preceding conditions."[5]

The planning of new residential satellite towns or newly founded state-capitals, like Thamesmead or Brasilia, were quintessential projects of the Modern Movement. For in the planning of a whole new system of transport fit for faster motorised vehicles, organising all city spaces according to their activities and connections to leisure and working spaces such as green belts and business centres, reconfiguring dwellings to suit a new way of life supported by a vast infrastructure of services and amenities, a whole new life style was being designed, it was the project of a whole new and uniform culture. "The feverish moderns swore allegiance, above all, to an avant-garde habit of mind that regarded intelligence as successive rather than coexistent; new ideas had to murder old ideas."[6] The concept of technological disruption and revolution in all fields marks the twentieth century, allowing the full crystallisation of "a society that is developed, industrialised, urbanised, capitalist, secular, and modern"[7] configuring a cultural model that, emanating from the industrial centres of the Western world, would spread out globally along with a technocratic system of capital.

While the search for new ideas was being led in all fields, modernisation also meant specialisation and the specification of the field in itself. Documental and archival works assume great importance in this process as it is necessary to register procedures, standards, and models as well as to keep a record of all that existed or was made or built until then. It became a common practice to assemble information of all sorts in vast national archives which serve as data banks, instituting data as a valuable resource, a raw material that has to be handled and processed by specialised technical workers.[8] This allows several analytical tools, and the role of the planner and the consultant to be formally inscribed into the discipline of architecture and urbanism, reshaping, affirming and solidifying the recognition of a professional body and its functions. It is in this context that "whilst the economic effects of oil revenues had not yet had any major impacts, the government of Kuwait in 1950 was remarkably foresighted in considering the possible consequences on urban development" appointing, in 1951, the British firm Minoprio, Spencely, and Macfarlane (MSM) "to prepare the first Master Plan to control future development."[9]

This was the first stone of an on-going project of nation-building in Kuwait and in other Arab states that saw themselves embraced by the incredible revenue of oil exploration. For this project, many professionals were recruited from Western firms, as the nation possessed a limited amount of technical professionals.[10] The whole reformation would pass as well through the educational and central administration systems which would host in the future the many Kuwaitis who were then pursuing higher education abroad.[11] The development of these Arab nations became closely linked to a prolific production of city studies, urban development plans, and architectural projects anchored on modernist premises. This would constitute a considerable body of work that, by March 1957, deserved coverage in a special issue of *Architectural Design*, titled *Architecture in the Middle East*.

The project of a modern and urban Kuwait became for many foreign firms a preferred site of experimentation, and a sound source of financial expansion opportunities[12] creating the conditions to further the modernist quest in new town designs and new road systems; while for others, such as Shiber, this was a much different project of cultural affirmation and national constitution in the territory, "a veritable urban drama of the desert and the twentieth century."[13]

> From the first "glance" at this extraordinary urban mammoth of the Arabian desert, I became convinced that here was a great potential for the Arabs to harness great opportunities into significant channels; that, despite the alluring surface of achievements many dangers were surreptitiously gnawing at the roots – at the very fabric – of this great Arab challenge in urbanism; [...] Kuwait was the Arab challenge par excellence.[14]

Shiber's clear statement, "the Arab challenge of the twentieth century," refers directly to urban development, to the settlement of the Arab peoples in their territory, but mostly to the affirmation of the nation in all forms, cultural, economic, political, and technological. "[...] Kuwaiti suburbanisation was implemented in order to urbanise and modernise the city as a symbol of a modern state."[15] This process of institution that so perfectly met in modern aspirations the driving force to build an image and change and dominate a territory becomes, throughout time, an identity quest that blooms in parallel with globalisation. As the production of oil assumed its central position in the global financial system, feeding motorised engines and stock markets, Kuwait grew vertiginously. By 1960, the transformation prescribed by the MSM Master Plan could be felt on the whole urban structure, and it began to gather critical voices that questioned the legitimacy and even the usefulness of many of these projects.

A Newly Constructed Criticality

At the 1960 Cairo International Symposium on city planning "The New Metropolis in the Arab World," Shiber warned the Union of Arab Engineers that "one day soon it will be too late and we will be drowned under the expensive debris of current Arab urban and architectural design."[16] In 1961, Sheikh Abdullah Al-Salem Al-Sabah signed the independence agreement, and during the next decade the country fostered the creation of many of its official institutions. This moment of state constitution, and the whole urban development that it demands, brought forward in a more physical and corporeal way the clear impact of this project on Kuwait's cultural and urban landscape.

During the 1960s and 1970s, critical voices grew in number among Arab professionals – further studies, several plan reviews, and numerous building commissions were seen as "the imposition of Western technology onto an established Arab society,"[17] composed of plans designed over aerial views in far away British offices. In the form of academic researchers and architectural practices, a local professional body was starting to assert itself and participate actively in the urbanisation process. People such as Shiber, and Sabah Abi-Hanna who founded what would later be the SSH office,

12. "Middle East difficulties – report of conference on the Middle East export challenge," *The Architects' Journal*, v. 163, n. 18 (1976): 870. "Lamb [the British ambassador to Kuwait] noted that there are also many opportunities in Kuwait for building for the private sector, particularly residential development for rental to non-Kuwaitis who are not allowed to own land."

13. Shiber, *Kuwait Urbanization*, 6.

14. Ibid., 9.

15. Asseel Al-Ragam, "The Destruction of Modernist Heritage: The Myth of Al-Sawaber," *Journal of Architectural Education* v. 67, n. 2 (2013): 244. "Therefore, Kuwaiti suburbanisation, unlike its Western counterpart, was not a reaction against urban industrialisation. Nor was it a response to population trends or 'urban flight'."

16. Asseel Al-Ragam, "Representation and ideology in postcolonial urban development: the Arabian Gulf," *The Journal of Architecture*, v. 16, n. 4 (2011): 461–62.

17. Karim Jamal, "Kuwait, a Salutary Tale," *The Architects' Journal*, v. 158, n. 50 (1973): 1453.

3. Aerial view of Ahmadi, Kuwait, 1950s.
© Kuwait Oil Company Archive.

Ghazi Sultan, the founder of the Kuwait Engineers Office (KEO), and Hamid Shuaib, who established the Pan-Arab Consulting Engineers (Pace), are the most conspicuous examples.

These professionals were all eagerly competing for commissions, but feeling nevertheless that "there was a bias in government toward foreign firms, as if Kuwaiti firms couldn't be trusted with big jobs,"[18] giving great support to the measure proposed by Salem Al-Marzouq (Sabah Abi-Hanna's partner in SSH), which was formally introduced in 1973 and that imposed on foreign firms the obligation to collaborate on each project with a local counterpart team. The main goals of this forced corporate marriage would be to cross areas of expertise: locals would give assistance in what would concern local culture, climate, geography, and traditions, and foreign experts would be bonded by a "training clause"[19] to their Kuwaiti counterparts, in order to provide them the tools to proceed autonomously with the development of the plans.

In *The Architects' Journal*, a discussion took place throughout several articles over three years, involving the British firm Colin Buchanan and Partners (CBP) which was responsible for several studies and revisions in the 1960s and 1970s. Karim Jamal and Ghazi Sultan, two Kuwaiti architects, the first being a part of the local planning counterpart teams, and the latter a director of the Master Planning Department in Kuwait in that

18. Rod Sweet, ed., *SSH Design – The first 50 years* (Kuwait: Al-Khat printing Press, 2010), 47.

19. Ghazi Sultan, "Kuwait," *The Architects' Journal*, v. 160, n. 40 (1974): 792.

period were also involved. The editors introduced the first article by Karim Jamal, in a provocatively commercial tone as "the other side of the coin – the consumers' point of view"[20] of British involvement in Kuwait, but at stake in the discussion are strong arguments from both sides that foreground the cultural dynamics involved, as the project materialises a struggle between two strands: a lineage of Kuwaitis spearheading a local cultural movement into modernity and the establishment of a national identity, and a strand of experimentalist foreign experts attracted by a fetishised place, offering cultural and financial exoticism.

"Wherever There is Oil, Man Begins to Write a Strange Story on The Face of The Earth"[21]

From the moment "when the magic wand struck the country and oil was discovered in the Burgan fields in the 1930s,"[22] the territory and the culture of Kuwait have been cut across and intersected by many different influences, aims, processes, and visions. Many superimposed projects became the fragmented image of Kuwait torn between a traditional past and a future of supermodernity. "The impact of revenue on the landscape is, in Kuwait, perhaps more dramatic than anywhere else."[23]

> [...] then, this scene by the author depicts what was, until two years ago, officially known as "Sharia el-Jedid" – New Street. Now it is called "Sharia Abdullah el-Salem." Called "New" only around fifteen years ago, the lightning speed of Kuwaiti development had already rendered "New" Street obsolete by contemporary urban standards even four years ago. Together with "Sharia Fahed" – the newest "new" street of Kuwait – "Sharia Abdullah el-Salem" forms one of two spinal cords of the booming Central Business District of Kuwait. [...] In a few years, New Street, rendered temporarily "old" by Fahed Street, will emerge, again, to be the newest new street of Kuwait. Structured around it will be rebuilt pedestrian shopping "precincts" or "enclaves" – the first of their type in any Arab city. Thus, the scene above is pregnant with meaning: it is a "bit" history, a "bit" the present, a "bit" the future, a "bit" the ever-dynamicism of evolving Kuwait. In short, it is the nexus between old and new, yesterday and today and tomorrow, between what will be and what had been.[24]

The contest between the 'old' and the 'new,' which fuelled the movement into modernity and continues to be the propeller force of our times, is also the contest between two sides of a dividing line or a wall that establishes difference not only between new and old, but also between central and peripheral, advanced and archaic or developed and under-developed, *the West* and *the Rest*. These are representations that structure the sedimentary layers of meanings and practices that build culture, constituting "*both* the organising factor in a system of global power relations *and* the organising concept or term in a whole way of thinking and speaking"[25] in cultural institutionalised bodies as well as in the spectres of cultural struggles.

In the particular case of Kuwait, the collaboration between Western and Eastern architectural practices, as it is portrayed by articles in the 1957 special issue of *Architectural Design*, and by the discussion hosted by *The Architects' Journal* in the 1970s, is intensely tinted by the cultural dichotomies that tend to separate further, instead of creating connections and opportunities for exchange between both 'sides' of the wall.

In these articles, the Western modernist enterprise often revels in assertions about their clients, describing the Arab peoples with "generalisations

20. Jamal, "Kuwait, a Salutary Tale," 1452.

21. Shiber, *Kuwait Urbanization*, 61.

22. Jamal, "Kuwait, a Salutary Tale," 1452.

23. Shiber, *Kuwait Urbanization*, 6.

24. Ibid., xvi.

25. Hall, *Modernity*, 187.

and abstractions,"[26] as *other* than "the co-operative type of individual that is required for the development of a modern, highly organised state."[27] The diverse population of the Middle East is often represented as a people that, too embedded in out-dated tradition, has no attachment or knowledge to grasp the scope of modernisation, "who have little or no conception of [...] town planning, as it is practised in highly-developed countries," while, in contrast, the task of the expert is to bring new models from "England who has led the world in town planning."[28] Many architects and planners point out the considerable "difficulties encountered during construction"[29] which include delays in receiving shipments, the lack of available raw materials and specific technologies, and the poor and inefficient logistic systems. These difficulties, in turn, directly imply the lack of expertise of the workers themselves, who would always be subject to training and teaching. Replying to this, Sultan affirms:

> [...] although in most cases the paper qualifications of the counterpart team were equal to those of the consultant's team, in reality the counterpart team was not as capable as the consultant's team primarily due to their work experience being in the Arab world alone. But they were nowhere as incapable as CBP made them out to be in their AJ article (22.5.74, 1131).[30]

Among Kuwaiti professionals, along with a growing sense of technical autonomy, voices emerged against a discourse that tends "to keep the region and its people conceptually emasculated, reduced to 'attitudes,' 'trends,' statistics; in short, dehumanised."[31] They defy the authority of the initially proposed planning and the revisions of many 'advisers' in numerous reports which they consider overall inadequate, and with "little impact as they have tended to be repetitive and general."[32] This project was considered "not a useful planning tool for Kuwait,"[33] which was "slowly but systematically destroying"[34] Islamic culture, using not localised approaches, but the mechanical application of procedures of a post-Second World War "boom urbanisation era in practically every corner of the World."[35]

The 'educational' exchange intended between foreign firms and counterpart teams was also regarded as a failure; the project "did not train an indigenous team of professionals, nor help to create a planning mechanism or establishment that would secure the continuity of the work."[36] Seen by Kuwaiti architects as a "missed opportunity for including local people,"[37] the continuous recruitment of foreign professionals was justified by the necessity to respond to the pressures of projects "both unnaturally contracted in time and exploded in size,"[38] while the counterpart team members "began to complain that they were being used as errand boys and were not really contributing to the study."[39]

It became clear that the involvement, or symbolic attachment, of foreign teams was not equal to the one of local teams. Though the latter were regarded as "simply not used to the sustained pressure of work which Western professionals take for granted," and thus "generally less productive,"[40] the former were accused of having "become used to 'dumping' Western type schemes on the Third World host countries, with no questions asked; they have collected their super-profits, and then promptly left."[41] The main issues raised against a good part of the projects proposed by foreign firms are essentially based on their lack of capacity to represent adequately the people who would receive the project – the local community was always portrayed through a biased lens that could only see them as the

26. Edward Said, *Orientalism* (New York: Vintage House, 1979), 300–01.

27. Raglan Squire, ed., "Architecture in the Middle East," *Architectural Design* (March 1957): 73.

28. Ibid.

29. Raglan Squire, ed., "Schools at Kuwait," *Architectural Design* (March 1957): 94.

30. Sultan, "Kuwait," 792.

31. Said, *Orientalism*, 291.

32. Jamal, "Kuwait, a Salutary Tale," 1454.

33. Sultan, "Kuwait," 792.

34. Karim Jamal, "Destruction of the Middle East?," *The Architects' Journal*, v. 164, n. 30 (1976): 161.

35. Shiber, *Kuwait Urbanization*, 11.

36. Jamal, "Kuwait, a Salutary Tale," 1455.

37. Ibid., 1456.

38. Ibid., 1452.

39. Sultan, "Kuwait," 792.

40. Ibid., 794.

41. Jamal, "Destruction," 161.

inhabitants of what was secluded behind those old walls they proposed to demolish. While Kuwait was involved in a performative search for a modern identity – of belonging to the physical and cultural territory – a contrasting involvement is reflected in the discourse and attitudes of many foreign firms that very closely link the exercise of modernisation in Kuwait with Orientalism, as it is described by Edward Said:

> [...] Orientalism, [is] a way of coming to terms with the Orient that is based on the Orient's special place in European Western experience. The Orient is not only adjacent to Europe; it is also the place of Europe's greatest and richest and oldest colonies, the source of its civilisations and languages, its cultural contestant, and one of its deepest and most recurring images of the Other.[42] [...] It is rather a *distribution* of geopolitical awareness into aesthetic, scholarly, economic, sociological, historical, and philological texts; it is an *elaboration* not only of a basic geographical distinction (the world is made up of two unequal halves, Orient and Occident) but also of a whole series of "interests" [...]; it *is*, rather than expresses, a certain *will* or *intention* to understand, in some cases to control, manipulate, even to incorporate, what is a manifestly different (or alternative and novel) world; [...][43]

4. Undisclosed author, *Kurtugraphia*, 2015, rollerball pen on paper. © rewotwint, courtesy of the artist.

What is at stake in power struggles in the cultural arena is mainly the matter of 'from where' and 'from whom' comes instituted knowledge – "the location of culture," as Homi K. Bhabha puts it in his homonymous work, published in 1994 – in other words, under which political agenda, commercial aim, and social code is assembled the *discourse* entitled to prevail and dominate over others.[44] The 'wall' draws the limits of *property*, distinguishing those who can hold cultural belonging, own and be owned by a place, as much as it defines the limits of *propriety*, instituting borders between what is and what is not proper of being integrated into cultural language – that is, what is welcome inside and what is left outside, marginal. Inside these walls other segments of distribution and classification are organised: myths, traditions, objects, innovation, and speculation all hold a specific space in the construction of cultural value. Much like urban space, culture is constituted of networks, infrastructures, scales of intensity, crystallised clusters of productivity

42. Said, *Orientalism*, 1–2.

43. Ibid., 12.

44. Homi K. Bhabha, *The Location of Culture* (London and New York: Routledge, 1994).

and shelved institutions, and voids or blank spaces that harbour pockets of marginality within the walls.

The power relationship between local and foreign architectural practices can be regarded as both a contest for authority of "the peoples of that region to struggle on for their vision of what they are and want to be,"[45] and as a reflection of a new form of imperialist process of subordination that found its vehicle in late-capitalism's cultural and commercial expansion logics. Undoubtedly, Orientalism is a scholarly cultural production that orients and develops a set of attitudes towards a people and its culture based on "deformations"[46] and static representations, retaining their incapacity "to represent themselves"[47] which has been, and is:

> [...] produced and exists in an uneven exchange with various kinds of power, shaped to a degree by the exchange with power political (as with a colonial or imperial establishment), power intellectual (as with reigning sciences like comparative linguistics or anatomy, or any of the modern policy sciences), power cultural (as with orthodoxies and canons of taste, texts, values), power moral [...][48]

As we move into the 1980s, reaching the 1990s with the invasion of Kuwait by Iraqi armed forces and the first Gulf War ending in 1991, we can observe that "a major change in the international configuration of forces" took place, distancing France and Britain from the centre stage in world politics, displaced by the influence of the American *imperium*[49] – the Kuwait Emergency and Recovery Office (KERO) tasked "to plan for the reconstruction of the country following its liberation"[50] was based in Washington DC during the war. And still the reaction of local professionals remained grounded on the same claims of being prey to profit-seeking enterprises that hold no connection to their country and culture. As KERO plans ahead, a several million dollars contract is attributed to USACE (the US Army Corps of Engineers) in order to plan and distribute the tasks of urban reconstruction and oil industry recovery,[51] while local observers assert that "the post-war rebuilding work in Kuwait's construction industry is not the 'bonanza of the decade' that many have envisaged."[52]

Orientalism finds momentum in a whole repositioning of forces, reconfiguring methodologies to fit new agendas deriving from military investment to corporate interest in the region, namely the US army and oil industry become tied to geographic analysis of the territory and to the study of local languages, accommodating geopolitical dynamics as the Cold War competition with the Soviet Union, and putting itself "at the service of government or business or both."[53] In Kuwait, the shift occurs from a modernist focus on urban and architectural development, mainly planned by UK firms in the 1950s and 1960s, to a late-capitalist impulse, mainly operated by US companies, focused as much on the engineering of the oil infrastructure and on military geopolitical control as on the promotion of consumer goods as beacons of a cultural standard. In fact, Said's critique of a corporate academia around Orientalism is very much in that sense connected to the "'expert' networks linking corporate business, the foundations, the oil companies, the missions, the military, the foreign service, the intelligence community together with the academic world."[54] In this sense, Kuwait becomes the contested site where several currents meet and combine – Modernism, Capitalism, and Orientalism on the one hand, globalisation and an Arab cultural quest on the other. The efforts of this decades-long process are continuously scrambled by a global game of forces that though politically

45. Said, *Orientalism*, xiv.

46. Ibid., 273. "Representations are formations, or as Roland Barthes has said of all the operations of language, they are deformations."

47. Ibid., 293. "They cannot represent themselves; they must be represented."

48. Said, *Orientalism*, 12.

49. Ibid., 285–86.

50. Huda Al-Bahar, "Kuwait's Post-War Reconstruction," *Mimar*, n. 40 (September 1991): 14.

51. Al-Bahar, "Kuwait's Post-War Reconstruction," 15–16.

52. Ibid., 17.

53. Said, *Orientalism*, 291–92.

54. Ibid., 301–02.

and economically rooted is, nevertheless, of cultural character, displacing the territory through a distorted centre-periphery dichotomy that frustrates the possibility of creating an image that can be accepted and coherent throughout.

An increasingly dense collection of articles addressing architecture in Kuwait is issued as we enter a new millennium, and further on, reasserting the interest of the matter for newly formed professionals and scholars. Haider Mirza Abdul Reda and Kuruvilla Varghese published an article marking the completion of the Liberation Tower, "the tallest structure in the whole Middle East and Europe [...] [and] the fifth tallest free standing telecommunication tower in the world"[55] at the time – a highly symbolic structure in this whole debate. Others, such as I. A. Touman and F. Al-Ajmi identify tradition and climate as essential conditions that have been constantly neglected in architecture,[56] Richard Anderson and Jawaher Al-Bader debate recent architectural production in light of the regionalism-globalisation dichotomy,[57] Yasser Mahgoub is dedicated to analysing the expression of cultural identity in Kuwaiti buildings,[58] and more recently Asseel Al-Ragam has authored several articles in which she analyses postcolonial urban development and modernist heritage in the Arabian Gulf and, specifically, in Kuwait.[59] These authors, who confirm the formation of a solid scholarship around the Kuwait urbanisation history, identify 'location' as a fundamental aspect of cultural and architectural construction. Beyond ideology and religion – the most transcendent and abstract aspects of culture – it is the *placeness* of society that posits embodiment, affect, and symbolic attachment, in other words, *belonging* sprouts from the fundamentally physical aspect of a culture that is its constant interaction with territory and climate.

In this long journey, as we reach the Kuwaiti modern metropolis of the twenty-first century, through this emerging body of critique, we can read that this now established local expert body, though nourished by global academic and professional experience, shares some of the same frustrations of their fellow professionals of the early years of urbanisation in Kuwait. Representation, ideology, cultural identity, heritage, environment, and tradition become the terms under examination in architectural production and urban planning, asserting that "[d]espite the awe-inspiring scale and extravagant building forms that most of the Gulf States exhibit today, there is an overarching sadness and sameness reflected in the pervasive 'Las Vegas' veneer that has been lacquered upon them."[60]

Much of this sadness is concerned with the impossibility imposed on Arab cultures of being able to overcome "a kind of extrareal, phenomenologically reduced status that puts [these cultures] out of reach of everyone except the Western expert."[61] Indeed, though multidisciplinary and transnational networks are today established globally, issuing knowledge from many places and defying notions of centre and periphery, it seems that *otherness* will hardly be taken at face value, and Western bias continues to distort the image of peripheral peoples into flattened reductions and myths.[62] "No one can escape dealing with, if not the East/West division, then the North/South one, the have/have-not one, the imperialist/anti-imperialist one, the white/coloured one."[63] Though much has been built and erected, it is still hard to see a clear image born from this project: the old walls have become hybridised by this cultural envelopment, displaying myriad textures mixing ancient mud-brick with high technology intelligent facades, a multifaceted dream that rises from the desert, as a mirage on the horizon.

55. Haider Abdul Reda and Kuruvilla Varghese, "Liberation Tower, Kuwait," *Journal of Indian Institute of Architects*, v. 6, n. 3 (1997): 25.

56. I. A. Touman and F. Al-Ajmi, "Tradition, climate: As the neglected concepts in architecture," *Building and Environment*, v. 40, n. 8 (2005): 1076–84.

57. Richard Anderson and Jawaher Al-Bader, "Recent Kuwaiti Architecture: Regionalism vs. Globalisation," *Journal of Architectural and Planning Research*, v. 23, n. 2 (2006): 134–45.

58. Yasser Mahgoub, "Architecture and the expression of cultural identity in Kuwait," *The Journal of Architecture*, v. 12, n. 2 (2007): 165–82.

59. Al-Ragam, "Representation and ideology," 455–469, and Al-Ragam "Destruction of Modernist Heritage," 243–52.

60. Anderson and Al-Bader, "Recent Kuwaiti Architecture," 144.

61. Said, *Orientalism*, 283.

62. Ibid., 312. "For a myth does not analyse or solve problems. It represents them as already analysed and solved; that is, it presents them as already assembled images, in the way a scarecrow is assembled from bric-a-brac and then made to stand for a man."

63. Ibid., 327.

5. The old Jahra Gate and the new city,
Kuwait City, 1960s.
© Kuwait Oil Company Archive.

These Walls
Are the Groundings
of Identities

These walls are what separates and yet assures continuity between the different cultural strands that have influenced the building of Kuwait; they stitch together different places, projects, and images into this territory and suture a cultural landscape constituted of difference and boundaries. "Identity [...] bridges the gap between the 'inside' and the 'outside' [...]"[64] negotiating subjective and collective images in relation to the ways in which one is addressed and represented by the cultural worlds one inhabits. If, in the beginning of Kuwait's urban quest, general notions of identity were still solid conceptual anchors for many nations and ethnicities, it becomes clear, while observing this complex and intricate process of cultural constitution, that "as the systems of meaning and cultural representation multiply, we are confronted by a bewildering, fleeting multiplicity of possible identities" and that a "fully unified, completed, secure, and coherent identity is a fantasy."[65]

Thus, in the context of globalisation, identification becomes the exercise of constituting "a narrative of the self" from a set of amplified experiences, "producing a variety of possibilities and new positions of identification, and making identities more positional, more political, more plural and diverse;"[66] and what is approached, here, as the constitution of an urban and modern culture in Kuwait can be seen as the construction of "nation as narration,"[67] compiled from the continuous thread of texts produced around this project. "A consistency between the story and the physical form is paramount to the precise soulful expression of the architect."[68] This narration gathered from multiple and diverse stories, different voices involved in the projects and their critique, produces a dissonant physical form, and a heterogeneous image full of soft edges and hard cuts where interventions can either melt into each other harmoniously or meet in friction, overlapping, dissolving, and superimposing layers of time in a fruitful and vivid debate. In this sense,

64. Hall, *Modernity*, 597–98.

65. Ibid.

66. Ibid., 598, 628–29.

67. "Nation as narration" is a concept put forward in Homi K. Bhabha, ed., in *Nation and Narration* (London: Routledge, 1990), and further explored by Neil Leach in the article "Belonging," *London: Postcolonial City, AA Files*, v. 49 (2003): 76.

68. Easterling, "IIRS," 9.

the cultural identification of the nation is constructed as the city, in an intricate conjunction of forces, built by a succession of performative acts – i.e. laying the foundations of landmarks and institutions, being appropriated by cultural and political agendas, negotiating its expansion, becoming a scenery of war and liberation, and keeping a continuous debate of the overarching process – which becomes embodied in its old walls and new streets, rendering a compelling cultural image of our times, which might allow us "to formulate new paradigms for understanding attachment to place that are in tune with contemporary modes of existence"[69] and in which dissonance and rupture are as meaningful as harmony and continuity.

In the revolving confrontations between the local and the universal – the "transcendent universal"[70] dreamt by the modernists – between past and future, tradition and progress, shifting time and velocity, processes of cultural hybridisation, homogenisation and translation overlap.[71] Realities and fictions are confounded and deformed. To be attentive to this narrative, as to many others, revisiting its inflections, its influences, outcomes, critiques, and the discourse in which it can be inscribed, may allow us to understand more of our current condition. There will always exist a dividing line somewhere, but a capacity to translate might allow us "to cut across and intersect natural frontiers."[72]

The old walls that once held tradition and heritage as solid cultural representations of a community, are now cut by speeding highways, intersected by building complexes, illuminated by neon and LED advertisements, and overshadowed by skyscrapers; cultural moorings are today deformed and dislocated, adapting and evolving fast. The old wall is fragmented. But though parts of it have been demolished over time, the entrance points persist in this 'strange story.' The five gates of the city are still there to remind us that the coexistence of multiple, counterbalancing, contradictory fluxes and dynamics – peoples and cultures – continues to shape this territory since ancient times.

The Kuwaiti people may now find themselves more attached to the landscape, more in tune with the flow of time, and more vigilant to the pressures and interests that influence their territory and their lives; their cultural struggle is fuelled by the economic emergence of oil, and shaped by a very specific movement towards globalisation that is imprinted on the landscape. Confidence and prosperity may be taken from the testimony of some true and strong partnerships, such as the fiftieth anniversary of the local firm SSH, and the many notable buildings that exist in Kuwait. Other experiences may have left a taste of regret behind; nevertheless, this narrative that comes to us from the Middle East by the hands of Shiber and the many others who followed his critical path, may suggest "that, though powered in many ways by the West, globalisation may turn out to be part of that slow and uneven but continuing story of the decentring of the West."[73] Following this idea, a broader concept of knowledge can be understood to play a powerful role acting as the immaterial capital of the people: globalised experiences, local history, and corporeal tradition can have the ability to shift political designs, social dynamics, and academic thought, contaminating with its multiplicity and fluidity the processes that institute culture. •

6. The old mud wall, Kuwait City, 1950s. © Kuwait Oil Company Archive.

69. Leach, "Belonging," 80.

70. Easterling, "IIRS," 4.

71. See Stuart Hall et al., *Modernity*, especially chapter 18, for insightful development of the concepts of cultural hybridisation, homogenisation, and translation.

72. Hall, *Modernity*, 629.

73. Ibid., 632.

The Architects' Journal 28 July 1976

Destruction of the Middle East?

Nearly three years ago KARIM JAMAL, a planner from Kuwait, wrote of his misgivings about employing foreign consultants in the Middle East, based on experience in his own country (AJ 12.12.73 pp1452-57). His criticisms were challenged by a British firm of consultants in a later issue (AJ 22.5.74 pp1131-32).

Jamal again returns to the attack and urges foreigners not to foist their own, western, ideas on to the so-called 'wealthy oil sheikhs'. The only expertise they can pass on is 'how not to do it'.

The World of Islam Festival (advertised in the poster above) includes exhibitions at several major galleries and museums throughout Britain plus a course of lectures and seminars through the summer. The festival offers Britons and visiting foreigners a chance to study and gain some understanding of the arts and ideas of Islamic culture.

It is ironic, paradoxical and shameful that although throughout London many exhibitions are showing the splendours of the Islamic civilisation, at the same time hundreds of useless schemes and projects are being thrust upon the Middle Eastern cities and countries (from the Gulf to the Atlantic Ocean) by the Japanese, East European and, above all, Western firms. These firms are slowly but systematically destroying the very thing we all are admiring at the moment in London.

No questions asked

Unfortunately, none of the exhibitors have taken the trouble to question and discuss the deliberate extinction of the traditional Islamic city structure (see AR May 1976) which has been taking place during the past 40 years and to examine what has been offered to replace it. On the contrary, a group of British firms met in London earlier this year (conference on the export challenge AJ 5.5.76 pp869-870) and were given the impression that 'working in the Middle East is risky, requires a full-time commitment and can result in costly bank over-drafts'. If the alleged situation is so bad, I wonder why increasing numbers of such firms (AJ 26.11.75 p1112) still shuttle back and forth to the Middle East? Is it because the prospects are much worse in Britain, or because, in real terms, these firms' bank balances are steadily improving?

What follows is my own opinion; it might offend many of these sensitive firms. First, any exploitative, profiteering and speculative business is 'risky' and suggesting meaningless schemes in the economically rich Middle East is no exception. Second, of course working in the Middle East 'requires a full-time commitment'. It certainly requires it in Britain too. However, these very firms have become used to 'dumping' Western type schemes on the Third World host countries, with no questions asked; they have collected their super-profits, and then promptly left. Now the Middle Eastern countries require that guarantees be placed so that firms are held accountable for their endless mistakes.

Middle East must protect its heritage

Let me illustrate the above statement by giving a few examples that I have experienced or witnessed. I can appreciate the anxiety and the frustration expressed by the firm of Robert Matthew, Johnson-Marshall & Partners whether in Kuwait, Abu Dhabi or, in this case, in Jeddah (AJ 5.5.76 p869). However, I certainly disagree with their interpretation and understanding of what happens 'in reality' in Saudi Arabia. I understand that the firm is the planning consultant to the city of Jeddah and the whole western region (a dangerous task to leave in the hands of one foreign firm). Therefore, they should recognise (if not be partially blamed for) the systematic dismantling of the old quarter of Jeddah and the gradual disappearance of its vernacular architecture. The expressed resentment as to how the Saudis interpret and exercise their own law is unjustifiable. The Saudis, and indeed all other middle easterners, must and should take all the necessary measures to prevent what is left of their old cities from vanishing and to make sure that all 'jobs are being done properly'.

Speculative market not stamped out

One has only to look around in Jeddah to see that the municipality there still has not succeeded in stamping out schemes built purely for this speculative market, or for hefty profits and commissioneering. Both the AJ and AR have published examples of such projects from time to time. May I suggest that while conservation, rehabilitation and improvements of the traditional areas is more difficult for foreign firms to put forward, it does involve smaller sums of capital and results in lower commissions.

The aggressive battle to promote products (eg armaments, nuclear reactors with their uncertainty) and expertise, no matter what, has been fought fiercely by the industrialised

ADEL ALBLOUSHI

To Whom Are We Giving Custody of Our Modern Architecture Heritage?

Introduction: the Polemic of Nostalgia

Grandfathers and grandmothers recount stories of childhoods spent in an urban environment that no longer exists. They can no longer identify the places that moulded them into the people they became: where they used to play soccer, meet their friends, or tried to mingle with potential partners (against explicit social norms). Their descendants can no longer study their own heritage, as Kuwait's history does not have the necessary referents to substantiate itself. It is simply written, or recounted, with a flexible, politicised narrative, but seldom tested against the immutable – the kind other societies are desperately trying to preserve.

Is it surprising that there is very little cultural value to whatever came post-*tabula rasa*? The counter-effect to such discontinuity in identity is an adequate measure of apathy. Yet one can always question whether there is simply a delay in enamorment; surely those shaped by this new and 'alien' environment may have legitimate reasons to be fond of it, as one becomes fond of a surrogate mother. Were they ever asked?

The value of any object is given partially by its own merit among similar objects, and partially through cultural and economic processes. Buildings tend to require higher maintenance costs and, as such, it is only natural that at least

some of these buildings would eventually become too costly to be profitable. At that point the continued existence of such buildings becomes a question of how persuaded the owners are to support their maintenance. Typically, when the environment is deemed worthy of preserving, or in other words, worthy of being called 'heritage,' there is a legal framework that aims to protect it from modification beyond recognition or disarray beyond repair. History shows us that before such policies are formulated there must be a cultural current that identifies the built environment, or part of it, as important and significant enough for any amount of effort (within reasonable limit) to be spent on preserving it.

After concluding that Kuwait's legal framework for preservation is still in its infancy compared to other urban environments, especially when the buildings in question were built less than 60 years ago, this article will take an in-depth look at how the cultural current of identifying 'heritage' is prompting institutions and individuals to pursue the goal of preservation. The main investigation will be into how the present and next generation of architects, teachers, lawmakers, cultural workers, and stakeholders can be persuaded to appreciate their modern heritage, if at all.

Basic Law

Kuwait does have in place a written framework to protect its built heritage. Bearing the name of the

Law of Antiquities, it was drafted into law by Amiri decree and has not seen either major or minor revisions. Despite it being issued before most of the bulk of modern buildings were built, or even before Kuwait acquired its independence, it nonetheless clearly states that Kuwait would indeed expend effort to protect its cultural heritage "throughout the ages" by preserving both movable and immovable antiquities. To be classified as an "antiquity" something has to be "man-made, produced or built forty calendar years ago," and thus has to be recorded, studied and preserved.[1]

There are obvious challenges imposed by the wording of this definition: Does "forty calendar years ago" take as a reference point the time the document was drafted, or the present day? Such loopholes can clearly be exploited by anyone who has a knack for grammatical and legal logic, and it would be crucial for the preservation of post-1920 edifices to clarify the intention of the document in a (hopefully near) future revision.

One might also find it striking that age is solely the criterion for assigning a building its heritage status. This will later be addressed by the National Council for Culture, Arts and Letters' (NCCAL) grading system. However, this is a major clue as to how heritage was being understood: intuitively rather than intellectually. Perhaps at the time – in the 1960s – it made intuitive sense that older buildings were important in terms of heritage, and the number 40, albeit arbitrary, was a nice, rounded number by which to set the age criteria. Perhaps intuition went deeper, recognising the many dimensions that make a building significant regardless of age, yet we have nothing explicitly written upon which to test this idea.

The Permit Givers and Their (Master) Plans

By hiring the expertise of local consultants, Kuwait Engineering Group (KEG) and the UK-based, Colin Buchanan and Partners, Kuwait Municipality conducted a third Master Plan review, more precisely in 2005, targeting a developmental period spanning from 2005 to 2030. The plan concerns mainly housing, education, and employment of the population, the facilitation of economic activities, the control of natural resources, and the management of the environment. Under the 'environment' umbrella, one can find a small section stating that "all historical buildings, structures and archaeological sites throughout the state will continue to be listed and identified in the National Register [...] [and] will be strictly protected from destruction or alteration."[2]

The Plan further elaborates that the above can be conceptually categorised into: heritage areas, listed buildings and archaeological sites. Identifying the artifices and sites is assigned to NCCAL, and their preservation should be the fruit of a joint venture between NCCAL and Kuwait Municipality's Historic Building Preservation Section.[3]

Nowhere else in the document are there any further guidelines as to how such protection will be accomplished. As far as the Master Plan is concerned, it is simply expected that those in charge will find a way to accomplish their tasks and whatever this involves with regards to making concrete plans for taking positive action, preventing negative intervention, and financing the whole ordeal. Yes, it unambiguously states that heritage needs to be protected and "preserved," however, it is perhaps not enough to just "preserve" these artifices, they also need to be *respected*, which requires a more sophisticated understanding of heritage vis-à-vis planning.

Previous versions of the Master Plan were even less concerned with preservation. For example, The Second Master Plan, first review by Salem Al-Marzouq and Sabah Abi-Hanna (SSH) and Shankland Cox and Partners,[4] and its successor, the second review by Colin Buchanan and Partners, Ove Arup and Partners, and Kuwait Engineering Group (KEG),[5] do not even mention in their headings anything remotely related to the topic of preservation. Only the initial Third Master Plan, which was commissioned to local consultants SSH, called for the preservation of Kuwait's heritage along vague lines, and, like its successor, assigned it to another party. At the time, that other party was an unknown entity, yet to be defined or formed. It is, then, no coincidence that the NCCAL's involvement started in 1997 when it established its architectural division.

It is worth noting that Kuwait Municipality commissioned its own historical preservation study in 1988, yet the document was simply a survey without any legal binding power.[6] One might think that this first step would have led to the logical consequence of policy formulation if it were not abruptly interrupted by the war of 1990; post-invasion Kuwait's priorities lay – understandably – in undoing the damage.

Institutionalised Heritage

Even within the NCCAL's bureaucratic machine, one does not find a clear consensus as to which side of 1960 the *Law of Antiquities* is supposed to refer to; however, circumstances have proven such concerns moot. While the Law unambiguously includes built artifacts, and moreover outlines the punishment for failing to follow its prescription, it was not – apparently – used for any building preservation endeavours until the late 1990s. When the NCCAL established its architectural division in 1997, one of their first major tasks was to create the first Kuwait Heritage Building Registry (KHBR), which had a larger scope than Kuwait Municipality's study of 1988. Obtaining approval from Kuwait's National Assembly in 1999 finally opened the door for NCCAL and Kuwait Municipality's preservation and restoration efforts.[7]

Kuwait Heritage Building Registry organises buildings into four grades: Grade-1 is for buildings of outstanding national value, which translates to a combination of building age, historical importance, intactness in form and materials and unique character. Permanent protection of its existence and character is granted. In Grade-2, the buildings are slightly less important compared to Grade-1, mainly due to their lack of intactness, though they are still of considerable value. Such buildings have to be generally preserved, yet alterations are permitted to restore lost features. Under Grade-3 are buildings with a unique architectural character and form that are in good physical condition. They are to be generally preserved, with alterations permitted after approval from the NCCAL. The fourth and last category, Grade-4, is reserved for buildings of minor historical value. A myriad of alterations are allowed in this category – after approval from the NCCAL – and in some cases even complete demolition and free rebuilding.[8]

How does the NCCAL decide which buildings to include under which category? It evaluates each building under ten criteria and assigns each a grade from 1 to 10. These criteria are: age, condition, use, location, architectural form, ornamentation, historical importance, socio-political significance, loss of characteristics and additions. After a simple linear addition, the total grade-number then determines the category.[9] Yet the document does not fully explain how an investigator is to assign a grade-number for each criterion; rather it seems to leave it to the latitude of each investigator, thus, injecting into the process a high degree of ambiguity and subjectivism.

The result was that whatever little pre-1920s urban fabric survived the ambitious rebuilding of Kuwait was dully preserved, while latter buildings entered the NCCAL categorisation process. In fact, the National Register includes to date around one hundred thirty-seven buildings, out of which forty-seven are of a religious nature, twenty-seven are governmental, twenty-six are residential, twelve are cultural, eight are commercial, another eight are graveyards, six are schools, one is a hybrid, another is an abandoned factory, and the last one used to be an embassy. Forty-two of these buildings are classified as Grade-1, fifty-eight as Grade-2, twenty-eight as Grade-3, and nine as Grade-4.[10]

In 2010, NCCAL published a book to showcase its accomplishments called *Kuwait: History, Heritage, Architecture 1900–1950*.[11] As one might conclude from the title, none of the buildings serviced by NCCAL were built beyond the 1950s. Although the number of projects in NCCAL's portfolio is about five times fewer than the KHBR, it seems to reinforce the perception that the older buildings are the most important. There is very little dispute about the significance of NCCAL's work to retain for society's sake an idea as to where we came from, yet it cannot be successfully argued that the more recent buildings are not as significant – or ever more so – in shaping who we are today.

Regrettable Decisions

Poorly understood buildings have little chance of being preserved. It is clear that the current mindset is focused more on the symbolic rather than the architectonic, and the extrinsic value of the built object rather than the intrinsic. One unfortunate happening is the ongoing demolition (at the time of writing) of Kuwait Airways Company tower completed in 1972 in the capital city. Despite the state-owned building recently becoming forty years old, enough to potentially benefit from the Law of Antiquities, it didn't get, perhaps to no-one's surprise and the regret of many, protected status. How one of the first high-rises in Kuwait City, which undoubtedly holds sentimental value for a large portion of the globetrotting Kuwaiti population, escaped the filtering process of the authorities is remarkable, yet not entirely outside the realm of understanding.

On the one hand, it seemed to matter little that from an academic point of view, Kuwait Airways tower

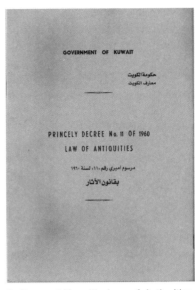

1. Cover of Kuwait's *Law of Antiquities*, 1960. © Government of Kuwait.

1. Government of Kuwait, *Law of Antiquities* (Kuwait City: Government Press of Kuwait, 1960).

2. KEG Consultants and Colin Buchanan and Partners, *Third Kuwait Master Plan Review – Executive Summary* (Kuwait City: Kuwait Municipality, 2005).

3. Ibid.

4. SSH and Shankland Cox Partnership, *Master Plan of Kuwait First Review* (Kuwait City: Kuwait Municipality, 1977).

5. KEG Consultants and Colin Buchanan and Partners, *Third Kuwait Master Plan Review – Executive Summary* (Kuwait City: Kuwait Municipality, 2005).

6. Kuwait Municipality, *Kuwait Historical Preservation Study* (Kuwait City: Kuwait Municipality, 1988).

7. Interview with Abdullah Al-Bishi, Kuwait City, April 2015.

8. NCCAL, *Kuwait National Building Register* (Kuwait City: Government Press of Kuwait, 1997).

9. Ibid.

10. Ibid.

11. *Kuwait: History, Heritage, Architecture 1900–1950* (Kuwait City: National Council for Culture, Arts and Letters, 2010).

was a pioneering project for the region, architecturally, urbanistically, politically, economically and socially; a concrete tower amid a sea of mud houses. Like a tree falling in a forest with no one to hear it, Kuwait Airways tower is falling in the urban context with no audience to recall its history or understand its significance. This lack of interest is reflected in the scarcity of documentation, posing a challenge to anyone trying to re-search the building post-eradication. On the other hand, the pragmatic forces seem to have decided that the tower's structure made it too danger-ous to continue operating, and in 2014 the Council of Ministers took a firm decision to demolish it.[12] One look at the design of the pompous (and tasteless) building that is sup-posed to take its place in the near future is enough to cast doubt on Kuwait Airways' financial ability to rehabilitate its original tower.

The list of demolished mo-dernist buildings is constantly grow-ing, and some of the victims were true cultural landmarks, such as the old Chamber of Commerce. Yet why the apathy? Could it be that all protests were muted or ignored? Is the exodus of locals from the capital the primary culprit? Are the stake-holders hoping for better profit? Perhaps there are answers to these questions; however, what is happen-ing to the old Kuwait Airways tower is not inevitable. Regardless of how the situation evolved to its current status, one thing is clear: there is a lack of understanding of architecture as a valuable intellectual endeavour that is capable of producing valuable objects, and consequently "preser-vation" never gains serious intellec-tual importance. Without an under-pinning logic, the legal framework is either too narrow or too inadequate to address issues outside its explicit scope.

The Aristocracy of the Free Market

Outside the realm and reach of public organisations, private entities can, even in a pseudo-pragmatic society such as ours, be very much concerned with the reutili-sation of older, partially defunct buildings.

In one such case, the Pearl Al-Marzouq complex, a modernist *beacon* built on a privileged site right on the tip of the small Ras-Al-Salmiya peninsula, underwent a facelift that was intended to lift it out of decay – the curse of the aftermath of modernism, it seems – and make it relevant to the contemporary archi-tectural scene. The whole incident arose out of the intersection of pure capitalist interests with the personal concerns of an expatriate architect, in a chain of events that seem pulled from a postmodern movie script.

The main character in the script is architect Naji Moujaes. Of Lebanese lineage, born and brought up in Kuwait, he completed his bachelor's degree in architecture at the American University of Beirut, received his master's degree from the University of California Los Ange-les – after studying for a semester in Switzerland, and practiced in New York. Undoubtedly, this kind of exposure to global cultural changes shapes one's evaluation of and attitudes toward the built environ-ment. Freshly returned from his academic and professional endeav-ours abroad, Moujaes noticed, was intrigued by, and finally became enamored with the Pearl Al-Marzouq complex. So much so that he strived to live in it, and after being placed on a waiting list, he rented an apartment in a nearby edifice, with a view to achieving his aim. Finally, after some time and much perseverance, he managed to occupy one of the units.

This led to the web-blog pearlmarzook.com, Moujaes' pers-onal study of, and watchdog over the life of the building.[13]

According to Moujaes, he answered his phone one day to an offer to purchase his website by Pearl Al-Marzouq's owners, Kuwait Real Estate Company. Moujaes' refusal led to his meeting with the upper management of Kuwait Real Estate Company and, since he was an architect, he managed to get involved with the renovation process. Initially, the owners had sought the help of the acclaimed local office AGi. However, upon seeing AGi's proposal of covering the sandstone facade with alumin-ium cladding, Moujaes expressed his concern over the lack of sensibility in dealing with the project. And so, the story goes, Moujaes' design studio, PAD10, received the commission to create a proposal for the renovation of Pearl Al-Marzouq.[14]

Moujaes prefers to call the process *re-tooling*, as opposed to *renovating* or *restoring*, as the word for him has more suitable con-notations with his actual interven-tion, which was driven by urbanistic, programmatic, and aesthetic con-cerns. Firstly, Moujaes noticed how the building's swimming pool enc-roached on the public realm, pro-hibiting public access to the portion of the beach directly in front of it, and decided not to undo this, but to extend this *re-publification* (to use Moujaes' own term) to the courtyard of the building and most of the ground floor. Secondly, the buil-ding's initial lobotomisation into three separate towers and a lower corpus, each with its own entrance, was dissolved, such that the lower corpus acted as the main entrance and lobby for all parts of the building, – and the complex acted as one edifice. Thirdly, Moujaes saw an opportunity to deal sensibly with the existing sandstone cladding – which was starting to loosen its connection to the structure it enveloped – and simply stapled it in place with highly stylised metal meshes, their form alluding to current aesthetic trends.[15]

As with any architectural project, judgement and criticism, both favourable and not, were exchanged in design and culture circles. But the fervor surrounding the discussion also revealed a deep-rooted interest and intrigue in the reuse of modernist buildings. One has to note that neither the NCCAL nor Kuwait's Municipality had any discernible interest in how this project unfolded. In fact, Moujaes recognises a reluctance on the part of the authorities to identify and fruitfully exploit and expand on the urban opportunities these modern projects have sometimes embedded in their original design intentions.[16]

This is to show that, when left to its own devices, the free market can very efficiently deal with issues of renovation and re-use without needing help or input from state institutions, with the condition that there is a willing private owner and a willing private service provider. Yet this process is inherently aristocratic, hanging on the whims of a select few, and it goes against the spirit of a collective heritage, which requires a much more democratic approach and a more active societal involvement. The conceptual construct we call *heritage* is the inherited property of the many, not the few.

Furthermore, aside from the building described above, one can safely assume that other significant buildings are owned and operated by the private sector.

It is highly problematic that there is a lack of legal framework to reconcile the act of preservation with the rights of proprietors. At the moment the state can either purchase buildings it deems significant, or be content to focus only on what its institutions already own and operate, which does not seem to be satisfactory.

The Need for Criticality

One might assume that such lack of concern with modern building preservation is typical of Kuwait's cultural context, but any doubts are dispelled by a little bit of research. There is a global crisis of heritage in general, but modern architecture has seen a disproportionate share of threats countered by a relatively slow global reaction and awakening. For example, Canada's first conference on the topic was held in 2005.[17] Meanwhile, masterpieces of the modern era, such as F. F. L. Wright's Unity Temple, are forever lost.[18] This should not discourage local efforts; rather, it should make those implicated aware that the situation is not entirely unique to Kuwait, and that there are lessons to be learned from precedents.

The first observation is that currently there is an intuitive understanding of preservation. It seems natural that strong symbols of Kuwait, such as the Water Towers, have to be preserved. Similarly, mosques and palaces seem to naturally fall under the umbrella of social acceptance. Yet the intricate relationships between the built environment and the functioning of any society can never be understood purely in the symbolic realm.

A complex and thorough survey is needed to identify buildings that are symbolically relevant (which,

as noted earlier, was already done in the 1980s). Also, in order to understand which buildings are truly relevant to the nation's identity, a more sophisticated understanding of the value of individual buildings is needed. Martin Heidegger's dissection of the words "dwelling" and "building" are telling of an undivorceable act of mutual shaping and re-shaping between the inhabitant and the inhabited.[19] The idea that one can understand a society without understanding its buildings seems paradoxical. It matters little which era or aesthetic current any particular building belonged to; its contribution is not negligible.

12. Saud Al-Fadhli, "Removal of Kuwait Airways Corporation Building," *Al Qabas,* August 31, 2014.

13. Interview with Naji Moujaes, Kuwait City, April 2015.

14. Ibid.

15. Ibid.

16. Ibid.

17. Susan Algie and James Ashby, eds., *Conserving the Modern in Canada: Buildings, Ensembles, and Sites, 1945–2005,* conference proceedings May 6–8, 2005, Trent University, Peterborough (Winnipeg, Manitoba: Winnipeg Architecture Foundation, 2007).

18. Patrick F. Cannon, *Frank Lloyd Wright's Unity Temple: A Good Time Place* (Portland: Pomegranate Communications, 2009).

19. M. Heidegger, *Poetry, Language, Thought* (New York: Harper Collins Publishers, 1971).

However, what can be seen on the ground is a direct jump from an intuitive understanding of heritage to legislation. Very little effort was dispensed in formulating a well-defined theoretical understanding of the value of objects in general and of buildings in particular. The many shortcomings of the current legislation can be attributed to this direct jump from the intuitive to the legislative.

What makes for a valid semantic model for assigning value to objects? An intuitive approach is to affirm that such questions have arbitrary answers, the formulation of which is our own responsibility. What is clear is that some objects have value to an observer, while others do not, and a complete apathy to the world outside might be deemed worrisome. Our concern is not this general; rather it is focused on architectural objects from the 1950s to the 1980s. Yet one cannot deny that without a general framework of consciously recognising value in any object, one cannot hope to focus on specific objects. To make things even more complicated, this problem needs to be addressed at the intuitive individual level, at the level of the collective consciousness, at the historical societal level, at the deliberate institutional level and at the policy level.

An edifice, like any other object, can be assigned intrinsic and extrinsic value. There is intrinsic value to a building – value to the object in and of itself – when it comes to how well it suits its program and context, and where it stands in the history of architectural achievements. When a building becomes deeply engrained in the fabric of cultural consciousness it acquires strong extrinsic value. Whatever the dynamic between architecture's intrinsic and extrinsic values, for a society to have a sensibility regarding them, it needs a strong body of architectural theorists, critics, and cognoscenti. Just like Kuwait University's Faculty of Architecture separated from the Faculty of Engineering in 2011, perhaps it is time for the architects from the Kuwait Engineering Society to separate and form their own group, one that is free to promote its own cultural and academic agendas.

The Academic Endeavour

Kuwait's official generator and filter of intellectual and academic thought is its state university. Simply called Kuwait University, it is charged, among other things, with shaping the thoughts and attitudes of future Kuwaiti generations. One might argue that the professional class most interested in issues of preservation might be the architects (the idea has some backbone), which immediately leads to the following question: How are we teaching our future architects about their built heritage?

The College of Architecture developed its own curriculum by studying a number of prominent architectural programs in the United States. The result might be aptly called a 'compromise' between these diverse curriculums; nevertheless, some embedded intellectual attitudes prevailed. One such attitude was a traditional disregard for architectural history – after all it seems to counter the idea of progress when the past is always worse than the present – and an implicit favouritism towards a sort of tabula rasa. The American educational landscape in the twentieth century was fascinated with notions of Pure Design, Modernism, Deconstructivism, Parametricism and so on[20] – largely formal, decontextualised, and idiosyncratic methodologies that had no need for historical context. The relentless quest for innovation and 'newness' shifted the concern from appreciating past buildings to deeming them inferior by default. One pitfall of these attitudes is that, given enough time, they tend to disregard themselves and their own fruits, reinitiating the cycle that begins with tabula rasa.

While latter revisions of the curriculum added a tad more emphasis on history and theory, there is nothing to suggest that the conservation of Kuwait's built heritage is of much concern to Kuwait University. There are neither specialised design studios on how to preserve Kuwait's culturally significant buildings, nor theoretical courses focusing on what value these buildings have or might potentially have for present or future society. There is, however, an intellectual dissection of Kuwaiti landmarks through the lens of architectural analysis theory, not conservation. The fundamental distinction is that, while submitting a building through the process of analysis, it can sometimes result in the building acquiring some cultural value indirectly. Analysis is neither concerned with, nor does it assume a priori that there might be any such value to be found. Furthermore, the subject matter in history courses is mostly of the generic sort: Architecture of the Ancient World from the Prehistoric to the Baroque and Rococo (History I), Architecture of the Islamic Civilisation (History II), Architecture in the nineteenth and twentieth century in the Western Civilisation (History III). Only in History II is Kuwait's architectural history considered, partially, and mostly superficially.[21]

It would be understandable to expect of Kuwait University more enthusiasm for architectural preservation, but at the same time one must not forget that the root of the problem is a societal one, and is not centred on one particular institution. What Kuwait University does, instead, is solving the problem of authenticity in a society that sees building design as largely an imported commodity-cum-service, by supplying the society with an increasingly large number of home-bred architects (and theorists). As they return to their particular communities in increasing numbers, they carry with them the intellectual lenses – contagious as they are hoped to be – through which built objects can be seen as valuable, both intrinsically and extrinsically. Perhaps it is a question of reaching a critical mass of alumni before we see rapid, fundamental change, but some change is happening, and it is rather significant.

First Glimpses of Hope

One cannot fail to notice the ambiguity of the Kuwait Historic Building Registry and its generous allowance for subjective input, which was both a problem to be fixed and an opportunity for creative solutions. Whatever the circumstances that surrounded the decision to follow UNESCO's Modern Heritage and DOCOMOMO's programme were, there is now an additional requirement for modernist buildings forty years of age or more. In the hope of easing an acceptance of preserving a certain modernist building, with its implied spending and at times the stripping of some rights from the proprietor, the NCCAL seems to pursue a sort of 'branding.'

DOCOMOMO's mission since its 1988 inception in Eindhoven, the Netherlands, has been to document and conserve buildings of the Modern Movement worldwide.[22]

It is perhaps noteworthy that DOCOMOMO does not have a chapter in Kuwait yet – it is a work in progress and one of the NCCAL's ambitions.[23] In any case, the end result is clear: there are at the time of writing no modern buildings in Kuwait that DOCOMOMO recognises as being worthy of documentation and conservation.

Let us assume for a moment that one or more buildings, for example Kuwait Towers, will eventually acquire recognition from UNESCO and DOCOMOMO. Would it make a difference? Perhaps. One must keep in mind that DOCOMOMO neither has any legal authority to intervene locally, nor does its recognition of a certain building have binding powers. The only leverage it offers is a sort of soft power. Nonetheless, if one decides to look at these sorts of recognition as brands, then it becomes clear how the perceived value of the recognised buildings increases. In a society obsessed with brand value and international prestige, it might be just the right catalyst.

While a 'brand' is a semantic shortcut to recognise an object as intrinsically valuable, the way it works is by assigning extrinsic (cultural) value to the object in question. Yet, there are a myriad of other ways to assign extrinsic value. Take for example the well-known effect that a compelling story about an item increases the price someone is willing to pay for it. Similarly, it seems that initiating the conversation about buildings slowly adds weight to their cultural worth, and perhaps heightens the need to preserve them. The NCCAL has been perceptive enough to ride the conversation bandwagon to further its agenda. For example, it initiated the *Al-Thuluth Al-Akheer* talk series,

2. Aerial view of Kuwait City, 1970s.
© Saudi Aramco World/SAWDIA, Tor Eigeland.

20. J. Ockman and R. Williamson, *Architecture School: Three Centuries of Educating Architects in North America* (Cambridge: MIT Press, 2012).

21. "Course Description," Kuwait University College of Architecture, accessed March 2015.

22. DOCOMOMO, "DOCOMOMO Constitution – Revision 2010," *Journal* (August 2010): 88–93.

23. Interview with Zahra Ali Baba, Kuwait City, April 2015.

3. Entrance lobby of the former Ministry of Information and Guidance (1959–1962) in Kuwait City, today's National Council for Culture, Arts and Letters headquarters. © Centre for Research and Studies on Kuwait.

the *Kethra* (abundance) exhibition at the 13th International Architecture Exhibition of la Biennale di Venezia in 2012, and *Acquiring Modernity* at the 14th International Architecture Exhibition of la Biennale di Venezia in 2014.[24]

The NCCAL's mission is clear: change attitudes through discussion and awareness.[25] With each of these conversations, the circle of involved participants widens. Better yet, the media coverage of these events exposes them to a national audience among which ideas of modernity and preservation have a better chance of trickling down into society, somehow finding their way to decision makers.

In parallel to NCCAL's efforts, Dar al-Athar al-Islamiyah (DAI) and its consultants have been working on an extensive catalogue of modern build-

ings in Kuwait. Together with this publication, it is supposed to offer a reference for future researchers willing to dig deeper into Kuwait's modern heritage.[26] It was about time; the preservation movement still needs intellectual weight of course, it is but a start, and more academic effort is needed to create a movement strong enough to alter, enrich, and strengthen the current legal framework.

What these efforts signal is a growing societal desire for introspection and for redefining its identity vis-à-vis its accomplishments. Armed with richer referents it is better suited to remodel its awareness, to re-arrange its priorities, and to re-evaluate its possessions. Some hope that the future will bring about an awareness that guarantees the preservation of some or all of Kuwait's modern era buildings.

However, at the heart of all of this is an aspiration towards better decisions regarding our built environment. The newer is not always better, and the older might be irreplaceable. ▪

24. Noura Alsager, ed., *Acquiring Modernity* (Kuwait: National Council for Culture, Arts and Letters, 2014).

25. Interview with Zahra Ali Baba. *Op cit.*

26. Interview with Roberto Fabbri, Kuwait City, April 2015.

THORSTEN BOTZ-BORNSTEIN

The Pietilä Kuwait Buildings Revisited

In 1969, Reima and Raili Pietilä were invited to participate in an architecture competition for the improvement of Kuwait's old town. From 1969–1970, the architects spent four weeks in Kuwait to become acquainted with the country's urban milieu. In 1970 they drafted a report titled, "City of Kuwait: A Future Concept." No winner of the competition was announced. Instead the planning board asked each of the four participating offices to develop a particular area of Kuwait's old town. The Pietiläs were assigned the development of the downtown shore area, located east of the Seif Palace.

In particular, they were asked to conceive three buildings: an extension of the Seif Palace, the Council of Ministers, the Ministry of Foreign Affairs.

A certain absurdity of paradigms determined the *style* of the Seif Palace Extension project and, indirectly, also the *style* of the Ministry. The original Seif Palace consisted of two relatively small buildings, constructed between 1907 and 1917. Both buildings had details such as *mashrabiyyas*, balustrades, as well as doors framed with brick reliefs.

The old Seif Palace was directly connected to the much newer but predominant clock tower complex designed by British architects Pearce, Hubbard and Partners in 1963. In 1988, the construction of an immense government complex southwest of the two Seif Palaces (old and new) began. This complex would be named the 'New Seif Palace,' making what had so far been called the 'New Seif Palace' part of the 'Old Seif Palace.' As a result, the entire 'old looking' part of the Seif Palace – that is the original two small buildings dating back to 1917, plus the new pastiche part

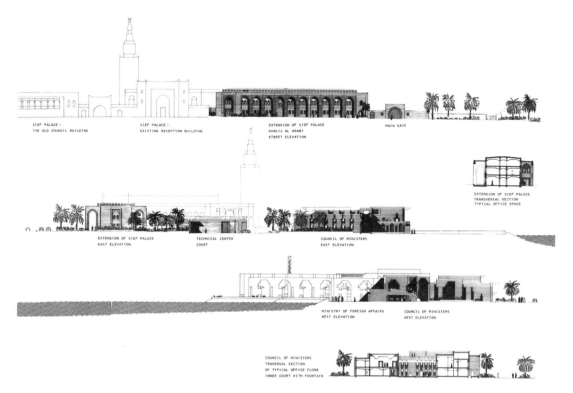

1. Elevations and sections of Seif Palace Extension and Ministry of Foreign Affairs in Kuwait City, Reima and Raili Pietilä, 1973–1983. © Aga Khan Trust for Culture, courtesy of the architect.

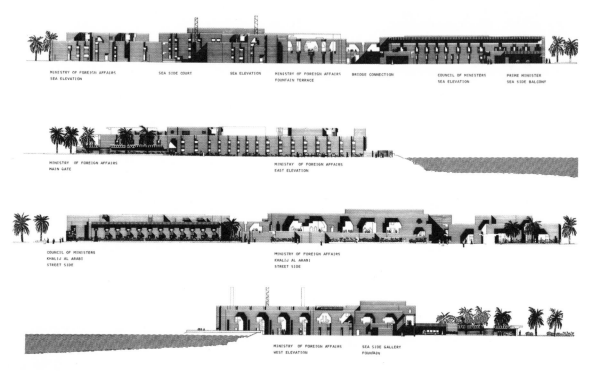

2. Elevations of Ministry of Foreign Affairs in Kuwait City, Reima and Raili Pietilä, 1973–1983.
© Aga Khan Trust for Culture, courtesy of the architect.

from 1963 – were lumped together and given the summary predicate 'Old Seif Palace.' Today, tourist websites such as Kuwait-info.com and even the government website evoke the impression that the entire Old Seif Palace was built between 1907 and 1917. The Archnet web entry on the Pietiläs talks about the "nineteenth century Seif Palace" adjacent to The Pietilä buildings, which is inaccurate, because what is immediately adjacent to those buildings is the 1963 addition.

The extension was made to what is today called the 'Old Seif Palace,' (the 'New Seif Palace' when the Pietiläs were working on it). More precisely, the building contract stipulated that the Seif Palace Extension was to follow the *style* of the original building, irrespective of the latter's questionable originality.

The Ministry

Pietilä had the double task of retrieving a non-existent past and anticipating an unclear future. How did he solve this conundrum? Was the 1963 Palace really an example of the new Islamic architecture that the advisory committee or Kuwaiti authorities had in mind? If so, it is safe to assume that it was not what the Pietiläs had in mind. Concerning the Ministry, they established a relationship with local traditions that transcended mere imitation and representation. They were obviously looking for a new vocabulary. However, in many cases, this resulted in a complete change of language that the local public might only understand with much difficulty. For example, the shapes of the colonnades were arguably too estranged and probably too experimental for the conservative local taste. The

aluminium soffits in the corridors were painted in blue and light green, which may have looked unfamiliar and inauthentic to the local eye, because reeds are normally used after they have been dried and are thus brown. Further, the size of the tiles significantly differed from the traditional size of mosaic tiles and the choice of their colours was not related to any regional set of colours.

Occasionally, by shying away from any literal reinstatement of shapes and items, the Pietiläs played with themes that were alien to Arab culture and seemed imported. The most radical example was the silhouettes of the spruce trees, which are typically European, or more specifically Finnish. For Finns, this tree symbolises a deeply felt relationship with nature and certainly made much sense for the Hervanta Com-

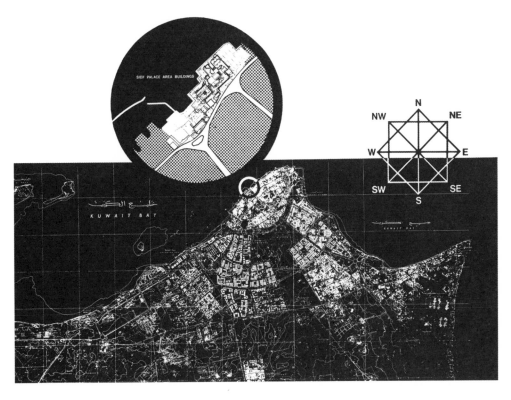

3. Site location of Seif Palace Extension and Ministry of Foreign Affairs in Kuwait City, Reima and Raili Pietilä, 1973–1983. © Aga Khan Trust for Culture, courtesy of the architect.

munity Centre, because this suburb of Tampere is located in the middle of the forest. What feelings or thoughts do Kuwaitis associate with such trees?

The 'Skin Technique'

As a result of its city-like floor plan, the entire Ministry complex appeared half-open. The Pietiläs also achieved this through the 'skin technique,' relying on the sophisticated use of traditional building elements, such as contours and arches. However, this was only a secondary effect: The interior of this modern building was defined by elements derived from Arab heritage, utilising the skin technique as a way of managing the tensions between identity and internationalism. The entire building proposal is indicative of the architect's surrealism, which is also present in other projects, such

as the Dipoli building (1961–66), and Malmi Church. However, in Kuwait the strategy was taken one step further. Here, there is surrealistic play with the skin concept – both inside and outside – making explicit comparisons with surrealist paintings, such as René Magritte's *Le Double Secret* or *Le Thérapeute*, possible. At the same time, Pietilä never gave in to any kind of concrete symbolism. Italian fashion designer

4. René Magritte, *Le Double Secret*, 1927, oil on canvas. © Artists Rights Society

Anna Battista has been fascinated by the Pietiläs' Ministry as an example of 'architecture through tailoring,' because, for her, the building offers a

5. René Magritte, *Le Thérapeute*, 1937, oil on canvas. © Artists Rights Society

perfect "outside to inside vision." She writes:

> Indeed the Ministry of Foreign Affairs building presented an outside wall cut-away to reveal an unexpected scale of openings to the wall that separated the outdoor and indoor environment. The transition zone was a bit like a colourful "lining" and seemed to have the same purpose of the lining in a jacket or a coat. This feature was used by the architects to create a visual access from the street to what went on inside the building. [...] Can you think of other buildings that could be compared to garments?[1]

The Ministry Transformed

What remains of the Pietiläs' 'transcultural' approach today? Ambitions such as theirs could have taken on a symbolic dimension in a place like Kuwait, where 70 percent of the population are foreigners. However, because of the context described above, it appears the statement could not live up to the idealist intentions of its creators. In 1994, major 'reconstruction' works began on the Ministry site, the most ambitious project being the elimination of the cutout wall openings (in spite of intensive research it has been impossible to obtain the names of the architects and companies that carried out these works). Further major transformations included turning the open corridor into a closed one by adding several supplementary buildings in front of the street side facade. Most of the added building parts feature arch-like shapes, decorated with modernist geometrical forms such as upright standing squares placed on the top of the arches or on rooftops. Initially, the use of the arch as a main motive has been against the guidelines for the design of the Ministry complex, as issued by the Ministry of Public Works in 1970, which strongly advised against monumentality.

The new additions, placed on the terrace from which one could previously see parts of the building's interior from the street side, have been furnished with a dome made of stained glass. Again this runs counter to the Pietiläs' intentions, as they conscientiously avoided domes. Underneath the new dome, heavy wooden doors mark the official – though practically unused – main entrance to the Ministry. Smaller, dome-shaped windows have been placed on the roof wherever possible. The yellow bricks have been removed from part of the original street facade wall, showing this section without cladding it in raw concrete.

Most recently, the east facade facing the fish market has been amended, with additions placed in front of the original buildings occupying a surface of 9000 square metres. The project value of this latest addition is fifteen million US dollars and the work was carried out by the office of Dar Saleh al-Qallaf Engineering Consultants. The aesthetics of these buildings draws on the theme of the upright standing decorative squares from the previous structure.

The most important consequence of the transformations imposed upon the building over the last thirty years is that the Arab motifs found in the interior are no longer visible through holes. The holes no longer exist and most of the motifs have been eliminated. Primarily, this means the skin concept has been removed, and, as a result, the skin has become a meaningless modern shell with a strange contour – through which motifs can still be seen, but have no function and look rather pointless and awkward. Many long-term residents of Kuwait never suspected these buildings belonged

to a ministry, and identified the area as an industrial zone. Partially responsible for this misperception is Pietilä's own decision to place the A/C centre and cooling towers on the street side, which diminished the aesthetic appeal of the complex from the very beginning. Secondly, by eliminating the openings, the language and structure of the building moved from being half-open to entirely closed.

Just a few years after the Ministry's completion, the systematic elimination of the Pietiläs' 'Islamic' motifs began. Coloured tiles were either torn off, or, in rare cases, painted over. The tiles that remain are only in the restrooms and kitchens. According to the Kuwaiti architect in charge of the current renovation projects (whose name has been consistently withheld from the author), the removal of the tiles was the most urgent task, as they "did not add to the building, but made it look uglier." The Ministry was apparently commonly referred to as a *public toilet* because of the tile theme.

A few years after its completion, the coral fountain was refurbished with black granite plates. The corals in tile were replaced by white marble stripes, on which golden arabesques are engraved. (The present architect, who was in residence in 2014, was not aware that the fountain featured coloured tiles, despite it being the most documented element in any international publication of the Pietiläs' Seif Palace project.) The remaining coral fountains had to be demolished when major additions were made to the terrace square. All other original fountains have either been modified or have disappeared.

Because the seaside terrace could rarely be used in the Kuwaiti climate, a covered *diwaniyya*-style reception room was constructed. The *diwaniyya* is covered by a white tent structure with a pointed top, from which hangs a chandelier imitating palm branches. The *diwaniyya*'s walls are clad with artificial fur that has been strewn with metallic pallets.

After conversing with several Kuwaiti architects, it is apparent that the planning history of the Ministry is one of a series of miscommunications between architects and their clients. Firstly, the complex was planned by the Ministry of Foreign Affairs and the Council of Minsters, but due to several misunderstandings, the buildings were built in a way that made them unfit for the latter's purposes. From the beginning, both buildings were used only by the Ministry and a new Council of Minsters was built elsewhere. These architects repeated a reproach that was also voiced by Roger Connah: "Why had there not been more openings to the seaside?"[2] Reima Pietilä himself answered this question, pointing out that in the hot climate, large window openings are not useful. More window openings have been created, however. The engineer the Pietiläs collaborated with, Vilho Pekkala, explains that, "the facades on which the sun shone were provided with shades made from concrete elements, which decreased heat transfer through the windows. At that time, thermal effective windows, as used nowadays, were unknown."[3]

Several architects responded to the Pietiläs' 'hot climate' argument with the counter-question – *why?* – with one asking 'why, if he was so concerned about the climate, did he design an open corridor as the main passageway between two major buildings, forcing people to walk in

the heat when going from one end of the complex to the other?' The Pietiläs would probably reply that, at the time, these were two separate buildings (the Ministry of Foreign Affairs and the Council of Minsters) and that only a very small number of people would have to walk from one end to the other anyway. The courtyard concept was gleaned from regional architecture. Was that a mistake? The Pietiläs believed they had done enough. They had designed the arcades and galleries surrounding the buildings as "climatic sun-protecting shelters [that] also provide ample opportunity for a poetic imagery of shape and shadow."[4] Climatic questions were meticulously considered, as explained by Vilho Pekkala:

> The exterior walls were of a brick-mineral construction. The mineral wool had a thickness of 50 mm and it was coated with aluminum foil to reflect the heat. This was a new solution and proved to be effective. Roof surfaces were white, given effective thermal insulation. [...] The Seif Palace included an air conditioning centre with large, ceramic, water-evaporating cooling

6. Coral fountains in the courtyard of the Ministry of Foreign Affairs, Reima and Raili Pietilä, 1985. These coral fountains disappeared when the additions were built on the terrace.
© Museum of Finnish Architecture, Reima Pietilä, 1985.

1. Anna Battista, "Buildings like Garments: Al Seef Palace," accessed June 12, 2011, http://irenebrination.typepad.com/irenebrinatio n_notes_on_a/2011/04/Seif-palace.html.

2. Roger Connah, *Fantômas Fragments Fictions: An Architectural Journey through the Twentieth Century* (Cambridge, MA: MIT Press, 1989).

3. Vilho Pekkala, "The Structural Engineer in the Realization of Architecture," in *Hikes into Pietilä Terrain*, ed. A. Niskanen (Helsinki: Rakennustaiteen Seura, 2007), 73–6.

4. Reima Pietilä, "Intermediate Zones in Modern Architecture," in *Reima Pietilä: Exhibition at the Museum of Finnish Architecture*, ed. Roger Connah (Helsinki: Museum of Finnish Architecture, 1985), 87.

towers. Local specialists later wondered how it was possible that such small amounts of energy were needed for the cooling.[5]

The five-metre-wide street side arcade kept the interior elevation in the shade. Apart from this, all windows were lowered thirty centimetres from the external surface.

In 1998, in order to improve the situation, the entire former cutout outside wall was closed and the terrace was transformed into a five-metre-wide air-conditioned corridor. A reception room, covered by a dome and made of stained glass, was built on the terrace. This is the most dramatic change the building underwent.

The Environment of the Ministry

The transformation of the Ministry's environment is as radical as that of the Ministry itself and needs to be analysed in order to understand the present status of the Pietiläs' buildings. The construction of a huge New Seif Palace began before the Iraqi occupation, a few years after the accomplishment of Pietilä's Seif area project. The project was carried out by the Kuwaiti Archicenter and was only concluded during the late 1990s, because the occupation halted all construction work. The project modified the coastline, being built on reclaimed land, right behind (as seen from the land) the Old Seif Palace, along a new shoreline that extends 280 metres into the sea. The Old Seif Palace became landlocked and the Pietiläs' Ministry was impacted by the development of the seaside with new installations, such as a dock for grand visitors' yachts and a heliport. Originally, the Pietiläs had placed the Ministry buildings close to the shore, aligned with the older Seif Palace.

The authors of *The Evolving Culture of Kuwait* highlight the fact that the Pietiläs "built along the coastline skillfully, deploying its natural formation and making the water front an integral feature of their design."[6] While they attempted to produce an "imaginative portrait of the spirit of Kuwait that would be seen from out in the Gulf,"[7] at present the building can hardly be seen from the sea. Furthermore, the 1,250-metre-long waterfront of the Seif Palace is far from being a living feature in the city, as public access to this area is strictly restricted. The colonnade of the Seif Palace Extension is not used either. The Pietiläs' interpretation of the central waterfront as, the main natural value of the old city, sounds today like a farfetched slogan.

Most of the Ministry's neighbouring buildings are *pan-Arab* in style: the 1963 Seif Palace, the New Seif Palace, and the 45,000-square-metre Grand Mosque, which was completed in 1986. Stephen Gardiner found this mosque, which has a 70-metre-high minaret, to be "a little conventional and over-concerned with perpetuating tradition."[8] A recent building on the same side of the Arabian Gulf Street is Al-Babtain Central Library for Arabic Poetry, completed in 2007. The library's main feature is a stylised – though still very literal – Islamic arch. Its main buildings evoke the shape of an open book. The library's website praises the architecture of the building because it uses "traditional Kuwaiti characteristics," such as "huge wooden doors" and a "precise choice of colours and their harmonisation with furniture and carpets." A new heritage village is under construction almost across the street from the Ministry. However, the most dramatic change has been brought about by the construction of

the new tower of the Central Bank of Kuwait, which is celebrated on the bank's website as a new landmark symbolising "the country's significant economic power in the twenty-first century." It supersedes Arne Jacobsen's old Central Bank building. The construction of this new tower was concluded in 2015 and is located right opposite the Ministry. The forty-storey-high slim pyramid was commissioned to the international firm HOK, which specialises in skyscrapers and is famous for the design of the Baku flame towers in Azerbaijan. The placement of such a tall building in this particular location contradicts all planning initiatives from the 1970s, especially those of the Pietiläs.

The idea from experienced planners to build more cultural buildings of national importance was adopted by the new planners, but unfortunately only after the Sharq area was neglected for almost thirty years. Al-Babtain Poetry Library is the first cultural building that has been added to the vicinity since 1986. The driving force of the recent renewal is the new Central Bank high-rise.

The Macro-Scale

The macro-scale of its surroundings affected the development of the Seif Palace. By the time the Pietiläs' Seif project was completed, Kuwait's urban condition had developed towards a cityscape without hierarchy or layering, dominated by a number of unconnected tall buildings and mega-projects with questionable cultural and environmental sustainability. This tendency remains particularly visible in the neighbourhood of the Ministry, where urban planning and architecture did not seem to matter for three decades. Given the urban development east of the Ministry, as well as the relative quietness of the New Seif Palace area, the Ministry is no longer at the centre of the crescent, enclosed by the first ring road. Instead, it is situated at the periphery of the urban context of the Sharq district. This gives the Seif Palace area a different value. Officially, almost the entire Ministry is located in the Sharq district, as the district border cuts from the Seif roundabout right through the Ministry premises, up to the parking lot. The rest of the Seif area is in Qibla. This means that, in spite of the geometric continuity produced by the parallel ring roads, the significance of the Seif Palace site has changed considerably, and the transformations have left the Ministry particularly isolated in geographical terms. While in the 1980s, the purpose of the Seif project was to revive the old central city by designing three new buildings, today the Ministry buildings find themselves locked away in the far western corner of the Sharq district. The Sharq side is dominated by the shopping mall, Souq Sharq, the first grand project to be built after the Iraqi invasion. Any natural connection with the Seif buildings and the area has thus been removed. Both the Ministry and the Seif buildings are prohibited to the public; the former can't be seen from the street anymore, being hidden behind the latest monumental additions. The arches and the emphasis on monumentality create a distance between the building and the spectator. As a result of the trauma of the Iraqi invasion, a machine gun mounted on an army vehicle is constantly pointing at passersby, which may cause them to feel uncomfortable.

The area that accommodates five buildings by world-class architects in three of the city centre districts (Qibla, Sharq, and Dasman),

is extremely incoherent. This is particularly extreme in the area opposite Souq Sharq, which remains a sand field, following the1980s demolitions, as seen in the Google Earth picture. The key buildings that attracted Gardiner's attention in 1980 are there, but any sense of urban coordination is lacking. Today, these are still located in former demolished areas and, as Shiber predicted fifty years ago, little thought was given to the orientation of the buildings or their structural order. The Museum of Modern Art is located in an old highschool building in the middle of these sand fields. No "tailoring" of the urban fabric has been done. There is a lack of coherence between the relevance of these buildings and the district of Sharq as a whole. To a large extent, the inconsistent handling of their relationship to each other – "Seif versus Sharq" – is the reason for the feeling of urban desolation that persists in this part of the city in spite of the realisation of multiple projects. The Pietiläs' main purpose was the informal integration of the area into the urban fabric and the metaphorical appropriation of the *genius loci*, so the resulting reality is rather ironic.

Conclusions

The Pietiläs' Ministry could have been a successful example of critical regionalism that is inspired by transcultural thinking. The confused perception of the building can be attributed to several factors: badly organised urbanism in Kuwait, inadequate building aesthetics, and general difficulties implementing critical regionalism in the non-West.

The Pietiläs' architectural agenda remained far from the Kuwaiti mindset, as it was influenced by an ambition to go beyond geometry, to create unpredictable shapes, and to implement a fragmented

"pluralising antisystem, antihierarchy, disentity, [and] the context of assembling-disassembling,"[9] which resulted in surreal abstractions. Conservative Kuwait was not the right place to experiment with such ideas. Khan noted in 1988 that "there must be mass appeal in the form that is communicable to and understandable by the public,"[10] and found that this appeal did not exist in the case of the Ministry. Connah had similar thoughts. The Pietiläs' expressions were too abstract, too ironic and too poetically vague. For example, they pointed out "the windows are guardian shapes, [...] [and] that the function of these wall openings is to allow friendly forces in and hold out enemy powers, spirits [...]"[11] Even to well-informed researchers it might not be entirely clear what is meant by this. The problem seems to be that the Pietiläs' locally inspired symbols, even in instances where they were recognised by locals, are mere symbols without deeper meaning or connection. In Kuwait, especially after the Iraqi invasion, the search for identity-symbols has evolved along

5. Pekkala, "Structural Engineer," 74.

6. Royal Scottish Museum, *The Evolving Culture of Kuwait* (Edinburgh: HMSO Books, 1985), 91.

7. Stephen Gardiner, *Kuwait, the Making of a City* (Harlow: Longman, 1983), 143.

8. Ibid., 77.

9. Malcolm Quantrill, *Reima Pietilä: Architecture, Context and Modernism* (New York: Rizzoli, 1985).

10. Sikander I. Khan, "In Search of a Direction in the Contemporary Architecture of Arabia" (Master thesis, Massachusetts Institute of Technology, 1988), 136.

11. Quantrill, *Reima Pietilä*, 130.

rather straightforward lines. If it is true that critical regionalism can emerge only through "a new kind of relation between designer and user,"[12] it needs to be stated that in Kuwait such a relationship has not been established.

The examples of critical regionalism most often cited by Kenneth Frampton are small-scale projects with a strong personal input. However, in the Kuwaiti case, the main problem was not the size or the official character of the building. On the one hand there is time and history from the region, yet ahistorical modernism attempts to base its expressions on *eternal* truths – or at least on a timeless concept of eternal innovation. It is obvious that this dichotomy is useless in the Kuwaiti context. Critical regionalism can only be understood in relationship with certain perceptions of modernity. The problem is that various perceptions of modernity are not necessarily the same in the non-West as in the West. Modernism as a utopian and purist ideology has been accepted by many non-Western countries in the past, and has more recently been rejected by neo-traditionalist or religious cultural movements. Different from this is the kind of modernity that is often on the Western mind today. This modernity speaks out against the above utopian proto-modernity, with its innocent faith in the future, belief in progress, and so on. The new, predominately Western, modernity sees itself as a 'critical' (some might say 'cynical') type of modernity that is disillusioned by humanism, though it still somehow clings to it. This new modernity sees itself mainly as a resistance movement attempting to slow down a soulless process of unification, industrialisation and mechanisation of an old modernity.

At the same time it has difficulties spelling out an alternative vision of the future. Critical regionalist thought is derived from this critical type of modernity, which is why it cannot be installed in regions where the image of the first type of modernity persists (either as an example to emulate or as an example to reject).

In a globally compressed world, determined by the transnationalisation of capital and internationalisation of labor, many people might desire not to transcend their ethnic and cultural roots but rather to reinstate them. *Liberty*, in this case, is the freedom to choose, emphasise, and demonstrate one's identity. But politics is also a factor. According to Nezar Al-Sayyad, "many Middle Eastern governments resorted to using local and foreign architects to help them create such a new national style."[13] It is not a coincidence that almost all the important building design commissions of the 1970s and 1980s were given to foreign architects who pledged to continue the Arab building tradition. New Arab architecture was a matter of national pride and identity to an exaggerated degree. A large part of the architectural activity in the region has been concentrated on official buildings and palaces, as, according to Kultermann, such buildings represent "an image of the country's power and authority."[14] It is not surprising that the Pietiläs' abstract "transculturalism," which was supposed to *undermine* authorities and hierarchies, has been found unacceptable. While critical regionalism sees the political instrumentalisation of vernacular architecture as a danger, for the Kuwaiti authorities architecture should construct national identity in a relatively direct fashion. This is especially true in the case of the Ministry of Foreign Affairs, which is supposed to show how official repre-

sentatives want to appear in the national arena. Here, critical regionalism offers no solution, since it constantly avoids univocal narratives and favors ambiguous hybridity. In a world without aesthetic hierarchies, all styles are equal and everybody is free to add his/her option to the transcultural mosaic. This is not the way an official building in Kuwait should be designed.

The Pietiläs asked Kuwaitis to adopt their pluralising aesthetic anti-system of anti-hierarchy and dis-entity, which was difficult for the local consumption-oriented community to comprehend. Another reason why the Pietiläs' language could not be accepted – closely linked to the one above – is that it was too abstract. Traditionally, abstraction is permitted and encouraged in Arab culture in the form of ornaments, but in the Pietiläs' vocabulary, the concreteness has been taken out of the Arab, as well as out of the Western. Both Arab culture and Western culture are represented in an utterly abstract fashion and are subsequently combined. To understand such forms requires an intuition shaped by a critical culture. Other examples are the mosaics with large tiles, reed soffits with aluminum sticks, and arches presented as strange hole contour?

Not everyone can appreciate this abstract kind of aesthetic play, which requires a certain taste or reflective mind to leap from concrete facts to abstract concepts. •

12. Alexander Tzonis and Liane Lefaivre, "The Grid and the Pathway," *Architecture in Greece*, n. 5 (1981): 5.

13. Nezar Al-Sayyad, "Space in the Islamic City," *Journal of Architecture and Planning Research*, v. 4, n. 2 (1987): 259.

14. Udo Kultermann, "Contemporary Arab Architecture: The Architects in Saudi Arabia," *Mimar*, n. 16 (1985): 42.

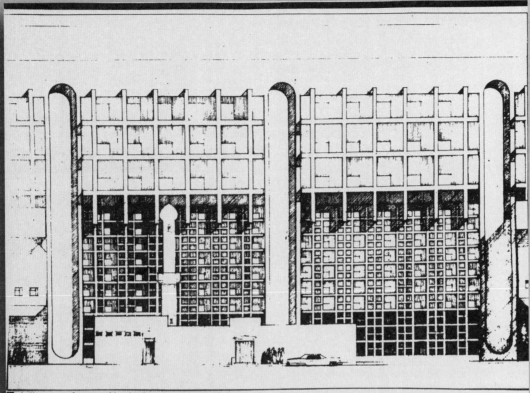

First attempt was the competition, but it went on to be modified...

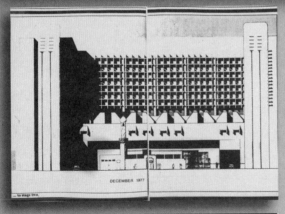

DECEMBER 1977

... to stage two.

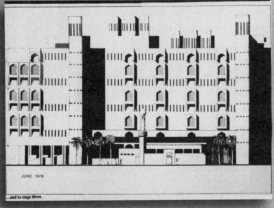

JUNE 1978

...and to stage three.

SUNSHINE AND THE RULE OF LAW

Tales from the Arabian nights? Anthony Blee gave Lynda Relph-Knight the run-down on the Kuwaiti law courts scheme.

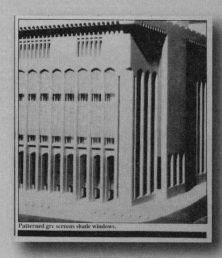

Patterned grc screens shade windows.

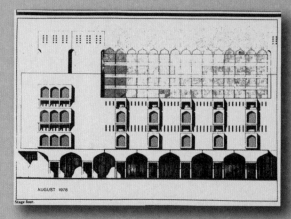

AUGUST 1978

Stage four.

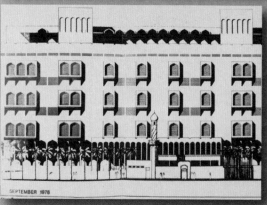

SEPTEMBER 1978

Client; Kuwait Ministries of Works and Justice. Architects: Sir Basil Spence International Partnership in association with Fitzroy Robinson Partnership. Consulting and Civil engineers: White, Young and Partners. Services: Williams Sale Partnership. Quantity surveyors: Edmond Shipway and Partners.

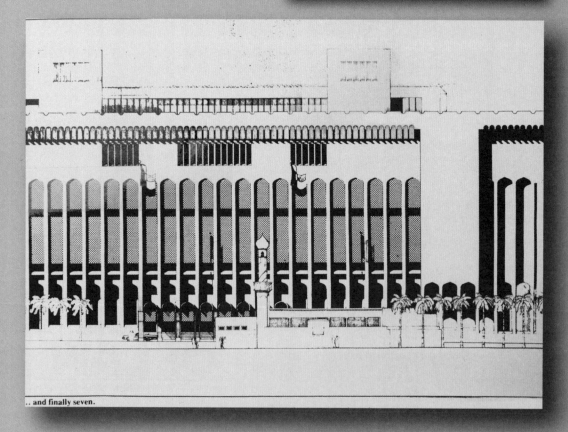

.. and finally seven.

Towards a Critique of a Kuwaiti *Nahdha*: Al-`Imara al-Haditha and the Competing Narratives on Architecture and Urban Modernity

ASSEEL AL-RAGAM

The decades between the 1950s and the 1980s represented a period of nation building in Kuwait. The 1950s Development Program (DP) marks the beginning of this period of rapid modernisation. The DP was a cultural, social, political, and an economic program, introduced by the state to distribute oil wealth among Kuwaiti citizens. However, it resulted in a deeply divided social structure and a stratified urban fabric. The DP also included urban and infrastructural changes, the modernisation of the old town, restrictive housing programs, and neighbourhood planning based on ethnicity and socioeconomic status. These 'modern' transformations represented an overarching state ideology aimed at increasing control of residents' everyday lives. These latent goals were ignored, at first, because of the economic and social opportunities provided by the DP. Thus, the multi-scaled networks established due to DP projects ensured state hegemony within a heterogeneous community and a politically volatile region. On the one hand, this thirty-year period was one of exhilarating and innovative creative activity that crushed crippling historical class dependencies and gender inequalities; on the other, it was a period of severed relationships between residents and the city's natural and built environment. This paper examines the processes and networks of the DP and illustrates how shifts in power can be mapped on the Kuwaiti landscape.

The study expands on arguments developed by the author in previously published research, including a 2008 PhD dissertation entitled "Towards a Critique of an Architectural *Nahdha*: A Kuwaiti Example."[1] The study relies on the primary sources obtained from Kuwait Municipality's archive and indexed in the final chapter of the dissertation; those include architectural and urban projects, drafts of master plans, sociological studies, and correspondence letters between invited architects, planners and state officials. In addition, the author revisits and expands on previously published themes such as the role of invited architects in relation to local actors and the multiple representations of Kuwaiti modernity. These arguments rely on primary sources that provide first-hand testimony of this period of development.[2]

Expanding the Geographical and Temporal Boundaries of Modernity

This case study on Kuwait stretches the geographical and temporal boundaries of modernity. Modernity is understood "as the modes of experiencing that which is new in modern society and its cultural manifestations."[3] Kuwaiti modernity can be traced through the various – and at times conflicting – definitions of what constituted the modern. Officials at the Kuwait Municipality and other planning departments represented modernity through nation building projects that were based on the privileged

1. Asseel Al-Ragam,"Towards a Critique of an Architectural *Nahdha*: A Kuwaiti Example." (PhD diss., University of Pennsylvania, 2008).

2. Saba George Shiber, *The Kuwait Urbanization* (Kuwait: Government Printing Press, 1964) and Saba George Shiber, *Recent Arab City Growth* (Kuwait: Government Printing, 1969).

3. David Frisby, *Fragments of Modernity: Theories of Modernity in the Work of Simmel, Kracauer, and Benjamin* (Cambridge: MIT Press, 1986), 2.

'citizen' and on discriminatory policies that fragmented the urban fabric along social, demographic, and ethnic lines. *Al-Nahdha*'s[4] progressive doctrine, discussed in more detail below, contributed to the evolution of existing familial, social, and cultural traditions. A new Kuwaiti middle class represented modernity through this progressive understanding of self. Local and regional architects of Arab descent debated a new relationship with the past to construct a modern present. In addition, international design professionals, invited by the state, proposed solutions inspired by a 1960s Western debate on the modern city, orientalist visions of the 'Arab City,' and 'makeshift' building in colonial contexts, most notably the North African *bidonvilles* or slum villages.

These different views found their expression in Kuwait's built environment, where, at times, perspectives and ideologies were negotiated within these modern spaces. These contrasting perspectives also led to abandoned architectural projects, changes to the course of development, and, more productively, novel experimentations in design and construction techniques. These distinct yet parallel narratives illustrate Kuwait's rich modern architectural heritage and also the limited role that the architect sometimes plays in relation to the privileged position held by high-ranking civil servants of the state. This reading emphasises the "role of local actors in mobilising development that are otherwise overlooked when too great an emphasis is placed on colonial agency."[5] Interestingly, the emergence of the press, as a cultural outlet, was an important stage for the debate on Kuwaiti modernity.

Intellectual *Nahdha*

In contrast to European and North American modern experiences emanating from a critique of industrialisation or urbanisation, a modern consciousness in Kuwait preceded any form of these modernisation processes. Cultural modernity was a response to the arrival of progressive Arab literature from Lebanon and Egypt in the form of magazines subscribed to by the Kuwaiti elite. In turn, a nascent literary *nahdha* was nurtured in Kuwait through social and professional clubs (*nawadi*), gradually penetrating different disciplines to give rise to feminist movements, a politically and culturally charged popular press, and a new building technique.

Since the nineteenth century, the Middle East as a whole has been undergoing radical change. Ibrahim Abu-Lughod describes the history of the region during the nineteenth and twentieth centuries as a "history of transformation," arguing that predominantly Muslim, introverted societies transformed rapidly into secular, outward-looking ones.[6] In Kuwait, measured change first unfolded during the course of World War I, when the Gulf region was usurped by Western imperial powers that formed various military alliances, and when regional cooperation furthered the economic interests of the imperialists and a few local elites. During the war, conduits for cultural exchange were established between the Middle East and Europe.

After the collapse of the Ottoman Empire, and more so at the end of World War II, additional changes occurred. The reshaping of the region into "modern" states by Western powers led to a new Arab awareness and a resistance to colonial empires. These developments helped bring about some of the most important ideological movements in the history of the Arab world in general and Kuwait in particular. Arab nationalism was rooted in *Al-Nahdha*, an ideology of progress and enlightenment. It began as a literary

4. *Al-Nahdha* is an ideology of progress and enlightenment. For more see George Antonius, *The Arab Awakening: The Story of the Arab National Movement* (New York: Capricorn Books, 1939).

5. Asseel Al-Ragam, "Critical Nostalgia: Kuwait Urban Modernity and Alison and Peter Smithson's Kuwait Urban Study and Mat–Building," *The Journal of Architecture* v. 20, n. 1 (2015): 16.

6. Ibrahim Abu-Lughod, *Arab Rediscovery of Europe: A Study in Cultural Encounters* (Princeton: Princeton University Press, 1969), 3.

movement in the nineteenth century and it spread to other disciplines, gradually penetrating the entire Arab region during the twentieth century. In 1946, George Antonius, an Arab-Lebanese author, documented this movement in the period between the wars in his book *The Arab Awakening: The Story of the Arab National Movement.*[7] Forty years later Albert Hourani, one of the more prominent scholars on the history of the Arab people, wrote on the importance of *al-nahdha* in the construction of progressive Arab thought.[8] The word *taqaddum* was used to describe change and progress, while *rajiya* and *ta'akhur* – meaning, respectively, backwardness and delay – identified conditions of stasis and stagnation.

By the mid-1920s, Kuwait was experiencing a similar renascence. This *nahdha* began as a relatively small literary movement, as recorded by one of Kuwait's first historians, Abdul-Aziz Al-Rushaid. Clubs (*nawadi*) were the first forms of civil society organisations to help nurture this rebirth. In 1923, the Literary Club was initiated by the Kuwaiti author Khalid Bin Suleiman Al-`Adsani. In 1947, to ensure that Kuwaiti literature reaches a wider audience, two prominent merchants established the first printing press in Kuwait. Among the first printed novellas[9] was *Al-Um Sadiq (A Mother Is a Friend)* by Kuwaiti author Farhan Rashid Al-Farhan. In 1948, the first cultural magazine, *Kathmah,*[10] debuted. Work by local authors was more widely distributed and dependency on Lebanon, Iraq, and Egypt for printing *en masse* ended with the emergence of local publishing organisations.

Modern Kuwaiti prose developed a marked change in literary style that could be detected in the works of Khalid bin Suleiman al-`Adsani, Hashim Al-Rifa`i, and Saqr Bin Salem Al-Shabīb, to name a few.[11] Their works addressed the subject of progress and the right to complete self-determination. Al-Rushaid celebrated the advent of this advanced Kuwaiti literature in his book *Tarikh Al-Kuwait (Kuwait History)*. Writing in 1926, Al-Rushaid stated:

> In Kuwait today an intellectual, scientific, and literary movement is directed by people who have witnessed the changing conditions of this modern period, which can only be described as a period of development (*taqaddum*) and progress rather than a period of stasis and regression (*ta'akhur*).[12] (Translations mine)

Al-Rushaid's book was published concurrently with the arrival of cultural literature from Lebanon and Egypt. Although the availability of these cultural magazines was confined to a largely elite population, some of the progressive ideas they contained were, in turn, disseminated through a more popular Kuwaiti cultural forum: the *diwaniyya* – a place of gathering where politics, culture, and social affairs were discussed. These modern conditions necessitated educated Kuwaitis to reconcile tradition with evolving social and cultural values.

These changes in society were instigated by exposure to new experiences. In the late 1930s, Kuwaiti men and women began travelling abroad, exploring new fashions, and alternative social and cultural forms. Despite there being many social groups that continued to adhere to traditional cultural and societal norms, the majority of the population participated in the transformation and evolution of existing familial, cultural, and social tradition. Haya Al-Mughni, a scholar in Kuwaiti gender politics, explained the social change that was necessary for the modernisation of Kuwaiti society:

1. Cover of *The Arab Awakening*, 1938.

7. George Antonius, *The Arab Awakening: The Story of the Arab National Movement* (New York: Capricorn Books, 1939).

8. Albert Hourani, *The Emergence of the Modern Middle East* (Berkeley and Los Angeles: University of California Press, 1981).

9. Muhammad Yusuf Najim, *Al-Thaqāfah fī al-Kuwayt mundhu bidāyātihā hattá al-ān (Culture in Kuwait from its Beginnings to the Present)* (Kuwait: Dar Suad Al-Sabah, 1997), 438.

10. Ibid.

11. Abdul Aziz Al-Rushaid, *Tarikh al-Kuwait* (Kuwait: Dar Qurtas, 1999), 124–27.

12. Ibid, 98.

The whole idea of *nahdha* was to move forward, to break away from old traditions and customs, and to build a modern infrastructure. The concepts used to describe the world and justify the necessity for change were *taqaddum* (progress) versus *rajiya* (backwardness). The latter was interpreted as being the result of rigid traditions and ignorance, whereas *taqaddum* was equated with scientific knowledge, cultural advancement, and democracy. The aim was to modernise Kuwaiti society and end its isolation from the civilised world.[13]

This Kuwaiti *nahdha* presented a formidable challenge to existing societal and cultural traditions, including the continuance of tribal governance. In addition, Arab nationalism became one of the most important issues in governance for the existing power structure. Increased political representation, greater press liberties, and educational and institutional reform were introduced in an attempt to control popular discontent. These transformations that were also caused by the new building development and its modern technology radically altered spatial experience, social and cultural customs and traditions, and aesthetic values, and gave birth to a new public space. In these spaces, social values, identities, and cultural aspirations were forged and defined. This reading draws connections between Kuwaiti modernity and the experience of space – not a simple, direct relationship between the two, but the complex and implicit association that, in fact, existed. This relationship has informed the appropriation of modern architecture and urban space in Kuwait.

Challenges of Kuwaiti Modernity

During a period of almost thirty years, from the early 1950s to the early 1980s, the Kuwait Municipality and the Public Works Department commissioned over forty design proposals, ranging from urban renewal schemes to the construction of civic buildings as part of a larger 1952 Development Program (DP). As documents, they were powerful representations of utopian ideals. In reality, they present evidence of the challenges faced by the state in mediating between modern reform on the one hand, and pre-oil traditions and alliances on the other. The 1952 DP resulted in comprehensive modern policies for health care, education, and housing. It provided a modern sewage system, healthier living conditions, greater employment opportunities, and economic diversification that, in effect, eased historical dependencies that had crippled a large segment of Kuwaiti society. Conversely, the DP explicitly and implicitly attempted to control class antagonism and the intersection of nationals and non-nationals, the latter achieved through a type of urban zoning and housing policies that excluded non-Kuwaitis.

Implementing the DP, though, depended, in part, on legislating urban policies. The first was the Land Acquisition Policy (LAP), on the basis of which the state, in 1951, expropriated private land from within the old town, mainly for the purpose of development, and at prices above market value. This land was mostly residential housing. The state, in turn, auctioned off land outside the city limits at nominal prices, with priority given to displaced individuals.[14] The expropriation and compensation process resulted in disputes over land ownership, and caused an exponential rise in land value. In effect, a policy that developed out of a desire to modernise the country and distribute oil wealth had an adverse result. A committee report sent to Kuwait from the International Bank for Reconstruction and Development in 1961 and 1963 wrote that:

13. Haya Al-Mughni, *Women in Kuwait: The Politics of Gender* (London: Saqi Books, 2001), 54.

14. Ghanim Al-Najjar, "Decision-Making Process in Kuwait: The Land Acquisition Policy as a Case Study" (PhD diss., University of Exeter, 1984).

The Government buys land at highly inflated prices for development projects and for resale for private buyers. Land purchases amounted to between KD 40 million and KD 60 million in most recent years. Whatever the political or developmental justifications for this practice, the prices fixed by the government for these transactions and the small amount thus far collected on the resale of the land make the public land transactions a rather indiscriminate and inequitable way of distributing the oil revenues. In addition, probably the largest shares of these funds are invested abroad, so that the land purchase program fails to accomplish its main objective of invigorating the Kuwait economy.[15]

The second policy, drafted and ratified in July 1954 by Sheikh Abdullah Al-Salem, was the Public Organising Line (POL). It mandated that all land outside the POL was state-owned and non-negotiable for private ownership. The purpose of the POL was to end land disputes and speculation, and importantly to stop the financial burden on the state from public land transactions. In August 1954, the POL was extended, and a decision was made that all land acquisition outside the city walls was to halt, with the exception of land purchased by the government. The POL, consequently, affected the LAP, and the latter's application was confined to property within the POL. Under these conditions, the LAP applied to only 3.05 percent (543.85 km²) of approximately 17,818 km² of Kuwaiti territory.[16]

Executing the DP also depended on forming civic institutions and planning departments. At first, the planning departments were the foundations for the early stages of state modernity. On July 19 in 1954, a Higher Executive Committee was formed, consisting of three members from the ruling family – Sheikh Sabah Al-Salem, Sheikh Jaber Al-Ali, and Sheikh Khalid Al-Abdullah – along with three non-sheikh members – Ahmed Abdul Latif, Abdul Latif Al-Nusif, and Izzat Ja'afar. A state council and a system of coordination between various government departments were also set up. However, undefined roles within these institutions resulted in administrative overlap. As a result, a reorganisation of the Kuwait Municipality was undertaken, and the Public Works Department (PWD), formed in 1945, was made to accommodate additional technical departments, including an inspection and construction department. Yet, within these departments individuals overextended their reach and dictated the course of planning to suit personal goals and vendettas, making this early period of government formation extremely chaotic and ineffectual.

In addition, British 'experts' were enlisted. As Simon Smith reported, "the political agent acquired additions to his staff, including an economic counselor [who] was permitted to receive instructions from and report [directly] to the Foreign Office."[17] Under these conditions, Herbert Jakins, the political agent in Kuwait from 1949 to 1951, recommended the appointment of a financial advisor. In 1951 Colonel G.C.L. Crichton, a former secretary to the government of India in the Foreign Department, was appointed as the financial "expert."[18] Crichton recommended establishing a board that would coordinate, plan, and execute development projects with the objective of estimating and controlling state expenditures. In 1951, establishing a Development Board (DB) was recommended to oversee the affairs of physical growth. The DB was charged with three main functions. It was responsible for the establishment of land-use guidelines for Kuwait City and the establishment of a coherent road network that would connect the city to various rural areas. In addition, the DB determined the necessary land needed to accommodate the expanding residential areas to the south and west of the

15. The International Bank for Reconstruction and Development, *The Economic Development of Kuwait* (Baltimore: John Hopkins Press, 1965), 4.

16. Ibid.

17. Simon Smith, *Kuwait, 1950–1965: Britain, the Al-Sabah, and Oil* (Oxford: Oxford University Press, 1999), 49.

18. Ibid., 25.

town.[19] Jakins secured the consent of Sheikh Abdullah, and General Hasted was appointed Controller of Development in January 1952.[20] Hasted took office as the chair of the DB, with Crichton – Controller of Finance – as secretary. The Kuwaiti directors from the Departments of Finance, Education, Municipality, Health, Public Works, and Awqaf (Muslim Endowments) made up the remaining members of the DB. They met from February 5, 1952 until April 16 of the same year.[21] With the addition of three members from the Municipality, the DB continued to meet under Hasted's leadership until November 1953.[22]

Much criticism, however, was centred on the idea that Kuwait's development rested in the hands of Britons (Hasted and Crichton), an argument that was, at times, overstated, as the paper illustrates, but was still compromising to both the government, which funded Arab ideologues in Egypt, Syria, and Iraq, and its people who rallied behind the Arab cause. Crichton was disturbed by the extravagance of Hasted's ambitious projects, which also facilitated tremendous profits for the Big Five. In the early phases of its implementation, the DP required skilled technicians who could carry out large-scale projects, which Kuwait lacked at the time. As a result, development work was contracted to five British firms. These firms came to be known as the "Big Five."[23] They included Holland, Hannen, and Cubitts; D.C. and William Press; John Howard; Taylor Woodrow; and Richard Costain Limited. Some believed that wealth was directed mainly to the Big Five contractors. Deliberate attempts were made by British advisors to misrepresent project estimates in order to ensure project approval, resulting in a lack of trust in the objectivity and reliability of British advice. Pelly, the political agent at the time, described John Howard and Company as having the worst reputation for greed and sharp practice of any British firm here. He also feared this would reflect poorly on British prestige. The political resident, William Hay, predicted that:

> The attempt to create a super welfare state where everybody will get everything for nothing does give us cause for alarm, not only because it means that none of the existing projects will pay for their maintenance, but also because the population will inevitably increase by leaps and bounds by the immigration of adventurers and vagrants.[24]

Hay's predictions came true and attempts were made to curb development speculation. Hasted was targeted due to his growing network of power. Disagreement ensued between Hasted and the DB, and between Hasted and Crichton. Crichton was finally unable to regulate Hasted's expenditures, and he criticised his "financial irresponsibility and extravagance."[25] Consequently, Hasted found it more difficult to exercise his duties. In February 1953, two events led to his resignation. First, a reshuffling took place in the DB and among the technical staff in the state Development Department. Second, the state Development Department merged with the Public Works Department. The merger was announced on April 6, 1952, during the sixty-first meeting of the Board. Hasted was appointed as chairman of a Technical Sub-Committee, formed to advise the DB on technical matters. British records report that Hasted and his British staff continued to administer the work of the main contractors, although he was gradually marginalised regarding new work. These conditions did not permit Hasted from performing the functions that he had been assigned to carry out. He resigned in April 1954, but not before he had outlined the main program

2. Cover of *Kuwait Today – A Welfare State*,1963.

19. Rula Sadik, "Nation-Building and Housing Policy: A Comparative Analysis of Urban Housing Development in Kuwait, Jordan, and Lebanon" (PhD diss., University of California at Berkeley, 1996), 225.

20. Richard Trench, ed., *Arab Gulf Cities: Kuwait City* (Slough, UK: Archives Editions, 1994), 607.

21. Ibid.

22. Ibid., 607.

23. Ibid.

24. Ibid.

25. Ibid., 607.

for the Development Plan and assigned much of the contracting projects to the Big Five.[26]

Importantly, the Big Five were required by the state to collaborate with newly established Kuwaiti companies in order to gain development contracts. The Kuwaiti partners, who did not possess the technical skills to carry out projects of this magnitude, most certainly benefited from that policy. They also had a vested interest in maintaining the status quo. The partnerships guaranteed work to the value of one million pounds (approximately two million dollars) for an unspecified period or profit on a cost-plus-15-percent basis.[27] Profits were divided equally between the partners despite lesser contributions from the Kuwaiti contractors. In addition, contractors were instructed by the state to carry out purchasing through the local market's industrial establishments. These companies expected to make large profits, particularly at moments when materials were scarce. Since building materials were largely controlled by a merchant oligarchy, contractors were forced to buy at inflated prices.[28] Competition between these contracting companies developed alongside great public criticism. Projects were awarded based on personal connections and power relations rather than merit. These networks and methods of operation continued until 1955 when the monopoly of the Big Five was finally broken.

Kuwait's Urban Modernity

The political ties between the British and Kuwaiti government secured for British architects/planners lucrative commissions as well as locations to test out their design ideas. In 1952 a large-scale urban project proposed by the British planners Minoprio, Spencely, and Macfarlane (MSM) was approved by the state. The proposal was mentioned in Hasted's 1952 Development Program report to Sheikh Abdullah Al-Salem.[29] The plan was commissioned in April 1951. MSM worked not only in Kuwait but also in Baghdad. Max Loch and Partners produced plans for the city of Basra, Iraq. Raglan Squire and Partners developed plans for Mosul, Iraq. Some of the envisioned urban models corresponded with the urban renewal policies and the new town plans that were developing contemporaneously in Britain. These models and plans mostly centred on theories of planned neighbourhood units, satellite towns, and garden cities. The application of these models in Kuwait considered the local context, and did not strictly adhere to the original ideas as developed by Clarence Perry, Ebenezer Howard, Frederic Osborn, Barry Parker, and Raymond Unwin.

However, the British were not alone. Architects from the region were also active in the transformation of modern Kuwait: Sayyed Karim and Saba Shiber are just a few notable examples. Karim was an important figure in carving a niche for modern architecture in the region. His publication *Majallat Al-'Imarah* from 1939–1950 presented contemporary architecture in Cairo. It continued under a slightly different name, *Majallat Al'Imarah wa-Al-Funun* from 1952–1959, but maintained its goal to define modern architecture as it related to the region. He worked in Kuwait and built private villas and office buildings. Kuwaiti architects and planners also had an important role in changing the course of state planning in the late 1960s. Many Kuwaiti architects, including Ghazi Sultan, after having studied abroad, returned and worked in state planning departments. Here, it is also worth mentioning Hamid Shuaib. Stephen Gardiner wrote that "Shuaib has had the single most

3. Advertisement of a building materials company in *Majallat Al-Imarah,* v. 5, n. 1, Cairo, 1945. © Sayyed Karim on behalf of *Majallat Al-Imarah* (also titled *Al-Emara*).

26. Ibid.

27. Ibid., 574.

28. Ibid., 609.

29. Ibid., 555.

constructive effect on the city since Dr. Shiber."[30] However, the paper's argument does not overstate the architect's role. Instead it recognises the architect's inherent limitation in relation to the overarching reach of state planning departments and high-ranking civil servants; the latter, at times, controlled whether a project was carried out or abandoned. As such, these projects cannot be viewed in isolation and instead, it is important to illustrate the multi-scaled networks mentioned above that developed around every commission. Throughout the implementation of the DP, different networks would rise or fall as alliances shifted.

In the case of MSM, two proposals were presented. The first abandoned the old town and established an alternate site. A second proposal was implemented that envisioned a policy of urban renewal within the historic urban fabric of Kuwait City, with housing in neighbourhood units outside the city wall. The city and its suburbs would be separated by a green belt. MSM were influenced by the existing historical references mapped in the 1951 aerial photographs by Hunting Aerosurveys. The plan proposed a road network influenced by the old fortification walls running east-west and caravan routes running north-south. Macfarlane stated that "inside the town wall [...] the present road pattern has been followed [...] to a large extent, the road pattern is fixed by the three existing gates through the town wall, though a fourth is proposed."[31] Two dominating geometries were superimposed. The first were concentric ring roads with a dual carriageway running east-west, and the second were radial roads with a single carriageway, running north-south. These roads converged at roundabouts. The main traffic routes and expressways provided for an increase in traffic volume. The roads were also conceived as avenues lined with trees, whose purpose was "to enable motor vehicles to move across the town with speed and safety."[32] Development roads, or avenues, were designed to accommodate "local movement of men and vehicles to and from the buildings they serve."[33] They were connectors between main traffic routes and commercial, residential, and recreational areas. The roads inside the wall were designed to connect different areas in all parts of the city. The proposed road network effectively divided Kuwait City into administrative, cultural, commercial, and financial districts; and the city was separated from the suburbs by a green belt. The historical relationship between the city and its residents was now severed.

Implementation of the plan proceeded in stages that were determined by the speed with which locations designated as 'development areas' were demolished. Disputes over land ownership were one of the major obstacles to carrying out the plan. At times, the course of development would change to benefit certain individuals. In general, demolition proceeded, along with reparations made for damage to housing frontages. Affected people were compensated monetarily. Garden and tree-planting schemes were proposed along designated boulevards. Despite the modern road network that facilitated traffic and shortened distances, much of the old town was destroyed due to speculation; undeveloped patches of land that remain to this day map a period of economic greed and uneven development.

MSM also suggested new settlements separated from Kuwait City by a green belt. Neighbourhood planning outside the city attempted to control urban growth, but instead resulted in urban sprawl. Because of MSM's proposal, Kuwaiti urban planning proceeded from the scale of the neighbourhood unit. Many Kuwaiti families were encouraged to settle in these planned neighbourhoods. Plots and houses within these neighbourhoods

30. Stephen Gardiner, Kuwait, The Making of a City (Harlow: Longman, 1983).

31. P.W. Macfarlane, "Planning an Arab Town: Kuwait on the Persian Gulf," Journal of the Town Planning Institute, v. 40, n. 5 (1954): 113.

32. Minoprio & Spencely and P.W. Macfarlane, Plan for the Town of Kuwait Report to His Highness Shaikh Abdullah Assalim Assubah, C.I.E, The Amir of Kuwait (1951): 5.

33. Ibid.

were restricted to Kuwaitis. Housing programs were also divided according to income; therefore, state control was not limited to economic and political development but also included social development in its control of housing policies and who can participate in these welfare programs. Neighbourhood planning within the DP was an instrument for the demographic split between nationals and non-nationals, for zoning of neighbourhood units according to ethnicity and socioeconomic status, and for restricting housing policies to benefit the privileged Kuwaiti male. Kuwaiti women married to non-Kuwaitis gave up the right to participate in these housing programs.

4. Safat Square in Kuwait City, 1960s.
© Kuwait Municipal Archive.

Social, Economic, and Cultural Effects of the Development Program

Despite these latent and, at times, explicitly restrictive policies, a vibrant construction industry emerged. As a result of the DP, the 1950s and 1960s saw a construction boom that served to diversify Kuwaiti industry.

The rate of development was unexpectedly rapid, at least in the first years from 1952 to 1954.[34] P.W. Macfarlane wrote in 1954 "at the moment constructional work, in varying stages of completion, makes the desert outside Kuwait [City] look as if an atom bomb had struck it."[35] One has to imagine the number of projects that were being carried out simultaneously in

34. Trench, *Arab Gulf Cities*, 591.

35. Macfarlane, "Planning an Arab Town: Kuwait on the Persian Gulf," 113.

order to understand the magnitude of the DP, especially for a small port town and a people that have never experienced such physical upheaval and growth at such an unprecedented speed. However, this dynamism was precisely what state policy sought to maintain, because it created employment and significant economic opportunities. A British official noted:

> The DP should be thought of not only as providing amenities for Kuwait but also as a means of distributing some of the oil wealth to all Kuwaitis. A steady flow of this income is most desirable if the community is to remain content.[36]

Simon Smith has opined that "Sheikh Abdullah's determination to channel oil revenues into development projects and create a modern welfare state clearly increased the numbers who had a stake in the survival of the regime."[37] The state encouraged the establishment of private Kuwaiti industries in order to produce locally manufactured building materials and construction technologies for the implementation of various architectural and urban projects. Local private industry, the state believed, would alleviate the economic strain placed on its bursar in funding a nascent construction industry. Wealth accumulated by these manufacturers and increased employment opportunities would result in a population vested in this dynamic because of the monetary and social advancement it offered.

By the mid-1950s, the monopoly enjoyed by the Big Five was broken. In 1955, there were twenty-eight registered Kuwaiti construction companies in partnership with foreign construction organisations.[38] In addition, Kuwait established industries that supplied modern building materials, including the Sand, Lime & Brick Factory that provided bricks, rock-filler, and hydrated lime, and a Cement Products Factory that fabricated cement blocks, paving stones, and molded conduits. A British official reported:

> A representative of the Sand, Lime & Brick Factory recently visited the United Kingdom on behalf of the government to enquire into the possibility of local manufacture of cement asbestos pipes. It is understood that none of the leading British firms were interested, and that the estimated cost of erecting and equipping a factory here was 1 million [pounds sterling]. The government now seem to have decided that local demand for cement asbestos piping will tail off after the present building boom and their proposal has now been shelved. A number of merchants, however, are still believed to be interested in the scheme.[39]

Kuwaiti engineering firms were also established that specialised in steel fabrication. Furniture and kitchen cabinetry were manufactured locally and on an industrial scale. Surpluses of local materials such as glass and brick were exported. A new market was established that specialised in construction materials, such as a glass-cutting factory, tile and brick factories, and carpentry workshops.

Al-`Imara al-Hadītha

These construction techniques and modern building materials served Kuwait's modern architecture. Design projects radically different from the traditional architectural vernacular were labeled Al-`Imara al-Hadītha or modern architecture. Visually, the new architecture veered slightly from the architecture of high modernism. Ideologically, it was constructed on a doctrine of progress that continued to shape a developing cultural modernity.

36. Trench, *Arab Gulf Cities*, 591.

37. Smith, *Kuwait, 1950–1965*, 136.

38. Trench, *Arab Gulf Cities*, 630.

39. Ibid., 673.

The lack of ornament and the use of concrete, glass, and steel characterised this new building method. It also differs somewhat from the codified 1930s International Style by the heavy use of shaded fenestration as a means for climate control. Elaborate facade detail in the form of *brise-soleil*, louvers, and overhangs compensated for the simplicity of this design approach. Many of these buildings were constructed with locally manufactured brick and reinforced concrete, employing modern construction techniques such as standardised architectural elements, pre-cast structural members, concrete, employing modern construction techniques such as standardised architectural elements, pre-cast structural members, concrete portal frames, and light steel trusses.

5. Aerial view of old Kuwait City, 1940s.
© Kuwait Oil Company Archive.

Nuanced spatial configuration and innovative facade treatment had also come to represent the modern. For example, state schools represented a stylistic shift in the state's architectural approach. Unlike the earlier civic buildings constructed in the 1940s, in which ornamentation and facade embellishment were influenced by Ottoman and Persian motifs, during the 1950s state schools borrowed from the tradition of the International Style in its straight lines, lack of ornamentation, and rigid geometry. Tripe and Wakeham (TW) developed a prototype that was adapted for all subsequent schools in Kuwait. Their designs departed significantly from Kuwait's traditional school vernacular. The TW model was characterised by a series of horizontal boxes containing modular class units. As there were no provisions for air conditioning in the first schools, the horizontal boxes did not exceed the width of one room, typically three metres. This dimensional constraint encouraged cross ventilation. The structural framework was made of reinforced concrete with standardised beam and column sizes on a three-metre gird. Flat roofs capped each horizontal box. These were typically constructed of pre-cast reinforced concrete panels. Local manufacturers provided locally produced insulation and waterproofing materials. Similarly, floors were produced using local pre-cast concrete slabs. In some of the schools, but mainly in the Technical College, glass mosaics were used to accentuate architectural features such as stairs, walls, and columns. Most building materials were locally sourced; while artisans, arriving from Lebanon, Syria, Iran, and Iraq, were trained in modern construction techniques upon arrival.

Residents expressed cultural aspirations within the very layout of these newly constructed spaces. For example, in February 1958, an estimated 20,000 Kuwaitis gathered at the Technical College in Shuwaikh to exhibit solidarity with their Arab brethren, and celebrated the anniversary of the United Arab Republic. During the summer months, the schools hosted various educational, social, and literary clubs. The public also converged in the courtyards of schools demanding greater state reforms. Modern social values and cultural aspirations unfolded and were nurtured within these buildings, making state schools not only an integral part of a Kuwaiti educational *nahdha* but also a locus for dynamic debate. Within their courtyards, the collective demanded an increase in political participation, greater employment opportunities, and press liberties. Paradoxically, these early explorations of architecture were also symbols of the state's modern status. For example, schools were used by the state to celebrate independence, using military parades to demonstrate state power.

6. Tripe and Wakeham prototype public school in Kuwait, 1956.
© Kuwait Oil Company Archive.

The Press and a Design Discourse

The local press was also a cultural outlet for the debate on Kuwaiti modernity. It represented the resident intelligentsia, who, over the course of the DP, shifted perspectives on the meaning of Kuwaiti modernity. At first, the MSM plan and the architectural projects were well received because of the monetary opportunities and progressive values they embodied. The excitement of better living conditions also prompted positive reviews. During the early stages of the DP, the press lauded and celebrated the new architecture as significant steps towards a comprehensive Kuwaiti *nahdha*.

Media independence and pluralism were among the effects of modern reform in the 1960s. Prior to these press liberties, Kuwaiti newspapers had been suppressed for a short period because subversive articles were seen as constituting a threat to the state, capable of inciting mass political movements and revolt against local and regional governments. Reacting to this threat, the state curbed press freedoms historically enjoyed by journalists working in Kuwait, and in 1959, several newspapers were banned. Nationalist reformist clubs that were critical of state politics were also dissolved. In 1961, as part of a project to reinstate press liberties, the ban on newspapers was lifted and with the aid of the Supreme Council, the state approved a Press Law that allowed Kuwaiti citizens to "own or run a newspaper."[40] A number of privately owned publications were established or, in some cases, resurrected from a state-imposed hiatus.

At first, articles on a Kuwaiti *nahdha* expressed cultural modernity through the tectonic qualities of modern materials and their advanced construction techniques. Innovative building techniques and the modern spatial organisation of *Al-'Imara Al-Hadītha* possessed the capacity to communicate visually the character and ideals of a new nation and a sophisticated populace. In February and May 1948, *Al-Ba'tha*, a Kuwaiti cultural journal, reported:

> Progress that incorporates numerous aspects of Kuwaiti life has begun to influence architectural vernacular. This new architectural technique is most suitable for a modern Kuwaiti life.[41]

40. Anita Burdett, ed., *Records of Kuwait 1961–1965* (Cambridge: Cambridge University Press, 1997), 624.

41. *Al-Ba'tha*, May, 1948, 74.

It pleases us to confirm that all state departments are constructed in the modern architectural style (*tirāz*) that corresponds to Kuwait's continued progress. Certainly, traditional architecture is no longer compatible with Kuwaiti modernity.[42] (Translations mine)

The progressive values associated with the new built form were a direct result of appropriating these spaces for social and political protest as well as for progressive cultural clubs. Appropriation, in fact, weighed immensely in assigning the new architectural style great value. Schools, as mentioned above, were host to collective demands.

Sawt Al-Khaleej (*Voice of the Gulf*, hereafter *SAK*) was particularly active in this debate. Founded by Baqir Ali Kharaibit on April 26, 1962,[43] it published articles on the use of modern materials such as concrete and glass in Kuwait and the cultural and climatic significance of their structural principles. Standardisation, particularly in prefabricated housing, was presented, at first, as an exemplary solution for the Kuwaiti housing problem. A 1964 article reported that "Kuwait is witnessing a *nahdha* [...] the speed with which this movement is taking place guarantees Kuwait's position among the advanced nations of the world."[44]

7. Thunayan Al-Ghanim building in Kuwait City, Sayyed Karim, 1959.
© Centre for Research and Studies on Kuwait.

With the rise of Arab nationalism, *Al-'Imara Al-Hadītha* was later discredited for its western aesthetic and social values. On May 29, 1963, *SAK* published an article questioning the state's motivations for hiring Western rather than local architects and planners. One example involved the planning of Rumaithiya, a neighbourhood unit. The article mentioned that VBB, a Swedish urban planning consulting bureau that was responsible for the master and regional plans for Sweden during the 1950s, had been hired to produce a plan for Rumaithiya. The plan, described by Shiber as a "simple, rational, and functional design, although somewhat uninspired aesthetically,"[45] was critiqued in *SAK* as lacking in climatic specificity. Commissioning a Swedish firm for this urban project had been perceived as an irresponsible decision on the part of the Kuwait Municipality. The article reported that Kuwait and Sweden do not share climatic or cultural similarities. The design, it was argued quite dramatically, had contributed to disruptions in the structure of the Kuwaiti family.

Many of the articles written in *SAK* were influenced by Shiber's design theories.[46] Shiber assumed his planning post at Kuwait's Public Works Department on June 15, 1960.[47] His articles brought greater awareness of Arab heritage and social theorists, particularly Ibn Khaldūn. These articles were important in the middle of the twentieth century when many Arab cities were undergoing similar processes of modernisation. His appeal to planning officials highlighted the possibilities that lay dormant in Kuwait City, noting the *fait accompli* of previous planning decades while simultaneously urging officials to reconsider the future of urban planning and architecture in Kuwait.

One might say that Chapter I of Kuwait's growth has already been written. It is a chapter full of surprises, boldness, experimentation, great expenses, and mistakes no one could avoid when confronted with the unique pressures and treasures of Kuwait. Chapter II in the development of Kuwait is up to the Municipal Council and authorities of Kuwait to write.[48]

Administrative Reshuffling

The debate on the modern city finds additional support in the late 1960s when a new vision gave architecture further importance. Despite state efforts to restructure the link between Kuwaitis and tradition, memories

42. *Al-Ba'tha*, February, 1949, 80.

43. Trench, *Arab Gulf Cities*, 697.

44. "Phoenicia: A Miracle Happens in Kuwait," *Sawt Al-Khaleej* (*Voice of the Gulf*), January 30, 1964, 8–9.

45. Shiber, *Kuwait Urbanization*, 222.

46. For more on Shiber see Asseel Al-Ragam, "Representation and ideology in postcolonial urban development: the Arabian Gulf," *The Journal of Architecture*, v. 16, n. 4 (2011): 455–469.

47. See Shiber, *Kuwait Urbanization*, 1.

48. Ibid., 161.

involving historical urban markers persisted in the Kuwaiti consciousness.[49] In terms of Kuwait City's physical growth, the 1960s were distinguished by a series of preparatory reports that included comprehensive social, demographic, and topographical data. This social planning exercise had greater influence on the physical determinants of the urban fabric.

In 1962, a Planning Board (PB) was established as an independent body for planning and development set up by and attached to the Council of Ministers.[50] Sheikh Abdullah Al-Salem Al-Sabah appointed Sheikh Salem Al-Ali Al-Sabah as president of the PB, and installed as members the ministers of Public Works, Social Affairs, Education, and Finance and Economy. In addition, three members were appointed to the PB by decree. The PB's main objective was to formulate general economic and social policies that would ensure "social justice and [the] securing [of] a continuously dynamic [Kuwaiti] economy."[51] The PB was also responsible for initiating and executing the supervision of development projects.[52] Members of the PB determined and defined long-term economic and social development goals. They were also responsible for the collection and preparation of statistical information and for requesting that ministry officials provide information concerning economic and social development in their respective departments. These many functions demonstrate the bureaucratic nature of state planning departments that might not have been effective or efficient at the time, but were certainly telling of the extensive reach these planning departments had in guiding development policies.

To some extent, the restructuring of the state departments helped define some administrative responsibilities between the Public Works Department and the Kuwait Municipality. At the same time, it further expanded the reach of the Kuwait Municipality. The Municipal Council (MC) assigned urban planning functions solely to the Kuwait Municipality. Prior to the establishment of the PB, a technical staff within the Public Works Department (PWD) executed planning functions. Communication between these departments and their respective urban planning responsibilities were largely undefined, which inevitably resulted in inefficiency and great overlap of activities. After 1962, the MC shifted functions concerning the physical growth of Kuwait to the Kuwait Municipality, a decision that brought, to a limited degree, an increase in its administrative efficiency, and to a greater degree, additional executive powers. Moreover, an MC charter was codified by Emiri decree, calling for ten council members of Kuwaiti nationality to be elected democratically, with an additional six members appointed by decree. The MC was responsible for providing urban and architectural policies and increased public participation in the development process. This also shifted the centre of power from high ranking civil servants in state planning departments to elected and appointed MC officials who now signed off on the implementation of architectural projects and, on a much larger scale, approved the distribution of land plots into residential, agricultural, and industrial areas. In effect, the MC institutionalised the processes and networks of Kuwait's development.

Additional changes occurred within the Kuwait Municipality, this time with help from United Nations officials. In November 1965, Colin Buchanan and two representatives from the United Nations, J. Thijsse and Omar Azzam, produced a report on policies considered necessary for the reorganisation of the Planning Department within the Kuwait Municipality. They suggested dividing the department into two branches: a Development

49. For more on Kuwaiti nostalgia and the city see Asseel Al-Ragam, "Critical Nostalgia," 1–20.

50. Trench, *Arab Gulf Cities*, 680.

51. *Kuwait: First Five-Year Development Plan 1967/8–1971/2*, v. 1, *Development Plans of the GCC States 1962–1995* (England: Antony Rowe Ltd., 1994), 8.

52. Trench, *Arab Gulf Cities*, 680.

Control Department and a Research Department. The former would administer public demands and inquires, while the latter would direct urban design.[53] The Research Department, would also oversee the execution of design projects.

In selecting design projects, the Research Department suggested a more competitive approach. An architectural competition was first carried out by the PWD in 1961, for the development of the Kuwaiti waterfront. Design competitions were still in their nascent stages and invitations to participate were limited to five architects/planners. Submissions for the waterfront project communicated abstract ideas through architectural drawings. Competitions proved successful in establishing a measure for design control. They were also responsible for a shift in the mode of representation from explanatory text to architectural drawings such as sections, elevations, and plans. Shiber wrote:

> The improvement of architecture in Kuwait has been due, in no small part, to the advent of the employment of the architectural competition as a means of soliciting good architectural design.[54]

The Kuwait National Museum[55] and the Al-Sawaber housing complex[56] were some entries submitted by international architects through this selection process.

Kuwait City, the APC, and Planning in the 1960s

In 1968, Colin Buchanan and Partners were appointed consultants for Kuwait's second Master Plan. Buchanan had previously worked in the region. Upon Buchanan's arrival in Kuwait, he and his design partner Allan McCulloch were commissioned to follow up on the work completed in the MSM Plan. Buchanan's sojourn in Kuwait continued into the next decade. In 1971, he proposed four studies for Kuwait's urban areas, including a national physical plan and a master plan for Kuwait City. Together, they were known as the Second Master Plan of Kuwait (KMP2). Buchanan's proposals responded to the contemporary Kuwaiti urban and regional context. KMP2 acted as a framework for all subsequent architectural projects, which had to engage the planning boundaries set by Buchanan. It outlined a growth pattern for the state that was distinguished from that of the previous decade. Buchanan suggested linear growth along the Arabian Gulf instead of concentric growth outside the city limits. KMP2 recommended the dispersal of employment, commercial, and government activities from congested areas to satellite centres in Hawalli, Salmiyah, Fintas, and Jahra. Within the city limits, potential areas for growth were suggested south and east of the existing Central Business District.

In 1967, several international urban planners were approached to advise on carrying out the portion of Buchanan's plan having to do with Kuwait City. Hamid Shuaib, the Kuwaiti architect and urban planner introduced earlier, began the selection process. Shuaib was the head architect at the Kuwait Municipality, who had transferred from the Public Works Department in 1964. Omar Azzam, a representative to the United Nations on Middle Eastern planning affairs, had been working in Kuwait, and had collaborated with Buchanan on policy making. Azzam was invited to join the committee. Together, they recruited Leslie Martin from England and

53. Shiber, *Recent Arab City Growth*, 720.

54. Shiber, *Kuwait Urbanization*, 289.

55. Asseel Al-Ragam, "The Politics of Representation: The Kuwait National Museum and Processes of Cultural Production," *International Journal of Heritage Studies*, v. 20, n. 6 (2014): 663–674.

56. Asseel Al-Ragam, "The Destruction of Modernist Heritage: The Myth of Al-Sawaber," *Journal of Architectural Education*, v. 67, n. 2 (2013): 243–252.

Franco Albini from Italy to be part of an advisory panel for the development of Kuwait City. Together, Shuaib, Azzam, Martin, and Albini constituted the Advisory Planning Committee (APC).

Shuaib in collaboration with the other members of APC was responsible for selecting and outlining a design brief for the redevelopment of Kuwait City. Four firms were selected: Alison and Peter Smithson from England; Peresutti, Banfi, Belgiojoso, and Rogers (BBPR) from Italy; Georges Candilis from France; and Reima Pietilä from Finland.

Design debates, during this period, are best understood as a critique of the transformation of the old town. A modern road network facilitated traffic in and out of town but Kuwait City lacked the qualities that could define it as a vibrant modern city. Instead, the demolished sites earmarked for construction were left vacant and were turned into makeshift parking lots. Many blamed the DP and those who executed this program for the city's rapid deterioration. By 1964, the lauding of Al-'Imara Al-Hadītha was overshadowed by a nostalgia for the loss of the traditional urban fabric.

8. Kuwait City Municipality drawing room, 1957.
© Kuwait Oil Company Archive.

> The Old City of Kuwait has now largely disappeared. There are still some traces of its physical form and architectural character in some of the residential areas that remain in the market and mosque areas, but a new road pattern has been established. Large areas of the Old City have been cleared and the new main shops are being developed along wide and busy roads. Car traffic is rapidly increasing and vacant plots are being increasingly used for parking. The character and coherence that the Old City possessed is vanishing but development with modern buildings has not replaced this with anything that can yet mark the new city of Kuwait as a great capital city.[57]

The APC shifted the course of development. In place of the large-scale urban redevelopment that had proved too chaotic and inefficient before, the APC suggested urban design interventions in targeted areas. Urban planning would affect the areas left vacant as a result of the MSM Plan. These interventions were meant to enhance the urban dynamic of Kuwait City and resuscitate culture, commerce, and social activities in the city:

> What is clear is that a remarkable opportunity to establish the character and environment of this inner city still remains... The problem is that during the development of the Master Plan for the State the Old City will continue to rebuild itself. The purpose of these studies for the Old City is to provide desirable objectives and guidelines in relation to its physical form which can be reasonably firm in defined areas, and in others sufficiently free to adapt themselves to the influence of the Master Plan and to less well-known requirements of the City itself.[58]

The four architectural firms had to engage with KMP2 as a starting point of reference. Each architect was assigned a different site in Kuwait City and was asked to develop innovative solutions to pressing architectural problems. The solutions would act as prototypes for future development, as did the TW models for school design. Pietilä was asked to develop the Seif area, a symbolic government district that housed the Amiri Diwan and was the seat of the Kuwaiti government. BBPR was appointed to enhance the commercial district south of Pietilä's. Alison and Peter Smithson contributed designs for government buildings in a site southwest of BBPR's. Candilis provided housing solutions for a district to the west of the Seif area. The design brief, according to the Smithsons, was vague in the sense that fixed programmatic needs were not outlined. The Smithsons stated, "we had no real client [or] program and therefore had to assume certain occupancies."[59]

57. "Proposals for Restructuring Kuwait," *Architectural Review* (September 1974): 178–182.

58. Ibid., 179.

59. Alison and Peter Smithson, *The Charged Void: Urbanism* (New York: The Monacelli Press, 2005), 157.

What the Smithsons failed to realise is that each architect was asked to demonstrate modern solutions for typical architectural and urban problems. The architects were invited to contribute to the debate on Kuwaiti modernity through their design solutions. The question the architects faced was what was the appropriate form that best represented this period of Kuwait's modern society?

Upon reviewing the contemporary conditions of Kuwait City, the four firms reached agreement on particular issues. They stressed the value of the waterfront as an important recreational area for the city. They agreed that the Seif area, including the Seif Palace, Arabian Gulf, government buildings, and mosques, should be considered a cultural district, and that designs should enhance this character. In addition, they recommended re-establishing residential areas in Kuwait City. Using these points of agreement as guidelines, the architects turned their attention to a pressing concern articulated by the APC: re-establishing architectural comprehensibility and character in Kuwait City. The architects were asked to "think about a city, and to express their thoughts as architectural ideas... not as written reports."[60]

In all four proposals for the city, the architects equated modernity with increased and exaggerated mobility, and accordingly, enhanced existing and proposed additional road networks. For the targeted areas, some of the architects were inspired by earlier design explorations produced in colonial settings, particularly makeshift buildings in North African *bidonville* and other squatter settlements. At times, the architects were influenced by an orientalist view of the "Arab" town that was set against Western modern cities. According to the Smithsons, the Arab City seems "to be a broadcast of houses, mosques, and bazaars [...] new to our Roman-seeded urbanism."[61] These inspirations were not images or symbols Kuwaiti planning officials identified with at the time.

Importantly, these projects by the 1970s consortium were implemented to varying degrees and, at times, abandoned. BBPR's project for the city and Pietilä's for the Seif Palace were carried out. Alison and Peter Smithson's government district along with Candilis' innovative urban housing in the city were not. In official records they were not carried out for financial reasons. The paper, however, argues that their lack of implementation is due, in part, to the limited influence architects have compared to the executive powers of decision-making networks in Kuwait. The centralised and complex processes of the welfare state are additional impediments. This suggests that the architectural project, although an important part of the development of Kuwait, was more of an instrument of a dominant network that sought economic gain rather than a tool to further social and cultural reform.

Conclusion

During a period of almost thirty years, from the early 1950s to the early 1980s, the state, in a fluctuating relationship with an increasingly sophisticated Kuwaiti public, attempted to forge a modern identity from a dynamic interconnection between a *nahdha* and architecture and urban projects. Institutional and economic reforms that took place during this thirty-year period were deeply rooted in social and political transformations that forced the Kuwaiti ruling family to initiate radical change. Arab nationalism became one of the most important issues in governance for the existing power structure. Increased political representation, greater press liberties, and educational and institutional reform were introduced in an

9. Old city gate in Kuwait City, 1940s. © Kuwait Oil Company Archive.

10. Textile shop in Kuwait City, 1961. © *Al-Kuwaiti*.

11. Fahad Al-Salem Street, the first modern avenue of Kuwait City, 1960s. © Kuwait Oil Company Archive.

60. Gardiner, *Kuwait, The Making of a City*, 66–67.

61. Smithsons, *Charged Void*, 136.

attempt to control popular discontent. In addition, the social, cultural and political nature of the DP furthered the growth of a local construction industry. The state encouraged the establishment of private enterprises that, in turn, produced local materials and construction technologies for the manufacture of various development projects. This construction industry alleviated the economic strain placed on the state's bursar in funding Kuwaiti modernisation. Wealth accumulated by these manufacturers resulted in increased employment and a population that was heavily vested in this dynamic because of the economic and social advancement it offered.

12. Street view of Central Business District Area 1, Kuwait City, 1967. © Kuwait Oil Company Archive.

An integral part of the DP had been the transformation of Kuwait City. MSM's proposal changed, as well, the course of Kuwaiti urban planning and provided an alternative mode of living for Kuwaitis. MSM's proposal for neighbourhood planning controlled urban growth. It also implicitly defined Kuwaiti modernity: to be modern in Kuwait meant living in a single-family house using modern materials and techniques in segregated neighbourhood units outside the city. This severed a historical link between residents and the city's built and natural landscape.

Thus, the 1952 DP was a cultural, social, political, and an economic agenda that orchestrated the masses into relative political and social stability. The DP was also responsible for the restructured societal bonds and the importance assigned to suburban living. In effect, the dynamic of the DP provided not only countless opportunities to many segments of society but also restructured historical alliances, dependencies, and, more importantly, identities that had obstructed social mobility for a large segment of the Kuwaiti people. *Al-'Imara Al-Haditha* possessed the capacity to communicate visually the character and ideals of a new nation and a progressive society. Such associations developed despite the inherently paradoxical political and economic motivations that had activated these material and technological developments, including repressive housing policies and nation building based on the privileged citizen. This modern architecture was lauded as a central part of a cultural revolution, mainly because it was associated with social freedoms.

By 1964, the lauding of *Al-`Imara Al-Hadītha* was overshadowed by a nostalgia for the traditional urban fabric. A new urban environment had inspired a turn to nostalgia. These feelings coalesced after the old architectural and social values were not replaced with anything that can yet mark the new city of Kuwait as a great capital city. This void posed a threat to a Kuwaiti identity. To move forward, some in Kuwait debated a new relationship between the past and the present. The 1968 urban direction by the Kuwait Municipality and the formation of the APC were some of the more constructive reactions to this critique.[62]

Subsequently, 1967 signaled a shift in the state design approach shaped by the Advisory Planning Committee. The architects, BBPR, Pietilä, the Smithsons, and Candilis, were asked to enhance the character of historical markers in their proposals. What the transformation of Kuwait City has clearly illustrated is that various local and non-local actors continued to define and redefine what it meant to be modern. Kuwaiti modernity was shaped by the nature of this shifting definition. The question that remained throughout this period was what architecture and urban form best suited modern Kuwait. Importantly, these proposals cannot be viewed in isolation; instead, one must examine the processes and network of actors that formed around these commissions. State planning officials, foreign and local architects, and contracting companies had competing interests in the implementation of a project. The variance between what was proposed and what was built also relied on a state ideology. Despite state rhetoric that promoted reform these decades of nation building built on policies and plans that privileged certain groups and marginalised others. The architectural project was an instrument for this process. However, as the paper argued different groups used these spaces to resist the dominant narrative and to shape their own histories

Finally, this study is not an exhaustive account of Kuwaiti modernity. It starts a discussion on the multiple and competing narratives that emerged during this period of creative activity and brings into greater focus what was at stake for the beneficiaries of these modern policies and for those marginalised. The successes and failures of Kuwait's modern project can be examined at the architectural scale that continues to be the stage where cultural aspirations and social values are forged and negotiated. •

62. Al-Ragam, "Critical Nostalgia," 1–20.

Sabah Al-Rayes

Sabah Al-Rayes (1940–) graduated in 1965 from Indiana Institute of Technology in civil engineering with a minor in architecture and metallurgy. He returned to Kuwait in the same year to work for the Ministry of Public Works. He is one of the founders of Pan-Arab Consulting Engineers (Pace), where he served as Managing Director starting in 1968. From 1968 to 1973, he served as an advisor to the Kuwait Ministry of Foreign Affairs Aid Program for Developing Countries. Al-Rayes has been the Executive Secretary of the Kuwait Society of Engineers from its foundation in 1967 and has served in numerous other roles, including as Director of the Kuwait National Industries Company (1973–76), Director of the Gulf Real Estate Development Company (1976–80), Director of the United Gulf Bank of Bahrain (1981–86), Director of the Arab Life Insurance Company of Jordan (1981–87), Chairman of Kuwait Precious Metals Company (1982–86), Vice-Chairman of Tunis International Bank (1982–85), and Vice-Chairman of Kuwait Department Stores. In 1984, he was granted an honorary doctorate in civil engineering from the Indiana Institute of Technology. He left Pace upon retirement.

Ricardo Camacho and Roberto Fabbri conducted this interview in Kuwait in March 2016.

Roberto Fabbri: *We have a brief bio of your good self and have divided our questions into three blocks: We would like to discuss the early days of your profession, then we will talk a little bit about Pace and your work. After that, we will focus on your involvement in construction and real estate companies in the 1970s. Finally, we'd like to address your later development in the 1980s, when you were in charge of other matters not related to construction.*

What was the situation like when you started working after graduating and upon returning to Kuwait? The city was going through a big transformation. What do you remember about that moment? What were your aspirations, goals, and what was it like working with key figures, such as Khaled Al-Essa at the Ministry of Public Works? What was the direction?

Sabah Al-Rayes: I really consider myself lucky to be from the generation that lived both when Kuwait was really poor – and I mean really poor – and then saw the effect of oil and the start of real estate development in the 1950s. Unfortunately, we also saw it decline.

I was a kid, about ten years old, when Sheikh Abdullah Al-Salem took over after Sheikh Ahmad Al-Jaber died in 1950. From then, you could really say, "This is the start of a completely new country," a country where, for many years, the budget of the ruler and the budget of the state were the same. If you look at the budget of Kuwait between 1900 and 1915, it was Sheikh Mubarak's personal budget. Little by little, they started separating under Sheikh Ahmad, who took over in 1921 and ruled until 1950. Of course, in 1936, they signed the concession agreement, and they started finding oil, and finally struck a good well in Burgan. But they had to cover it because of the Second World War, and then, right after the Second World War, the British and the Americans came in, and we as kids started feeling it. Suddenly, there was a place where we would go in Ahmadi during the New Year and watch football between Hubara Club and the Frigates and the Destroyers and the military ships that come, with their crew and their football. And that was really something, seeing those blonde, white footballers.

In Kuwait, you had these small streets and the souq, and suddenly the whole city was really destroyed from 1957 on. For a kid that had lived in these neighbourhoods and suddenly saw the bulldozers in front of you – maybe we didn't understand much about it until we graduated and read that it was a master plan. We didn't know what a master plan was.

When the first Master Plan was put forward in 1952, it was a beautiful master plan. I think the planners did a fantastic job under the circumstances because they did not have any historical data, nothing about population, about growth, about traffic, about anything. And really, to come and submit a plan like that, I think it was beautiful, and what they did was a great idea, and General Hasted had a lot to do with it.

I left Kuwait in 1958 and went to the United States after graduating from high school. I really wanted to study everything. I took classes in architecture, civil engineering. So, it was nice for a kid that really loved to read – loved to learn. Anyway, I graduated in 1965 and came back and joined the Ministry of Public Works (MPW). There were seven of us in the Ministry, and we were entrusted with significant responsibilities. After a few months of being trained under a resident engineer who was very good – a Palestinian – I was entrusted to be the resident engineer for low-income housing. The first day the contractor came to me and said, "Sabah, I want you to determine the type of foundation for the houses because the contract calls for a resident engineer to determine the type of foundation based on the load-bearing capacity of the soil."

Come on – we learned this in school, but then we were in reality – this soil can bear three kilos, or half a kilo? How do I know? So, I ran to the chief engineer and said, "Listen, that's a big responsibility. Who am I to...? Really I don't know."

He said, "Don't worry. I'll send somebody with you." He sent one of the foremen who had experience and told me that this soil is this [kind of soil]. It takes so much. This is sandy soil. It takes [such-and-such].

Anyway, we managed, but that was a big responsibility for a kid to take. We overcame that and probably, about a year later, I got a call from the minister who said to come to his office. So I went to his office, and he said, "Sabah, I want you to handle the legal matters for all the claims against the Ministry of Public Works."

I said, "What? Claims? I'm a civil engineer."

And he said, "Don't worry. Don't worry. You'll be ok."

"What do you mean?" I said.

"I'll appoint you to deal with legal matters." And then he called the head of the legal department to explain the context, and it became an instruction from the minister that I would handle the task.

The Audit Bureau had just been formed three years after independence. It was the moment when all of the institutions were being established, and, to handle the audits, they appointed somebody that was very tough. He had no problem auditing all the ministries, except the MPW, because our contracts were either cost-plus or re-measured, and with cost-plus, you don't have a budget – it costs so much, and to re-measure again would be impossible. So he insisted that all the contracts be lump sum so he could audit them. The MPW at the time was almost controlled entirely by the British professionals. All the surveyors in the ministry were British citizens. Finally, the auditor's refusal to audit the contracts of MPW and the refusal of the ministry itself to be audited were referred to the Council of Ministers, who issued the decision that all contracts should be stalled until we looked into the matter.

And imagine, that at the time Kuwait was booming. You have thousands of contracts, and suddenly, everything stands still. So now here I am in the middle of a very serious matter. The Council of Ministers decided to go ahead with the auditor's suggestion. So all contracts had to be changed to lump sum payment, replacing those under the parameters of cost-plus or re-measured. An exception was made for some infrastructure projects.

Here I am, a young 26-year-old kid, with these claims in the millions, and here I have to decide. So what happened? We agreed that of course this should go to court. The court decided that there were too many cases, so they formed an arbitration tribunal, headed by a judge and myself as a representative from the MPW. The third member, a representative from the contractor, would vary.

I gained tremendous experience because I looked into all these problems. I started settling out of court with the contractors – "We will extend the contract for you but don't file a claim, so no payment whatsoever." They approached me to try to bribe me to side with them. That was my first experience with contractors who try to buy you.

So, that was just a small example really of the responsibilities given to us, as young engineers and architects, to handle the development of the state.

After three years of experience working with the ministry, I thought, it's definitely not for me. I cannot be an employee, so I submitted my resignation. Khaled Al-Essa, the minister of public works, called me and asked, "Did we do anything wrong?"

I said, "No, no, no. Please don't misunderstand."

He asked me, "What are you going to do?"

So I said, "I'm going to open my own consultancy."

"Are you kidding? There are more than 150 consultants." At the time, there were no restrictions whatsoever on opening a consulting office – you had Egyptians, Palestinians, Jordanians, Lebanese, all nationalities. A lot of them were not even qualified. It just happened.

Definitely, there was a niche for me. And sure enough, I established Pace in July 1968 and built it to be the biggest or second biggest practice in the Arab world. We did a really fantastic job. If it weren't for the help of KEO International Consultants and Faisal Sultan, I probably wouldn't have made it. Faisal, who was a colleague, established KEO in 1964, and, as soon as he learned that I opened, he started referring international consultants to me. So with any other consultant that came to him for the same project, he would say, "Sorry, I have a friend, that maybe you could associate with." And he referred some really good contacts. I recall one time there was a tender out on the Shuaiba oil pier – it was by invitation only – and I got a call from Faisal Sultan. When I arrived, there was an American guy sitting with him.

Faisal said, "Sabah, these guys are from Frederic R. Harris" – a firm that specialised in oil piers – and he wanted to associate with me. But we had an association agreement with another competitor. So I went with this fellow to my office, and we signed an agreement. Sure enough, we won the project against KEO. And the first call I got was from Faisal to congratulate me.

This is really how it was. There was plenty of work. And funny enough, all of us that had established our engineering and architecture firms had initially worked with the MPW for a few years, gotten sick of it and opened our own firms. It was Faisal Sultan, Mohamed Nahyan, myself, Sadeq Marzouq, and so on and so forth. All of us came from the MPW. Hamid Shuaib was an exception because he worked with the Ministry of Health.

We opened the office in 1968, which was really the peak, the boom. At that time, the Ministry of Planning had realised how important planning was. When the first planners did the Master Plan, they did not have anyone to talk to. Nobody. Who would they talk to? The first Kuwaiti engineer graduated in 1959. Then, of course, the various departments in ministries

realised that they needed somebody, and that's when Saba George Shiber was appointed. I met him when I joined the MPW in 1965, and we became friends. I became the general secretary of the Kuwait Society of Engineers, and he was an active member. We traveled to Cairo to attend the Union of Arab Engineers, and I also traveled with him to Singapore for a housing conference.

Through Saba George Shiber, I met almost all of the people that were involved in city development: the consultants, advisors and members of the committees. I got to know many of them on a personal level and I must say that Kuwait did a fantastic job selecting those professionals because all of them were really top quality.

Ricardo Camacho: *May I interrupt here? To understand better, when you say, "Kuwait did a great job," to whom are you referring?*

SR: I think it was mainly Saba George Shiber.

RC: *But who brought Saba George Shiber to Kuwait?*

SR: That was in 1960. What happened is that Sheikh Abdullah Al-Salem, when he took over, wrote to the British government requesting assistance for the town's development. The British government suggested General Hasted, who had a military and architecture background, saying "he's a doer." They appointed him, and the Sheikh really depended a lot on that fellow. He was instrumental in bringing what was called the 'Five Sisters' companies (George Wimpey, Taylor Woodrow, Richard Costain, and more) because there were no contractors as such. At the time, there was only the Contracting And Trading Company (CAT), a Lebanese contractor which had already built the Shuwaikh Secondary School. That contract marked the start of cost-plus. Ahmed Jaafar, at the time the head of the financial department (KOC) – let's say the Ministry of Finance – suggested appointing CAT due to its Lebanese background.

When General Hasted came, the cost-plus budget had been implemented, so he carried on with it with the 'Five Sisters' companies to do all the schools, hospitals, and so on. Everything that was built by the 'Five Sisters' was on a cost-plus basis.

RC: *From our research, there were a series of companies, of course including CAT, but also including Ahmadiah and others, that were established in the 1940s in Haifa or 1950s in Beirut and that initiated their activity working for British Petroleum (BP) from Syria to Iraq. The majority of these were sub-contracted by larger British or American contractors, such as Bechtel, which, at the time, was the main sponsor of the School of Engineering and Architecture at the American University of Beirut (AUB).*

These relations were instrumental to hiring such companies, including mainly those established by AUB graduates, such as the engineer Emile Bustani, the founder and owner of CAT. Actually, the presence of companies like Bechtel and Wimpey in Ahmadi, before 1950, was instrumental, bringing many of these Lebanese contractors and AUB graduates to work in Kuwait. Apart from CAT, you had the Consolidated Contractors Company (CCC/CONCO), who initiated their activity in Kuwait immediately after Sheikh Abdullah Al-Salem became the emir. One of the first requests from the Sheikh to General Hasted was the construction of an Arab village in Ahmadi, which had not been initially considered. With that said, can we assume that this request was a tentative approach to not only serve a local community but also bring a regional agenda into the planning and architectural agenda?

SR: Sheikh Abdullah Al-Salem took over in 1950, two years later the Egyptian revolution started, and we, as kids, were pro Gamal Abdel Nasser. At the time, there was only *Sawt Al-Arab* radio (*Voice of the Arabs*) [the Egyptian Arabic-language radio service where Nasser spread his message of pan-Arab unity], so definitely this had some sort of effect. But the turning point was 1956 when the Suez Canal was nationalised. One could see how the attitude of the Kuwait Oil Company changed in Ahmadi, from not having an Arab at all to appointing three members onto the board: Faisal Al-Mazeedi, Ahmed Jaafar and Suleiman Al-Saeed.

If we look at the development of Ahmadi, in the beginning it was segregated: Arabs southward and then Brits on the northern side. And that was it. You could not cross that line. When General Hasted came, appointed by Sheikh Abdullah Al-Salem, he headed all the technical components of the Ministry of Public Works, and Sheikh Fahad Al-Salem was appointed to the municipality.

RC: *Contemporary historians describe Sheikh Fahad Al-Salem as pro-Arab. Can you comment on his role as the head of the municipality during the late 1950s?*

SR: Fahad Al-Salem appointed the mayor of Aleppo as his assistant. So now you have an Arab here, and he really wanted to have somebody, and finally Hasted resigned. I really think that both of them, in addition to the mayor of Aleppo, did a good job. The mayor of Cairo [reference to Mahmoud Riad who was the director general of Cairo Municipality] also was appointed as an advisor to the Ministry of Public Works, and later, of course, you had Omar Azzam. If there was anything, it was not because Fahad Al-Salem was siding with Arabs or not, but, at the time, Arab nationalism was rising. The influence of Gamal Abdel Nasser, when he got on the radio and gave his speech and said, "OK, you guys, in this place, revolt." It was definitely Gamal Abdel Nasser who was embracing it from 1956 on, after the nationalisation of the Suez Canal, and we felt it in Ahmadi.

RF: *After years, when you returned from your studies, was Shiber still there? Perhaps in another role?*

SR: He started with the municipality, and, by 1965, they had established the planning bureau, which, at the time, was headed by Ahmad Al-Duaij who requested that Saba Shiber join. Shiber was an intellectual. He loved to read and write. He wrote about Yemen but never visited Yemen. He was really something. I think the history of architecture should do more justice to Saba.

RC: *So, if he was in office during those years, why did he disappear from public view? All the references state that he left Kuwait in 1964. What Roberto is asking is what was his role in Kuwait until 1968, when he passed away?*

SR: From 1964 to 1968, Shiber was in the so-called Ministry or Department of Planning, which did not have any teeth – you have to realise that. This was a department doing reports, and, as usual, all reports go into the drawer and die there. So Saba Shiber did a lot of reports and research, but the remaining department did not have a role in the country's development, and Saba George Shiber was left alone.

When Sheikh Abdullah Al-Salem took over, he realised suddenly the tremendous rate of unemployment among young people. He started hiring people to work in ministries, who had no training, no qualifications. And he devised the expropriation scheme, which did two things: It gave the planner a free hand in the city; the second thing was that when we bought your house,

we would pay you 20 times more than what it was really worth, so no one could say, "No I'm not going to sell my house." Everybody sold their homes to the government.

Going back to your question concerning why between 1964 and 1968 Saba did not do anything: During this time, in fact from 1965 to 1968, I was seeing him almost on a daily basis.

RC: *So he was living in Kuwait?*

SR: Oh yes, and not only living in Kuwait. My office in the MPW – the compound was in Sharqiya, and we had a shed that was our ministry and the other shed was the Planning Ministry. So I walked to his office or he walked to mine everyday, and, in fact, we had our lunch together. Always writing and writing and writing. He was working on one of his books.

RC: *The green-blue one, Recent Arab City Growth.*

SR: Yes, it was so foolish to overlay those prints on the book to make it so hard to read. It's a lot of information, but I wish it could be reprinted in a better way.

RC: *Can you tell us more about his brother? He is present everywhere, but no one can tell us much about the practice that he developed in Kuwait.*

SR: His brother Victor? I really was not very familiar with him. I got to know him a bit more after his brother died. At the time, I was the general secretary of the Kuwait Society of Engineers and, when Saba died, Victor made a small ceremony and I gave a speech about Saba. He was very much moved, and came to me and said thank you so much. Then we became close.

RC: *You referred to Omar Azzam before and also Mahmoud Riad, which is another fellow that is everywhere but also one whom no one can tell us much about in Kuwait. There were some projects Pace developed where Mahmoud Riad had some sort of role: the stadiums and the Kuwait Sport Clubs.*

SR: No, it was given to Rifat Chadirji [partner of Iraq Consult (IQC)], and he was working with Pace, in a way, but, as Pace, we didn't have much to do with the project. I established my firm in 1968, and the first two projects were for Mubarak Al-Hassawi, who I knew very well because he hired me to work for the Department of Customs in 1954. Al-Hassawi gave me those two projects, and I really didn't know much. I established the firm, but this was my first job.

At the time, they had some good architects in Iraq: Hisham Munir, Jaafar Allwai, Qahtan Madfai, Rifat Chadirji. So I agreed with Rifat to do those two projects: the architecture. We would do the services. We agreed and he did the architecture drawings. The facade was beautiful, but there were some problems in the plan. For example, from the elevator to the last apartment, you had to walk 75 metres. And my question to him was: Imagine, Rifat, a pregnant lady carrying her groceries and she has a baby with her, walking from her car to the elevator, then to her apartment. Don't you think all of those corridors are too much? His answer was, "Listen Sabah. I want people to live my building not to live in my building." And that was the end of our relationship.

RC: *We did not interview Rifat Chadirji, but some of his colleagues: Maath Alousi and Saad Al-Zubaidi who were coming to Kuwait regularly for this project. Both of them said they never understood the relation. Maath Alousi said that somehow they were against* the association because they saw Pace as a competitor. From the other end, you were starting an office and these projects were very important to establish a process, a way of working, the office itself. With that said, was the relationship with Iraq Consult (IQC), which was already a big corporation at that time, a useful contribution?

SR: No, no. It ended before it started. It really ended with the submission of those plans. After that, I made a settlement with IQC, we paid them, and completely changed the plans and only kept the facade, of course with some amendments.

I ended the relation after he said, "I want people to live my building." He was a very difficult person to work with, and the relationship ended there. After that, I realised how he had a very big ego. I worked with many people that were icons of architecture and engineering, but I never felt that any of them were treating me as if I didn't know anything. If I really owe someone for making Pace what it is, it's Louis McMillan (The Architects Collaborative, TAC). He even showed me how to keep time clocks, how to really run an office.

RC: *To conclude the relationship with Iraq Consult, there was the cinema in Jahra, one of your earlier projects, was IQC also involved. Can you tell us a bit more about that process?*

SR: By then I'd already been exposed to, as I said, Walter Gropius, Louis McMillan and all of TAC (The Architects Collaborative). You know TAC, at the time, was really at the top. And then I had met with SOM Chicago and SOM New York and all of those architects and engineers, and then there is this fellow that thinks he's better than anybody else in the world.

The stadiums, I'm sure we didn't have much to do with. Now, we'd been appointed as the consultant for the cinema. We did the Jahra Cinema, in Sulaibikhat. We did Abraq Khaitan. I think three or four cinemas. Of course a cinema is something that is very, very specialised. It's not just a building. I recall that the first time in my life that I did acoustic calculation was for myself, because at the time we didn't have anybody else and I did part of it and finally we found somebody to really do all of that.

RC: *Some of the cinemas during those years were designed by Sayyed Karim. Can you tell us your impressions of Sayyed Karim's work in the city, considering that he designed many buildings.*

SR: Sayyed Karim designed the building in Mubarakiya Street, which unfortunately now has almost been taken down. He did Hamra Cinema and I think he did the Andalus cinema also. He did so many other buildings, you know. In my view, it was like when you come to a place where hardly anyone really knows how to play football and then you bring a Messi. Sayyed Karim was definitely not a Messi, but someone that played better than the others.

RC: *Yes, and actually again he was another personality, like Shiber, that has disappeared completely. Is it again a phenomena of the climax of Arab nationalism?*

SR: I really don't know. This is something that I see you are really touching on. It's very interesting. They rise and then they suddenly disappear. I really don't know.

RC: *Companies like Pace and Dar Al-Handasah, for example, were always progressing, while the individual practices of people like Rifaat Chadirji or Sayyed Karim disappeared from practice while they were still young.*

SR: I don't know. Neither Rifat Chadirji or Sayyed Karim worked as professionals. I think for architects working in Kuwait in that period there was plenty of work. But at the time, there were no good examples. The first good example that was built was the municipality building, which still stands today, a fact for which I'd say, "Chapeu!" That was Sami Abdel Baki. But before that, there was the Ministry of Information and Guidance – which is now the National Council for Culture, Arts and Letters – which I really don't think is an icon. I don't know who designed it. Some people say it was Sayyed Karim. Some people think it is an open question.

RC: *He actually did the first proposal for that site. But we don't know if he finally did the one that was built.*

SR: But really, I'd say that the turning point, if there is a turning point in architecture, was the Kuwait Fund building, and I had to fight my way to get that approved. It was Abdulatif Al-Hamad who hired TAC, and then TAC contacted us. And we did most of the services at the time. I had to also get a license for this building. At the time, imagine the municipality had what they called the "elevation [building facade] committee," and none of the people in that committee knew anything about architecture. All of them were not practicing architects, and if you had asked them if they had done any building in their life, the answer would be no. So, when I submitted TAC's drawings, they were rejected, because it was a box. And I said, that's what we want: a box, a *sondouq* [word for fund and box in Arabic].

Well, you could sit with the committee members and they would theorise whatever they wanted, saying that the design was not good enough. I was really upset. Imagine the resistance, and it is still an icon today.

RC: *It's a very good building.*

SR: But I think that really was the turning point. After that, many clients came to us asking for a beautiful building: simple yet really striking, something like that. When we did the Andalus Complex for Mubarak Al-Hassawi, it was a big hit and people started imitating it. And, in fact, Al-Hassawi came and said we should sue them. And I said, "No, we're starting a school. Let them." The fact that you're being copied, means that your work is good.

RC: *There was also another building 'that made school,' with many similarities to that: the shipping company headquarters in Shuwaikh.*

SR: We did that.

RC: *Without no support of Iraq Consult, right?*

SR: Of course, that was done in-house. I tell you, we did not learn anything from Iraq Consult. We learned a lot from TAC. If anyone had an effect on Pace, it was TAC.

RC: *So, the Nugra Complex represents a lesson learned from TAC? Although, it might be better than what TAC was doing.*

SR: TAC was the first to build an exposed concrete facade and use sandblasted concrete. The first place where bush hammer concrete comes into play was with the Kuwait Fund building. We used that technology in the Nugra South Complex, Behbehani and Khalijiya towers and the Imad Centre because we realised that the owners looking for no maintenance. At the other end, the municipality never imposed on any building owner the obligation to maintain their building.

RC: *But was the Nugra Complex totally designed in-house? There was significant attention paid to building development as it was constructed in three phases. It is a real estate-oriented manner of development? Who designed the brief?*

SR: I had a very good relationship with Sheikh Jaber who was then the Minister of Information, and I was doing Nugra Complex for him. I got a call from his secretary, saying Sheikh Jaber wants to see you immediately. So I go to his office. We're friends. Yes, he's a minister, and I'm a consultant, but that was the first time that I had gone to his office and he did not ask me to sit down. The minute I walked in I said "*Salamu aleikum.*" I don't recall he even replied.

He said, "Is it true that you have designed my building [Nugra North Complex] without any shops on the street?"

I said "yes."

"Is it true you've designed my building as one storey?"

I said "yes."

He looked at me and said, "Listen, you go back and design it with shops all around the plot's perimeter and build it as high as the municipality allows. You understand? Go! Come back on Wednesday."

This was on a Saturday. He did not allow me to open my mouth, kicked me out, and I went out shaking. I came back to him on Wednesday. I was really afraid. And he said, "Where are the drawings?"

I said "Sorry. I don't have any drawings. I came to resign from the project."

I said that and he starts shouting: "You refuse?! How dare you refuse?"

Honestly, I was shaking, and I almost fainted, I really didn't know how my knees could carry me. I knew how rude he could be. I think he probably repeated "You refuse?" 1,000 times. And I was really shaking. Then, suddenly, he stops and looks me in the eye and says, "Sit down. Sit down. Sit down."

So I don't know what to do. I'm waiting for his verdict. He wanted to kill me? He looks at me – there's some silence – and says, "Listen, you go back, do whatever you want, yalla, go!"

Now I started regaining my courage. And I said, "Thank you, but you've asked me two questions and I want to answer."

He said, "No, no, no."

I said, "No I want to answer. You asked me whether I have planned to put shops around the perimeter of the building and I told you no, because I have studied this. If I had put shops around the perimeter, I would end up with twenty-two shops. But if I make it a shopping mall, I will have one hundred thirty-two shops. And I, as your consultant, decided that it's better to have one hundred thirty-two shops rather than twenty-two shops. So I took that decision."

"As for your second question, if it's one storey. I said yes but it is not really one storey. There are three. It's a basement, a ground floor, and a mezzanine, that look like one story when you see the plan. Moreover, I did this as a first stage. We will build the shopping mall, and we will get key money from deposits and rent that we can utilise to build the second phase, which will be the highest that the municipality allows. This is my second plan. I took that decision without asking you because I thought it should be done in two stages without having you put more money in."

He said, "Okay. Okay." After that day, he became one of my best friends. I will never forget the shift in personality. He had been very tough. But then I discovered that he had one of his employees, a Lebanese man, who wanted to give the project to Dar Al-Handasah, and, because of my relationship with him, he gave it to me.

RC: *Changing the subject, but keeping the conversation on the same building typology, we would like to better understand how the new souqs were developed in the confined commercial zones during the 1970s. There are points of view that credit Khaled Al-Marzouq for Souq Al-Kuwait and Souq Al-Kabeer and argue that they were the pioneers of these projects. Although, we have a different opinion. We think that first there were the 1968 studies, then Belgiojoso's (BBPR) and the Zoning Plan for the City centre were instrumental for that to happen. We also learned from TAC that Roland Kluver was a major advisor regarding the buildings program brief.*

SR: Roland was a senior partner with TAC. He was a great friend of mine. I don't know whether [he is] still alive or not, but he is a very fine person. But he did not really have much of a role with the municipality. The role was entrusted to the master planners and the people that did various projects here [referring to Belgiojoso]. I'm not aware of Roland doing anything. Coming back to your comment about Khaled Al-Marzouq, I give him a lot of credit because he had guts. When we did the Ahli Bank (ABK), it was part of the banking district within which there were two parking plots, refered to as the Manakh and Mubarak al-Kuwait. Then Khaled Al-Marzouq took the latest open plot at Souq Al-Kabeer where a disaster had happened, killing 42 people. Khaled Al-Marzouq took over those plots and he was courageous enough to say, "Okay, I'll take the BOT contract." And he built it and utilised it in a way. It was public parking and all of that.

RC: *So, somehow the idea that Khaled Al-Marzouq 'designed' the building program for Souq Al-Kuwait and that had an impact on the other souqs is true?*

SR: Yes because, after that, there were investment companies and not individuals. And here it was Al-Marzouq but operating through through the Aqarat Al-Kuwait [the Kuwait Real Estate Company]. After that, there was the Kuwait Investment Company and the KFTCIC [Kuwait Foreign Trade Contracting and Investment Company], as well as the National Real Estate Company in Wataniya. All of those followed suit after Khaled Al-Marzouq. Al-Manakh was built. Al-Safat was built. Al-Watiya was built by the Sheraton. All of them came after.

RC: *So the planners had no impact on this decision?*

SR: No. I'm not saying the planners didn't. It was a plot that was available for parking. When it was designed there where sixty-six lots in the city, allocated for multi-story car parks.

RC: *I'm just insisting on the subject because it represents a very relevant achievement in our point of view.*

SR: It was designed by SOM.

RC: *I'm referring to the mixed-use building program itself. All these multi-story car park souqs that were built together are relevant for the discussion of larger matters such as the relation between planning and architecture, or, one can say, worldwide urban design at that time. For that debate, it matters to know if it was something that happened due to the context, or if there was a dialogue between architecture and planning.*

SR: As Schwartz said, "It doesn't take a hero." The hero – you know what he said? – he said we, as planners, as war planners, we make plans and all of this, but the hero is the one that implements it. He is the true hero because we, as planners, plan the war, but who implements it? The soldiers.

For a city completely for pedestrians, it became completely the opposite. There was no room for pedestrians. We had to shout and really raise our voices. Where is our city? Where is our city? Where did the concept of malls and all of this come from? Kuwait was already malls. If you look at the old souqs, they were all connected to each other. They were all shaded. Yes, of course, it was primitive, but, if you look at Souq Al-Gharabally, Souq Al-Lahm and Souq Al-Khodar, all of them were integrated. That was the souq district which was the 'mall.' The concept was there. Who ignites that? The plots were there and available, but nobody took them, for years, until Khaled Al-Marzouq did. And when he did, for sure it was a good concept. He triggered that.

RC: *Yes, but, when someone brings all that together into a building, it's a big move. The idea of a self-contained unit where you have all of your life within a building: It's a fantastic idea, of course. It's an idea anyone could have had, but as you said it happened there.*

SR: Of course you have to deal with the weather. Kuwait is unbearable for three months of the year. Even during Abdullah Al-Salem's era, somebody had suggested covering Kuwait.

RC: *Yes, it was Sheikh Sabah Al-Salem in an interview for Life Magazine in 1965. But another misconception, here, is the acceptance that Souq Al-Kuwait was designed by SOM, when the project was already there, designed by the Italian studio BBPR, and the structure they proposed is pretty much the same.*

SR: Maybe I could shed some light on this. Khaled Al-Marzouq is a businessman. He goes by the metre. 'How much is this metre going to bring me?' When we negotiated Wataniya, I was able to sell the concept of TAC to KFTCIC [who was the client]. And fortunately, all of the people that were with KFTCIC really trusted me. "Trust me it is going to be beautiful. You will make money. Trust me," I told them. And this had a lot to do with it. With Khaled Al-Marzouq, it was "why do we have to do this when it does not bring me income? Why theses spaces and this architecture? Why are there villas up on the roof?" [reference to Souq Al-Wataniya]

I'll tell you. With SOM, we won a very big project at the time: the Conference Centre, in front of the Sheraton, a beautiful concept. Following the competition results, I got a call from Sheikh Jaber Al-Ahmad who was at the time the Crown Prince.

He said, "Listen, Sabah. I don't know your friends, the Americans, but I know you. This is a very important project for me, and I want you to report to me every month on its progress."

To do that, I took two of my staff, Hakam Jarrar and Abdel Rahim, and sent them to work in Chicago with Fazlur Khan and Bruce Graham.

When the ante project was finished and we were at a stage where we needed approval to go a step further, we had a full scheme, elevation, sections, samples of materials and all of this, I went to do the presentation. At the time, he [Jaber Al-Ahmad] would not allow anybody else to attend meetings on the project, just myself and the Minister of Finance. So I was doing the presentation for him, and as I went through the plans and the elevations, he stopped and said:

"I don't like the elevations." The Minister of Finance said, "We will change them." I did not say anything. I just continued to present as if I did not hear anything until the end.

Then I said, "Okay, Your Highness, you said you didn't like the elevations. Why didn't you like the elevations?" So I get a hit right here from the Minister of Finance, like how dare you ask? Again I ignored that. It hurt, believe me, but I said, "Why don't you like it?"

He said, "Well, it is not Islamic." I said, "Why is it not Islamic?"

He said, "It doesn't have arches." I said, "Well, but Jahra Gate doesn't have arches."

He said, "No, but I want something impressive." I said, "Islamic architecture is not really impressive from the outside."

"I want people to be impressed by it." I told him, "When you get inside, it explodes in front of you and you see it."

Then he said, "Okay, *trust in Allah*. You go ahead."

From "I don't like it" to "Go ahead and do it" – 180 degrees. I got it approved, as I was walking out of the conference room. I met the Minister of Finance leaving his office, and I was really upset. He said, "How dare you ask or argue?"

I said, "How dare you say you would change it. Who's going to change it? You're going to change it or am I going to change it? If I'm going to change it, I want to understand what he likes. He wants something with arches. There are more than 100 types of arches, which arch?" It was a back and forth with the ministers. It is really hard to gain the trust of your client, and I think that is something I was successful in.

RC: *Do you think that Souq Al-Wataniya was successful after it was built?*

SR: It was. All of those apartments that were designed for housing were not really used for housing. That is not because the project was not good or successful, but because of the rules and how they were implemented, and also the greed of the owners. Do I rent this apartment for 500KD per month or as an office for 1000KD?

RC: *So all the arguments that people back then did not want to come back to the city to live in the apartments is not valid? There were people willing to move there?*

SR: Unfortunately everything was against pedestrians, against people living in the city. And I see it, as someone very proud. We did value engineering for the Mirqab project and decided it should be a commercial building rather than for housing. Okay, then do you value engineer for a garden that has zero return? Why do you plant trees? Why do you, if that is the concept of doing value engineering? They took value engineering as something – oh wow, I know value engineering.

RC: *Yes, they took it as a goal instead of a tool. Of these car parks, there is one project that remains unclear to us, which is Souq Al-Watiya. In the Wataniya and Safat souqs, the relation between Pace and TAC is clear. However, with Souq Al-Watiya, we have a design proposal by TAC that was not the one to be implemented.*

SR: Maybe TAC did the first, but that was a prefab – I don't really recall. Al-Watiya: now we go back half a century again, the whole concept. First of all, you cannot really see it from anywhere. It's behind the Sheraton Hotel, behind that street facing the Al-Bahar building. It's in the middle of nowhere. So really I don't know.

RF: *The other project was the invitation for the National Assembly's competition.*

SR: Now I don't know if I can recollect. We were asked, I don't remember by whom, whether it was the Municipality or the Ministry of Public Works...

RF: *By the advisory group, maybe?*

SR: Yes. We were asked to design the parliament building. We decided to form a consortium, and we rented a space, an office. We furnished it and all of this, between Pace, KEO, Hamad Thunyan [a member of Gulf Consult]. At the time Sabah Abi-Hanna and Salem Al-Marzouq had not formed [SSH]. And, in fact, we had Bader Al-Salem in charge of that office. And I think it was in the Yaqoub Al-Humaidhi building on Soor street.

We worked on that because we were promised work from the Credit and Saving Bank. At the time, they were entrusted with housing. We were promised, if we are successful with the parliament building, that we would do the other building in the future.

But this consortium really never got off the ground because what we'd been promised never materialised. We finished that parliament project, which was designed for the Municipal Council and never really for the parliament. Then we had to redesign it for the real parliament. It did the job for a while, until they appointed Utzon.

RC: *We also have a question regarding the crash of the Souq Al-Manakh and its impact. The souqs that we have been debating also represent a moment of significant optimism: the ambition of a new and modern city. Of course, from the mid-1970s toward the early 1980s, there was a financial affluence that fed this boom. The buildings that were built during this period, and you mentioned several, were in their majority, very pragmatic, functional and efficient. The buildings were a direct response to purpose.*

With the Souq Al-Manakh stock market crash, everything became sparser. Real estate became weaker in terms of development. Can you give us your insight about what happened after the crash regarding consultancy work and building development in the city?

SR: Well, of course the crash had a tremendous effect on the development of Kuwait, to the point that the Master Plan had to stop. Twice, the Master Plan was reviewed: during the 1990 occupation and after the Souq Al-Manakh stock market crash. Both had to be addressed because things had changed completely. One of them was economical, while the other was of course a political and military change.

During the Souq Al-Manakh crash, these people created their own central bank and their own economy, to the point where money within the system itself was about 5 billion KD, while the checks that were written there were worth 25 billion KD. So the crash was expected. I was interviewed by *The Wall Street Journal* at the time and I said, "I'm proud I designed the Souq Al-Manakh, but I have not stepped into it." I really never stepped into the Manakh while it was the Souq Al-Manakh, because "they" always said, "when you go to Manakh, you have to leave your brain outside." And I'm not the type to leave my brain outside anywhere. What happened is that one fellow predicted that the market would crash any time. And he had a check for 10 million, and it was due, let's say, in April. So he went in March to cash it. There were not enough funds in the account of his friend. So, from his internal information – imagine – they told him that there was a shortage of 1 million KD. So he went and deposited 1 million KD in that account, and cashed it for 10 million, so he only lost 1 million. When this fellow realised that he did not have anything, he wanted to do the same thing, and so on. And suddenly the whole thing just collapsed, because it was not sustainable.

RC and **RF**: Thank you very much for this talk. •

SABAH AL-RAYES

The Boom

NAJI MOUJAES

This transcript has been taken from the conference "Modern Architecture Kuwait: The Architecture Debate Series," held at the Yarmouk Cultural Centre in Kuwait on May 1, 2016.

Edward Nilsson, TAC lead designer at Souq Al-Wataniya served as Guest Speaker, while debators included Professor Asseel Al-Ragam and Naji Moujaes, founder of PAD10.

Ricardo Camacho moderated the debate.

The transcript includes the responses from Naji Moujaes only.

The debaters were asked to give concise answers to ten questions, supported by visual material – one image per question.

On the occasion of the opening of the exhibition "Modern Architecture Kuwait: 1949–1989," Dar al-Athar al-Islamiyyah organised and hosted a series of architectural debates with local and foreign practitioners. This series was designed to deepen the knowledge of Kuwait's national architecture, and to foster a greater appreciation of the preservation of collective heritage.

In August 2012, the first conference on modern building heritage took place in Kuwait simultaneously with the first representation of Kuwait at the 13th International Architecture Exhibition at *La Biennale di Venezia*. The event included a series of round-table debates between architecture and planning practitioners and the local community. The success of this event triggered several years of research, now in a double-volume book, *Modern Architecture Kuwait, 1949–1989*, commissioned by Dar al-Athar al-Islamiyyah, with support from the Kuwait Foundation for the Advancement of Sciences. Unfamiliarity with Kuwait's national history and architectural heritage is a major loss for the country. Since this research was initiated, at least three major buildings – all subjects of study – have been demolished to make space for high-rise office buildings, while others have been modified or covered in shiny aluminium cladding. Understanding these previously unknown and uncorrelated incidents is fundamental to providing tentative answers to a series of hypothetical questions: How were architectural design processes and practices developed from the early 1950s until now? How was, and is, architecture practiced in the absence of historical heritage, major local architectural references, and strong morphological elements?

The rise of state-sponsored funding in the 1970s transformed this temporary utopian community, imposing spectacular building developments on the modern town. After the 1973 oil embargo, new buildings were informed by the relationship between Kuwait and the global economy, introducing common architectural paradigms of the post-modern era.

However, buildings such as the new souqs – built between 1974 and 1980 and designed by Pace + TAC and SSH + SOM in the city centre – combined the functionality and efficiency of modernist architecture with recreational needs. Either with The Architects Collaborative (TAC) or with Skidmore, Owings & Merrill (SOM), investment in the production of 'place' over the modernist 'space,' brought a new level of interest to the city's urban environment and modern development. A new hybrid typology based on the old commercial street – the souq, vernacular neighbourhood, and car parking – was finally able to mediate levels of comfort throughout the city. These eight buildings are still prominent in the city to this day.

*RC*_Saba George Shiber's recognition of Kuwait as a "fluid city shell" is a diversion from dependence on large planning operations and state building programs.

Since the construction of Fahad Al-Salem street, an emerging private real estate sector has transformed the pre-oil mercantile tradition into building design and material trading.

Was the city planning of the 1970s drawn up to regulate the expectations of the real estate market, design and construction industries?

NM_ Fluid, being an internal dynamic condition of relationships, and shell, the broad external framework that internalises such fluidity, both describing the hope and frailty implicit in Kuwait as a city in flux.

In many ways, Shiber's "fluid city shell" concept reflects his agitation and anxiety amid the rush, as seen in his book, manifested with cries on lost opportunities, emanating from inherent potentials of unlimited budgets manifested thus far with a private development spine, along a car artery.

On Fahad Al-Salem street, Shiber mentions in *The Kuwait Urbanization* that, "More design goes into such articles as a Dior dress or a door knob than in the study of costly and enduring urban emergents. More design effort was put into the storefronts […] than in its overall civic, or urban design [...] This is a pity," he concludes. The design of storefronts and their displays is driven by private initiative and ambition, while the overall civic or urban design is driven by a young state, which defines, shapes and maintains civic space. This suspension of responsibility of the private sector, developers and citizens, reaffirms Mohammad Al-Assad's observation that there is a widespread feeling that the city is the mere responsibility of the state, while the state itself has shown a *laisser-faire* approach to policy, doing nominal works that are ill-fated and lacking a commitment to maintain them.

RC_ The most relevant and evident results of this energy are the new multistorey souqs and the first towers in Sharq, built during the 1970s. Today these souqs are being renovated and new towers built. How can

1. Jahra roundabout in Kuwait City, 1958. © Kuwait Oil Company Archive.

these be understood – as the direct result of planning and regulations or evidence of market demand?

NM_ The aftermath of planning has evidenced sparse developments, with vast vacant lots and weakly defined and maintained public frameworks, indicating that the contemporary mechanism for renovating some structures is to defer to the status quo, however problematic it may prove to be. On market demand: an oil glut, all sense is lost, including the market to its demands; this is known as 'Dutch Disease.' This mono-economy somehow sedates an otherwise frenetic real estate market; the latter loses any sensibility for its demand, especially considering "the artificially inflated land value" within the city, as stated by Michael Kubo in his travel grant report to the Aga Khan, *The Incorporation of Architecture: Bureaucratic Modernism and Global Practice after 1945.*

While the towers are emblematic of the prowess of 'private' financial institutions, the souqs are more of an arranged marriage between the public and the private

(these souqs were built on publicly-owned land during the 1970s, through Build–Operate–Transfer (BOT) contracts). To understand their impact on the city, we can examine Darwaza Abdul-Razak area, where the Joint Banking Centre towers are across the road from Souq Al-Kuwait. The residual public areas around the Joint Banking Centre reveal minimal but maintained landscaping, a Miesian urban setback that follows an architectural framework. As for the Souq, the developer took an *ad hoc* approach, after it was a sort of wasteland patched with *astro turf,* cut around leftover stylised pergolas.

Such randomness is typical of the way in which these BOT projects were managed, bridging the gap between the mandate renovation for qualified developers and an inactive municipal body. With the termination of the thirty-year contract for the Souq's operation and its subsequent BOT renovation, a serious opportunity has been missed to mediate between the Mubarakiya traditional souqs and Souq Al-Kuwait – one of the few surviving pedestrian experiences within the city.

RC_Being client driven, many of these buildings were designed by a certain elite of foreign architects, selected based on professional recommendations or through personal connections. However the failure of many of these buildings has been associated with lack of commitment from their designers, or lack of awareness of context, building materials, and regional practice. Why did Sawaber housing project fail?

NM_ Firstly, there is professional colonialism, which is far worse than stylistic colonialism. A mandate to have an international designer spearheading the project and local offices processing the paper work and all technical aspects lobotomises them of all sensibility towards the role of the project, its context and community.

The consequences are: the formation of local offices as a one-stop shop for foreign architects, focusing on everything and mastering nothing. In a way this paralysed the offices from taking the lead in most cases, as they propped up international consultants at the expense of leading in a particular discipline. Also, it became unlikely that specialised consultants (specification writers, landscape architects, specialised engineers, QS firms, etc.) could focus on their specialties due to the confusion surrounding their scope of work.

Secondly, the right question should be, Why did Sawaber succeed for so long, when public housing projects failed in many cities around the world? Sawaber succeeded as an architectural proposal, even with all the compromises, as it introduced elevated streets (segregating pedestrians from cars), re-introduced urban density and public communal spaces back into the city, and added shade to communal areas by stepping the

buildings. Practically, it failed when the plug was pulled ten years ago by the Public Authority for Housing and Welfare, which stopped maintaining the buildings. On the other hand, the present replacement housing project in Northwest Sulaibikhat embodies everything that caused public housing programs to fail in the 1970s.

RC_The diversity of production sources, together with a strong motivation for experimentation, generated a series of remarkable architectural and urban models during the 1970s and 1980s that remain challenging alternatives for collective housing today, such as Sawaber or Loulou'a Al-Marzouq. Are these experiments the result of local context or the design process of owners and architects? Can you elaborate on any relevant building characteristics to support your argument?

NM_ While Sawaber was part of the public housing welfare program, Loulou'a Al-Marzouq embodied the complete opposite – private housing for the affluent. At the tip of the Ras Al-Salmiya peninsula, seemingly ready to sail out, the Loulou'a captured the imagination of the rich expatriate elite in Kuwait, who perceived it as a private residence, a home far from home, with an elevated vantage point over the city and sea.

Doubling its footprint with skip-stop elevators made its preservation worthwhile, and it somehow escaped the fate of fifty percent of Ras Al-Salmiyas demolished buildings in the last decade.

Its pitched red roof and sandstone warm facade infused a Mediterranean feel to the Arabian Gulf. The commercial elevated plinth regulated by pilotis, a pool area encroaching on the sea opposite to an enclosed private courtyard, and a

hybrid of house typologies, was inflated to multiply a collective experience, bringing to Kuwait the excitement of a dense urban mix. Somehow, it was convincing for well-to-do locals to substitute the privacy of their single residences and claim their prime duplexes and penthouses, mixing with white-collar expats. Until today, part of the building is on hold, captive to such dreams.

RC_Referring to the new public buildings erected in Kuwait in the late 1970s, Lawrence Vale wrote: "Most of these buildings [were] being treated like isolated islands in a sea of parking lots," highlighting how the lack of an organic urban connection system led to the production of a cityscape made for cars more than for pedestrians.

Do you agree, and, if yes, can we attribute such a phenomenon to the absence of public interest in many of these building operations or lack of social and urban responsibility from designers and design firms?

NM_ Any city in the making with car access and loose legislation may run such risks. On an optimistic note, one of the trends that shaped the city counter to this is Souq Al-Kuwait. A hybrid of building with vertical parking, where cars are stacked between offices and shops to extend, internalise and acclimatise the urban experience. This symbiosis of the vital elements of the city was lessened over time due to the bypassing or lack of enforcement of drafted laws. Car-parking areas exempt from the new office buildings littered cars onto adjacent vacant plots.

However, the BOT contracts governing the wellbeing of such hybrid buildings are mere sheets of below-budget bill-of-quantities, with no qualifying clauses meant to be preserved. There, a 'qualifying' regulatory authority must step into the process to render it more culturally and environmentally relevant.

In order to build on current booms and past models: what if we learn from other cities with tough climates? – using for instance the strategy of urbanist Vincent Ponte's underground city for Montreal, by having the Avenues Mall less of a commercial strip and more of an underground or raised network of connections between disparate city blocks. The Shopping mall could be less of a big box and more of an urban acclimatised shopping connection, animated by museums, art galleries, and bookshops.

RC_Alison and Peter Smithson, who were invited to Kuwait in 1968 to prepare urban form studies for the old city, advocated for buildings that could help to define national identity. They called for buildings that, in their words, carry qualities that would differentiate Kuwait from other Arab cities, such as Cairo or Beirut. They envisaged buildings within the frame of Arab urban traditions adapted to modern life, contrary to the idea of variation models from America, Europe or from Europeanised North Africa. With this said, do you think that the projects developed after the 1968 call for "urban form studies" were able to build a city that differentiates from Cairo or Beirut?

NM_ The mat-building was strategically antithetical to the organic old city, thus positing itself as a clear alternative. The mat plan simplified the functional zoning and considered the newly emerging needs of a modern state, with a sectional complexity capable of providing shade and space through functional zoning. This *tabula rasa* extended the building facade and the plot limits, internalising the urban experience of the old city and dissociating itself

from dense settings like Cairo and Beirut, not mentioning their already dense urbanity. Still, with Jørn Utzon's National Assembly, the facade was re-introduced as an urban space, with an ambition to mediate between parliamentarians and their constituencies. There were threats to value engineer the symbolic structure, whereby the architect asserted that he must do it, and luckily he got his way.

RC_From his presentation "Architectural Conception of Buildings in Accordance with Twentieth Century Islamic-Arabic Style," at the Conference on Building Maintenance in Kuwait in January 1969, Macklin L. Hancock called for an Islamic-Arabic inherited approach to "understand how this could be achieved [using] materials to help keep maintenance costs low [and] effective solutions to technical problems unique to this part of the world."

During the 1970s, practices such as Iraq Consult, Pace, KEO, KEG and Sabah Abi-Hanna (later SSH) initiated a remarkable body of work related to the private development of mixed-use programs, which utilised, in their own ways, the aesthetic values identified by Hancock. Can you elaborate on this assumption?

NM_ Nationalism as a way to strengthen identity was simultaneous to the Modern Movement, and was a common motivation pursued both by the local offices and international consultants. Modernity somehow captured the imagination of a nation that was seeking stature. It was more a pan-Arabist motivation, rather than an Islamic movement at that time. Islamic iconography and style was more apparent in the post-modern era, as we can see in the transformation of Arne Jacobsen's Central Bank of Kuwait facades.

When we look at design production in local offices during the 1970s and 1980s, it seemed less stylised. Geometrically abstract, the concrete constructions with deep and minimal fenestrations were driven by climatic motivations.

Hancock's coupling of Arab and Islamic influences ran the risk of one stifling the other, as Ghazi Sultan's article, "Designing for New Needs in Kuwait," suggested.

Lastly, the illusion of low maintenance, locally misinterpreted as 'no maintenance' is what degrades modern structures and cities to a point of no return.

RC_Kuwait capital city has suffered from gradual deterioration in areas once characterised by their modern architecture. Today, the city faces the challenge of urban renewal. During this process, the conservation of the existing buildings, regardless of their use and institutional value, has been the subject of denial and many have been demolished and replaced. This refusal to preserve buildings has been encouraged by a political and academic elite, as well as architecture and planning practitioners, who have labeled such buildings as 'foreign' and therefore implicitly indifferent to local history and builing traditions. Only recently, with narratives of 'nation building' through memory and identity, has an emerging community of young, well-educated artists and professionals from varied sectors in society started to ascribe 'archeological status' to buildings and urge their preservation.

Please elaborate on the differences and similarities between the movements to preserve Bait Lothan and Sawaber.

NM_ This is a wave of arguments and counter-arguments, whereby the first sets a pretext for demolishing 'foreign' constructions, and the latter argues that we as a culture and a nation are a sedimentation of all these accumulated built works, which are representative of a history that is built and not one that is eclectically selected to construct a mythical past.

Considering the history of Kuwait's modern and pre-oil constructions as 'archeology' may be problematic terminology that has been sanctified in some ways.

More accurately, to borrow from the Landmarks Preservation Commission of NYC, it must be replaced by "architecturally, historically, and culturally significant buildings and sites" that are granted "landmark or historic district status" and regulated "once they're designated." Landmarks can be "individual landmarks, interior landmarks and scenic landmarks." They are regulated rather than owned, which is key.

For Bait Lothan and Sawaber, to preserve first and foremost you need to maintain and program with economic viability, with cultural and architectural significance playing a role. In Sawaber, maintenance stopped a decade ago. The movement for its preservation should have happened back then, as the deterioration of the buildings today may, by itself, undermine such a movement.

A building must be re-imagined, reprogrammed, and re-situated to fit its present context, as in Loulou'a Al-Marzouq, where primarily it encroached on the public beach, but now, with its central garden, is itself a public venue.

RC_The building conservation and the emergence of different commitments towards the rehabilitation and adaptive re-use of modern buildings in Kuwait is confined to the lack of recognition and an almost non-existent framework for legal protection.

The local authorities approach to building conservation, by entities such as the NCCAL, is based on the idea of building fossilisation. Every building becomes a monument to itself or a museum. Can you comment on the cases of Kuwait National Museum, Loulou'a Al-Marzouq and Kuwait Towers recent intervention works?

NM_ While monuments are usually fossilised to capture memory rather than imagination, private developments are not; they need to be relevant and help shape our present surroundings.

Loulou'a Al-Marzouq belongs to the latter, as it was retooled according to programmatic thinking rather than aesthetics. In this situation, we were activists, before we were hired as architects, by creating a community blog to document the building's history, architectural significance, and to monitor its systematic degradation. The owner was sympathetic to it and finally implemented measures: the main access was reoriented through the central courtyard, with all the apartment vertical cores also accessed through this area.

The pilotis buoyancy of the building was reclaimed by promoting commercial exposure to both sides, the central courtyard and building perimeter. The transparency of the retail units allowed for a ground floor that could be seen from outside, through to the central courtyard garden.

In the apartments, bay windows replaced the facade closet blocks, opening the building up to view its unique surrounding, and the falling sandstone was overlaid with expanded metal mesh to hold the stone in place.

Still, the dynamics among different parties: the incapability of the authorities to comprehend the

benefits of retooling the building, and the management of the facilities are future challenges that will set a precedent for the re-use and retooling of modern structures especially as this structure has proven its communal relevance.

RC_Kuwaiti citizens often show a lack of attachment to many of these buildings. The local authorities have taken very few measures in the past to promote their proper conservation and restoration. Among the worst examples of preservation are state-owned buildings, such as the Mubarakiya School and the former Ministry of Information and Guidance, actual head offices for the NCCAL.

Can you suggest how this culture might change?

NM_ Actually, I feel it is the other way round, whereby Kuwaiti youth want the city to believe in them. As we have seen in the recent past, and currently, many are coming up with initiatives and small businesses all around the city, sometimes claiming worn out structures to revive them and their surrounding neighbourhoods.

Local authorities must pick up this momentum and reach out to these private initiatives, securing proper urban programing think tanks, amenities, infrastructures, and most importantly spaces and connectors that bind these sporadic initiatives to reclaim and sustain a street life that has long disappeared.

Additionally, Kuwaitis and non-Kuwaitis, who feel affinity to the place and what it stands for, must not hold back from claiming a leading role in re-imagining the city as a space in which everyone should claim his or her own place, forming a sense of belonging.

With the ruthless non-dialogue all across the Arab world, we at PAD10 imagined a space for dialogue.

Along the 1 km stretch of sea front, car-free with the Gulf road diverted underground, the National Library, the National Museum, the National Assembly, *Bayt Bader, Bayt Sadu,* and last but not least Dar al-Athar al-Islamiyya have become pavilions within the park. All at walking distance from one another, they connect the city back to the sea and the people to the pillars of a nation that is representative of their hopes and aspirations. •

2. Aerial view of old Kuwait City, 1940s.
© Kuwait Oil Company Archive.

3. Detail of Dasman Complex facade, KEO, Kuwait City, 1975–79.
© Dar al-Athar al-Islamiyyah, Nelson Garrido, 2015.

4. Aerial view of new neighbourhood units, Kuwait, 1980s.
© Kuwait Oil Company Archive.

Maath Alousi

Maath Alousi (1938–) graduated in architecture from the Middle East Technical University (METU) in Ankara, Turkey (1957–61) after completing his first year at the Agriculture College in Baghdad. He pursued an interest in large-scale projects and architectural heritage from the very beginning, joining Rifat Chadirji (1926–) at Chadirji, Sherzad and Abdulla Ihsan Kamil (later Iraq Consult – IQC). Alousi was awarded a scholarship at the Architectural Association London in Educational Buildings at the Department of Tropical Studies, which he completed in 1964. Upon the establishment of IQC in 1965, Alousi was responsible for the design studio and production drawing studio. His first works in Kuwait were Al-Hamad Villa (1964–67) and Al-Hassawi Residential Complexes (1968–70), in association with Pace. In 1974 he left IQC and established the Technical Studies Bureau (TEST) office in Beirut with three other partners. While at both IQC and TEST, Alousi helped to design, supervise, and complete the Kuwait Sport Clubs (1970–74), which were a series of four sports complexes with stadiums. When TEST split in 1980, the Alousi Associates Technical Studies Bureau TEST-Baghdad continued Alousi's practice, and is still responsible for the Ministry of Planning's head offices (1980–82) and many other projects in Kuwait.

Sara Saragoça Soares conducted this interview via email in March 2015.

Sara Saragoça Soares: What led you to enroll in the Architecture degree program at a school such as METU (the degree was established in 1956 by Holmes Perkins, the professor who taught Ghazi Sultan at the GSD and, as such, was one of the strongest references in the Kuwaiti architect's work). Were you one of the first to graduate from there in architecture?

Maath Alousi: I joined METU in 1957. My uncle was the ambassador of Iraq in Ankara and he was very well informed about the school. It was an obvious choice to study architecture there, both for me and my family.

    Dean Perkins, as I remember, used to spend some time with us, but never full-time. I didn't know that he taught Ghazi, who I met much later during my trips to Kuwait.

SS: What was the impact of such a degree on your early education? As far as we know, the degree in architecture at METU was strongly related to other disciplines such as landscape and restoration. Did being under the umbrella of UNESCO determine this? How would you describe the degree and its impact on you and your colleagues back then?

MA: In the first few years, the departments of architecture and business administration had foreign faculty members. I don't recall any foreign professors in the civil or mechanical engineering departments. Gönül Tankut (1932–2005), Abdulla Kuran (1927–2002), Prof. Robert Matters and Marvin Sevely (former Gropius' student and UN representative), and later William E. Cox (who worked with Louis I. Kahn and was a UN representative) and Joe J. Jordan, all had a big impact on us, coming from different cultures. Our high school was inferior compared to others, so thank goodness I had my freshman year at the Agriculture College in Baghdad. I always appreciated the standards and values of those professors.

SS: Did you refer Gönül Tankut there first for any reason? Was she already preservation oriented back then? Was she part of the UNESCO program that funded the degree?

MA: Tankut assisted Prof. Abdullah Kuran and Prof. William E. Cox. Yes, she was preservation-oriented. Prof. Cox was very much influenced by the American architect Louis I. Khan. He used to express his admiration for Khan's works, like the Treton Bath House in New Jersey and the Richards Medical Research Laboratories at the University of Pennsylvania in Philadelphia. These were some of the projects we had to study in detail at that time.

SS: Were any of the following your colleagues at METU – Prof. Kemal Aran, Prof. Dr. İnci Aslanoğlu, Prof. Dr. Gönül Evyapan or Prof. Dr. Sevgi Aktüre?

MA: Inci and Kemal were one year ahead of me. Gönül Evyapan (nee Aslanoğlu) is Inci's younger sister. Yildirim Yavus (who latter became dean at METU and also taught at King Faisal University, Damman), Ayşe Gedik (who is still at METU, teaching in the Dept. of City and Regional Planning) and Özcan Esmer (also teaching at METU Dept. of City and Regional Planning) were in the same year, and were very close friends. Sevgi Aktüre I don't recall.

SS: During your time at METU, was the Danish architect Johan Otto Von Spreckelsen (renowned author of l'Arche de la Défense in Paris) at school? If yes, was he an important influence? Were there any other foreign faculty members from the Netherlands, or from Lebanon, that you recall? If yes, what was their experience or interest in the region's development, particularly the Middle East and the Gulf? Were they aware of urban development taking place in Baghdad and Kuwait?

MA: I was not aware that Spreckelsen was at METU. I met him and his wife, as I recall, in the late sixties, when he was working in Baghdad for a government design department. Our relationship was more social than professional, though he did have professional relationships with some Iraqi architects outside his government job.

SS: Other faculty at METU during that period was Frederick Alois "Fritz" Janeba (1905–1983), former student of Adolf Loos in Vienna and Bauhaus, who was living in Australia and was appointed by UNESCO to teach the basic design course. Was he there while you were?

MA: No.

SS: Was Behruz Çinici a big influence in Turkey at the time? Did his work influence your early practice in any way?

MA: I was not familiar with Behruz Çinici's work. Turgut Cansever (1921–2009) was the architect that caught our attention, with projects such as the METU Campus International Design Competition (1959) and the popular Türk Tarih Kurumu in Ankara, completed in 1966.

    The architect who impacted my work was Prof. Abdullah Kuran. He was my tutor for history of architecture, and my advisor for the Design Studio for more than one semester. He made me believe the inspiration for work on a place should come from its inherited architecture. He taught us how to respect our architectural heritage.

SS: Was the architectural and building scene in Baghdad or Kuwait discussed at METU? With so many faculty members aware of the work of Alvar Aalto, Walter Gropius, Josep Lluís Sert and others, were the competitions and proposals for Baghdad reference projects to study?

MA: No, they were not discussed.

SS: Did your interest in environmental and large-scale projects start there? – For example, the reforestation project initiated in 1961 for the new METU campus that completely changed Ankara's periphery?

MA: Yes. My final thesis was on faculty housing, on a site near the lake of Gulbashi, a water reservoir surrounded by wooded hills. This site was the first choice for the new campus; later they moved to the present site, which is more than fifteen km from Ankara.

SS: Being one of the first students to graduate in architecture from METU (1961), what were your initial motivations when researching where to work and what to do? After 1961, did you return back to Baghdad and start work straight away at Iraq Consult? How would you describe the office in those days (before moving to the new office in 1965)?

MA: One month after my graduation, I joined "Chadirji, Sherzad and Abdulla Ihsan Kamil," which was the name of the practice then. I was the first architect to join them. Because of his health condition, Mr. Kamil wasn't a frequent participant, but he did ask me to assist in some projects, one of them being a proposal for Tahrir Square in Baghdad.

We were all part-timers. Rifat was Deputy Minister of Housing, Sherzad was Professor of Structure at Baghdad University, and Professor Kamil was teaching and a member of the Amanat Al-Asima's council.

SS: Can you refer to some other significant projects that you worked on during this time?

MA: The Iraqi Insurance building, the Tobacco Monopoly building on Jamhouria Street, Rafidain Bank on Rasheed Street, and many private residential buildings. These were all prior to my sabbatical for the Architectural Association in London.

SS: How would you describe the role of Rifat Chadirji in the daily routine of the office back then? What was the relationship with professors Ihsan Kamil and Ihsan Sherzad? We had the opportunity to go over the documents from the Gulbenkian Foundation Archive on 'Al-Shaab Stadium' (formerly Saddam Hussein Stadium, the national stadium of Iraq) and the Arts Centre, which gave us a good idea of the dynamic between the three partners.

MA: When I joined the practice, Rifat was the leader and decision maker, but everyone's roles were well-defined, they were a team of serious professionals. The Stadium and the Modern Art Museum were already under construction and the office was responsible for site supervision.

SS: Were these two projects, funded by the Caloust Gulbenkian Foundation, important for the work developed later by the office? – For example, was the stadium, design by the Portuguese architect Francisco Keil do Amaral, an important reference for the Kuwait Sports Club project?

MA: Yes, the stadium did help. However, our role was site supervision only. I had no contact with the Portuguese designers.

Later, I had to deal with two projects and present them to the Gulbenkian Foundation: Orphanages for Arbil and Duhok. Both were completed and were nice buildings, but I have no evidence of them.

SS: Were you involved in developing relationships with clients, such as the Gulbenkian Foundation, for example? Did you visit Lisbon during the design process for the orphanages?

MA: No, I met their representative in Baghdad.

SS: It seems that your relationship with Rifat Chadirji was special. In Chadirji's book, "Concepts and Influences: Towards a Regionalised International Architecture," you are at the top of the acknowledgements list, after engineer Levon Artin. Can you tell us more about the circle of colleagues around him?

MA: On Mr. Kamil's retirement, after he had dedicated himself to the practice, his share was given to Mr. Artin, who was the structural engineer at the practice since the beginning of their collaboration. A year later, Artin confounded his time to the university job, and his work responsibilities were added to mine.

SS: Can you please rephrase the last statement? Is it correct that Mr. Artin joined the practice in 1952? When you say Mr. Artin "confounded his time to the university job," you mean that Mr. Artin left the practice in 1962 (one year after you joined), to

dedicate his time to his faculty role at the university, and all responsibility under Mr. Artin was passed to you on his departure.

MA: Artin collaborated with the partnership in 1952. IQC's internal partnership took place in the late sixties. In the early seventies the Iraqi Authority passed a law prohibiting university professors from working outside their schools. Artin didn't want to take the risk of keeping both jobs. He preferred teaching and was unofficially the engineer responsible for structural and civil engineering design at the office. Ihsan Sherzad was very much involved in politics, being a regular member of the Cabinet, representing the Kurds.

My relationship with Rifat was always special, even before joining. I was aware of his work, and we come from the same neighbourhood in Baghdad, from A'dhamiy. We had distant family relations. On my return from METU, the first architect I met in Baghdad was Rifat. He was a very close friend of my cousin. The meeting (interview) took place at his office in the Ministry of Housing. I reported to work in the afternoons in his private office (in those days they only operated in the afternoons). For the morning job, he made me join the Housing Directorate to become familiar with local building materials. Our professional, social, and cultural relationships were always very close and very special.

SS: Were Rifat Chadirji or the IQC influential in your application to proceed further in your studies at the Architectural Association, particularly in the Tropical Studies Department? It's interesting that other colleagues of yours also took the same trajectory, such as Sa'ad Al-Zubaidi some years after.

MA: My nomination for the AA was through a scholarship that I won from the design department at the Ministry of Housing. It was a bonus for completing an urgent urban design of a Civic Centre for a housing project. The IQC was still not established back then. I didn't select the AA as such, the scholarship was from the British Council, offered to the Iraqi government.

The opportunity arose for Saad to join the AA when we decided to participate in The Mosque of London competition. Saad managed to both attend the AA and work for the competition at the same time. At that time, we collaborated with the Architects Co-Partnership of the UK.

SS: Was the Civic Centre related to any of Doxiadis' housing projects? Was this the first project you developed on your own in Baghdad?

MA: I was nominated by the Housing Ministry. No, the project wasn't one of Doxiadis. It was my first urban design project.

SS: What was the role of the Architects Co-Partnership in the London Mosque competition? Was Leslie Martin from the London County Council involved in the competition process? Was Abdul-Sattar Al-Ayash involved? Do you know why General Ramzy Omar's proposal from 1954 was rejected? Did Ramzy Omar also run for the Kuwait National Assembly competition?

MA: Architects Co-Partnership provided the local assistance, research on the bylaws. Their studio produced the competition documents. No, I didn't know of Ramzy Omar's entry. I think he was a jury member for the Kuwait National Assembly competition.

SS: Once in London, who had a stronger impact on your interests, the faculty and school environment, or the architectural scene, such as A&P Smithson, Fry&Drew, Cedric Price, the Archigram? (Peter Cook and Ron Herron proposals of the Plug-in-City and Instant City are contemporaries of yours).

MA: I must say it was the school: The Bedford buildings, the member's room, the library and dining area(s), and the whole cultural climate of the school and London. The sixties, Beatles, Biba, Hair, the South Bank and the Old Vic, Pyjama Tops, etc. The most important was my membership at the Institute of Contemporary Arts at The Mall.

SS: *When you mention the "Old Vic", are you referring to the theatre? By the "Pyjama Tops," do you mean the play with Luan Peters and Kirsten Lindholm? What exhibitions were on at the ICA while you where there? Was the Independent Group with the Smithsons and Reyner Banham or Eduardo Paolozzi still active back then at the ICA?*

MA: Exactly. As for ICA I don't remember who was exhibiting there.

SS: *While in London, did you ever go to Iraq Airways' branch in Piccadilly? Can you comment on the work of Alison and Peter Smithson there?*

MA: I had a feeling the office of Iraq Airways was designed by Qahtan Awni, a pioneering Iraqi architect, who may have been associated with A&P Smithson. The Smithsons got my admiration and full attention after the construction of The Economist buildings masterpiece.

SS: *You may be right about the possibility of an association, although it is still strange. This is a project from 1960, and I always had my doubts about how randomly the Smithsons got the job. The proposal was implemented in a very theatrical way that resembles Awni's work and an interest for the exotic, which is more rare to find in Alison and Peter's work.*

MA: Regarding Qahtan Awni (1926–1972), it's good you mentioned the Iraq Airways branch. He was also a big friend of Rifat's and from the same neighbourhood as ours.

SS: *Do you know anything about Awni's relationship with polish architects Aleksander Markiewicz and Jerzy Staniszkis that you can share with us, considering your involvement in the Ministry of Housing?*

MA: At the Ministry of Public Works there were two Polish architects: Piotr Gerard – from the Educational Building Department, which I headed, and Lech Robaczyński – the other architect working for the Civil Building department handling Mustansiriyah University buildings; Igor Platonov – from Belgium, working for the Major Building department and handling the Baghdad University project, Abu Ghraib Prison, the Ministry of Planning Building and the Medical City complex. I have no idea about other expatriate architects. Some were collaborating with local offices, but none with us (IQC).

SS: *How would you describe the impact of AA faculty, such as Arthur Korn, Bill Allen, David Oakley, Otto Koenigsberger or T.G. Ingersoll?*

MA: Dr. Otto Koenigsberger was the real spirit behind the department. At a later stage in my career, his ideas and intervention were very useful and valuable for my work in the Congo Brazzaville (*Palais Du Peuple*, the Presidential Palace).

SS: *Can you elaborate more on this? How was it influential and which "ideas and intervention" were relevant for your work? Do you know about his involvement in A&P Smithson's proposal for Kuwait in 1969?*

MA: No, I didn't know of Dr. Koenigsberger's involvement. T.G. Ingersoll was the unit master, assisted by Allen Mayhew. For the Educational Building, it was Professor Barbara Price from the Ministry of Education. She had vast experience in the construction of school buildings post-war.

SS: *Can you refer to any of Professor Barbara Price's works that most impacted you? Both Price and Mayhew joined the school in the years you were there. Was the course in Educational Building somehow related to Charles Abrams' (maybe your former professor at METU) recommendations for the Singaporean government?*

MA: Professor Price Iretired from the Ministry of Education, she was an expert in school building systems. Schools were her concern at the Tropical Department. Mayhew was assisting Ingersoll.

SS: *Considering the relationships of Maxwell Fry, Bill Allen, and David Oakley to Kuwait, was the country used as a case study at any point during your studies? Was Baghdad architectural venue a reference at that time at school? Was the work of Gropius, Dudok, Le Corbusier, Sert or even James Mollison Wilson in the region known there?*

MA: I don't recall any such involvement.

SS: *Was the work of Iraqi colleagues, such as Badri Qadah, Jaafar Allwai, Abdulla Ihsan Kamil, Qahtan Madfai, Rifat Chadirji or even Makiya known in Europe? Were there any other influences from the region that were understood and dissected at the time at the AA, like the work of Hassan Fathy or Sayyed Karim, or even of any Lebanese architects, such as Antoine Tabet or Pierre Khoury?*

MA: None of the above were known at the AA. I managed to present some of our work (IQC) at the Exhibition Corridor, but had no feedback or interest. Tabet and Khoury were known because of a publication on "Architecture in Lebanon" (Soraya Antonius, Khayats, 1965).

SS: *Can you elaborate more on this small exhibition you organised at the Corridor? When was it, what was the content and works or architects displayed?*

MA: It was in early 1964, nothing of significance, the drawings displayed were of the Tobacco Monopoly building, Jomhouria Street, Rafidain Bank, and some private residences.

SS: *Was urban design an important component of the Tropical Studies degree? Was it discussed in terms of relevance in regions with hot-climates, such as the Middle East; not just in terms of the environment, but also identity, material culture, politics, or context?*

MA: No importance, planning and urban design in general were introduced to us by Professor Arthur Korn, with no cultural relevance to our specialisms.

SS: *So, for instance, the work of Jane Drew and Ove Arup for the Kuwait Oil Company as part of the publication on "Tropical Villages," published in 1947 by Fry & Drew, or "Tropical Architecture" by the same authors, from 1956, were never part of your curriculum at the AA Tropical Studies?*

MA: I don't recall any such involvement.

SS: *Did you find any relevance in Saba Shiber's work in the region, specifically in Kuwait?*

MA: I came across Mr. Saba's ideas and influences on my visits to Kuwait because of the Sports Club project. I went in detail through his publication, and his urban planning solutions raised many questions in my mind.

SS: *Can you elaborate more on the questions Saba Shiber raised for you regarding Kuwait?*

MA: I didn't like his ideas on open public spaces. He was uncertain about local influences on the future of Kuwait's urban context.

SS: *Being an urban-oriented architect from the very beginning of your practice, was the work of Doxiadis, specifically the Baghdad and Mosul projects, of any relevance for you?*

MA: As for the Doxiadis' Ekistics, they were very relevant from the early days. I had a role in keeping up with their housing projects, in Thawra district, Saddam and Sadr city, and the Baghdad West Housing project. I was also working on their civic-centred and school designs. Sulaymaniyah Sarchnar industrial housing was my responsibility for site inspection, Mosul was not.

SS: *Did Hassan Fathy, as part of Doxiadis' team, have any influence on these projects? Do you think these projects had any relevance for the low-income housing schemes developed in Kuwait after 1957 and 1965 by Dorsh Consultants, Jafar Tukan, Luigi Moretti or even Energoprojekt architectural team?*

MA: Doxiadis' 'grid iron pattern' was applied in Pakistani housing projects prior to the Iraqi low-cost housing schemes. I believe this concept generated the ruralisation of the urban centres of Iraqi cities. Hassan Fathi was part of Sayyed Karim's team for the design of an urban centre project, called 'New Baghdad' in the early fifties.

SS: *After graduating from AA, did you move back to Baghdad immediately or did you stay in Europe, either for work or travel?*

MA: The AA scholarship was a sabbatical leave. I went back to the practice soon after, which was re-named Iraq Consult and had moved to a new office that was specifically designed for it.

SS: *When back in Baghdad, what was the first project you worked on?*

MA: I didn't have a specific responsibility for more than two years, and was busy developing the ideas of Rifat. Upon my return from London at the end of 1964, I was responsible for running the architectural studios. We had two studios, the design studio and production drawing studio. Later on we had a third one for preparing data sheets, and a fourth that was a building extension reserved for *ad-hoc* projects.

SS: *Can you elaborate a bit more on these "ideas of Rifat" you worked on between 1965–66?*

MA: The detailing on windows, fireplaces, private residences and landscapes.

SS: *When did you come to Kuwait for the first time, or first establish a relationship with the country? Did you ever meet the Baghdad town planning officer, Mr. Shafi, from Kuwait? Were there many Kuwaiti students at the school of Architecture in Baghdad or among your practitioners? If yes, can you give us some of their names and works?*

MA: No, I didn't meet Mr. Shafi. Sami Al-Bader, a friend and my local partner for TEST Kuwait office was at Baghdad University, in the Architectural Department. He worked with Hisham Munir… Sami passed away a long time ago.

SS: *At this point in the interview, we would like to talk about specific buildings you worked on in Kuwait, if you don't mind giving us small insights into each of them in terms of context, design motivations, project methodology and approach to various stakeholders during the design and construction stages. Also, can you describe a bit more about the feedback from clients, politicians, local architects, and civil society regarding each project. Here is a list of projects we would like your comments on: The Al-Hamad Villa, Salmiya.*

MA: The design was prepared in IQC Baghdad. Periodical supervision was also conducted from Baghdad on frequent one-day trips. We had no local presence at the time. We specified the use of Iraqi local bricks, brought from Basra.

SS: *The Al-Hassawi Housing Complex in Hawally and Salmiya.*

MA: Sabah Al-Rayes and Hamid Shuaib's newly established office (Pan-Arab Consulting Engineers, Pace) required some professional assistance. The preliminary drawings for the above two projects were carried out in IQC Baghdad. The working drawings were prepared at their office in Kuwait, supervised by Mr. Attila Saeed, a senior architect from the Baghdad office. I used to conduct follow-ups during my frequent visits to Kuwait.

SS: *Was there any specific agreement, between Pace and IQC, regarding further collaboration beyond the two housing complexes? Was Mr. Saeed the IQC representative inside Pace? Did you meet the other partner, Mr. Charles T. Haddad?*

MA: There was no specific agreement. Yes, Mr. Saeed was an IQC member. Mr. Charles was one of the hidden partners and I met him.

SS: *Did Rifat Chadirji establish any particular relationship with these projects? Were the projects relevant to IQC's practice, considering they were perhaps the first IQC projects outside Iraq?*

MA: Sure, we treated the design as one of IQC's projects, but we didn't use them for marketing purposes.

SS: *The Cinema of Jahra.*

MA: IQC had no role in that project.

SS: *The drawings for the Cinema for Jahra are signed and stamped by IQC, and were submitted in 1969. Is your statement related to any disputes during the development of this project? Charles T. Haddad told us about specific disagreements between the IQC team and Mr. Sabah Al-Rayes over the arches during the development of Al-Hassawi housing complexes.*

MA: I have no idea, maybe the project was developed with Rifat? From the beginning I was against this venture, why should we train a competitor?

SS: *The Kuwait Sport Club stadiums.*

MA: The clubs were commissioned by the Ministry of Public Works, on behalf of The Minister of Social Affairs, then Mr. Abdul Aziz Mahmoud, represented by Mr. Abdul Rahman Al-Mazrou'I and Ahmad Al-Sadoun, who at the time was the Chairman of the Kuwaiti Football Federation. Documents were prepared at IQC Baghdad. Kuwait Sporting (in Kaifan) was the first to go to tender. We had an arrangement with TEST Kuwait, which was under Fareed Khorsheed's office for the local backup staff.

Al-Qadsiya (in Hawally) and Al-Arabi (Al-Mansoriya) clubs had the same tender documents for each, with new site arrangements and administrative buildings. We had a contract for the design of the three clubs and negotiated with Ahmad Al-Sadoun over the implementation of the same design for Kazma Stadium, by then the National Stadium, but it didn't work.

SS: *Mr. Sameh Al-Nimr, a mechanical engineer, who worked at first for IQC and then for Pace, preferred that the project be reviewed by the Egyptian architect Mahmoud Riad, who was a UN consultant for the Ministry of Public Works at the time. Can you confirm this?*

MA: We were not aware of any of the above. This must have taken place, if it is true, behind the scenes, and without our knowledge.

SS: *The Banking Studies Institute, Mirqab.*

MA: Design and production documents were prepared in the head office in Athens. The production studio left Beirut and was established in Athens in 1976, following the war in Lebanon. The construction supervision was by TEST Kuwait.

SS: *This project, together with the Ministry of Planning, are among those you seem to have been more involved in. Can you elaborate a bit more on the architectural concepts and urban strategies beyond these projects, as we would like to situate them contextually in terms of your main works in Kuwait.*

MA: The Ministry of Planning was all about the location and the L-shape was to create an open public space. The Banking Studies Institute was an exercise in the open landscaping of offices.

SS: *The competition for the Kuwait Society of Engineers' headquarters.*

MA: The entry for the competition was prepared in Baghdad. We proposed Iraqi local brick as the building material. I remember it was the first time we introduced rounded corners.

SS: *The Salmiya District Centre.*

MA: TEST acted as local associates for this project, and local planning input was provided by my partner, Mr. Abdullah Sabbar. I myself acted as the local architect. My role was limited to provide architectural concepts through rendered perspectives of the district's public and common spaces. The perspectives were produced in our studio in Athens.

SS: *Was Abdullah Sabbar part of TEST? He delivered his thesis at the AA in 1971 on Kuwait Old Town. Was this relevant to the proposals for Salmiya and Hawally District Centres? Regarding the architectural renderings, were there any major references by either you or the client?*

MA: Sabbar was my principle partner from the start. I met Sabbar in the early seventies. Sabbar from Collin Buchanan team and me from IQC were both part of a team devising a regional plan for Kurdistan, and a development plan for Erbil Citadel in Iraq. Later we joined to establish TEST Beirut. I know nothing about Sabbar's thesis.

SS: *The Ministry of Planning*

MA: Ministry of Planning drawings and contract documents were prepared in Athens, construction started in late 1979, shortly after.

I was involved in Baghdad, winning the Haifa Street competition, which required my extensive presence in Baghdad. For the first year, I managed to shuttle by car between Kuwait and Baghdad. Later, I was denied travel and for two years was not able to go, which is why I have no idea of the building's final outlook.

SS: *Al-Qabas newspaper*

MA: The design of *Al-Qabas* newspaper building was originally drawn up when I was still at the IQC in 1972. It was a sub-commission by Fareed Khoursheed of local TEST Kuwait. After four years, the extension of the same building was carried out by TEST's head office in Athens.

SS: *While working in Kuwait did you came across any other relevant international practices, such as The Architects Collaborative (TAC) or Dar Al-Handasah? Do you know how TAC started in Kuwait and who were the main designers of Dar Al-Handasah?*

MA: TEST prior to becoming a pan-Arab practice, as a local Kuwaiti office, was commissioned the first extension of the Sheraton Hotel; the second extension, 'the tower,' was designed by TAC. The building supervision was carried out by TEST's local office. I didn't come across Dar Al-Handasah during those years.

SS: *When you refer to "TEST prior to becoming a pan-Arab practice," what do you mean?*

MA: I meant by pan-Arab, offices/branches all over the Arab world.

SS: *This first extension of the Sheraton by TEST is unknown; the TAC tower extension is always referred to as the first. Can you please clarify the scope and dates for this extension you mentioned?*

MA: The first extension of the Sheraton was the construction of a trapezoidal pool and a restaurant, which may have disappeared by now. My last visit to Kuwait was in 1981.

SS: *Can you describe the establishment of TEST and how the projects in Kuwait were managed by the firm – operating from offices in Kuwait, Baghdad, Beirut or Athens.*

MA: As mentioned, TEST had some sort of professional relationship with IQC. TEST had a number of interesting consultancy commissions from all the Gulf states.

SS: *How were these commissions achieved? What contexts or personalities were relevant to them? Can you please mention some of these projects in Kuwait and abroad?*

MA: Fareed Khoursheed of TEST Kuwait had a good relationship with Al-Nisf family. At a certain point, TEST Kuwait couldn't handle the scope. At the same time, I decided to leave Baghdad. Beirut was my first choice; the Group offered me a proposal to join them and to be in charge of TEST's head office in Beirut – 'the production centre.' In a few months we established branches in Baghdad, Mutrah, Dubai, Dammam, and of course Kuwait.

SS: *Do you mean the scope couldn't be handled in Kuwait? When you mention the "Group," can you describe who they were and what sort of relationship you had with them?*

MA: Test had commissions from all over the Gulf. The partners were: Fareed Khorsheed, Maath Alousi, Safa Al-Killidar, and Abdullah Sabbar. All designs and tender documents were prepared at the head office in Beirut, or later in Athens. Local offices were responsible for marketing, local research and site supervision.

SS: *Can you tell us more about Athens and Beirut? Where these locations relevant to your production? Did you engage in any local collaboration, or were there other practices you remember when working for Kuwait that you eventually partnered with or could have joined?*

MA: Athens and Beirut were the headquarters and the production centres. I was running them. Other partners were doing marketing and follow up, or working on *ad-hoc* projects, like Salmiya and the Ministry of Electricity workshop in Kuwait.

SS: *Thank you.* •

The Making of an Arab Architect

RICARDO CAMACHO

The architects who exercise the craft differ. Some are intelligent and skilful. Others are inferior. [...] There are other similar kinds of architecture activity. The workmen who do all these things differ in skill and intelligence [...] [These] crafts are perfected only if there exists a large and perfect sedentary civilisation [...] [Architecture] is the first and oldest craft of sedimentary civilisation. It is the knowledge of how to go about using houses and mansions for cover and shelter [...] Thus, it is unavoidable that it must reflect upon how to avert the harm arising from heat and cold [...] building conditions are different in the [various] towns. Each city follows in this respect the procedure known to and within the technical [competence] of [its inhabitants] and corresponding to the climate and the different conditions of [the inhabitants] with regards to wealth and poverty [...] All these questions are clear only to those who know architecture in all its details.[1]

Saba George Shiber, former city planning advisor to the government and municipality of Kuwait, frequently used quotes from *Al Muqaddimah* (Ibn Khladun's major work from 1377) in different articles he wrote between 1960–68 criticising the general practice of architects and planners in the region, particularly the building production in Kuwait. Karim Jamal,[2] also an advisor to the Municipality, viewed the foreign influence of architects and planners in Kuwait, as an "imposition of Western technology onto an established Arab society,"[3] which became the ground for "dumping Western type schemes [...] with no questions asked."[4] This critical judgment of the referred practitioners extends beyond Western individuals and corporations. Jamal also critiques regional practices, such as the firm of Jafar Tukan, the acclaimed Palestinian-Jordanian architect who graduated from the American University in Beirut (AUB) in 1960, and George R. Rais, the Lebanese architect and scholar that collaborated extensively with Assem Salaam and Theo Kaanan in the design of some of the landmarks of Beirut. Jamal's critique that targeted his colleagues extends beyond traditional practice. In his first article for *The Architects' Journal* in December 1973, Jamal also claims that the advisory work of foreign experts, such as Egyptian architects Omar Azzam – UN consultant with a PhD from ETH Zurich, and Mahmoud Riad – former city planner of Cairo who graduated from Liverpool University in Civic Design, had "little impact, as they have tended to be repetitive and general."[5]

In addition, and contrary to the testimonies of Sabah Abi-Hanna, Abdulaziz Sultan and Sabah Al-Rayes on the impact of foreign architecture firms and practitioners on the establishment of the Salem Al-Marzouq and Sabah Abi-Hanna (SSH), Kuwait Engineers Office (KEO) and Pan-Arab Consulting Engineers (Pace), the major consultants to this day in Kuwait, Karim Jamal insisted that they (the foreign) "Did not train an indigenous team of professionals [...] that would secure the continuity of the work, [which was a] missed opportunity for including local people [...] the continuous recruitment of foreign professionals was justified by the necessity to respond to the pressures of projects."[6]

1. Ibn Khaldūn, *The Muqaddimah: An introduction to History*. Transcribed from, Saba George Shiber, *Recent Arab City Growth* (Kuwait: Government Printing Press, 1969), 256.

2. Jamal's qualifications include: a bachelor's degree in Architecture from the University of Colorado Boulder in the United States (1944), a master's degree in Tropical Studies from the Architectural Association in the UK (1971), and a Ph.D. in Planning from University College London in the UK (1976).

3. Karim Jamal, "Kuwait: A Salutary Tale," *The Architects' Journal*, v. 158, n. 50 (1973): 1453.

4. Karim Jamal, "Destruction of the Middle East?," *The Architects' Journal*, n. 30 (July, 1976): 161.

5. Karim Jamal, "Kuwait: A Salutary Tale," 1455.

6. Ibid., 1454.

Shiber refers on multiple occasions to the lack of essential staff in the region: "No Arab city is equipped as adequately as it should be to collect, collate and scientifically analyse information needed for synthesis and design."[7] But he also reports that, even in Kuwait, "a city that has the means to afford competent architects," those who conduct such work are, "so underpaid that they are often forced to resort to unorthodox means to supplement their meager wages. Such means range from outright bribery to private practice that usually becomes more important than their civic responsibilities." Shiber also points out that, "Even when an architect works within a municipality, he is often inadequately trained."[8]

The Principles

The development of the modern architect in the Middle East was primarily influenced by European education models, such as the *École Polytechnique*, the Royal School of Engineering and the *École Nationale Supérieure des Beaux-Arts*. Later the influence of the *Staatliches Bauhaus* and the Swiss *Technische Hochschule* were dominant in the *Levant* schools, while fresh graduates where commonly sent abroad for further education at the Civic Design and Tropical Studies departments in Liverpool and London respectively.

At the Eighth Congress of the International Union of Architects (UIA), dedicated to the training of architects in 1965, the scholar Abdel Baki Mohamed Ibrahim (A.B.M. Ibrahim) criticised these education models and the principles of functionalism, purism, rationalism and expressionism while presenting the Egyptian case. He described these as being related to visual and superficial aspects of architecture. Ibrahim highlighted an individualism and self-esteem among the "pioneers,"[9] specifically *Congrès International d'Architecture Moderne* (CIAM) group members in their roles as practitioners and professors, emphasising the lack of integration between their practice and their different philosophies and theories, which he saw as the main reason for the chaos in which the discipline was dropped into. This "chaos of principles and theories" has, he suggested, left a young generation of Arab architects "not knowing their way through."[10]

Following the holistic approach of Buckminster Fuller, also present, Ibrahim asserted his belief in the scientific approach, also advocated by Shiber, acknowledging in his own words "two gaps in architectural thinking (that need) to be filled" – the "human and spiritual," and "general planning problems facing the future of humanity."[11] He pointed to the benefits of a "monastery for architectural education" for extended study, referring to Al-Azhar, a religious centre for higher learning in Cairo established in 975AD. He also advocated for an exchange between scholars from different universities, suggesting *The Grand Prix du Caire*, following Western tradition of awarding travelling and in-residence scholarships to young graduates (such as *The Grand Prix de Rome*), as well as architectural competitions, which according to him, are an educational media which can contribute in a relevant manner to the formation of architects. Ibrahim also identified as main challenge to architectural education in Egypt, that it is still part of the Engineering program, with a curriculum based on lecture courses, which according to him were insufficient for the architectural student to gain the ability to construct. Consequently, Ibrahim justifies the emergence of a "continuous carnival of buildings alongside the streets of Cairo,"[12] with the lack of quality among the local young architects, solely searching for affirmation and recognition.

1. Alison and Peter Smithson, index of flow pattern routine for "Urban Form Studies for the Old City of Kuwait," 1969–1974. © Frances Loeb Library, Special Collections, Graduate School of Design, Harvard University.

2. Letter to Hamid Shuaib from Alison and Peter Smithson, January 11, 1973. © Frances Loeb Library, Special Collections, Graduate School of Design, Harvard University.

7. Saba George Shiber, *Recent Arab City Growth* (Kuwait: Government Printing Press, 1969), 177–184.

8. Ibid.

9. Term borrowed from Nikolaus Pevsner, *Pioneers of the Modern Movement from William Morris to Walter Gropius* (London: Faber & Faber, 1936).

10. A.B.M. Ibrahim in "The training of the architect: reports by the Eighth World Congress of the International Union of Architects," Paris, July 5–9 (1965).

11. Ibid.

12. Ibid.

From the second half of the nineteenth century onwards, the demand for ostentatious private villas and opulent department stores,[13] the commissioning of European and American private companies for public works, the establishment of Christian religious missions in the region, as well as the concern for building preservation, 'beautification' of public spaces and the advent of city planning, diversified the professional practice of architecture beyond state work. Several local architects that were educated and trained abroad emerged in academic and institutional roles during the first decades of the twentieth century, such as Mahmoud Riad, who completed his master's degree from Liverpool in 1931, and gained his experience at Shreve, Lamb and Harmon,[14] first as an intern drawing details for the Empire State Building in Manhattan, and after completing his studies, in Jerusalem as a site architect in the construction of the YMCA complex. Riad, who served as a technical advisor for the Ministry of Public Works in Kuwait from 1965–1975, pursued a career as a public servant in Cairo while developing a liberal practice. A.B.M. Ibrahim mentions in his presentation for the 1965 UIA Congress, that "quite a number of Egyptian architects [such as Riad] who recently completed their education in England, France, Switzerland and the USA, [the education models he criticised] returned back to represent the bulk of the teaching staff in architectural departments in Egyptian Universities."[15]

Becoming an Architect

The first modern universities to teach engineering and architecture in the region were established in Istanbul (*Sanayi-i Nefise Mektebi-i Âlisi* in 1883 and *Hendese-i-Mülkiye Mektebi* in 1884),[16] Cairo (*École Égyptienne des Beaux-Arts* in 1908[17] and the Royal School of Engineering with the architecture department established in 1916), Jerusalem (Bezalel Academy of Arts and Design in 1906) and Haifa (*Technikum* in 1912). In Beirut, the *Université Saint-Joseph*, established in 1875 by Botros Bustani offered the first degree in engineering in 1913, and the American University of Beirut (former Syrian Protestant College established in 1866) in 1920. The degrees in Damascus, Baghdad, and Tehran were established in the 1940s, while degrees in Saudi Arabia only appeared during the 1960s and in the remaining Gulf states from the 1990s. Cairo, Beirut, and Haifa became the main centres for the regional education and production of architecture. Foreign educated architects, such as Lebanese Ilyas Murr graduated from the Massachusetts Institute of Technology in 1905 and Egyptian Mostafa Fahmy from *École des Ponts et Chaussées* in Paris, 1912, were among the first locals to practice. Following WWI, a prodigious generation of locally educated modern architects emerged, including Antoine Tabet, who graduated from *École Supérieure d'Ingénieurs* at the *Université Saint-Joseph* in Lebanon in 1926 and, Egyptians Hassan Fathy and Mahmoud Riad from the Egyptian University School of Engineering in Cairo (the former Royal School of Engineering) in 1925 and 1927 respectively.

During this period, Haifa, under British mandate, attracted a new generation of European educated architects who practiced in Palestine after WWI. The construction of a new city, planned by Scottish architect Patrick Geddes in the spirit of Liverpool Civic Design School, brought influential practitioners to Haifa, such as Le Corbusier's disciples Samuel Barkai and Ze'ev Rechter, the former educated in Venice and Paris (1926–1933), and the

13. Rudolf Agstner, "Dream and Reality: Austrian Architects in Egypt, 1869–1914," in Mercedes Volait, ed., *Le Caire–Alexandrie. Architectures européennes, 1850–1950* (Cairo: Institute Française d'Archéologie Orientale, Centre d'Études et de Documentation Économique, Juridique et Sociale, 2001), 149–155.

14. Mahmoud Riad interned at Shreve, Lamb & Harmon, designers of the Empire State Building, during construction in 1931.

15. Ibrahim, "The training of the architect."

16. Sibel Bozdogan, *Modernism and Nation Building: Turkish Architectural Culture in the Early Republic* (Washington: University of Washington Press, 2001), 28.

17. S.A. le Prince Youssef Kamal, *École Égyptienne des Beaux-Arts fondée* (Cairo: Imprimerie Paul Barbey, 1908).

3. Kuwait City Municipality, 1960.
© *Al Kuwaiti.*

latter, Rome (1926) and Paris (1929) respectively. Among the first graduates from Bezalel Academy of Arts and Design in Jerusalem was Dov Karmi, who pursued further studies at Ghent University (1929), and Ben-Ami Shulman, who was born in Jaffa and graduated from Brussels under Victor Horta's influence in 1931. However, the most influential of this generation of architects from the Haifa (UNESCO Modern Heritage site) were Richard Kauffmann, who studied in Amsterdam (1909) and graduated from Munich in 1912, and Arieh Sharon, who graduated from Brno (1920), and Bauhaus (1929) where he was trained under Joseph Albers and later with Hannes Meyer, before returning back to Palestine in 1931.

In Cairo, Mostafa Fahmy, Antoine Selim Nahas and Hassan Fathy made a name for themselves after their master's studies in Liverpool (1923) and Paris (1925 and 1930), assuming foundational roles in the modern education of architecture, and being the first heads of departments at the Egyptian University School of Engineering, assisted by two other remarkable architect's, Ali Gabr and Mohamed Raafat, both educated abroad.

Sayyed Karim, who graduated with a PhD from Zurich ETH in 1938, eventually became the one who most contributed to the professionalisation of architecture in the region.

The Pan-Arab Architect

The *Al-Emara* magazine,[18] following the spirit of *"L'Esprit Nouveau,"* *"Vers une Architecture"* and *"L'Almanach d'architecture modern,"* together with the Arab Engineering conferences initiated in 1945, were determinant to

18. (Also titled *Majallat Al-'Imarah* before 1952) was published from 1939 to 1950, with the exception of 1943–44. The publication was later continued as *Al-Emara and El-Fonoun* (*Majallat al-'imārah wa-al-funūn*) between 1952–1959. The repository lies in the Fine Arts Library at Harvard University.

4. Doldertal Apartment Houses, Marcel Breuer and Alfred and Emil Roth, Zurich, 1936. Commissioned by Sigried Giedion. © *Al-Emara*.

19. Thonet Frères, Letter to Le Corbusier, September 1, 1926. Ariane Lourie Harrison, "Le Corbusier: Architect, Agent de Propaganda," *Perspecta*, n. 45 (2012): 101.

20. Ibrahim, "The training of the architect."

21. Ibid.

22. Ali Gabr, "*Imarat al-'ahya' al-wataniya*" (Architecture of Native Slums), *Al-Emara*, n. 1 and 2 (1941): 51–65.

provide a common context for this generation and open doors to their practice beyond borders. Sayyed Karim's magazine mainly addressed precedent projects in Europe and locally developed or under-development projects, showcasing the work of Karim's professors at ETH and his own work in Cairo, among other colleagues' work in the region. In the first two issues, the obsession with his professors is evident, publishing projects such as the Zurich Doldertal Apartments by Marcel Breuer and Alfred and Emil Roth, completed in 1936 for Sigfried Giedion, or the Reinickendorf Weiße Stadt (UNESCO Modern Heritage site) in Berlin, completed in 1931 by Wilhelm Büning, Bruno Ahrends, and Otto Rudolf Salvisberg, Karim's thesis advisor.

The Berlin neighbourhood was subject for other articles in *Al-Emara* and an important architectural reference for the work produced in Haifa, the 'white city.' Through case-studies such as these, Karim's office research – regularly published in the magazine – evolved into a series of articles on building typology, constructive systems, and industrially manufactured materials that exposed local architects to a broad knowledge base. The magazine also provided exposure through advertising for contractors and manufacturers. As Le Corbusier in *L'Esprit Nouveau*, Karim became a spokesman (agent de propaganda) of the highest authority, from whose influence the construction industry "obtained [...] much business."[19]

The systematic use of resources, such as photography and building plans and sections, affected not only the practice, but also architecture education. In his UIA Congress presentation, A.B.M. Ibrahim highlights Cairo's Ain Shams University Department of Architecture as an outstanding example of research as an educational experience using spatial composition through tridimensional representation which he referred to as "design through movement: a new media for drawing."[20] This revolution in methods and processes led to a "direct drift away from genuine local Egyptian architecture and the dependence on foreign references or examples."[21] Medhat Mohamed Al-Abd's, a graduate from Ain Shams in 1959 and Sayyed Karim's work in Kuwait are obvious examples of such change in the local architecture production. In fact, the exposure of *Al-Emara* brought the first commissions to Karim from outside the country. First, as United Nations planning consultant he developed work in Baghdad (1946), Jeddah (1949), Riyadh (1950), Mecca and Medina (1952), and latter Kuwait (1957–1965).

Ali Gabr, a regular contributor to *Al-Emara* and professor of Saba George Shiber in Cairo, continued the tradition of Mostafa Fahmy in preserving the values of class distinction that protect educated architects from being mistaken for common builders. In his article from 1941, Gabr presents a criteria for the design of popular housing through seven points: the class of residents, its financial status, their spacial needs and requirements, the number of rooms, room dimensions, spacial configuration of the dwelling, and the building economy in terms of construction systems and materials, without "compromising beauty and function."[22]

One year after Shiber graduates from Cairo (1946), Gabr and another of Sayyed Karim's collaborators, Tawfiq Abdel-Gawad, a graduate in Civic Design from Liverpool (1939), assumed the control at the Cairo office and magazine in the absence of Karim. Both changed the trajectory of *Al-Emara* magazine from there on. Contrary to the first years when the magazine based most of its research on Western cases, Abdel-Gawad transformed *Al-Emara* into an instrumental tool to advise the state regarding what to build and where, from building programs to conception, far beyond the limits of Cairo.

Abdel-Gawad was the most active editor of the magazine for the next ten years, (under the early years of Gamal Abdel Nasser mandate), and published comprehensive studies on a range of different scales and typologies, from rural settlements[23] and schools[24] to apartment buildings.[25] Gawad was by then the head of the Architects Society, engaged in the Department of Rural Affairs in 1939, where he worked in the conception and construction of the first rural model villages – *qarya namuzagiyya* – which was the most notorious of these projects and the first to be completed, near Al-Marg in 1941. In the same year, Hassan Fathy was commissioned by the Royal Society of Agriculture to study the improvement of farmers' houses. Gawad's plan for an area of six hectares established clear hierarchies between inhabitants and animals in a regular plan, with fluid and organic circulation between rows of houses and wider tree-lined streets. With the common facilities located at the perimeter, the 121 houses, built in mud brick, were conceived to appear modern, with walls that "looked exactly like plaster cement."[26] After completion, the village temporarily housed refugees fleeing the Egyptian coastline, who had suffered from heavy bombing during the first months of 1941. After the war, it was transformed into a convalescent centre for tuberculosis. In an *Al-Emara* article from 1957, Gawad hardly criticised Professor Gabr's design criteria for popular housing, not only questioning Gabr, but also Karim and Fathy, regarding the extent to which they were committed to the needs of lower-income groups, which, according to him, were still to be studied.

However Gawad's critic doesn't emphasise on Gabr's use of aesthetic values to distinguish different social backgrounds of the clientele; rather, he advocates that such codes, which were present in organisational schemes, tended to be projections of the personal tastes and preferences of the architects. This attitude towards architecture is evident in the works of Medhat Mohamed Al-Abd and Sayyed Karim in Kuwait, in examples such as Salam Palace in Shuwaikh, or the Ahmadi Cinema, which revealed a progressive and modern exterior image in opposition to the stylised interior. Karim, Gabr, and Gawad dedicated a substantial part of the magazine to discussions of style, composition, and stylistic architecture. In an article from 1952, Gawad stated:

> The modern attitude towards simplifying forms and building codes has greatly affected facade design by simplifying them also. Facades have become plans free of ornament and cornices at the same time that the architect now relies on beautiful proportions and new materials, and has applied them in different areas of the building. He also relied on protrusions, balconies and verandas.[27]

This obsession for facade composition exposes the real motivations of *Al-Emara* contributors. Even Gawad, was more concerned with the building image (facade) and its impact on local traditions and identity, than the building's climatic performance. In the same article, and regarding the specific context of urbanism, he insists that, "these formal innovations (building response to climatic performance) should not negatively affect the privacy of the neighbours by being too close or intrusive."[28] The optimism and fascination for the 'new' eventually led many of these practitioners to misinterpret tradition as an aesthetic and formal quality only.

Such hybrid approaches and attitudes towards design and built landscape, which A.B.M. Ibrahim referred to as "romantic school" (UIA, 1965) and Shiber the "jigsaw puzzle,"[29] were propagated throughout the region,

5. Pharmaceutical Laboratories for La Roche AG, Prof. Otto Rudolf Salvisberg, Basel, 1936. © *Al-Emara.*

23. Tawfiq Abdel-Gawad, "Replanning the Egyptian Villages," *Al-Emara*, n. 1 (1953): 5–12.

24. Tawfiq Abdel-Gawad, "Schools Premises, State Foundation, Index of Builidng Types," *Al-Emara*, n. 2 (1957): 5–62.

25. "Modern Flats," *Al-Emara*, n. 1 (1957): 25–44.

26. Abdel-Gawad, "Replanning the Egyptian Villages," 5–12.

27. Tawfiq Abdel-Gawad, "Brazil and Modern Architecture" *Al-Emara*, n. 8, 9 and 10 (1952): 27.

28. Ibid., 31.

29. Saba George Shiber, *The Kuwait Urbanization* (Kuwait: Government Printing Press, 1964), 306.

mainly in the Gulf, where the lack of preparation to cater for the will to be modern and affluent led to a massive production of domestic architecture that Shiber described as a "phantasmagoric architectural 'forest'."[30] In Egypt, Nasser's post-revolutionary propaganda transformed this notion into a particular nationalism that didn't last long within the regime but left a strong legacy among a new generation of graduates from Ain Shams, Helwan and Cairo Universities. These are the 'pan-Arab' architects that migrated to successful practices in the Gulf, and now an important phenomenon to consider when questioning the motivations and arguments of practitioners and project owners on this region.

Solidarity and Modernity

In the foreword to *Al-Emara*'s first issue of 1949,[31] Sayyed Karim looks in retrospect at the benefits the magazine brought to people in general and to the arts researcher in particular. Karim assumes the role of a visionary that is fighting "radical concepts" and "dark attitudes" following "the artistic beauty" extracted from the basic "meaning of life."[32] He also highlights the strength of the youth and the wisdom of the elderly, with no hierarchy or difference between social classes, gender and origin, in achieving Egypt's development and to, "get over the black smoke," in a clear reference to the country's political context. He concludes the text with a *motto*, "Those that stand will die and those that move on will live forever."[33]

Solidarity within a new Arab world was hailed by Gamal Abdel Nasser and Afif Al-Bizri in 1958, upon the first agreement for the establishment of a pan-Arab state, the United Arab Republic, in the aftermath of the United Nations' Partition Plan for Palestine (1947). This was determinant for the exchange of architecture and planning professionals throughout the region, first under a cooperative framework and later as an individual initiative. Under such context, the following years of practice in the region can only be understood in depth by looking at training programs like the "Village Welfare Service in Lebanon, Syria and Palestine,"[34] initially established through cooperation between the Institute of Rural Life at the AUB and the Department of Education in the Government of Palestine, with the purpose of contributing to rural development by encouraging AUB students to work in remote villages during their summer vacations. According to Albert Hourani, AUB had "become in practice, and without the deliberate intention of its authorities, the intellectual centre of Arab nationalism."[35] For Arab students, the idea of social service was related to Arab solidarity. The program rapidly expanded across the Levantine territories, and by 1938, apart from Ramallah, Safad, Jibrail, and Beka'a, camps were established in Aleppo and Damascus.[36] Soon the program evolved into the Civic Welfare League (*Rabitat Al-In'ash Al-Qawmi*), where students became involved with a wider range of concerns, even more cosmopolitan such as the training of prisoners and orphans in Beirut. Following WWII the school devoted its attention to improving its academic standards and social service became part of the academic curriculum, including the Civil Engineering degree. For instance, the thesis projects of Yusuf Shahin Sayegh, on the "Preparatory Boarding School in Haifa,"[37] 1945–46, and the "Model Village"[38] by Mounir Tahir Kathib (Munthir Khatib) in the same year, as well as "The New Palace of Baal in Ain-Baal Lebanon,"[39] by Sami Abdul Baki from 1946–47, reveal major concerns within the discipline. The first addresses an interest in social

30. Ibid., 321.

31. Sayyed Karim, "1939–1949," *Al-Emara*, n. 1–2 (1949): 5–6.

32. Ibid., 5.

33. Ibid., 6.

34. Stuart C. Dood, "The village welfare service in Lebanon, Syria and Palestine," *Journal of The Royal Central Asian Society*, v. 32, n. 1 (1945).

35. Albert H. Hourani, *Syria and Lebanon: A Political Essay* (Oxford: Oxford University Press, 1946), 85.

36. *Village Welfare Service 1937–38*, Annual Report. American University of Beirut Special Collections Archive.

37. Yusuf Shain Sayegh, "Preparatory Boarding School in Haifa" (Diploma thesis, American University of Beirut, 1946).

38. Mounir Tahir Khatib, "Model Village" (Diploma thesis, American University of Beirut, 1946).

39. Sami Abdul Baki, "The New Palace of Baal in Ain-Baal Lebanon" (Diploma thesis, American University of Beirut, 1947).

service, the second focuses on planning, and the third preservation. Abdul Baki's project calls for the "restoration of family glory" through "oriental design, so that classicism and orientalism go hand in hand in the beauty of the place."[40] Among his references is Violett-le-Duc, who provides Baki with an evolutionary reading of the building, positing that intervention in an old structure is an opportunity to integrate new material and construction technologies. "The changing social conditions and advancement in technological contributions have given the problem flexibility," Baki claims. He understands this has released the building "from the limitations of masonry construction with thick walls to a regular grid of pillars," highlighting the ability of new materials, such as "plastics and glass," to expand the relationship between interior and exterior, and "the ability to heat and light interiors" as a way of providing a "different quality to the shelter in which we work, play and rest." In his proposal, Baki references among his main achievements the varying sizes of the proposed openings, as a way to break the monotony of the building facade. He also claims the use of black stone, as the condition to provide "the building with a sentimental vivacity," while "the whole expresses the character of the building, that of an oriental palatial residence."[41]

Being more politically aware and more focused on issues of space program, Sayegh, in his thesis introduction, clearly states that:

> The choice of the problem [referring to his thesis scope] [identifies] the countries of the Near East [...] [where] education has assumed a great importance [in particular Haifa] with a population of 50,000 Arabs [...] and poor educational facilities [...] This regrettable state of affairs should be remediated. It is the duty of the educated people, and civil engineers especially, to convince the notables of the district of the necessity of taking the matter into consideration. [...] school accommodation is perhaps more complex than any other professional task he [the architect] may have been given. Each succeeding year has witnessed the development of education, [...] the way the school relates to the community has changed. [He suggests that] particularly in the larger cities, a further use of the school house as the community centre [...] as it increased the problems [challenges] present in the design and planning of a school building [in addition to] the essentials of hygiene and sanitation. Ventilation and lighting [...] the health of the students [...][42]

In his analysis of the problem, Sayegh devotes attention to the buildings' foundations, considering the drainage of underground water and the geotechnical capacity of the soil. He continues to use a functionalist and pragmatic approach throughout the building program, applicable to the size and proportions of the classrooms, the width of the aisles, and circulation.

With programs such as this, the influence of AUB throughout the *Levant* and surrounding countries increased, and the school was reportedly requested to provide trained men and women by mandate officials, to foreign and local businesses, and native governments and firms. George Sarton refers to AUB as, "a nursery of good men and a perpetual fountain of good will."[43] Among them were some of the most significant city planners and architects working in the Gulf during the second half of the century.

Following the *Nakba*, a series of incidents between 1947–49 that led to the partition of Palestinian territories, the diaspora of intellectuals intensified their contributions to the empowerment of solidarity and pan-Arabism at AUB. Betty Anderson refers on multiple occasions to this energy encouraging a growing civic conscience and commitment towards the development of the Arab World.

40. Ibid.

41. Ibid.

42. Yusuf Shain Sayegh, "Preparatory Boarding School in Haifa" (Diploma thesis, American University of Beirut, 1946).

43. George Sarton, "The Incubation of Western Culture in the Middle East" (lecture presented at the Coolidge Auditorium of the Library of Congress, Washington, March 29, 1950).

6. Model of the new town Sabahiya presented at the Kuwait International Airport, 1970. © *Al Kuwaiti.*

This commitment towards the development of the Arab World is evident in Shiber's "anxiety [...] with the building of the Arab city," as Sheikh Sabah Al-Salem Al-Sabah exposed in the forward to *Recent Arab City Growth* (1969),[44] but also in the political ambition of individuals such as Maurice Gemayel, faculty member at AUB and author of "*La valorisation du Liban: plans et programmes,*"[45] who in 1955, in his role as president of the Central Planning Bureau of Lebanon, announced the Pan-Arab International highway, connecting the *Levant* with the Gulf ports of Baghdad, Kuwait, and Damman.

The pan-Arab motivation had a direct impact in the curriculum of the recently established architecture engineering program at AUB, and under Professor Raymond Ghosn. In 1955, some final-year students submitted their thesis projects on a motel for the pan-Arab International highway, somewhere in the Saudi Arabia-Iraq border between Jordan and Kuwait. Contrary to the thesis of Sayegh and Abdul Baki that are less architectural, these project reports were by then full sets of projects, including: cost estimates, financial feasibility studies, schedules and the planning of works, structural calculations, architecture, interior design, landscape, structural reinforcement, plumbing, electrical, ventilation, and lighting design. The media surrounding the initiative included schedules, text and bi-dimensional drawings, as well as site plans and tridimensional birds-eye view perspectives, exterior and interior renderings, and even detailed elements such as structural components and furniture axonometries.

44. Shiber, *Recent Arab City Growth*, 17.

45. Maurice Gemayel, *La valorisation du Liban: plans et programmes*, v. 1 (Beirut: 1951), in Mūrīs Jumayyil and Wākīm Bū Laḥdū, *Maurice Gemayel: Le pionnier de la planification* (Beirut: Joseph D. Raidy printing press, 2001), 401.

These fresh graduates also engaged with contemporary discourses of vernacular, spatial identity, and leisure. In his project report, Nabih Majdalani recalls the resting houses where camel and donkey caravans that used to cross the desert were stationed. Majdalani saw the large number of motor vehicles and the 30,000 tourists that would come every summer to Lebanon from "Bahrain, Kuwait, Iraq, Syria, Qatar and Egypt"[46] as a main motivation for the erection of a modern motel halfway between the Mediterranean and Gulf coasts. The author also refers to the modern ability to enjoy travel, evidenced by the touring culture of motorway stations as leisure environments and the potential for developing trade out of this connection between east and west. In this regard, the author's proposal extends far beyond the disciplines of architecture and engineering, suggesting a corporate approach towards hospitality, including estimating operational costs and a national motel company to manage the initiative. In selecting the location the author considers: traffic congestion, accessibility to drainage, visibility and level, frontage to the highway, setbacks and regulations concerning the actual highway plans, position towards highway exits, and distance from other similar facilities to avoid insufficiency and competition. In determining capacity, the author considers a set of assumptions for traffic load, electricity and water consumption and also source of supply.

Moving East:
the Arab Diaspora

Other Palestinian AUB graduates were the city planner and Pace co-founder, Charles Haddad, architect Victor Shiber (Saba Shiber's brother), Ayman Taji and engineer Hasib J. Sabbagh, as well as Said Tawfiq Khoury and Abdel Mohsin Al-Qattan, who were the first two engineers with an established contracting company in Haifa during the 1940s – Consolidated Contractors (CONCO). Al-Qattan, after being in charge of the Department of Water and Electricity in Kuwait, established Al-Hani Construction and Trading Company in the country. According to Kamal Shair, Al-Qattan was instrumental in introducing Dar Al-Handasah to Sheikh Jaber Al-Ali Al-Sabah, who "wanted to know what educated Arab nationalists were thinking, and what their attitudes were to the issues of the day" and very supportive of the idea of establishing "an Arab consultancy to challenge the existing hegemony of Western consultants in the region."[47]

However, before Dar Al-Handasah's contract for a ninety megawatt power station in Kuwait, in 1957, CONCO and the Contracting and Trading Co. (CAT), led by Emile Bustani, another AUB graduate, were already in Kuwait since 1952, after the first contracts for the Iraq Petroleum Company in Syria and Iraq under the American Bechtel Group, a strong supporter of AUB's School of Engineering. Both contracting companies developed diverse practices in Haifa during the 1940s. Under the British mandate, the coastal city became the central port and hub for Middle-Eastern crude oil. The young contracting firms were then exposed to the construction of refineries, heavy industry, power stations, and ultimately to Tel Aviv construction. Both contractors were relocated in Beirut and contributed to the effort of building heritage preservation, following the independence, especially CAT who worked for the Association for the Maintenance of Ancient Residences under Professor Assem Salam, who later recruited Saba George Shiber. Emile Bustani, a member of the Lebanese parliament, was fundamental to the establishment of the National Authority for Reconstruction, following the 1956

46. Nabih Majdalani, "Motel in the Pan-Arab Highway" (Diploma thesis, American University of Beirut, 1955).

47. Kamal Shair, *Out of the Middle East: The Emergence of an Arab Global Business* (London: I.B.Tauris, 2006), 67.

earthquake in the South of Lebanon, heading operations with the support of the United States Overseas Mission (USOM)[48] and the British International Co-Operative Alliance (ICA). The Reconstruction Board recruited, among others, Saba Shiber, who was working for the Saudi/American Aramco (Saudi Arabian Oil Company) and had recently been awarded a PhD from Cornell University, as well as Sami Abdul Baki and George Ayoub. The three then joined the Associated Consulting Engineers (ACE) after 1959. The team under Michel Ecochard's coordination was appointed to carry out the planning of Saida and several low-income housing schemes. The extra-curricular training camps at AUB's School of Engineering, established by Professor Ghosn following the tradition of the Village Welfare Service, were assigned to join the effort. Sabah Abi-Hanna was among the architectural engineering students to join the initiative, surveying damage in small villages and providing construction and design services for the reparation of damaged housing units. Two weeks after the tragic event of March 16, among others, three future practitioners in Kuwait, students of Ghosn, submitted their thesis projects to complete their architectural engineering degrees. The final projects of Charles Haddad, Victor Shiber and George Ayoub demonstrated the ability of the degree program to respond to the specific planning and housing unit design context reported by Frederick W. Lang:

> As the terrain is primarily mountainous, there was no similarity in sites, nor was there any possibility of standardisation of site planning. The abundance of stone, availability of locally produced cement and lack of locally grown lumber, made masonry and reinforced concrete construction traditional and logical. Community planning and the potential relocation of villages was greatly complicated by recognising that the various religious groups would not be happy in changing their traditional location. Planning was also handicapped by the difficulty of formulating and passing legislation to govern the terms of repayment of the cost of repairs or new houses. The lack of housing statistics and time did not permit a completely refined study and planning [...].
> To accomplish the necessary standardisation, a modular system was selected, utilising a standard 4x4 square metre cell. One cell would be purely for living space, the second for sleeping space, plus a porch, and the third a kitchen plus porch and toilet. To provide maximum earthquake stress resistance, construction methods were standardised with reinforced concrete columns, each corner tied together at the floor line by four reinforced concrete beams and a reinforced concrete roof slab. The walls were either stone or concrete blocks filled in between the columns and tied into them through extensions of reinforced rods. This design also permitted professional builders erecting the basic skeleton and then the home owner completing the building himself [...] This architectural and structural solution met with universal approval, as evidenced by its voluntary use by home builders adjacent to, but beyond the control of the earthquake reconstruction area.[49]

However, in November 1956, the ambitious Charles Haddad landed Kuwait, where he found at the Department of Public Works, other AUB graduates, such as Mounir Khatib (Munthir Tahir Khatib) and Sami Abdul Baki, who were later joined by other colleagues, such as Victor Shiber, Varouj Azadian, Fawzi Germanus, Souhayl Bathish and Sabah Abi-Hanna. In May 1957, Doxiadis Associates was hired for the inception of the National Housing Program in Lebanon, with the persistence and support of USOM. The program also included "rural housing, slum clearance and amelioration for the next thirty years,"[50] and the implementation of the Mkalles Demonstration Project, supported by the United States Government. In 1958, with Lebanon in turmoil and political controversy, the recently established Dar Al-Handasah moved their entire office to Kuwait City, where they began work on Power

48. Frederick W. Lang, *Housing Activities In Lebanon 1956–1958: A Summary of Operations* (Beirut: USOM Housing Division, 1958).

49. Ibid., 6–7.

50. Ibid., 15.

A new village

The following building materials have been delivered to construction sites within the one-year period:

Portland Cement	105400 m.t.
Reinforcing Steel	13462 m.t.
Gravel	224876 m.3
Sand	189749 m.3
Lumber	8530 m.3

The Government of Lebanon enacted a special Earthquake Reconstruction Tax levied against cinema admissions and internal mail stamps. From these and other funds the GOL provided within one year the NRB LL. 33,000,000. Added to this is the value of LL. 6,200,000 of USA financed materials.

As USA aid has been completed in record time and our objectives accomplished, USOM/L withdrew from participation in the continuance of this program approximately one year after its initiation.

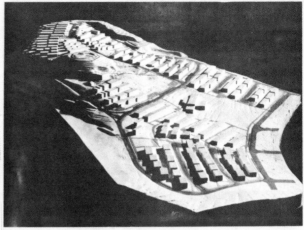

Model of Mkalles Demonstration Project.

Plans and specifications were completed for the construction of initial Demonstration Projects, on land purchased by the GOL, as follows:

Project Location	Total Number Housing Units	Housing Units First Stage	Construction Cost First Stage
Mkalles	1,100	587	LL. 2,200,000
Warwar at Hadeth	600	262	1,100,000
Bedawi at Tripoli	600	322	1,260,000
TOTAL	2,300	971	LL. 4,560,000

These are estimated costs. To provide for unforseen additional costs, and where required supplying the sites with electricity and water, it is recommended that an additional 10% be allowed to cover unknown contingencies.

7. Model of the Mkalles Demonstration Project for resettlement in the south of Lebanon as part of the USOM operations following the earthquake of 1956. © *Housing Activities in Lebanon 1956–1958, A Summary of Operations* by Frederick W. Lang, USOM Housing Division.

Station C. The majority of the office had graduated from AUB, among them the partners and faculty: Kamal Shair, Samir Thabet, Victor Andraos, Nazih Taleb, and notably Khalil Maalouf, who eventually remained in Kuwait for longer periods. Among the designers were AUB graduates: Raymond Ghosn, Robert Wakim, Ghassan Klink, and latter Jafar Tukan, who also eventually stayed in Kuwait during the early 1960s. This movement and the early visit of AUB's School of Engineering Dean, Ken Weidner in 1957 eventually led, at the request of Sheikh Jaber Al-Ali, to the establishment of an internship program at the Department of Public Works for AUB students. In 1958, Fawzi Germanus, Souhayl Bathish, and Sabah Abi-Hanna were integrated as interns under the supervision of Professor Mounir Khatib.

By then, AUB's program was still a four-year bachelor's degree, with a first common year for all engineering degrees. The choice was to be made after the summer camp. The architecture curriculum was then developed across a number of design studios and graphics courses. The studios were offered in semesters and tackled specific conditions, from the use of typology, and site selection, to adaptation and constructive systems, materials, and social development. The remaining curriculum was strongly grounded in intensive engineering courses, such as structures, and concrete and fluid mechanics, among others. The program was devoid of any theory or the history of art and architecture. According to Abi-Hanna, the strong focus on engineering left little time for researching architectural issues or developing students' own interests within the discipline. The curriculum only changed after 1963, with the beginning of a five-year program of architecture,

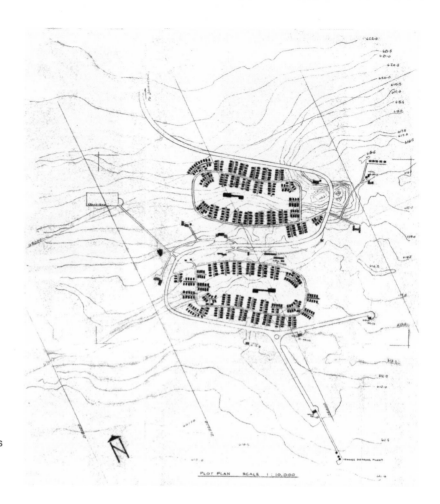

8. Charles Haddad's design concept as a student at AUB: "A Development for Bedouin Settlement," Syria, 1956. © AUB, Special Collections Archive.

PLOT PLAN   SCALE 1 : 10,000

and the nomination of Raymond Ghosn as school Dean. "Philosophy of Architecture, Man's Cultural Evolution, History of Architectural and Engineering Works" (AUB Catalogue of 1963–1964) became part of the curriculum, adopting American post-WWII models inspired in the Bauhaus school.

Charles Haddad:
The Desert Planner

In their 1956 graduation theses, Victor Shiber and George Ayoub developed civic buildings continuing the school's tradition of socially responsible awareness, beyond the excitement of modern pan-Arab territory explored by their colleagues the previous year. However, Haddad's project stood out, pursuing a scale of operation and interests that was far beyond his colleagues' and faculty – A Development for a Bedouin Settlement.[51] Haddad describes the object of his project as follows:

> A good portion of the Arabic speaking world today is still living in groups and human masses moving from one place to another after fertile grazing lands and abundant water resources. These groups of people, seen everywhere in the Arab States, form somewhat a threshold of resistance against the progress of the country in all active fields; a direct result of being unable to stay and stick to a certain area to cultivate and use its natural resources completely.[52]

51. Charles Tewfic Haddad, "A Development for Bedouin Settlement" (Diploma thesis, American University of Beirut, 1956).

52. Ibid.

These were Palestinian refugees, "holding to Syria, Iraq and ~~Trans~~jordan" (the author manually corrected his typing of Transjordan), walking through the desert of Syria, from where the author himself walked to Kuwait in November of the same year. Haddad identified himself as one of them, apart from referring to Syria as his home he also described himself in the following way:

> The designer, an educated man of his community feels that it's part of his duty to care for the progress of his nation and the welfare of his fellow men, committing to both with all his talents as far as his capacity permits. This is his sole motivating power, and is behind his choice of this subject for the reclaiming of the desert.[53]

In reference to the Syrian Desert, where the project was to be located, described in very precise and knowledgeable terms, Haddad adds the "bedouin tribes living in the desert" to this migratory population. He calls on regional governments to note that "in a span of five years maximum, [...] illiteracy" had to "disappear," and that "productivity [the contribution of these bedouin tribes to national economy] must rise."[54] The author concludes by reclaiming the use of the desert, which he says should "start on a large scale, and most importantly of all bring intellectual, wise living to [these] three million Arabs," by defining "a system of living," which, according to him was experimented by "officials in India, Pakistan, Egypt and Algeria"[55] as an "agricultural settlement erected where the soil is fertile and the water is abundant." Later, the author refers to the planning work of United Nations' Relief and Works Agency for Palestinian Refugees in the Near East (UNRWA) as an example to follow in the tradition of Richard Kauffmann's Jezreel valley settlements (1921). However, he argues it should be Arabs and their governments doing this, seeing as the Bedouins and refugees are Arabs. He also claims these settlements are fundamental to the "conquest of the desert" and in transforming this population into a contributor to the nation's prosperity. Haddad refers to New Gourna as a "project well executed and well planned, marking a milestone in the lives of Arab peasants."[56] In his project brief, Haddad clearly states that, "It must be designed as a Neighbourhood Unit,"[57] with no reference to Clarence Perry, Camillo Sitte, Raymon Unwin, Patrick Geddes or even Ebenezer Howard. Haddad's uses *The Urban Pattern: City Planning and Design*,[58] particularly to Radburn in New Jersey, as a fundamental reference in his argument. According to him, the idea of the neighbouring unit is not understood as a planning method for urban expansion but more of a social tool for integration and solidarity. As an example of social integration, the author refers to *Beit Shaalan* in Damascus as an example. After the British mandate in Palestine, many who were in exile in Syria found shelter in the Shaalan district. The author's family was eventually among them.

However the construction of his design narrative for the proposed settlement is grounded on rural and natural values. In the report he refers to the lack of literature and references available back then in the field of agricultural development and highlights the AUB summer school experience as an important milestone in his education. According to the author, he worked in the UNRWA Palestinian Pilot village during the summer of 1955. Haddad revealed clear arguments for the proposed strategy and highlighted the importance of the street in a rural environment as a fluid and organic element in opposition to the formal grid or radial systems. The author states

53. Ibid.

54. Ibid.

55. Charles Haddad, during his studies became aware of Hassan Fathy's work in Egypt, Doxiadis experiences in Pakistan, Maxwell Fry and Jane Drew in India and the policies of rural resettlement in Algeria during the Civil War (1954–62). Haddad, "A Development for Bedouin Settlement."

56. Ibid.

57. Ibid.

58. Arthur Gallion and Simon Eisner, *The Urban Pattern: City Planning and Design* (NY: John Wiley & Sons Inc., 1993).

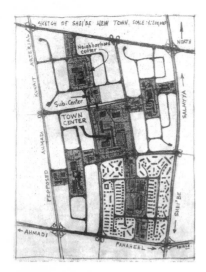

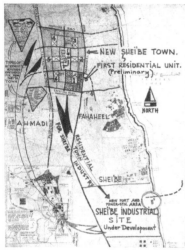

9. Sketch of the new town Sabahiya by Saba George Shiber, 1964.
© *The Kuwait Urbanization.*

10. Urban matrix of tri-town area (Ahmadi – Fahaheel – Sabahiya) by Saba George Shiber, 1964.
© *The Kuwait Urbanization.*

59. Haddad, "A Development for Bedouin Settlement."

60. Gallion and Eisner, *Urban Pattern: City Planning and Design.*

61. Haddad, "A Development for Bedouin Settlement."

62. Ibid.

63. Ibid.

that, "informality in the design is considered, but balance is well observed,"[59] arguing that the 'Garden City' model is a model for rural development. The proposed "curvilinear street" is described by the author, who quotes Gallion and Eisner, "to give some balance of character to the subdivision and subdue the deadly monotony of parallel streets stretching to infinity."[60] This narrative continues with the description of the proposal:

A winding main thoroughfare 24 metres wide was chosen. Within its symmetrical open loop two closed one 14m wide are layed. Staggering from their sides are cul-de-sacs 120 x 10 metre at 50-metre intervals or so. It might be thought that this distance is small, but will greatly help to keep traffic speed to a minimum, something that is very desirable in villages. Between each two cul-de-sacs and in the back byres, alleys of 10 metres wide are designated to farmers and cattle returning from the fields. Between the two closed loops and along the sides of the main thoroughfare is the balancing mass of the civic centre, equidistant from the furthest home on both sides by a maximum walking distance of 1000 metres. Each closed loop houses 2500 people and has its own kindergarten, elementary school and communal garden.

The accuracy continues further with a clear definition of the paved surfaces of public space to the main thoroughfare, where traffic is more dense, allowing pedestrians to cross via an underpass, preserving the natural and rural identity of the dwelling areas and the integrity, maintenance-wise, of the transportation route. Regarding the landscaped component of the plan, Haddad acknowledges the population is used to living among nature, maintaining that the landscaped parks and green belt are fundamental as "a sustainer of life, not a refuge from it,"[61] to attract a nomadic population to a sedentary way of life. He also acknowledges that landscape must be considered in a special way, suggesting the landscaper must select the regular plants, "he has to adapt living materials to the site [...] The free landscape commencing where we need it most at the walls of habitation [...] only cooperative effort can achieve the communal garden and ensure its permanent value [...] the hotel is situated in one corner to benefit from this advantage – an oasis in the desert."[62] In the description of the building uses for the central area, the authors refers to the possibility of a small museum, considering the pre-existing Roman settlement in the area, (Dayr Ash-Shamali, south of Al-Dumayr, Syria) or even a decomposition plant, where refuse is dumped and later "sold to the farmers and inhabitants as fertiliser," an experimental station for farming or a generating station for electrical power.

In his approach to the dwelling unit, Haddad enforces the need for training and introducing future settlers to a new sedentary life. His major concern is that "the community has to be taught to stick to its home." According to Haddad, only after this process "will they be able to live as one community, taking care of their own interests [...] they will understand the meaning of life and the value of their country." He concludes: "At that moment we will have the power to challenge and say that such a project is successful." As for the material condition of these units, Haddad acknowledges that he "read about the Gourna Development, and that truly there, the architect Fathy knows what he is doing. He has adapted thousands of years of heritage and material use to the context and structures of the day. He is the type of man that lived in the Egyptian 'reef' [countryside] and studied how to represent it with modern yet not strange architecture." Quoting Fathy, "it would be a form of treason to deliberately turn our backs on this age-old tradition in the name of false modernism."[63]

Haddad puts the comfort of the dwelling unit above any other motif as the main driving force for the selection of material and constructive system. Claiming that the house must assure thermic comfort at the cheapest cost, the author suggests the use of adobe brick. He describes in exhaustive terms all the processes of fabrication and application, from the collection of natural soil to the laying of bricks on the wall, claiming that the system "is a national method of building in many lands," and that, "modern buildings in different parts of the world are being erected" in this way.[64] Haddad exhaustively considers calculations for the adobe walls, including the reinforced concrete foundations, artificial lighting, water supply, drainage, sewage and refuse disposal, as well as the mix of construction materials and financial feasibility, proposing support from the Syrian Government and Arab League.

A few years later, similar problems were present in the borders of the urbanised Kuwait, as Haddad reports in several of his course assignments while at MIT (1970–71). After returning from his master's degree in City Planning at Yale University, Haddad became the Head of Planning division at Kuwait's Municipality and was finally able to implement his "bedouin" village plan in Sabahiya. The Municipal Council had previously approved Saba Shiber plan for a Kuwait Oil Company (KOC) workers town in the same location, aiming for an "inter-mixed community" considering "economy in land and street surface for public and recreation areas."[65]

With no access to increased income and no land, the former desert population in Kuwait became sedentary and dependent on governmental charity – the attribution of citizenship and consequent exposure to housing and social security programs. The exodus to vacant urban areas together with the massive influx of the migrant labour force to Kuwait during those years, in its majority originally from rural environments, characterised the nature of spontaneous settlements. By the early sixties, shanties had expanded and occupied twenty different locations, close to main roads and employment centres, with a capacity of 120,000 inhabitants by 1975 (12.1% of the total population).[66] Many of these ne immigrants organised by provenience and ethnicity started to erect temporary shelters (shacks) on any vacant lots close to their work, with little if any regard to land ownership. On the other end, the Bedouin population settled near the oil-fields or near the work in which they were engaged, in places such as the one where Sabahiya would be constructed.[67] This context defined the opportunity Haddad was expecting since 1956.

The Rise of the Practice in Kuwait

The evolution of architectural education and practice in the Middle East cannot be disassociated from Haddad's ambition. The impact of modern urbanisation in the region led to a series of unprecedented reciprocities between geographical, economic, political, and social realities. In Kuwait, the first shipment of oil in 1946, and the economic exposure of the Gulf region in the aftermath of the Suez Crisis (1956–57), transformed the small desert city-state into a "suddenly rich"[68] strategic destination, where "outsiders [blew] up a storm."[69]

Widely discussed in the West, the displacement from the city to urban society[70] that started to gain momentum all across the region after the discovery of oil, posed a series of challenges to the existing narratives of

64. Ibid.

65. Saba George Shiber, "Various Building Types for Low income Housing" (presented at Municipal Council, Kuwait, April 7, 1962).

66. Frost & Sullivan Inc., "Report on Housing and Home Furnishings in the Middle East," 1975.

67. M. Al Hashimy, *Nomad and nomadism in Kuwait* (Kuwait: The General Administration for Planning Affairs, Department of Social Planning, Planning Council, 1976).

68. Paul Edward Case, "Boom Time in Kuwait," *National Geographic*, v. 102, n. 6 (December 1952): 799.

69. "Kuwait: The Fabulous Sheikdom," *Life Magazine*, v. 46, n. 9 (1959): 56–68.

70. Henri Lefébvre, *The Urban Revolution*, trans. Robert Bononno (Minnesota: University of Minnesota Press, 2003).

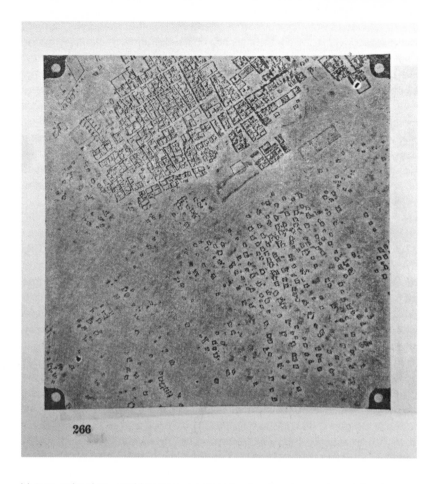

266

11. Aerial view of Bedouin settlement
near Hawally, Kuwait, 1961.
© *The Kuwait Urbanization.*

71. Macklin L. Hancock, "Architectural
Conception of Buildings in Accordance with
Twentieth Century Islamic-Arabic Style"
(presented at Symposium of Kuwait
Municipality, Kuwait, January 25–29, 1969).

history, urbanism, architecture, geography, landscape, and social sciences. Arab planners such as Charles Haddad, Saba Shiber and Riad Al-Nakib, together with Western architects such as Peter and Alison Smithson, Reima and Raili Pietilä, and to a certain extent the work developed by The Architects Collaborative (TAC) in association with the local Pan-Arab Consulting Engineers (Pace) – involving individuals such as Abdallah Sabbar – determined through Kuwait the context for modernity in the region from the late 1960s onwards. At different moments, while sharing similar objectives, they sought to identify the specific characteristics of the processes of urban renewal and transformation in highly contested territories, such as Kuwait City during the 1960s and 1970s, and the construction of the region's identity in the twentieth century, addressing the relationship between architecture and ideology in the way it determines the use and location of private and public space. Finally, one can say that Kuwait allowed for the development of models of urban intervention that are specific to this region today.

In January 1969, Macklin L. Hancock, in his presentation[71] at the Municipality conference on construction materials and low maintenance, called for an "islamic-arabic" understanding of how this might be achieved, considering "materials which will help to keep maintenance costs low." By calling for a study of the "aesthetic values" of regional architecture and "effective solutions to technical problems unique to this part of the world," Hancock suggested the importance of a school of architecture and the long-term interests of the Government of Kuwait through an "increase in the quantity and quality of Arab architects." For the Harvard Graduate School of Design professor, the country's problems were a "combination of radically increased Arab purchasing power, combined with ready availability of foreign skills and materials [which were] to eliminate the need for traditional solutions," stating that, "this poses a distinct threat to Arab cultures."

The Canadian architect's communication confirms a new conscience towards the importance of context and particular material conditions. However the motivations to create new instruments for territorial planning and architectural practice were not able to respond to the "rapid development of an area like the Gulf, where the pace of work required does not permit the architect the luxury to think out each problem in the depth necessary."[72] The phenomenon of rapid development and the affluence of the public and private sectors made it difficult for local practitioners to distinguish their limits.

In Ghazi Sultan's "Criteria for Design in the Arabian Gulf Region," the author recognises that, "to be able to cope intelligently with this recurring problem, a general list of criteria must be developed to assist the architect to check and come to grips with the alternatives facing him." Ironically, the two most distinguished Kuwaiti practitioners in the years that followed, Hamid Shuaib and Ghazi Sultan, both educated in the Anglo-Saxon West, were responsible for maintaining an emphasis on buildings and their materials and technological performance as the central objects in the architecture and urban design processes. The first graduated from Oxford Polytechnic (1958), earned a master's degree in Civic Design from Liverpool (1964), and spent a short experience at London County Council with Leslie Martin; while the second graduated from the Carnegie Institute in Pittsburgh, under Ulm Associate Professor William S. Huff, and earned a master's degree in urban design from Harvard GSD. They became the leading figures of Kuwait's planning and architectural practice until the late 1980s. The two influenced the development and implementation of the second Master Plan, and its successive revisions, as well as the selection of Western designers and planners, to whom major buildings and plans were commissioned during the years of progressive development, mainly during the 1970s.

The emphasis on the performance of buildings, whether aesthetic or technological, as the central model for informing architectural and urban design practice in Kuwait, a legacy from British Petroleum architects and planners in Ahmadi, was severely fought by Jane Drew, first in Ahmadi and later by Saba Shiber in Kuwait City. However, the ability of practices such as Wilson and Mason or Sayyed Karim during the 1950s and 1960s, in mastering the aesthetics of a building to please its stakeholders and in promoting the construction industry, were dominant. The establishment of such modus operandi eventually led the country and its city to surpass the construction of a modern subjectivity based on the progressive transformation of distinctive values, which Haddad recalled in "Bedouin Settlement,"[73] such as identity, authenticity, the natural, leisure, and pleasure.

Keith D. Watenpaugh in his book, *Being Modern in the Middle East: Revolution, Nationalism, Colonialism, and the Arab Middle Class*,[74] refers to a speech by newspaper editor Fathallah Qastun, on January 2, 1910, on "Becoming Civilised." According to Watenpaugh, Qastun questions the impact of European culture in the region under the Ottoman Empire. He argued that the influence of Western civilisation caused material and cultural harm, but also served as the means by which to conform to local traditions

72. Ghazi Sultan, "Criteria for Design in the Arabian Gulf Region," *The Arabian Journal for Science and Engineering*, v. 7, n. 2 (1982): 165.

73. Haddad, "A Development for Bedouin Settlement."

74. Keith David Watenpaugh, *Being Modern in the Middle East: Revolution, Nationalism, Colonialism, and the Arab Middle Class* (New Jersey: Princeton University Press, 2014).

12. Cinema Al-Andalus under construction in Hawally, Sayyed Karim, 1960. © AUC Rare Books Library.

and customs. This basis, which Qastun refers to as the "true civilisation" (*al-madaniyya al-haqqa*) is the "essence" of the West, which he considers vital to the survival of his society, as opposed to "the mere reproduction of the superficial trappings of European manners and fashions."[75]

'Beautiful or Ugly'

In December 1967, Sheikh Sabah Al-Salem Al-Sabah, in the foreword to *Recent Arab City Growth*,[76] exposed the "anxiety of the writer [Saba Shiber] with the building of the Arab city on the soundest basis from scientific, practical, economic, social, engineering and aesthetical points of view." And continues:

> Arab-Islamic heritage [...] safeguarding [...] continuing the process of building cities and erecting buildings. [...] We are of the belief that the author [...] has etched many broad-lines for the future Arab city, which surpassed all expectations of Arab ambition and utilised Arab labor to raise standards of living [...] We hope it will have a [...] pragmatic echo in the various quarters, particularly urban-architectural-engineering.

In the same book, the undersecretary of Kuwait's Ministry of Public Works, Saud Al-Fouzan, emphasises modernisation through city urbanisation as a motif of Arab pride, but at the same time a major source of problems for citizens. In the preface, Shiber highlights the relevance of three upcoming events: the First Conference of the Organisation of Arab Cities in Beirut, August 1968; the Eleventh Conference of the Federation of Arab Engineers, Kuwait March 1969; and the Third Congress of the Afro-Asian Housing Organisation in Dar-es-Salam, October 1969, as a good cross-section of Arab professionals and officials discussing the problems of building in the city and region. In this book, which resulted from his experiences mainly in Kuwait, Shiber refers to the city as "perhaps, the most affluent in history," and attempts to provide the reader with a cross-sectional Arab portrait, "to shed light on the many aspects of the Arab city: old, present and, perhaps, future?"[77]

In his own introduction to the book, Shiber borrows the concept of the 'modern city' as a revolution from V. Gordon Childe,[78] while the modernisation of the Arab City as an evolution from agrarian to urban society from Lewis Mumford. He understands the city as as process (frequently quoting Alfred North Whitehead's *Process and Reality*) and as a collective act of unity (Max Weber). He is aware of the dynamic and the required balance, mainly regarding economic and social stratification and segregation. Understanding the ecology of the place through the interactions between man and nature (with broad references, such as Gerhard Rosenberg and George Stapledon) allows Shiber to understand the relevance of the moment for the construction of a whole nation beyond its functional existence and the welfare ambitions of its rulers.

The comprehension of urban form in its generative conditions (Eliel Saarinen and Arthur Korn as opposites) serves as an argument for Shiber's obsession with the idea of the 'beautiful or ugly.' He aims to avoid the 'ugly' by accepting that the physical urban form is a "blend, or amalgamation of forms" that must be "judged on how they are modeled to serve [...] collective living." He surmises that the purpose of planning is considering "how to polarise the many forces at play, so that, across all the ranges of the city, its sensuous and visual attributes are maximised," and elaborates extensively on

75. Watenpaugh, *Being Modern in the Middle East*, 1–31.

76. Shiber, *Recent Arab City Growth*, 17.

77. Ibid.

78. V. Gordon Childe, "The Urban Revolution," *The Town Planning Review*, v. 21, n. 1 (1950): 3–17.

13. Model of Ahmadi Cinema, Sayyed Karim, 1962.
© Kuwait National Cinema Company.

the idea that "beauty must be sought in urban form." Disagreeing on "the dictum that form follows function," Shiber states clearly that, "functional guides, especially in urban formation, are not guarantors of beauty."

With this in mind, Shiber projects onto the historical moment of the 'post-oil discovery' Arab World, an opportunity to remake an Arab territory that is "conducive to political, intellectual and industrial achievement," and is "visually expressive in form."[79]

> Could not Arab planners today similarly animate the enthusiasm of the Arab masses by a City Marvelous movement, [reference to the *City Beautiful* movement] attuned to the dynamics of the age, challenging if not defying, the Arabs?[80]

With little reference to the narratives of religion, Shiber's idea of Arab World geography is based on the *Umayyad* dynasty expansion from the Arabian Gulf to the Atlantic Ocean. Almost 1,300 years later, the oil discovery is the opportunity Shiber envisions to "remake" this territory, which according to him must be politically unified under the denomination of United Arab States.

With clear statements such as – "What is Past is Prologue" – Shiber introduces this territory to Arab architects and planners evoking their own architectural and urban tradition in what he calls, "a pictorial roundup of city and building."[81] The first chapters of his extensive publication (almost 1000 pages) also known as *Recent Arab City Growth* are entirely dedicated the *"awakenings, [...] setting and anatomy of Arab Town."* In the introduction of the same book he recollects the work of Ibn Battuta, Ibn Haukal, and Ibn Khaldun, and the uniqueness of the urban-architectural heritage of Yemen or Morocco, as the basis for the understating of this Arab-Islamic unified territory. The 150 illustrated pages of political maps and diagrams include "Israeli occupations," diverse mediums of representations of cities and buildings, such as aerial views, paintings, sketches from the author, plans, and photography. In these, the Arab city is displayed in relation to the desert, the sea, and its monuments. The people are portrayed in all their mani-festations, from agriculture and sea-related activities to phenomenons such as the displacement of people from the "Arab heartland" (Palestine), as Shiber calls it, and their resettlement in refugee camps.

79. Shiber, *Recent Arab City Growth*, 25.

80. Ibid.

81. Ibid., 22.

14. Aerial view of Sabahiya, Kuwait, 2017. © Kuwait Municipality.

Apart from few modern achievements acknowledged by Shiber, which include 'T Consult' proposals for agricultural settlements in Kuwait and pilgrimage sheltering in Mecca, or Macklin L. Hancock's waterfront proposal for the facade of the city as an "attempt to nationalise development"[82] in Kuwait, Shiber highlights the need to preserve the native character of Gulf coastal towns. In a preparatory work paper he wrote prior to his death, for the Eleventh Arab Engineers Conference which took place in Kuwait in 1969 entitled "Whither our Arab Urban-Architectural Heritage,"[83] Shiber calls for a deeper understanding of an Arab "culture-in-transition" that had "to make the necessary accommodations, readjustments and syntheses." Constantly referring to it as "disturbed," he criticises architects attitude towards the preservation of an inherited architectural tradition by "cladding or clothing buildings with shapes, decorations and colours that appeal to us from the

82. Hancock, "Architectural Conception of Buildings."

83. Shiber, *Recent Arab City Growth*, 330–370.

past." In another press article entitled "From 'Ass-Thetics' to Aesthetics" confirms that money affluence of the post-oil "decades of boom" have led to "mammoth and successful urban ventures of uglification," using the example of "architectural change in Kuwait," which he refers to as "an inorganic type that has gone wild in an avid search for shapes and fetishes that do not relate suitably to the fundamentals of sound contemporary architecture – in the deep and comprehensive meaning of contemporary – nor does it take into active cognisance the climatic, social and economic factors as determinants of architectural form." Very critical of the early urban proposals of Abdullah Ishan Kamil and Rifat Chadirji (IQC) in Baghdad, Iraq, Shiber uses their major projects in the city centre such as the Unknown Soldier and Tahrir squares, to point out "the lack of harmonious spatial juxtaposition" of these modern interventions, in opposition to TAC's proposal for the university campus. Recognising the quality of the western architects, which he describes as "the reputable firm of Walter Gropius excelling in the field of civic and architecture design," he describes the project as follows:

> Here, modern urban functionalism and aesthetics have been scientifically employed. A close view of one of the buildings ensemble on the same campus ground depicts the 'open court' concept applied with sensitivity and thus appreciably contributing towards a rich, habitable and cultural environment.[84]

However, Shiber's wise criticism of the architecture and urban scene in the region, away from personal motivations or emotional instincts, allows for the recognition of the architectural work of Rifat Chadirji as pioneer, referring that his proposal for the Awqaf building in Baghdad as "a return to a more sober and organic form deriving inspiration from the heritage of Iraqi habitat and expressing affiliation to the tradition of functional, frank and puristic Yemeni urban architecture."[85]

When referring to building production in general, he quotes Ibn Khaldun, "The architects who exercise the craft differ. Some are intelligent and skilful, others are inferior."[86] •

84. Ibid., 173.

85. Ibid.

86. Ibn Khaldūn, *The Muqaddimah: An introduction to History*. Transcribed from, Shiber, *Kuwait Urbanization*, 17.

Charles Haddad

CHARLES TOUFIC HADDAD (1934–) was in the second class to graduate from the American University of Beirut's Bachelor's degree program in Architectural Engineering (1956), moving on to receive a masters degree in City Planning from Yale University (1961), and, in 1970, he was made an MIT SPURS Fellow. He commenced his practice in Kuwait after 1956, at Kuwait municipality's Division of project planning, first in the Roads Department and, after 1964, as the head of the division and as a member of the counterpart team to the state's Physical Development Plan. Between 1960 and 1962, Haddad was a planner with the New Haven City Plan Department. From 1964 until 1972, he served as the Executive Director for the Kuwaiti's residential-commercial survey program and as the principal designer in charge of various residential neighbourhoods for Kuwaiti municipality. Haddad is the co-author of "Housing for Kuwait University Graduates," a survey commissioned by the Kuwaiti Prime Minister in 1969, and another by the Kuwait Municipality titled, "Rules and Regulations for the Subdivision of Residential Land." Haddad was one of the founding members of Pan-Arab Consulting Engineers (Pace) in 1968, and, between 1972–78, he was the director of Pace International Corporation in Cambridge, Massachusetts. In 1978, he left Pace and, a year later, established his own practice Charles T. Haddad and Associates (CTHA), which today has become The Associated Engineering Partnership (TAEP) which he continues to manage.

Ricardo Camacho conducted this interview in Kuwait in June 2014.

Ricardo Camacho: *So I have several questions. It's always difficult to understand, among the architects that have worked here, the boundary between the practices of architecture and urban planning. What are your impressions regarding the ways in which these two practices related to each other during Kuwait's modernisation?*

Charles Haddad: The manner in which distribution of the money in oil developed was through the acquisition of property. This acquisition was confined to individual houses, which were irregular – small: forty, fifty, one-hundred square metres each – and did not lend themselves really to development on a large scale unless the government were to take over, add them all up, and then subdivide them. When the government did intervene, the properties were subdivided in a regular manner, meaning into square or rectangular blocks. There were some that were designed within a specific geometry, following a street pattern that was laid over the acquired property – it might have been a curve – and it affected the configuration of the building and so on. There is one building, here, in Kuwait, opposite the Khaleejia Complex, which was built in 1956 by the architect Kamal Al-Sayegh, and it houses the Mogahwi printing press. This was built in 1956, and it is a curved building.

RC: *This is where? Opposite the Khaleejia tower?*

CH: And it was a printing press, so it was easy to put a curved line parallel to the road. And then it goes to Bader Al-Mulla road.

RC: *Yes, Soor street?*

CH: Yes, Soor street. So really the attempt, or the plan, or the strategy, was to distribute the income from the oil to Kuwait's inhabitants through the acquisition of individual properties, and then to give them new sites to build on. The new sites were always rectangular, either thirty metres by twenty-five metres, or forty metres by twenty-five metres, and this is why there is a difference between the old houses, the shapes and things, and the new neighbourhoods outside Soor Street.

RC: *So, in this sense, the gaps that urban planning opened up – by definition or by context – were an opportunity for architects to*

work. On the other hand, when you have a regular grid, the planning will have a major impact on the definition of the urbanscape.

CH: Yes.

RC: *But when that impact isn't brought about, then the building is the element that can solve the problems posed by the urban context.*

CH: Yeah, it was difficult. It was difficult to subdivide a property or a superblock in an irregular way, unless it existed, and it was known for its irregular shape. I don't have immediate examples where buildings were designed irregularly because they were taken as regular.

RC: *To respond to the site's pre-existing elements, even if recent?*

CH: To respond to the site. But I'm sure there are examples where the government wouldn't acquire the property, and, therefore, it did not add it to another acquired property or subdivide it proportionally according to the original area or the original ownership. The majority of blocks were regularly subdivided for residential areas outside Kuwait City. The commercial areas within Kuwait City were also subdivided regularly, but the planners took the use that predominated the urban scene into consideration. There is no relationship between a 1,000-square-metre lot there and a 1,000-square-metre lot in old Kuwait at all. There were no houses that were 1,000 square metres – and this is without an inner courtyard.

It was solidly built. In fact, I look now at some buildings – you know, on Istiqlal street (road 30) going toward Jabriya – and I question their size. But, I do understand that, as certain families who have children and the children grow, part of life is probably to have the children marry and stay with their parents until another developed lot is ready. I remember when, a long time ago, we used to design villas. I had an American girl married to a Kuwaiti national who came here and had a twelve-metre by seventreen-metre lot on which she wanted to build a villa. I mean this is completely in the American way: un-American. Twelve metres by thirty-six metres. I don't know what happened to her, but I hope she is living there and joyfully.

RC: *But what was the role of the local planners? Because, during the 1950s, all the urban planners that were here or that worked here, were mainly Europeans, but, the architects that came here – they were Arabs and then the first Kuwaitis entered the field. So, what was the role of these architects, including yourself, in the modernisation of the city? How important was their background, the agenda, whether political or not?*

CH: I am sad that Arab architects were not educated as Arab architects. They were ready to look at foreign magazines and develop an architecture that they picked up in college, in school or as tourists. I've never heard of somebody – if he's in Damascus – going to Beirut to look at the architecture there, though there is good architecture in Lebanon. But, it does happen vice versa. So architects who came to design public buildings, which were easy to copy, like a superblock (reference to CBD Areas 1,2,3 and 9), would take and put buildings in.

RC: *But in that sense, what do you think the impact of education in the region was? Because, at that time, there were schools with clear and strong references, such as the American University of Beirut (AUB) or the Baghdad School?*

CH: The bloodline wasn't flowing properly. I mean, architecture is a latecomer to people's lives. I mean interior design, yes. They would return to the arabesque and whatever, but I feel sad every night now listening to the destruction that's happening in Syria. And, and that is a place where I lived and with which I can associate. I may have been able to walk the streets at the time and not be sensitive to its merits or to its positive points and so forth. But if you want to – not study it – but, if you want to learn more about it, it is something that pulls you to it, and you can benefit, understand or gain from it. The Architects Collaborative (TAC) was instrumental for all of us, because of their experience in Baghdad, at the university there, many years before they came to Kuwait. At least twenty years before they came to Kuwait, there was a learning period for them in Baghdad. You can see it in their architecture here – through the use of arches and several other features. While, if you go to other areas that were designed as superblocks, such as market alleys in the CBD Areas 2 and 9 – I mean areas that are 100-metres long and probably thirty-metres wide and were divided into shops along the way with the central corridor – they didn't have the detailing that TAC brought in. And this is where, when you ask me about architecture in the Middle East at the time: there was no one, fine! There was no one, but there are people who attempted in Egypt and Iraq, and succeeded.

RC: *Hassan Fathy?*

CH: Fathy. Fathy, he tried very hard to do things, and he had nice details. And I'll tell you, I, for one, lived, during my third year in engineering (1955), in a village that was built completely out of mud, and it was intended for Palestinian refugees. At the time, I was 18 or 19. My father had a position with the United Nations, and he arranged for me to train in the building of the camp: adobe construction, which was formed on the ground and then dried in the sun and aired. And I remember a most attractive woman: a Palestinian peasant – can you imagine? – who would carry the dried adobe blocks on her head and walk like a spear. So straight. So beautiful. And then she'd have, this thing on her face, the veil. And between here and here: this will be dark, and this will be red, from the sun not going in. I would return from the field around twelve o'clock or one o'clock, and the room would be cold, a chilled room. And we would wait in the desert in the evening after supper, and the weather would become cold, and then, at around ten o'clock, we'd go into the rooms, and they would be warm. It was unbelievable.

RC: *But, when you came to Kuwait after finishing your degree, what was your main background, or your feelings toward architecture? Were you connected to any practices, to any architects, to any buildings, to a sort of reference that you described before?*

CH: The nature of the country, the desert and the way the initial construction happened was not conducive to developing the old society again, or improving on or developing it. It wasn't.

RC: *It happened too fast?*

CH: First of all, it was too fast and each instance happened too far away from others. I mean, don't forget that Kuwait was a very small piece of congested, developed land. And, they were dreaming about developing a city like London that would have three ring roads. It was up to the fourth ring road. Even the forth ring road was not part of the city, because it was a cemetery. And then, they fell into the other trap – they had a lot of Palestinians there who were educated and they were diligently working for the

government and they were Muslims, which was very important, and they didn't want to take these people and give them Kuwaiti nationality. They didn't want to. So, the alternative was to dilute that force, that entity, or that grouping, by bringing Bedouins from Syria, Jordan, Iraq, and Saudi Arabia. Then, they put them in different areas, which was fine because they were not literate, and they didn't talk to people – meaning in the same language. They were not engineers. They were Bedouns. So, I think the Kuwaitis made a mistake by not pursuing an aggressive policy with foreigners.

RC: *But, even with that mix you are talking about, other educated people came from other parts: Sabah Abi-Hanna, for example.*

CH: No, Sabah Abi-Hanna came after.

RC: *He came after? I think he came for an internship in 1957.*

CH: Yes, he might have come, but I graduated in 56. He graduated in 58.

RC: *Yes, he came. He came for training before completing his degree.*

CH: Yes, which is the same one I spoke to you about: my experience. This was a prerequisite. But, I was the first fellow who came from AUB as a graduate, and I was the first to be paid 1,600 Indian rupees. They used to pay fresh graduates 1,400 Indian rupees. Not for me as person, but for the AUB class that wanted to come here, they increased it. They increased the salary from 1,400 to 1,600.

The reason classmates didn't come from Beirut is because there was an earthquake in Lebanon. And the city took practically everybody to work on the damage.

RC: *To rescue?*

CH: To serve, yes. Not to rescue, but, because there were cracks in the buildings, they would go into the houses, order five cement bags of whatever aggregate and so on, and pour it on part of the ceiling that had fallen but is still structurally stable, or plaster a room that had cracked. This was my class's job when they graduated, and they were taking it all over. I decided to come to Kuwait for one reason: I didn't see myself mixing with the Lebanese in Lebanon, my countryside, you know? I felt that way, being a Palestinian. And Sabah was a friend. He was okay, but we didn't do much together. Although, we tried to establish a firm together called Delta Associates.

RC: *What were your major references at school back then? Like, your professors, colleagues? Could you point out one or two names that had a major impact on you?*

CH: I mean, my parents were educated, so there was a strong influence there. There was a strong pull at home. And the pull – my father was German-educated, so, at heart, he was a rigorous man, but he brought us up well. We were three children, and he was a tough disciplinarian. A lot of my teachers knew of my father, because he was a highly placed government employee in Palestine, in Jerusalem.

RC: *Getting back to the people at school and then to Kuwait, there was, for example, Victor Shiber.*

CH: He was a classmate.

RC: *Yes, he also came to Kuwait after you, I presume?*

CH: He came to Kuwait in 1960–1961, and the reason he came to Kuwait …

RC: *His brother?*

CH: His brother, but let me tell you. Shiber's father is an architect, and they come from a good, well-entrenched family, from Jerusalem. And his father had a property on Mount Scopus, in Jerusalem, where he wanted to build an architecture school. Then Palestine came, so it wasn't – I saw the plans for it in Beirut. I didn't understand much of it at the time, but there's a man who spent time and money on something that he believed in. But politically, he couldn't do it. So, when Saba came from – I met Saba in 1955 in Beirut, when he came from Cornell, and the Shibers were very proud of their father, their brother, unlike us, where we would not mention our achievements and just remain quiet, and so on. It was a habit probably, because of our education. I don't know. But they were very proud of their brother, talking about him in his absence and what he had done and what he would do. And they fostered that by writing articles and books and whatever. So, he came here, and he was – I don't know if he made enemies when he came here – but he came at a time when the sheikhs were getting up. The man whom you might have enjoyed talking to died a few months ago: Said Breik.

RC: *He was still alive? I didn't know that.*

CH: Yes, he was alive. He died, very sadly, like a recluse. And there's another one: Tareq Bushnaq. Tareq was a graduate from Yale, also. But he was lazy, he was not a hard worker. I don't know for what reason.

RC: *During 1960 and 1964, there was time to think about Central Business District (CBD) areas and to develop detailed urban designs.*

CH: Yes. Now, one thing that I want to mention here is that development followed the availability of funding. As they exported more oil, they had more money to spend. However, because of the pressure they'd evade payment for the property. The acquisition of property – I remember mentioning that to you – was not started in this portion for the area from the Seif Palace down to Dasman (Sharq). Rather, it started from the Palace to the American hospital. And this is what they called Qiblia, where the Sunnis lived. From the Grand Mosque to the Dasman Palace were the Shias. So there was, through planned acquisition, an attempt not to give Shias money, though the area on the west side was limited, because of where the Salam Palace is, and the areas along the beach were geotechnically weak. They couldn't build, in fact, and the area was slated for light construction as an industrial area, built to one storey only. And this is why it was zoned for industry, not to build.

RC: *But this was something known before 1951?*

CH: Yes, they call it Sabb. The land is called Sabb.

RC: *There were some key projects in that area immediately after you came, such as the Thunayan Al-Ghanim corner building facing Jahra Gate.*

CH: This was designed by an Egyptian architect, Sayyed Karim. It was the first free plan office building that was built on Fahad

Al-Salem street. But they didn't permit him to build additional floors. So, if you get away from it and look towards it, you will see columns from the roof going up.

RC: *But, on the opposite side, there was a building, where the Sheraton – the former Ministry of Finance building – is today. That was higher, the building with a chess facade, white and blue? I don't know the name because it was demolished, and it's where the extension of the Sheraton was built.*

CH: The Sheraton itself was one of the subdivisions that Al-Shaya had his eye on. He was a member of the municipal council, and he always wanted that piece of land. He entered into negotiation with the Municipal Council to get it, and he got it, eventually. I was in the Municipality at the time, but I'm coming – you know where the Sheraton and Fahad Al-Salem street are?

The Thunayan Al-Ghanim building was built before Shiber. It was being constructed in 1955. As for the Secondary School of Shuwaikh, when I came on November 5, 1956, they were putting the final coat on the globe of the college, and painting it and so on. So, you can see that the school was completed in 1957. It took a long time. Do you know why it took a long time? Because the contract that was given to CAT was a cost-plus contract. All contracts were given on a cost-plus basis. There were five companies in Kuwait that were using cement bags to strengthen the foundations of any building, and cement would come in fifty kg bags.

RC: *Was this secondary school a project developed by AUB graduates?*

CH: CAT, as a company, had good ties with AUB. So, who it was exactly, I don't know. But it's highly probable that they had somebody from AUB. AUB was recommended to design the school, because the design was – I don't want to say it was nothing special – but it was designed like that, and it was easy to place detail on it.

I cannot recall who designed it. I remember, a few weeks before I left, there was an attractive woman, who wasn't wearing a veil or anything. She was the wife of the Palestinian Al-Ghusain, who was the Kuwaiti ambassador in Washington. She drove her big car on Fahad Al-Salem, parked beside the mud wall and walked across to get something from a shop. That was the status of Fahad Street when I left to Yale: mud roads, still sunbaked brick walls on the side, not much of an asphalt road. And when I came back three years later – I worked one year and studied for two years – I came back and I was disoriented. I just couldn't. I left Kuwait as an employee of the Roads Department, which – although I was an architect – belonged to the Ministry of Public Works. And when I was hired, Mr. Abdul Haq Abdul Shafi, the town-planning officer in Kuwait and Iraq who worked on Le Corbusier's plan for the Sports City was the chief planner. And, the inspector general – you should have heard of him: Fouad Abdel Baki – as I told you, I was the first one to come from AUB. He introduced me and he said, "He's a new graduate from AUB. I want you to take care of him. Thank you." So we went to Mr. Shafi's office and he asked, "What do you like to do?" and so on. And I mentioned planning. My mother always told me that I should be a planner.

RC: *For any reason?*

CH: Yes, probably prestige. So I went. I was given a table, and, for two years, I drafted road profiles. And then, during my third year, I noticed I was missing something, and I applied and was accepted.

So it happened that way. So I go into the Planning Department and there was another man in the planning department, a relative of Saba Shiber. His name was Sami Shiber. He worked there for three to four years. A very quiet man, ultra religious, he did design several areas. He was more involved in the commercial areas, and he was a happy man but very limited in dialogue. He was not an extrovert. Saba was an extrovert. I mean, he talks. He shuts you up, because he wants to talk. The other one was more British, a quieter man. But he did work with us for two to three years here as a planner.

When I came in 1956, Fouad Abdel Baki had a brother who was an architect and a civil engineer: Sami Abdel Baki. I think Sami was educated in Germany, and Fouad commissioned him for a job to design the municipality. The municipality is one of the oldest institutions in Kuwait. This is the only way that the merchant families could govern or have a say. And so, it was completed while I was away.

But one important thing about the municipality: because of his ties with Germany, they say that it's copied from a building in Munich. I don't know.

RC: *The old Chamber of Commerce, in Area 3, the one that was demolished now?*

CH: They demolished the Chamber of Commerce, or the Kuwait National Petroleum Company (KNPC)?

RC: *The Chamber of Commerce.*

CH: The KNPC is still there?

RC: *Yes. And the KNPC is also from Dar Al-Handassah.*

CH: The architect who designed it was a Palestinian national named Jaafar Tukan

RC: *Jaafar Tukan?*

CH: Yes, he designed the KNPC. And you can see, he was a graduate from AUB – yes! From the mosaic in the window, it is there.

RC: *It is there? In the building? Jafar Tukan also designed the housing development for Riqqa.*

CH: Yes, which one? I would be interested to pursue this with you. On that, is it Sabahiyah you are referring to? You are referring to houses that had roofs.

I am not going to sabotage anybody. The master plan for the village was done by me, and I have my fingerprints on it. They took a quarter of that town to develop it for housing, and we were contacted. That was project number two or number three at Pace.

We were contacted by Adrian Wilson (1898–1988), an architect from Los Angeles, who never heard that spaces could be air conditioned by pumping or generating gas. And Adrian Wilson brought in something new, in that respect. He told me, "Charles" – you know, because we were at Pace – he told me, "Charles, the worst thing about an architect's job is sitting on his ass, waiting for a decision from a client." He was a very nice chap. He didn't do well in Kuwait, but he was doing well with the American military out of Los Angeles. He had a big office on Wilshire Boulevard. Now, coming back to Adrian Wilson, the person who introduced me to him was Charles Chidiac, and he is running for president in Lebanon now.

RC: *Another project that was concluded after you came was the Khaldiya Campus, the old secondary school for girls that was turned into a university.*

CH: Sayyed Karim, the one who built the Thunayan Al-Ghanim, is the same architect. But Egyptians like to call him Sayyed Kurayem. The auditorium, we were afraid that it would fall.

RC: *Yes? Wasn't it the Austrian architect, Rambald Von Steinbüchel-Rheinwall?*

CH: At the time people – having said this just for your information – there was somebody in Kuwait doing pre-stressed post-tension beams. And the first beam was in this movie theatre, where Al-Hamra was. It was fifty metres, I remember.

RC: *This cinema is from 1958?*

CH: That was the first movie theatre. There was another movie house down at Ahmadi called Magwa, and there was Magwa Sharqia. A Greek Egyptian fellow engineer, George Stamatos, invited us all when he was going to pour the beam for the balcony.

RC: *And about Dorsch?*

CH: Dorsch, a German. He did the Qadisiya Master Plan, but he also did the Sabah Hospital.

RC: *He did Sabah Hospital? There are some English fellows listed as the designers of Sabah Hospital. So Dorsch worked on Sabah Hospital, on the main buildings?*

CH: The one main building, the block. I know that, when they came, they were supposed to take the full job there.

RC: *So, can we move on to Pace?*

CH: Yes, we can. However, anything that was built in brick was built by the British. Buildings and ...

RC: *Everything that has the brick facade exposed? Yes, you have all the schools from Tripe & Wakeham.*

CH: All something – yes, the five schools.

RC: *But, did you work on any building by yourself before Pace's foundation, because you mentioned Delta?*

CH: Delta was before Pace. I didn't design anything, no.

RC: *So how did it start?*

CH: Pace? I know how it started, and I'll tell you. But you might find it amazing. Hamid Shuaib and myself were working with the Kuwaiti Municipality. I was Head of Planning Projects. Hamid was not an undersecretary yet, but he was being pushed to be one. And as a Kuwaiti, it was easy to make friends with Hamid, because he was married to a British girl. The third partner was Sabah Al-Rayes. I didn't know him from before.

The 1967 War happened, and it was a defeat for the Arabs, as you are aware. And it was a bad shock, really, for all of us. And, I, my own self, decided that it would be difficult to continue in Kuwait unless I made use of my time in a good way, rather than as a terrorist or whatever. Nobody would have heard about a terrorist then. I spoke to Hamid about it, trying to find a way where he might be able to help, as a government employer, as a Kuwaiti. We discussed it, and we met once or twice in my place. Hamid used to close his eyes. You know Hamid?

RC: *I never met him. I know his son.*

CH: He [Hamid Shuaib] would close his eyes and smoke. He was okay. And he decided. I threw out the name of Mr. Shafi, the chief engineer in the Kuwait Municipality Planning Department. Now, the reason I wanted to bring Shafi in is that he had a very strong reputation in Iraq, and, Kuwait's future, I thought, for infrastructure projects and so on, would be in Iraq. He agreed.

So I told him to go ahead and seek permission from Sheikh Jaber, the ruler. He was on good terms with Hamid. British educated, married to a British woman: everything was perfect. And he went and spoke and was given permission. That was all. Now, we founded the company with minimal capital, with each of us paying 1,700KD. And then, after a few months, Hamid came back and he said, "Charles, we have to have somebody who runs the company during the day." And so he brought in Sabah Al-Rayes.

RC: *So, the company was founded in 1968?*

CH: I even have the papers that I thought – it was the first of May 1968. And, I signed off, and left the company on August 15, 1978.

RC: *The idea of a corporate practice was an ambition from the very beginning, am I correct?*

CH: You are truly correct.

RC: *I also found in our research that many people from Iraq worked for Pace in its early years.*

CH: Yes, the first architect whom we brought in, and his buildings are still standing, was Rifat Chadirji.

RC: *As an associate office?*

CH: Two firms together.

RC: *Iraq Consult with Pace.*

CH: Yes, yes. Rifat Chadirji. You know when you deal with people of different cultures, you have to size them up. Unfortunately, Sabah Al-Rayes didn't sympathise with Rifat Chadirji. And it was complicated with – I forgot the name [Maath Alousi] – an architect from IQC who came here to work with us. The deal was, okay you do the concept design. We'll get the job, then you send an architect to work with us, to develop the working drawings. And that was an excellent formula for success. We would pay for the salaries. We had a say on the final design. If we liked it, we could continue with it. If we didn't like it, we would ask you to change something or whatever.

And this was the relationship that we had with Iraq Consult. Rifat Chadirji was a man who was ready to work in Kuwait, and he was given five sport complexes – the Kuwait Sport Clubs and the Kuwait Sports Centre – before he worked with us. It was a political decision to give him these sports complexes: Shaa'b (Mansouriya), Qadsiya (in Hawally)...

RC: *The projects that were built in 1970 were commissioned to Rifat earlier?*

CH: Yes, yes. But he had the power, as much as they had the intention, to go ahead with them very quickly.

RC: *The MEP's (mechanical, electrical and plumbing projects) were done by Pace, no?*

CH: No, we were not involved in those.

RC: *So they had no local consultant for the stadiums?*

CH: No, there were – as I told you – special commissions from Ahmed Al-Duaij. And I remember Rifat Chadirji coming to the office after being awarded this.

RC: *So, this was when? Do you remember when he was awarded?*

CH: I want to say 1968.

RC: *But 1968 was also the time of the Kuwait Sports Centre competition, with Nervi, Felix Candela, Kenzo Tange, Frei Otto. All these people worked for the Sport City?*

CH: Yes.

RC: *So, your collaboration with Rifat was for the housing complexes in Salmiya and Hawally?*

CH: Yes, yes. One in Salmiya and one in Hawally.

RC: *But there was also the proposal for the Kuwait Society of Engineers building, in Bneid Al-Gar. which was done by Rifat Chadirji. This had no relation with Pace?*

CH: I cannot recall. Don't forget that I went to MIT, after the establishment of Pace. I went in 1969 and stayed until 1971.

RC: *Yes, exactly. Which were critical years for the project. In those years, Pace developed other relations, for example with T Consult.*

CH: Sabah brought T Consult in for the Ahli Bank. They really wanted an operation with us. The Architects' Collaborative (TAC) came in later, and brought several jobs with them, which we were happy to embrace.

RC: *But before going into TAC, let's stay here, because T Consult is a very enigmatic company for me. Even Saba George Shiber writes about them. They did a proposal for an agriculture town. So you don't know of their presence here before Sabah Al-Rayes brought them in to work with you?*

CH: Let me put it this way: I wasn't active enough to know of what they might have been doing here, before. But what I know is that a Swede named Jessie Mangat, who became partner at Gulf Ltd. with Mustafa Al-Sane, Khaled Al-Shaya, and Waleed Al-Nisf, worked with them and they adopted him.

RC: *There are two critical projects that were done by Pace more or less at the same time as the Ahli Bank, which were the cinema in Jahra, and the Kuwaiti Shipping Company in Shuwaikh.*

CH: The shipping was done by Pace, and Hamed was the one that designed it. We didn't have anything to do with the movie theatre. And I don't recall that Jahra Cinema had a number. And I mean the Al-Hassawi projects – which were our friend Mubarak

Al-Hassawi's projects with Mr. Chadirji – were 68001 and 68003, and 68002 was the medical college in Yemen. These are the three projects that I signed off before going to MIT.

RC: *The medical college in Yemen was done by whom?*

CH: By an Iraqi architect. I don't remember his name, but he worked with us. There were two people that we brought in: Akram Al-Ogaily, who was later the co-founder of Archicenter and was a structural engineer at the time, and an architect, who designed the Behbehani building here.

RC: *The tower?*

CH: The tower. He was the last architect. But, by that time, I was out. There was a structural engineer called Sa'qb Yousef, an Iraqi.

RC: *Before you left, there was still the competition for the National Assembly in 1968. Here again, Rifat Chadirji took part in the competition. Was there any reason why Pace was not involved?*

CH: The reason that I would give you, and you have to investigate it further, is that Hamid Shuaib was on the selection committee. I have a card from Utzon bearing his signature.

RC: *In the new souqs, was there any sort of ambition for a larger scale?*

CH: One was the SSH souq that collapsed [Souq Al-Kabeer]. It was designed according to different codes, because it was owned by Khalid Al-Marzouq. He always pretended that he could mix codes together. So he designed it according to the German codes for the columns, but to the British for the beams. They removed the concrete formwork earlier, you know, taking the wood under the slabs before the concrete cured, and this is why it collapsed.

RC: *The other two projects were the Hilton Safir Hotel, which was built with the demolition of the old Hilton, and the construction of …*

CH: Yes, Bneid Al-Gar and the trapezoidal plan. Pace undermined the original design and took the tower. I. M. Pei designed the housing. But there was an architect also, who was with Pace: the Iraqi architect. I cannot remember his name. And they knocked down the other trapezoidal building: the original Hilton. The trapezoidal building was designed by an architect retained by the Hilton, who designed all the hotel chain buildings [J. Ritchie]. Later on, he moved to the Hayat Regency, and he designed the Hayat hotels.

RC: *And the Kuwait Fund?*

CH: Abdulatif Al-Hamad wanted to help TAC. TAC was having financial problems, and he decided to give them this building to design, the lower one. And he even allowed them to copy it from a building in Boston [Boston City Hall 1962–68]. But they lost due to the copying. They even lost money on the copying because they didn't manage it properly. I know this from my dealings with them.

RC: *I wanted to ask you about the Nugra Complex in Hawally.*

CH: The first one, with the long facade? Okay, I take credit for that design because the way to change it to a commercial frontage was to do a calculation, which I submitted to the Municipal Coun-

cil. I didn't use my office at Pace, but I was Head of Planning Projects then. I didn't want buildings to have commercial frontages, and then above them directly residential or office units. This is the only building where a collective number of shops was put in at an elevation equal to the main street, and the construction that was normally on top was moved to the back, separate and with a different entrance.

RC: *This is amazing. I don't know of many other buildings, here, in Kuwait, in which the site's pre-existing condition was well resolved by the new building.*

CH: You can say that Charles Haddad did this.

RC: *You have this very low ceiling at the residential tower entrance that allows a sort of outdoor lounge.*

CH: It was designed like that from the start. The only problem that they [Pace design team] didn't resolve was the air conditioning equipment. That space between the residential units and the shops should have been used as a plaza for the children in the buildings.

The concept of the design was done by TAC, but was not continued by them, and Sabah Al-Rayes took it over. Sheikh Jaber never paid us for it, and this is why he [Sabah Al-Rayes as Pace Managing Partner] was able to move into it as a tenant.

RC: *The Pace office?*

CH: To the offices. And you know, the concept of dividing the shops, separating them from the houses, allowed you to build – as a landlord – shops and to develop the shops before you go into a larger investment.

RC: *So, it was done in two stages? First the shops and then the housing?*

CH: Yes, I would say.

…continues

Charles Haddad: Part Two

Ricardo Camacho conducted this interview in Kuwait, in June 2014.

CH: The map of the north and the south of Jaber Al-Ali was designed by Pace, along with the connecting bridge.

RC: *The bridge was also designed by Pace?*

CH: Yes, yes, it took some time to develop, to convince someone to put in a bridge that was air-conditioned. I don't know how it functions now. It's out of my realm, that area. I never lived in Hawally.

[…]

Do you know the mosque in Salmiya? Like the Fahad Al-Salem mosque? Square minarets?

RC: *Yes, it was designed by Sabah Abi-Hanna.*

CH: Yes, by Sabah Abi-Hanna. But she took Sabah to Jerusalem.

RC: *Who took him?*

CH: Sheikha Badriya. She also took him to Egypt and made him photograph this mosque, and this mosque, and this mosque. And she told him, "I want this minaret, this dome, this..." I don't want to say it looked like a Coptic Church, but the dome, the layout looked like it was. And he made a photo montage of that mosque. Now, opposite that mosque, there's a school.

RC: *Yes.*

CH: Opposite the school – which is now, I think, used by the American University of Kuwait – was a dormitory for female school teachers. But beginning a few years ago, before the invasion, the state stopped educating non-Kuwaiti children in their schools. So there was no need for the teachers, and this is what happened.

RC: *Talking about this area, we continue straight on Salem Al-Mubarak street all the way to Ras Al-Salmiya. On the left there are five to six townhouses that are very well-designed.*

CH: The Al-Bahar family. These are Sabah Abi-Hanna buildings.

RC: *Yes. Behind Lou'lou'a Al-Marzouq, there is a palace with a...*

CH: This was done by Ali Reda. He's Saudi, long established in Kuwait and in Saudi Arabia, and very well off. Regarding the Khaled Al-Marzouq building [Lou'lou'a Al-Marzouq], at that time, Al-Marzouq was riding a wave of popularity among the sheikhs, because Sheikh Jaber came to power and he liked Al-Marzouq a lot. And, as you remember, there is one building in the area that is nine stories high. There were several others later on, but he broke the rules.

RC: *Yesterday, you spoke about Sabah Abi-Hanna. Sabah recalled [in SSH biography] that he wanted to have his own office while he was still living in the house of a friend. Later he opened an office on Fahad Al-Salem street.*

CH: That's right, and the building still exists. Pan-Arab Consulting Engineers (Pace) was under him. We were on the third floor, and he was on the fourth. It is the building next to the Thunayan Al-Ghanim. When you go inside, there's a parking garage. That was his first office, and that was Pace's first office, as well.

RC: *Yesterday, we started talking about these big projects that were contracted to Pace in association with TAC. One of the questions I have concerns materials and construction systems. Was this all brought in by TAC, or was there any input from Pace? Was there a sort of construction material laboratory in Kuwait to test materials, to certify them?*

CH: Yes, there was, and the person was a good British engineer, Ray Jones, who took care of it. But, the problem with the testing lab is that it tested concrete cubes, making boreholes to ensure foundation capacities. As for abrasion tests, for reinforcing bars, they used a somewhat similar test that was not complicated.

But I want to comment that, at an early stage, the government established a company and invested in precast concrete construction. Unfortunately the company didn't participate in a broad range of construction projects in Kuwait, because people thought that precast concrete limited architecture.

RC: *But for the Public Authority of Housing, or even its predecessor the Credit and Savings Bank, this was the right motive.*

CH: Brick was. Everything was built with brick. The Ministry of Housing failed with the Al-Sawaber project, which used precast concrete. So people started to keep away, especially when they knew that they couldn't knock down walls and increase the size of a room.

RC: *At the time, there was a big discussion about transportation systems, and, when the multi-story car parks (the new souqs) were built, there was an assumption that precast concrete would solve the housing demand, increasing the speed of construction, as well as allowing buildings of a larger scale.*

CH: I'll tell you, it was a decision that was not taken at the level of Kuwait's Municipal Planning Authority [inside Municipality], and it was a hard decision to swallow, because we knew that the scale of Kuwait was going to change. But without knowing cars – I mean, I was working in New Haven, and Paul Rudolph was building his garage on Temple Street down to the Oak Street connector – I came and couldn't imagine the car park being placed here. It was too much. Now, as a footnote to this, the garage was demolished this summer.

RC: *But, for example, in this situation, you were at the Municipality, which had some sort of agenda regarding the planning of the city, and, on the other hand, there was Pace. And, of course, these projects and these commissions also radically changed the scale of Pace as an office, right?*

CH: Yes, they had decent projects.

RC: *So how did you yourself stand between those two positions at the time?*

CH: I want to tell you one thing. We won the commission. And I don't think we won it because we had the better design or something else, but because we were Pace. But this is when working with TAC was quality, having these projects allowed us to get more work.

RC: *But did you survey other offices to collaborate for these projects?*

CH: No. I mentioned yesterday that our arrangement with Chadirji was to send somebody to work with us. The same arrangement was in place with TAC.

RC: *But was there any public competition for these car parks (the new souqs)? Any design competition?*

CH: Yes, we didn't win though. We didn't win them all. It's TAC that got them, not us.

RC: *Yes, TAC won them, but TAC was invited to work on those projects?*

CH: Yes.

RC: *Do you remember any others that also worked on the new souqs, other than TAC?*

CH: Not really. But, you know, the ones that collapsed were designed by Sabah Abi-Hanna. There were garages designed by others.

RC: *After the experience of working on these "garages" (the new souqs) with TAC, Pace, as an office, changed.*

CH: There was a strong impact, but it kept a base of staff working on it at the office. I cannot recall the other projects, but I don't think the character of the office was diluted under parking garages.

RC: *But, for example, the capacity to do Khaleejia, Behbehani, Social Security and the Safir Hotel (former Hilton) towers right after the garages...these are big projects. And very complex projects, even beyond architecture in terms of engineering these are very demanding projects.*

CH: Yes, they were, especially in an environment like Kuwait.

RC: *So, these projects were possible because you had gained experience in building the garages, in terms of the know-how of construction systems and materials, in terms of efficiency?*

CH: Yes, we were able to maintain a staff that could be taken out and put on other projects, and this is where we succeeded, I think. Yesterday you started speaking about the management of the office and how the office was coordinated. A lot of that depended on the use of the manpower available to us, and on developing things ahead of time, so that we could have resources and the ability to shift to other things.

RC: *The quality of those projects, together with Nugra (mixed-use complex in Hawally), was exceptional, and something that could have only come from a very mature organisational structure. It was a very strong office to carry out this diversity of work.*

CH: Diversity and the requirement to do them properly.

RC: *So, it seems that there was a kind of momentum around this. Is there anything that you would point to that allowed this to happen?*

CH: A lot that happened started at the bottom level. It might have come from senior staff, but there was a dedicated staff team there, and they were not Palestinian. They were Indians and Iraqis. In fact, I remember one who was Armenian, and one who was Syrian. Are you familiar with Pace's logo?

RC: *Yes.*

CH: It took me so long to do that, because we were four partners. The sign of the cross in the middle which nobody knows. You know it, don't you?

RC: *Yes.*

CH: So even that angle has a significant relationship to the...and there are circles in it that are a neat square and then half and half. And it was designed by a Syrian from Tartus. You know, now, when I hear the news, they are fighting there, I think of him. And he would work extra hours and do extra detailing. Their drafts-

manship – don't forget that we were drafting by rapidograph pens at the time – and it hurt me to throw away the drawings that took such a long time to draw and then just scrub them and tear them down. So, doing something like this was based on a well-steered staff that was focused on quality and good workmanship. And, irrespective of the training the staff had, I should be honest with you that it came from working with both TAC and Chadirji (Iraq Consult). That is how quality work was infused into things.

RC: *Do you think the same could apply to SSH or to KEO?*

CH: I wanted to come to KEO, but KEO had a completely different focus. They didn't care about international work. I cared. I cared because of Dean Ghosn. You've met him?

RC: *You are talking about Raymond Ghosn (1921–76), from Beirut?*

CH: When I decided to do a master's degree, I went to tell him goodbye, because I needed a decent recommendation. I went to tell him goodbye, and he said, "Charles, if you really want to benefit from it, you should stay another year or two and work there." And I did that. I worked for the city for two years, in planning. This is why my inclination was more towards planning than architecture. And there were many, I mean, if we would have taken on T Consult, we wouldn't have benefited as much.

RC: *During the time you were at Yale, was Marcel Breuer there?*

CH: Yes, but he had just left.

RC: *So this idea of infrastructure and a focus on mass construction, seen in the so-called 'brutalism' evident in TAC buildings here, is something that you became familiar with after being at Yale.*

CH: Yes, and I went and met Gropius, when he was still alive.

RC: *And the competition for the Hayat Hotel with William Pereira?*

CH: That I was influential in. And Bruce Graham told me I never...

RC: *Bruce Graham from SOM?*

CH: Yes, from Chicago. I was selected to go and negotiate the SOM agreement with the Hayat Regency for the Hayat Regency Hotel to be built opposite the Sheraton. And the Alshayas were strong enough to kill that project in that location, because it would have affected the Sheraton, how many people would come to the Sheraton, and so on. I went to Chicago for three days and met with Bruce. I met Fazlur Khan at the time. There was another fellow with a hairless head that was a partner, and a younger chap who was very nice too. I negotiated the agreement with them, clause by clause. They were the consultants that Hayat Regency had selected, and the designers for the Hayat family. And then, everything was over. He told me, "Charles, I am interested in buildings, in agreements where buildings are built and do not remain on paper." He was very sad when the project didn't go ahead. You know, they designed the whole thing and the feature was – if you haven't seen it – a catenary roof.

RC: *Yes, but it has the four towers and the slope.*

CH: Yes, but the towers were probably not very prominent. I'll tell you something, now that you have mentioned this. When I go to Sri Lanka, I stay at an SOM hotel designed exactly in the same way. And they used wood and cloths to break the space. The Cinnamon Grand Colombo is its new name now.

It is the same design. But this one was larger, because it was around eighty metres by eighty metres.

RC: *But there was a competition with other entries?*

CH: It wasn't a secret. Well, it was a secret, because there was an Italian guy who was with the Hilton. And the Italian guy went to this chain of hotels. He was from Alexandria, Egypt: a fat fellow who always had a big cigar.

RC: *But, for example, why was it that someone like William Pereira, from Los Angeles, who had finished the Sheraton in Doha, entered a competition for the Hayat Regency here?*

CH: This was in 1972? Well, I wasn't aware of why he didn't participate in the submission earlier, and then it was decided to give it to SOM. I don't know.

RC: *But then, there was the competition for the Joint Banking Centre.*

CH: It was after this one. I wasn't working with SOM, but I was at their office. And I saw the design of the three towers. I mentioned to you that they didn't want to share it with me, because Sabah Al-Rayes had teamed up with SOM, and they knew that I was with TAC.

RC: *But how did this happen if you were both at Pace? In terms of the client, were there two different Pace submissions?*

CH: No, the agreement will not come with the local unless the foreign wants. SOM could have gone to someone else. The client wanted SOM. I was with SOM at that time, for the Hayat competition. They were designing the Joint Banking Centre, and I saw a glimpse of it: three towers that were pyramids. And I didn't know what the difference was between them, because I wasn't permitted to really see it. But the one at TAC, designed by someone with the name Bauer – I can't remember, but he was a senior architect. He didn't show the design to me. So, I wanted TAC, and Sabah Al-Rayes wanted SOM. And it was not a nice thing, because, as an office, there were two international offices vying for us, but we were not sure how to deal with them.

RC: *But did you have a role in the nomination of Paul Rudolph to the jury?*

CH: No, nothing. The answers lie with Hamid Shuaib and Ghazi Sultan.

RC: *And what happened with the Meridian Hotel, where the J.W. Marriott in Salhiya is today?*

CH: This is a long story. The government rents that property to the Salhiya Real Estate Company. And it is rented at two-fils per m2. It is an extension of the cemetery, and, eventually, they brought in an hotelier to change the design or alter it and make it into a hotel. This is why the entrance and the reception area at the hotel are not grandiose.

RC: *But who designed this project?*

CH: An Egyptian [Ahmed Nour, Seif Heikal, and Nabil Saleh from KEG], not Pace.

RC: *Even the Muthanna Complex on the other side of the street? It was also very contested.*

CH: The Muthanna Complex, yes. It was contested because it was given to the Kuwait Finance House. I don't know how they gave them the land and so on. It was an inside deal.

RC: *Was the project done by Pace?*

CH: No, by Kuwait Engineers (KEO).

RC: *So, after this, when you quit Pace, can you tell us a little bit about the experience of running an office on your own?*

CH: The request to leave Pace came as a surprise to me. We had just established an office using my own funds in Cambridge, Massachusetts. And, I didn't have any desire – though, my wife is American – to go and live in the United States. We were happily married here, and had four children by that time. And so, I established the office there, because of the quantity of work that was coming from TAC. And TAC required an office close to its operations in Cambridge, where the services were carried out according to their requirements, rather than do the work in Kuwait. DHL wasn't known at the time, and neither was email. So Sabah himself said that it was best for Charles to go. Hamid couldn't leave his job, and Sabah was the partner in charge, as a Kuwaiti heading the company. So, I went there.

We rented a house in Concord, beside Louis McMillan's house, commuted to Cambridge and hired somebody by the name of Martin Solomon, who was probably seventy-four at the time. He had worked with Metcalf & Eddy, an environmental engineering company based in Massachusetts, which worked extensively in the Middle East. He was a good engineer, and I learned a lot from him. You know, it's funny, you can always continue learning from anybody, if you want to learn. I never took any money from Kuwait. And, in fact, when they told me, "We will buy you out here. You buy us out in the United States." I lost a lot of money by doing that, because, there, the accounts had not yet been recorded. However, I knew that it was serious to have that request come from Sabah. Hamed wasn't 100 percent in agreement with it, and he told me. So I drafted a sales agreement, and part of the sales agreement was that I'd buy the American, Cambridge office, and they would buy me out of Kuwait. They accepted that I would register as a consulting office in Kuwait, because it was a limited liability company, and my name was in the charter. I didn't want to lose that right, as the government wasn't issuing licenses to foreigners anymore. So, I did that. I had the support from certain influential people in the government, but Hamid was a good guy as well. And it was bit of a tough battle to fight against his good will.

So there wasn't any problem there. Eventually we had to go to court, and I took part of the money I wanted. It is very complicated to evaluate a company using percentage of completion accounting. During all of this time, I was readying myself to start the office. I delayed my severance from the office for a year, in which time I collected all the evidence I wanted to build the case. The dispute rested on twenty-seven projects, I think. And, in these twenty-seven projects the percentages were not complete, and I wasn't sure how to do it. However, we did it, and we submitted it. The auditor that Sabah appointed was Bader Al-Bazie from Kuwait Finance House and his own auditing company. He was a respectable and an honest man. I asked around for one million Kuwaiti dinars, and I got just above half a million, allowing me to finance my other office. All the money really went there. I didn't buy a house with the money, but gave it in full to the office. And this is the end result. I remained without a Kuwaiti partner for seven years. From 1978 to 1985: seven years without a Kuwaiti partner. And then someone suggested Khalid [Al-Fouzan], and we met and shared ideas. He was very acceptable and very receptive to the way I ran things. He has changed a lot since, and I think it is positive change, not negative. I don't think we disagree anymore, and his shouting now is a synonym to my shouting in the early days. So, we have changed roles.

RC: *But during the seven years, did you try to implement an international culture in your office, because you started when displaced in the US, but your work was here?*

CH: No, I quickly closed the office in the United States. It took three years to finish the work, and Martin was instructed to close the office. And, you know, bankruptcy proceedings in the United States are not like bankruptcy in Kuwait.

Oh, I want to tell you about a building that I built as Charles Haddad. It was my first building. You know Al-Ghanim, on the airport road, with the vertical sun breakers? It's 100 metres long, the building that I designed. You go to the airport road, and it is on your right: Al-Ghanim, showrooms. I remember that was my first job.

RC: *The airport road? Then, it's the 55?*

CH: Well, do you know where the Arab Organisation is?

RC: *And then you continue, and all the printing presses and the newspapers appear to your right, until the fourth ring road, where you have this national printing press. There is a long building that was also designed at Pace.*

CH: Yes, that was done at Pace, but I was there, and I was instrumental in the detailing. A British architect did it: 100 percent by a British architect that we brought in. He was a dedicated person, along the lines I mentioned to you, and he wasn't even a graduate architect.

Anyway, going back to the building designed by Charles Haddad. I remember taking a pad on a Friday and going and parking in front of it and making alternative sketches as the sun rose. I had to use these sun breakers as columns, because the foundations were already poured and I had to use the foundations. •

Sharing and Building Modernities: Egyptian Architects in Kuwait 1950s–1990s

MANAR MOURSI

The primary goal of this magazine – the first of its kind in Egypt – is to serve the art of architecture [...] by opening a door and setting up a forum for the exchange of honest opinions and ideas [...] With this work alone, we will soon be able to proudly assert that Egyptian architecture is on the right track, with a distinctive voice, built on strong foundations.[1]

Egypt, which was previously considered a regional role model in terms of its architecture, and which contributed so much to the development of neighbouring Arab cities through its architects, lost its canonical position and stature. Instead, the very cities that had looked up to Egypt and its architects have now become the embodiment of what Egyptian architecture should have and could have been during that period of time.[2]

A discourse on the state of Egyptian architecture was never more present than between 1939 and 1959 in the pages of the first Arabic language architectural journal *Al-Emara*, established by Egyptian modernist architect Sayyed Karim. If the magazine was, as Karim described it, "the forum for the exchange of honest opinion and ideas," then the newly formed independent states of the Arab world were the terrain in which these ideas were tested, circulated, and shared. Fifty years after the launch of *Al-Emara*, in the 1989 preface to the book *Twentieth Century Architecture in Egypt*, Karim laments the loss of Egypt's position at the centre of architectural and urban development in the region. Reflecting on those fifty years however, one cannot deny the formative role Egypt played in developing the urban fabric of the cities of the Arab World.

Urban history is often told through the lens of what remains of its built landscape, but the drawing board and the building sites were not the only spaces in which Egyptian architects effectively disseminated their ideas. Magazines, conferences, education and institution building were other avenues through which they etched their presence onto the built environment of the region.

Taking Kuwait as a case in point, this article seeks to shed a light on the often overlooked contribution of Egyptian architects in the city from the 1950s to the 1990s. Though it might be but a minor chapter in the history of Kuwait's modernism, it serves nevertheless, as a counterpoint to the predominant narrative of a singular first-world influence on Kuwait's twentieth century architectural and urban development. This chapter links Egypt and Kuwait in the last fifty years of the twentieth century via two key Egyptian figures of modernist architecture and urbanism, Sayyed Karim and Mahmoud Riad, and the more widely recognised Hassan Fathy, as well as lesser-known practices established by Egyptian architects such as the Arab Consultants, credited with the design of public and private buildings dotted throughout the city.

1. Sayyed Karim, 1939, Opening to the inaugural issue of the first Arabic language architectural journal, *Al-Emara*. Sayyed Karim, "What is Architecture?," *Al-Emara*, n. 1 (1939): 10.

2. Sayyed Karim, 1989, *Egyptian Architecture in the Twentieth Century: Its Past, Its Present, Its Future*. Preface to *Twentieth Century Architecture in Egypt*. Sayyed Karim, "Egyptian Architecture in the Twentieth Century: Its Past, Its Present, Its Future," Preface to *Twentieth Century Architecture in Egypt* (Cairo: Anglo Egyptian Library, 1989).

Disaggregating Kuwait and Egypt's urban and architectural relationship involves unpacking first the layers of Egyptian cultural and political regional influence and assessing its reach in Kuwait. In the political realm, Egypt's fight for independence no doubt had strong reverberations in the region. The Suez Canal crisis nurtured the Kuwaiti desire for independence. During the crisis, support for Nasser was synonymous with strikes and a boycott of French and British products. Looking up to Egypt, Kuwaitis aspired to take full control of their resources. This can be gleaned from a series of entanglements in the immediate aftermath of the Canal crisis, where then British-controlled Kuwait Oil Company (KOC) was repeatedly and publicly attacked in the Kuwaiti press for "stealing" Kuwait's oil and resources. The *Al-Itihad* newspaper, published by the *Kuwait Students in Egypt Association*, demanded the KOC openly reveal the quantities of oil they produced to the public, as well as their costs and sale prices, so that "the Imperialist Company cannot play with the people's destiny and openly steal their resources."[3] A strong wind of empowerment, rebellion and incitement was therefore blowing from Egypt. It is no coincidence that just five years after the Suez crisis, Kuwait was already requesting its official independence from Britain.

Though officially the Kuwaiti position steered away from the Arab nationalist stance, on the street Egypt's president Gamal Abdel Nasser had a strong popular base. An event which illustrates Nasser's popularity was a gala dinner permitted by the Kuwaiti authorities in celebration of the union of Egypt and Syria in 1958. In the lead up to the dinner, crowds gathered on the streets chanting slogans like, "Awake from your sleep."[4] Speeches held in a public square included Kuwaiti Jassim Al-Qatami, who claimed it was time to dissolve the current regime's tribal rule in the growing tides of Arab nationalism. Though his passport was torn to pieces by the authorities afterwards, this event somehow demonstrates the reach and appeal of Arab Nationalist discourse in Kuwait at the time.[5]

On 25 June 1961, immediately following Britain's relinquishing authority in Kuwait, Iraqi president of the time, Abdul Karim Qasim, announced that Kuwait would be incorporated into Iraq. The military threat was seen by Britain and Kuwait as imminent. The subsequent British and Egyptian military interventions on behalf of Kuwait to stave off any attack strengthened the political bond between Egypt and Kuwait.[6]

On the media front, Kuwait's press, newly established by Kuwaitis educated in Egypt, was reported to be "copying articles directly" from Egyptian counterparts.[7] Egypt's public radio station, Voice of the Arabs, was the most popular station of the time.[8]

Cinema, literature, music and theatre were other manifestations of the reach of Egypt's soft power in the region. The first cinematic projection and opera had taken place in Egypt almost a century before any other Arab country, with the celebrations for the opening of the Suez Canal in 1869. In the Cairo of the 1950s, theatre professionals returning from educational missions abroad were already experimenting with new forms such as realism, melodrama, and the absurd. They would later help in establishing theatre companies in other Arab countries. In Kuwait, Egyptian dramatist Zaki Tulaymat formed The Arab Theatre Troupe in 1961, the mission of which would be, in Tulaymat's words, "a revival of Arab glories."[9] Meanwhile, young Egyptian-educated Kuwaiti thespians returned to Kuwait, writing and directing the first plays and activating the theatre space.

3. Reem Alissa, "Building for Oil: Corporate Colonialism, Nationalism and Urban Modernity in Ahmadi, 1946–1992" (PhD diss., University of California, Berkeley, 2012), 81.

4. Miriam Joyce, *Kuwait, 1945–1996: An Anglo-American Perspective* (London: Routledge, 1998), 41.

5. Ibid.

6. Curtis F. Jones, *Divide and Perish: The Geopolitics of the Middle East* (Bloomington: Author House, 2011), 137.

7. James Jankowski, *Nasser's Egypt, Arab Nationalism, and the United Arabic Republic* (Boulder: Lynne Rienner Publishers, 2002), 56.

8. Ibid.

9. Said Sadek, "Cairo as Global/Regional Cultural Capital?," *Cairo Cosmopolitan*, eds. Diane Singerman and Paul Amar (Cairo: The American University in Cairo Press, 2006), 180.

Education and institution building, not just in the realm of theatre, were the primary conduits for the transmission of Egyptian values and ideologies in Kuwait. By the mid-1950s, sensing this threat, the KOC's British managing director advised that, "It was most desirable that more students be educated away from the Egyptian influence."[10] Egyptians however maintained their dominance of the educational bastion with special missions, sending teachers and specialists to form, along with Palestinians, Kuwait's nascent educational system, including the establishment of Kuwait University in 1965, while Kuwaitis were being sent to Egypt to study at Egyptian universities.

In the architectural field, Egypt's university system, though fairly young, was one of the most established in the region. Founded in 1887, the *Muhandiskhana*, or engineering school was built following the models of European-style higher technical schools. Architecture was a branch of this engineering school and was seen as an essential cog in the machine of modernisation.

Already by 1887, Egypt's urban landscapes had undergone a radical transformation. The inauguration of the Suez Canal, and a visit by Khedive Ismail to Paris' Universal Exposition were catalysts for this desire to modernise the cities of Egypt. For the inauguration of the Canal, entertainment was to be provided to the international honorary guests in the form of theatres, gardens, and hotels, which needed to be designed and built. For this task, the Khedive invited European engineers and professionals to "Haussmanise" the city.[11] A vast market for engineering and design professionals thus materialised, attracting flocks of foreign architects.

The urban transformations, which Cairo, Alexandria and the canal cities underwent at the time, spurred a recognition for the need to secure and train local skills. The engineering school was therefore set up in 1887, followed very shortly by the School of Fine Arts in 1909, which also included an architecture department. Young graduates of these universities were sent abroad at the government's expense for further training in prominent European schools in Paris, Liverpool, and Zurich. Others went at their own private expense including, most notably, the father of Egyptian architect Mostafa Fahmy. The University of Liverpool was chosen as a destination due to the British occupation's influence, and because it offered the only academic course on Urban Civic Design at the time. The French Beaux-Arts School was in some ways a natural extension to the prevalent classical architectural and urban styles already existing in Cairo. The Swiss Eidgenössische Technische Hochschule (ETH) on the other hand, with its focus on engineering, science and technology, was considered a zone of openness to innovation and freedom from the classics, as described by Architect Yehia El Zeiny in a 1947 issue of *Al-Emara*.

The first graduates of the missions returned to Cairo in the early 1920s, shortly after the 1919 revolution and independence from the British in 1922. Independence did not necessarily entail full immediate autonomy from British interference. Nevertheless, an impact was felt, whereby, rather than occupying the usual subordinate ranks in the Egyptian civil service, Egyptians where now occupying governmental elite positions, "particularly in technical offices, such as those attached to the Ministry of Public Works, where local officials were soon to replace foreign experts in all upper ranks."[12] This was the case with Mahmoud Sabri Mahboub, who a few years after joining the service, was already heading the Tanzîm Department at the Ministry of Public

10. Alissa, "Building for Oil," 80.

11. Mercedes Volait and Joe Nasr, eds., "Making Cairo Modern (1870–1950): Multiple Models for a 'European-style' urbanism," in *Urbanism – Imported or Exported? Native Aspirations and Foreign Plans* (Chichester: Wiley-Academy, 2003), 21.

12. Mercedes Volait, *Architectes et architectures de l'Egypte moderne (1830–1950): genèse et essor d'une expertise locale* (Paris: Maisonneuve et Larose, 2005), 448–50.

Works. This department had been the central authority in charge of most of Cairo's municipal affairs and civic activities. As director of the Tanzim office, English-trained Mahboub undertook the task of a "comprehensive survey" of the city and proposed a general town plan for Cairo's improvement and extension.[13]

Other graduates followed in Mahboub's footsteps, amongst them, Liverpool-trained Mahmoud Riad, who joined the Ministry of Endowments (Wakf) in 1932. After seven years of service, Riad was appointed as Head of the Architecture and Engineering Department within the Ministry. He held this position until future appointments as Director General of the Popular Housing Division at the Ministry of Social Affairs in 1949 and Director General of Cairo Municipality from 1954–1965.[14]

Riad's approach to town planning can be gleaned from his final thesis project for the diploma course of Town Planning at Liverpool University.[15] Titled, *The City of Cairo: Proposed Development Scheme for the Central Area*, it recommended the rebuilding of the downtown area. "Examining his scheme one might suspect that what Cairo was lacking, in his opinion, was monumentality, as the plan concentrated mainly on this aspect." Riad proposed the opening up of three new large avenues, to be lined with monuments, plazas, and gardens. This grand design approach to town planning, with "axial compositions, perspectives and large parkways," is also evident in Riad's later proposal for Mohandiseen, a new residential neighbourhood for emerging middle class professionals on the West bank of the Nile.[16] In addition to his work in town planning, Riad ran his own private architectural practice with a diverse portfolio, including iconic civic and Modernist buildings in Cairo, like the Arab League headquarters and the recently demolished National Democratic Party building, which was originally intended to house Cairo's municipality.

As the representative of Cairo's municipality, Riad was invited in 1961 to the United Nations' Expert meeting on metropolitan planning held in Stockholm. It was this participation in an international forum that perhaps catapulted the second part of his career as technical advisor to the Ministry of Public Works in Kuwait. Already, Riad was facing political opposition to his proposals and plans in Cairo, the pressure of which eventually culminated in his resignation from his position as director of the municipality in 1965. In that same year, Riad was invited, along with fellow Egyptian architect Omar Azzam and Dutch architect Jacques P. Thijsse, Professor of Comprehensive Planning at the Institute of Social Studies in The Hague, to go to Kuwait to consult on the new development plan for the city. He was also invited to propose a design for the Kuwait Sports Centre in Kaifan.

At the time, the municipality of Kuwait was already acknowledging problems of urban sprawl, low density, lack of infrastructure and an unrealistic land and property market. These problems were to be addressed in a new development plan. However, what was proposed neither dealt with demographics, detailed traffic studies, or with the challenges of the city centre expansion. If anything, "it intensified the problems of low density, urban sprawl, and the extension of roads and services outside the centre," despite the original objectives.[17] Realising this, the government felt a more comprehensive planning effort was required and requested further advice from the United Nations. A committee of three advisors, including Mahmoud Riad, was formed to make recommendations on the management and control of the rapid development. The municipality's invitation letter to Riad

13. Mercedes Volait, "Town Planning Schemes for Cairo Conceived by Egyptian Planners in the 'Liberal Experiment' Period" in *Mass Mediations: New Approaches to Popular Culture in the Middle East and Beyond*, ed. Walter Armbrust (Berkeley: University of California Press, 2000), 87.

14. Ibid., 96.

15. Mahmoud Riad, "The City of Cairo, Proposed Development Scheme for the Central Area" (Diploma Thesis, Liverpool University, Liverpool, 1932).

16. Volait, "Town Planning Schemes for Cairo," 96.

17. Suhair Al-Mosully, "Revitalizing Kuwait's Empty City Center" (Masters thesis, MIT, Cambridge, 1992), 103.

1. Mahmoud Riad (second row, second from the left) in a group photo during his tenure as technical advisor to the Ministry of Public Works.
© Mahmoud Riad Private Archive.

conveys this mood of uncertainty towards a new plan: "Before adoption of the Master-plan in question, we would like to invite your considered opinions on the subject [...]."[18]

The global landscape post WWII was fertile terrain for the growth of new institutions under the umbrella of the United Nations. Within a more utopic and idealistic world view that was thirsty for the maintenance of international peace, these UN bodies were seen as instrumental institutions that would protect, unify, and encourage cooperation, as well as social and economic development. More critically however, a post-developmental perspective argues that the concept of development was constructed as a mechanism to control Third World countries and was merely an extension of the colonial and cultural imperialism project. The most prolific of post-development theorists, Arturo Escobar, a Colombian-American anthropologist, argued in his 1995 book *Encountering Development: The Making and Unmaking of the Third World*, that the "development era" was a product of Harry Truman's foreign policy ideas, rather than true philanthropy. By referring to South America, Africa, and Asia as "underdeveloped" and in need of structural changes to achieve progress, Truman "set in motion a reorganisation of bureaucracy around thinking and acting to systematically change the Third World." Escobar contends that the establishment of the development apparatus functioned to support the consolidation of American hegemony. The UN, with its various bodies, was the vehicle with which western economic structures and ideas on society could spread as universal models for others to emulate.

From this perspective, the UN consultants on modern town planning were sent to underdeveloped countries to help shape their cities, thereby became agents of this apparatus, whether knowingly or unknowingly. Lucia Allais' work on preservation in the modern period and its relationship to international institutions and global practices asserts that the UNESCO "acted as an agent of a type of urban planning that Lewis Mumford would call 'the highway and the city,' by replacing the Beaux-Arts of the immediate postwar with more strictly 'functionalist' ideas, drawing from a modernist palette, including zoning, tunnelling, and parks."[19]

18. Kuwait Municipality Planning Board – Programming and Progress Administration, letter to Mahmoud Riad, March 4, 1965.

19. Lucia Allais, "Will to war, will to art: cultural internationalism and the modernist aesthetics of monuments, 1932–1964" (PhD diss., MIT, Cambridge, 2008), 306.

On the ground, consultants like Riad, who themselves came from underdeveloped and anti-colonial contexts, were certainly unaware of this undertone to their UN missions. In fact, Riad's relationship to the Kuwaitis, which was further developed through his more permanent assignment as a technical advisor to the Ministry of Public Works, was as more of a confidant, big brother and role model from a neighbouring Arab nation, someone who could be trusted to liaise and mediate between the Kuwaitis and the Western influx of architects and professionals operating in their city. By the time Riad entered the scene, Kuwait did not yet have a class of engineers and architects who could negotiate the terms of construction with the foreign consultants brought in to work for them. This is the niche into which Riad inserted himself.

In an interview with Abdul Rahman Makhlouf, an Egyptian town planner who worked in Abu Dhabi in the late 1960s, Makhlouf explains why he came to Abu Dhabi to replace Japanese Katsuhiko Takahashi, "Sheikh Zayed had decided he wanted someone to help him who didn't always need a translator. So when a representative from the United Nations program for technical assistance came through the Gulf, Sheikh Zayed asked him if he could find him an Arab planner."[20] Not only was Riad's extensive portfolio and experience reason enough to recruit him for the position of technical director of the planning board, the idea of a translator and mediator who understood the language, culture, religion and politics of Kuwait must have certainly added to his appeal during the recruitment process.

One of Riad's first assignments in office was the supervision of the design of Kuwait's International Airport Terminal and Kuwait Sports Centre, projects on a scale he knew all too well from his previous experiences in Cairo, where he had just overseen the development of Cairo's International Airport and International Stadium Projects. Riad's role in the technical department can be understood best as somewhere between a client representative, commissioner and curator of the city. Bar the Kuwait Sports Centre, which he designed in 1965, Riad wrote the briefs, managed and oversaw the architects' work, and negotiated the terms with which the projects were to be executed. His role can be deciphered between the lines of the letters and exchanges he had with figures like Kenzo Tange, Reima and Raili Pietilä and VBB and Sune Lindstrom, who discussed with him specific amendments and suggestions to their projects, and in some cases seemed to be pitching services.[21]

Coming from the repressive context of 1960s Cairo, where he was essentially pushed out of office due to interference in his projects by governmental bureaucrats, probably made Riad all the more aware of the significance of the role a mediator could play in shaping the form of the city and its discourse – a role perhaps even more significant than the influential yet stunted one of architects and planners.

Kuwait and Cairo's intimately bound relationship in planning and architecture had already begun almost a decade before Riad's arrival through the architect and urban planner Dr. Sayyed Karim. Karim was the son of Egypt's Minister of Public Works under King Fouad, Ibrahim Karim Pasha, who was friendly with the Kuwaiti Emir, Sheikh Abdallah Al-Salem Al-Sabah. According to Karim, in an interview conducted with him for Kuwaiti magazine, *Al Yaqaza*, the Emir called Karim's father to personally invite his son, who he heard was an engineering expert, to consult on some of the buildings built by the British that were experiencing structural damage. Karim elaborates on

20. Abdulrahman Makhlouf, "Plans the Earth Swallows: An Interview with Abdulrahman Makhlouf," interview Todd Reisz, *Portal 9*, n. 2 (2013).

21. I was able to access the family archive of letters and correspondences thanks to Mahmoud Riad Jr. who has also published these letters online on the family website: http://www.riadarchitecture.com/

how upon arriving in Kuwait, he examined the cracks in the concrete and conducted some experiments on the affected buildings. Upon further research, the source of the problem was identified to be a flaw in the elements of the cement mix used by the British. Impressed by Karim's discovery, the Emir decided to commission a series of building projects to him.

It is not clear whether it was through his work with the UN as a planning consultant on the neighbouring cities of Baghdad (1946), Jeddah (1949), Riyadh (1950), Mecca and Medina (1952), or whether it was through the circulation of his magazine and discourse in the conferences for Arab Engineers, which he organised, that Karim originally became known to the Emir. As a prolific visionary, Karim had studied Cairo and published proposed plans for its expansion that were never implemented. It was these plans and studies that gave him recognition with the UN. Consultants invited from the UN to Cairo's municipality researched the city and encountered Karim's body of work. Impressed with his comprehensive survey of the city and proposals for its development, they invited him to join the UN as a city-planning consultant, a position he held from 1949 onwards, opening up new opportunities and allowing him to transition from local projects in Egypt to planning cities and building extensively throughout the region.[22]

Karim's ideas were also circulated through the magazine he established and the conferences he organised. With the increasing number of engineering graduates, a society for Egyptian architects was established in 1919. This was followed by a larger syndicate for engineers in 1946. Both sought to enhance the exposure of the fields of engineering and architecture and to set rules and legislation to govern how the profession was practiced. Meanwhile, conferences for Arab engineering and the magazine, *Al-Emara*, which was conceived by Karim, further propelled the professionalisation of architecture in the region.

The first Arab engineering conference was held in Alexandria from March 15–19, 1945, exactly three days before the Arab League was officially formed in Cairo on March 22. Though the alignment of these dates was probably coincidental, it is still telling of a momentum that was building in the Arab world towards nationalism and unity, and illustrates a desire for regional integration and development to more easily confront imperialistic initiatives in the region. In the opening speech for the session, engineer Sayyed Mortada beckons in "a new era in the history of engineering in Egypt and the East, for it is the first time engineers from this region gather to exchange opinions on issues of concern to the general public [...] The reality is that we now, more than ever, are in dire need of a dialogue on different aspects of our practice. We need, together, to work on developing our civic resources, as well as increasing the standard of life for all citizens."[23]

The conference was a platform for Arab engineers to share experiences, forge collaborations and enhance their networks. Housing, water and transportation were running themes discussed and presented at these conferences, with a focus on planning projects at the national level. After the opening remarks at the Alexandria conference, Karim took to the stage to present to the audience what he coined as a project for "Fouad's Cairo" – a plan to follow Khedive Ismail's plan for Cairo in ambition.[24] He also outlined other proposals he had been working on, which were then presented throughout the conference by his colleagues and collaborators. These included plans to ameliorate the standards of education through civic architecture, housing in poor neighbourhoods, healthcare, tourism and historic

22. Hisham Zaki Mahmoud, *"Al-Abqari Alathi La Ya'rifuhu Ahad (The Genius That Nobody Knows: Engineer Sayyed Karim),"* Shams Al-Hayat, n. 126 (2009).

23. Sayyed Mortada, "The First Engineering Conference," *Al-Emara*, n. 2–3 (1945): 7.

24. Sayyed Karim, "The Engineering Conference and the post-War Projects," *Al-Emara*, n. 2–3 (1945): 10.

preservation. Other than presenting visionary plans and policy proposals, Karim and his collaborator Tawfik Abdel Gawad, also advanced the main tenants of their manifesto on Modern Architecture, a discourse they had recurrently introduced to their readers via the pages of *Al Emara* magazine. The Kuwaitis' first attendance at these conferences was in 1960.

Like the conferences, *Al-Emara* was an even earlier attempt to establish a space for discussion on current architectural projects and trends, as well as urban policies and planning. According to Karim, who tells the story of his magazine in its tenth year anniversary issue, the publication was established after much prodding from architectural colleagues, who he met at international Modernist Architecture conferences, as well as his mentor and professor Salvizberg, who promised to attend the magazine launch from Zurich. Indeed, fulfilling his promise, professor Salvizberg bought a ticket to Cairo in 1939 to celebrate the first issue of the magazine. In Karim's account of the founding of the magazine, he likens not having an architectural magazine while having an active space of architectural production, to a country that knows how to read and write but has no printing press.[25]

Karim's magazine developed and contextualised the modernist ideology he had absorbed throughout his time in Switzerland. It also served to circulate and disseminate his projects to a wider public, in an attempt to educate potential clients and collaborators on his practice. The opening salvo to his magazine's sixth issue in 1940 posed the question: could national identity be expressed in built form? The history of pre-revolutionary Egypt, which pre-dated the magazine, established the debates between several factions of society on what exactly constituted Egyptian national identity. As Egyptians struggled to free themselves from British occupation, Pharaonism, derived from Egypt's ancient past, homogenous ethnicity and territory, gained currency as notions of identity. Other opposing visions emerged post-independence, including secular liberalism, Arab nationalism, as well as reform and traditional Islamism.

In architecture, these contending visions often manifested themselves in one building, which could include a Pharaonic scale with Islamic detailing, for example. The Beaux-Arts-educated classicists embraced the ideas of Pharaonism or Islamic expression in their work, most notably Hassan Fathy and Mostafa Fahmy. Meanwhile, Swiss educated Karim, aware of these contrasting visions, articulated a clear orientation towards an international modernist voice in architecture in his first issue of *Al-Emara*, which juxtaposed itself with a secular modernist perspective of Egyptian identity:

> Architecture is no longer an ornamented beautiful object [...] nor an external outfit [...] nor a borrowed dress which distinguishes its owner from the rest based on class and privilege [...] The modern car has replaced the jewel studded carriage, supported on arms and shoulders [...] Architecture is no longer a canvas with strict symmetries and proportions [...] Architecture has begun to be liberated from the past and is headed with all its prowess towards science and innovation, supported in its development by research, industrial production, and intellectual effort [...] Architecture has started to move towards the spirit of the time, with an articulation of the social and economic requirements and needs of its occupants [...] it is just like any modern machine in its adaptability to function and the service of humanity [...] Architecture is starting to develop a common language across borders and is moving towards an international style as nations become inextricably linked on a global scale [...] It is our role as architects to move towards this modern future built on science. We need to join the world stage in developing and applying research adapted to our climate and social

25. Sayyed Karim, "1939–1949," *Al-Emara*, n. 1–2 (1949): 6.

2. Cover of the first issue of *Al-Emara* magazine, Cairo, 1939.
© AUC Rare Books Library.

conditions. The concept of holding on to old traditions is wrong, and so is advocating for the maintenance of old styles because they are part of our national identity […] Maintaining tradition is regressive; had our forefathers maintained tradition, we would still be living in caves […] Architecture is an art, its beauty measured by its honesty and functionality […] it is built on industry and science with modern materials to accommodate modern comfort and lifestyles.[26]

With these words, Karim articulated his radically modernist dictum, which he elaborated on further in future issues of the magazine by his partner and collaborator Tawfik Abd Al-Gawad. Abd Al-Gawad's presentation in the 1950 fourth edition of the Arab Conference of Engineers, published in *Al-Emara*, outlined the contours of three conflicting positions that were then already prevalent in architecture. These positions can be summarised as being oriented towards holding on to past traditions in architecture, be they Pharaonic, Islamic or Arab, a second position which attempts to amalgamate traditional forms with modernism, and a third archetype – the school that embodied Abd Al-Gawad and Karim's forward-thinking visions of modernist architecture, materiality and language. Abd Al-Gawad conveys his message clearly regarding what was then already emerging as a major alternative discourse:

> They speak today of a revival of old traditions and we are in the age of the machine. They support their claims by saying that the religion of our nation is Islam so our Arab buildings must be a symbol of Islam. They do not realise that Islam is not restricted to Egypt only or to the Arab East, but is an international, not national religion. As Islam is the *Sharia* of each age and time, a *Sharia* free of stagnation, free of restriction and complication, free of imitation, so must our buildings be honest and correct in their articulation of their meaning and significance, representing the modern times in which they were built. This makes me want to pose a further question: Does Islam have a particular dress-code to which it is restricted? The answer is no. Because we took off those old outfits. So have modern buildings, they have rid themselves of the old materiality in favor of new materials and construction methods as well as new industrial programs […] There is a revolution in all of the arts today including architecture. Surely we feel some sadness and pain leaving behind all that is old, but we have embraced the future with some courage, confidence and faith.[27]

Karim's gravitas and conviction towards international modernist discourse is evident in his built works. No hints of Islamic architecture can be seen in his aesthetics, bar the distant relative of the mashrabiya – the *brise-soleil* – though Karim did not even acknowledge the genotype of this sun-screen and its distant Islamic relative. In Kuwait, in addition to being commissioned to design two palaces for Sheikh Abdallah Al-Salem and Abdallah Al-Mubarak, Karim was also given the task of designing three schools – Al-Mubarakiya, as well as a middle school for boys and a mixed primary school. It is no surprise that Karim, an Egyptian, was assigned the task of designing some of the earliest schools to be built in Kuwait after those designed by Tripe and Wakeham. As key contributors to the development of the educational system, it follows that the Emir would entrust this task to an Egyptian architect. The Al-Mubarkiya School was the first to be built in Kuwait in 1911. It was housed in a traditional building on a much smaller scale until Karim was asked to design its expansion in 1957.

By this time, Egypt had already been using reinforced concrete in construction. The first use of concrete in Cairo can be traced back to as early as 1863, when it was introduced by French contractor Nicola Marciani. Francois Coignet, who is considered among the first pioneers to pour

26. Sayyed Karim, "What Is Architecture?" *Al-Emara*, n. 1 (1939): 10–11.

27. Tawfiq Abd Al-Gawad, "Architecture in the East: Between Appearance and Essence," *Al-Emara*, n. 6–7 (1950): 67–68.

reinforced concrete in the world, was responsible for the construction of the buildings for the Suez Canal Company in 1892–95, in Port-Tawfik and Port-Said.[28] In 1951, foam concrete – an experimental porous cement material, invented in 1944 by French engineer Rene Fays – was also used in construction in Cairo.[29]

Local cement industries and contractors were already producing cement in Cairo and perhaps Karim brought these contractors with him to Kuwait. The advertisements in his magazine were mainly those providing complementary amenities for a modern living experience – such as air conditioners and electronic appliances – as well as contractors seeking collaboration with architects, and those providing construction materials and services. One of the advertisers that appeared repeatedly from the earliest issues onwards, stands out as the potential partner in the Kuwait projects – the Misr Concrete Development Company. In addition to setting up his own office in Kuwait and attracting the first set of Egyptian architects to the scene, Karim can also be credited for bringing in Egyptian contractors. Tawfik Abdel Gawad, in his seminal book on Egypt's twentieth century architecture, reinforces this position: "Al-Emara magazine opened its doors to architects, engineering firms and construction companies to extend their practices to the Arab World and to replace foreign companies. It paved the way for large contractors to set up offices outside of Egypt."[30] Other potential contractor partners in Kuwait could be Osman Ahmed Osman, founder of the colossal Arab Contractors, who, according to Karim's son, worked in Karim's office and was introduced to both the Saudis and Kuwaitis through Karim and was thus able to start his contracting practice through projects in Kuwait and the Gulf.

Karim's buildings relied on concrete almost exclusively. His architecture was functional, materialist and industrialist. In the pages of his magazine, he advocated the use of concrete and experimentation with it. In Kuwait, Karim introduced the brise-soleil through both the Al-Mubarkiya school and the Al-Andalus cinema projects, built roughly at the same time – around 1957. From the 1930s to the 1950s, before the widespread use of mechanical HVAC systems, the brise-soleil functioned as a mediator between the building and the external climate, shading openings, and avoiding heat loads and reflection caused by glazed surfaces. The brise-soleil were designed to be attractive from the street, while from the inside, their effect was to create a sense of enclosure and peace by establishing a distance between the exterior and the interior. There was no longer just a thin layer of glass between outside and inside; instead, a thickness was provided by the brise-soleil's fixed concrete slats and sun protection grids.

To maximise natural lighting and increase cross ventilation in the classrooms, a long and narrow plan was implemented by Karim for Al-Mubarakiya. The building was slightly curved, in recognition that the main mode of transport to the school was by automobile. The entire building plan followed this slightly curved form, to allow an easier and safer drop-off zone.

Karim's design for Al-Mubarakiya appears to be in conversation with the work of Brazilian modernists Lúcio Costa and Oscar Niemeyer, and gives a nod to Le Corbusier's later work, namely the Ministry of Education in Rio De Janeiro (1936–1943), the Unité d'Habitation at Marseilles (1947–1952), as well as the Secretariat in Chandigarh (1953–1959). Five years before Al-Mubarakiya's commission, Karim's 1952 issue of Al-Emara was devoted entirely to highlighting Brazilian modernist projects. A 1953 issue of the

3. An advertisement for an Egyptian contractor in Al-Emara, n. 5, Cairo, 1945. © Al-Emara.

28. Alaa Elwi El-Habashi, "The Building of Auguste Perret in Alexandria: A Case for Preservation of Modern Egyptian Architecture: Historic Preservation" (Masters Thesis, University of Pennsylvania, Philadelphia, 1994), 10.

29. Mercedes Volait, "Egypt (1914–1954): Global Architecture before Globalization," in Architecture from the Arab World (1914–2014): a Selection, ed. George Arbid (Manama: Ministry of Culture, 2014).

30. Tawfiq Abd Al-Gawad, Misr Al-'Imara Fil-Qarn Al-'Ishrin (Egyptian Architecture in the Twentieth Century) (Cairo: Anglo-Egyptian Bookshop, 1989), 23.

magazine also featured Le Corbusier's *Unité d'Habitation* housing project in Marseille, the first project Le Corbusier built after WWII. Aesthetically, the *Unité* marked a radical break in Le Corbusier's architectural style: the abstract plane, the smooth surfaces and the slender columns of his purist style were abandoned in favor of brutalist, muscular and sculptural forms.

Le Corbusier, in collaboration with Costa, Niemeyer and a team of Brazilian architects, had already experimented and built the first brise-soleil wall in the Ministry of Education in Rio. Le Corbusier continued these experiments with the facades of the *Unité*, and in Chandigarh. Searching for universal solutions to warmer climes, a structural system that he called "respiration exacte," was intended to produce "one single building for all nations and climates." Le Corbusier's inspiration for the brise-soleil system came from his study of North African and Arab vernacular architecture. Though the first built manifestation of it was in Brazil, in 1933, he had already developed the concept for the unbuilt design of the Durand in Algiers.[31] He had seen that screens could be arranged "to provide a 'valve' capable of allowing sunlight to enter in the winter, while providing shade in the summer.[32] The brise-soleil system was based on the wooden screen *mashrabiya* of Arab buildings, and the brick louvered claustra, seen in Morocco and Iran. Le Corbusier was attracted to the effectiveness of these vernacular devices to provide shading, reduce glare and facilitate natural ventilation. Thus, he sought to interpret these shading systems using modern materials with equivalent functions.

Meanwhile, in Alexandria, Auguste Perret was also developing a pre-cast brise-soleil system, which he introduced to the upper parts of the windows of a villa he designed in 1922 and another building he designed in 1938 – but he would have probably dismissed the practice of making entire walls of plate glass and then masking the whole facade with a screen of permanent concrete ribs as irrational and contradictory, which Le Corbusier is more frequently credited for.[33] Surely Karim, in addition to following the work of Le Corbusier and the Brazilians, was also exposed to the home-grown example and precedent of Perret's work in Alexandria.

For Al-Andalus cinema, Karim used an entirely different system of brise-soleil than the one he designed for Al-Mubarkiya school. This time, there was no egg-crate system with depth and thickness, but instead an amorphous outer covering to the main facade which created harmony for the street viewer through its patterned effect. This can possibly be explained by the fact that, unlike the school, the cinema required less sunlight and less shading. On getting the cinema commissions, Karim revealed in an interview with *Al-Yaqatha* that each night after dining with the Emir, they would watch a movie projection in the palace's cinema hall. One night, Karim told the Emir, "The people of Kuwait have complained to me that in order for them to go to the cinema, they have to travel to Egypt or Lebanon. They are asking why they can't have their own theatres where they can watch movie and theatre productions in the capital, which is destined to be a global capital."

According to Karim, it was from this point on that the Emir commissioned him with the construction of four cinemas, which he worked on between 1957 and 1965. Al-Sharqiya cinema had already been open since 1954, but it was just an open space with a projector, nothing like the fully programmed cinemas of Karim, which often included outdoor and indoor halls, and other semi-public spaces, such as cafeterias and shops on their ground floors.

31. Mohsen Mostafavi and David Leatherbarrow, *On Weathering: The Life of Buildings in Time* (Cambridge: MIT Press, 1993), 93.

32. Mohammad Arif Kamal, "Le Corbusier's Solar Shading Strategy for Tropical Environment: A Sustainable Approach," *Journal of Architectural/Planning Research and Studies*, v. 10, n. 1 (2013): 20.

33. Peter Collins, *Concrete: The Visions of a New Architecture* (Montreal: McGill University Press, 2004), 218.

4. Al-Andalus Cinema in Hawally,
Sayyed Karim, 1974.
© AUC Rare Books Library.

Coming from Egypt, Karim was aware of the powerful role a cinema could have in spreading lifestyles and ideas, but also in broadcasting his portfolio to the public. As Ifdal Elsaket points out in her thesis, *Projecting Modernism*, by the late 1930s, the cinema had become one of the most significant and ubiquitous cultural institutions in Egypt.[34] It was the urban space par excellence located in bustling settings, particularly downtown Cairo, surrounded by department stores, casinos and cafes. The Cinema signified a space of sociability and modernity, but was also a space where social and political tensions were played out. Other than its influence through the cinematic production that was projected on its screens, the cinema was also an active space of protest and politics. "Scattered through the British Foreign Office records are references to the use of cinemas as venues for worker and student union meetings during the interwar period."[35]

In a way, Karim must have wanted to reinvent this space of vitality in the more tabula rasa setting of Kuwait. He intended to achieve this through the mixing of programs – shopping, casinos, cafés, theatres, and cinemas in one complex. Further, Karim's Swiss education probably exposed him to the work of Swiss architectural theorist Sigfried Gideon. In 1943, Gideon coauthored a manifesto titled, *Nine Points on Monumentality*, and an essay on "The Need for a New Monumentality," which called for the construction of civic centres "symbolising the idea of 'community', in which all the visual arts would collaborate."[36] Elizabeth Mock, a curator at the Museum of Modern Art in New York, wrote about these ideas of new monumentality in 1944: "There must be occasional buildings which raise the everyday casualness of living to

34. Ifdal Elsaket, "Projecting Egypt: The Cinema and the Making of Colonial Modernity" (PhD diss., University of Sydney, Sydney, 2014), 91.

35. Ibid., 87.

36. Alan Colquhoun, *Modern Architecture* (Oxford: Oxford University Press, 2002), 213.

a higher and more ceremonial plane, buildings which give dignified and coherent form to that interdependence of the individual and the social group[...]"[37] Karim's subscription to this school of thought is evident not only in his cinemas, which acted as monumental institutions for communities of people in Kuwait, but also in Egypt, where he initiated projects for civic centres in peripheral cities such as Mansoura, Assiut, and Aswan.

5. Egyptian pavilion at New York World Fair, Mostafa Fahmy,1939. © *Al-Emara*.

The monumental scale Karim introduced through the cinemas he designed in Kuwait, can also be traced back to the Neo-Pharaonic architectural expression in Cairo decades before Karim's arrival in Kuwait. The apotheosis of this scale was evident in the design of the Egyptian Pavilion at the 1939 New York World Fair, published in the third issue of *Al-Emara*, with a description of the pavilion by the architect himself, Mostafa Fahmy, who was one of the first graduates from the Ecole des Beaux-Arts in Paris. The classicism the school reinforced in him is evident in his oeuvre. Fahmy was concerned with Pharaonic revival, and he combined the monumentality of Pharaonic architecture with elements from Art Deco and Islamic Architecture, using modern materials. This is also evident in his design of the mausoleum for Saad Zaghloul in Mounira.[38] Since Fahmy taught Karim at Cairo University, he must have been familiar with his professor's theories and work.

Finally, the monumentality in Karim's design could also be attributed to the monolithic capacities that concrete afforded him, where architecture

37. Ibid.

38. Al-Gawad, *Egyptian Architecture in the Twentieth Century*, 418.

was no longer a sum of 'parts.' For Cinema Al-Hamra, Karim was able to use a pre-stressed concrete beam for the first time, designed by Greek structural engineer George Stamatos, enabling large spans.[39]

Aside from the monumental language of Karim's cinemas, his architectural vocabulary repeatedly revealed a layered treatment of intersecting volumes, which composed the entirety of his built programs. He also highlighted the modern machine-age through monumental car drop-off spaces and entrance vestibules. The buildings were often lifted off the ground on pilotis, and interior courtyards were carved to split the spaces between winter outdoor theatres and summer indoor theatres, as with Al-Firdous Cinema.

Karim's Modernist ethos of transparency and honesty were evident in the form of the cinema hall of Al-Ahmadi Cinema, which followed the sectional diagonal of the theatre's seating. His design for Al-Andalus cinema mimicked the form of a giant TV screen, whether intentionally or not, with the brise-soleil's facade simulating the pixilation of a screen. Though Karim expressed his concern for environmental issues in his work, through his measured use of openings in the facades, his designs were often not context specific. The design of Al-Ahmadi Cinema's was an exact replica of a civic centre designed by Karim in Mansoura, Egypt.

Unlike other foreign architects, who later flooded the scene in Kuwait, Karim's work displayed an enthusiasm and zest. Uninhibited by requirements to justify 'Islamic' or 'Arab' architecture or to orientalise himself, Karim's work was emblematic of a generation of daring and experimental Egyptian architects. The cinemas and Al-Mubarkiya School were the most iconic of Karim's buildings in Kuwait. He also designed the Emir's private residences, the printing press, military hospital, and two other schools.

It is not known why Karim stopped practicing in Kuwait after 1965. In an interview with his son, Ibrahim Karim, I was informed that, due to conflicts with the Nasserist regime over the planning of Nasr City, Karim was placed under house arrest, with all of his assets frozen. It is perhaps this political handicap that hindered his movements. Other reasons could be that Karim's modernist, industrialist aesthetics did not fit with the zeitgeist of Kuwait in the late 1960s, early 1970s, where winds from the past had strongly established an atmosphere of nostalgia. This mood is evident in an article published in *Sawt Al-Khaleej* in 1965, titled, "The Kuwaiti Family: Living between Two Worlds."[40] The article lamented Kuwait's then-current state of indiscriminate modern adaptation, without taking into account traditional family values. Karim's architecture, with its programmatic implications and brutally modernist style embodied this heavily criticised new modern-era of cinema-going, educated Kuwaitis.

The search for an architectural language which could express this longing for the past was a propitious setting for the work of Hassan Fathy to appear in Kuwait. In his discourse, Fathy too had agonised intensely about the region's "rapid cultural transformations, a product of decolonisation," and "the accompanying agendas of modernity and nation-building." In the 1945 issue of *Al-Emara*, Fathy's scathing critique of adapting Western models of architecture called for "connecting to what we have disconnected from – our rich heritage and past [...] we've reached a point where we've been eating the leftovers from others' tables."[41] The leftovers and the "other" are clearly a reference to the colonisers. Fathy's presentation on "Planning and Building the Arab Tradition" in the 1960 conference of "The Metropolis in the Arab

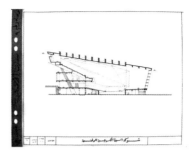

6. Section drawing of Ahmadi Cinema, Sayyed Karim, 1962.
© Kuwait National Cinema Company.

39. This was mentioned in an interview with Charles T. Haddad, the transcript of which is included in this volume.

40. Asseel Al-Ragam, "Critical Nostalgia: Kuwait Urban Modernity and Alison and Peter Smithson's Kuwait Urban Study and Mat-Building," *The Journal of Architecture*, v. 20, n. 1 (2015): 37.

41. Hassan Fathy, "Some of the Problems Confronting the Egyptian Architect." Op cit.

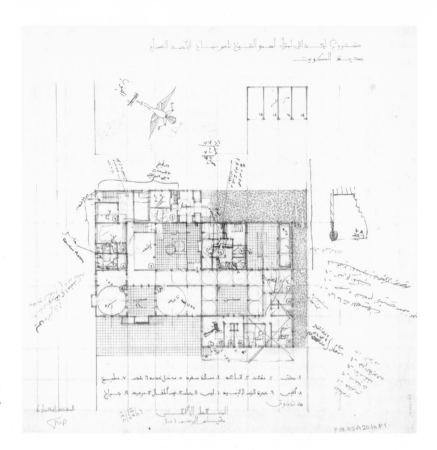

7. Working drawing of the Residence of Sheikh Nasser Al-Sabah, Hassan Fathy, Mahboula, 1978–84.
© AUC Rare Books Library.

World" went further in elaborating his discourse. The presentation focused on his experiment in building a village in New Gourna in Upper Egypt. The first section was aptly titled, "The Failure of the 'Modern'." He discussed the benefits of using traditional materials, mourned the decline of craftsmanship, and called for the re-establishment of what he described as the "trinity: architect, craftsman and client."[42] In Fathy's opinion, the Arab tradition is particular and significant, with consistent elements like the courtyard and the dome. Though existing in other Mediterranean settings, these elements, for Fathy, took on additional ethereal meanings: "To the Arab, the courtyard is more than a space that controls temperature [...] it is more than an architectural device for privacy and protection. It is, like the dome, part of a microcosm that parallels the order of the Universe itself."[43]

Educated in the Beaux-Arts, Fathy graduated at around the same time as Karim, but unlike Karim, subscribed to a school of traditional revivalism. Commissioned by the Egyptian Department of Antiquities in 1945, his most momentous project in Egypt, New Gourna was built with the goal of relocating a community of Nubians that were to be displaced after the building of the Aswan High Dam. The village was built using traditional materials and designs, including domes and courtyards. Political and financial complications, as well as residents' opposition to relocation, prevented the project from ever being completed. The domes that Fathy employed in the housing for the villagers, were perceived as a symbol of death, used traditionally only in mausoleums. As for the courtyard, it was considered a form exported from Cairene houses, rather than adapted from

42. Hassan Fatthy, "Some of the Problems Confronting the Egyptian Architect." Op cit.

43. Hassan Fathy, "Some of the Problems Confronting the Egyptian Architect," *Al-Emara*, n. 5–4 (1945): 57.

an existing local language which the villagers related to. Fathy was accused of developing an architecture that was based primarily on an imagined history and an invented tradition. In the end, New Gourna was also as Ijlal Muzaffar put it, "a project where community and tradition were invoked to displace rural populations from tourism sites and carry out the modernising agenda of an oppressive state apparatus and its international sponsors."[44]

Despite the failure of Fathy's work in Gourna, he succeeded in propagating his discourse through the publication of a seminal text in English on his experience there, published in 1973 and titled, *Architecture for the Poor*. This book allowed Fathy's work to be appreciated by international audiences, and he began to serve in 1976 on the steering committee for the nascent Aga Khan Award for Architecture and was awarded local and international prizes for his work. It was through this moment of international acclaim that he was eventually invited to Kuwait in 1978 to work on a private residence for Sheikh Nasser Sabah Al-Ahmad Al-Sabah.

Fathy's loyalty to Beaux-Arts symmetry can be seen in his first floor plan for the house, while his insistence on local materials, domes and courtyards were ingrained in the house as his signature aesthetic stamp. Beyond this project, the paucity of Fathy's built work in Kuwait is not at all a proportional reflection of his influence both in Kuwait and in the region. In a way, Fathy's work, both built and published, was where new parameters were negotiated for a forthcoming generation of post-modernist architects that included his students, who continued to practice in Kuwait, such as Soheir Farid and Rami Al-Dahan.

The Kuwait of the 1980s was a veritable crucible of architectural styles. The city had experienced a radical shift, with architects of international renown claiming it as their playground for experimentation. These included: Kenzo Tange, The Architects Collaborative (TAC), Arne Jacobson, Arthur Erickson, Mohamed Makiya, Reima and Raili Pietilla, and Skidmore Owings and Merrill (SOM), among many others. The political landscape of the Arab world changed dramatically from the mid-1960s to the early 1980s. The defeat of Arab armies during the Six-Day War in 1967 by Israeli troops constituted a pivotal moment in the Arab world. This loss, along with economic stagnation in the defeated countries, was blamed on the secular Arab nationalism of the ruling regimes. A steady decline in the popularity and credibility of secular, socialist and nationalist politics ensued. Islamist movements gained ground and flourished as an alternative to fill the identity vacuum. The Islamist ideology can also be read within a broader religiously-oriented nationalism that emerged in the Third World in the 1970s. Gulf countries were also gaining more agency in the region, through their economic power and rising oil prices. The remittances from Egyptians working in the Gulf signaled the start of a new era, in which, rather than exporting their modernism in a uni-directional trajectory, Egyptians were now on the recipient end of Gulf ideology and influence, which included a focus on Islamic and traditional themes. This socio-economic and ideological shift in the region had architectural ramifications, with growing popularity for an 'Islamic' language, albeit in modernist form and construction materials.

This identity turn in architecture can also be attributed to the work of some of the foreign architects practicing in the region. To justify their work, even the most radically modernist, infused their discourse with references to the context, if even invented and imagined. Their architecture included references to an Islamic heritage and was often decorated and dressed with

44. Ijlal Muzaffar, "The World on Sale: Architectural Exports and Construction of Access," in *Office US: Agenda*, eds., Eva Franch i Gilbert, Amanda Reeser Lawrence, Ana Milijacki and Ashley Schafer (Zurich: Lars Muller Publishers, 2014), 231.

'Islamic' and 'Arab' attire. This trend is most evident in the design of the Kuwait National Assembly Building in the early 1970s by Danish architect Jørn Utzon. His plan featured a colonnade of thin piers that support a draped concrete roof over an open plaza. Utzon claimed that "the cloth-like sensation of the roof references the iconic tent construction of the Arabian Bedouin people."[45] Appropriating a local vernacular typology, Utzon drew inspiration from Arabian bazaars in his layout of the government working spaces, which were clustered around central courtyards. "Selectively abstracting and modernising certain historical motifs, such as arcades of pointed arches, he superimposed a 'local' language onto a modern set of forms."[46] Arab ornamentation is abstracted and applied throughout the building in an attempt to appeal to a "somewhat fantasised Kuwaiti culture."[47]

Debates on what constituted 'Islamic' or 'Arab' architecture in the region began to emerge in new architectural journals published in the Gulf and in Egypt, as well as in conferences focused on the built environment. Some went as far as to illustrate how Sharia could be translated in an urban setting.[48] These debates resonated with the international discourse on architectural postmodernism, which called for contextualisation and appropriation of historical themes and ornamentation. Postmodernism was somehow the future's idea about the past.

It is in this context that the Arab Consultants office was established by Egyptian architect Said Abdel Moneim in 1969, just as international offices were starting to compete for terrain. Over the course of more than thirty years, the office built a robust portfolio of over fifty projects in Kuwait. Initially the Arab Consultants' practice relied on residential projects, mainly single family homes. Their design of the KFTCIC Residential Building in Salmiya in 1972 was a transition from the private realm to larger scale projects.

The influence of TAC and Pace's iconic Kuwait Fund building can be seen in many of Arab Consultants projects, including the KFTCIC Residential Building, the Carlton Hotel in the early 1970s, the Kuwait Finance House in the 1980s and Al-Hajri Building in the 1990s. The extrusion of the TAC *parti*[49] – of an overhanging roof held by piers or columns to a tower form, allowing for shading, is a scheme that Arab Consultants regularly experimented with. Other consistent features of their work are a tripartite composition for the facades, which can be traced back to a Fatimid tradition in Cairo, as well as an emphasis on symmetry, axes and grids. Their Carlton Hotel project demonstrates sensitivity to climatic conditions, with only small openings for ventilation in the bathrooms on the hottest facade facing south-west. Shading for the south-east and north-west facades came from the overhanging top two floors. The architectural language of the Carlton, with its deep piers is the most resonant with the Kuwait Fund's piers.

The next project of significance in Arab Consultant's portfolio was Al-Awadhi Towers in Sharq, built exactly one year after the Carlton Hotel in 1976–77. Again, the tripartite composition of the facade and the environmental concerns were the key elements in the overall architectural expression. This project also marked the introduction of mixed-use programs to Arab Consultants' work, as well as the use of pre-cast concrete elements and abstract Islamic references. The Al-Awadhi Towers were designed with the intention to include showrooms, offices, and banks. The ground floor, which acted as a common base for the three towers, had a shaded arcade for shopping and other commercial activities. The Islamic ornamented *muqarna* vault form was employed on different scales on the facade to provide

45. David Langdon, "AD Classics: Kuwait National Assembly Building/Jørn Utzon," accessed February 17, 2016, http://www.archdaily.com/568821/ad-classics-kuwait-national-assembly-building-jorn-utzon

46. Ibid.

47. Ibid.

48. Ahmed Farid Moustapha, *Islamic Values in Contemporary Urbanism* (Jeddah: 1986), 4.

49. A *parti* is the basic concept of an architectural design.

shading. On the ground level they extended to double height arches for the arcade, while in the middle section of the building they spanned the entire length of the five stories, thus allowing more sunlight in. The exposure to the sun, permitted in this section, was most likely justified by the shading provided from the overhang of the top two levels. Meanwhile, the top two levels were characterised by smaller openings and a density of deep *muqarnas*, intended to keep the windows shaded, since they had no upper overhanging levels to protect them from the sun. The plan and section were simple, with cores attached as appendages to each building, a remnant of a brutalist approach of transparency in terms of function, expressed in the exterior. The distribution of offices and shops in both plan and section was symmetrical and axial. Like the Fisheries Headquarters, Al-Awadhi towers included a tripartite facade, but here, it is much less noticeable, due to the uniformity of the panels covering its skin. The building's skin, clad in the prefabricated concrete *muqarnas*, along with bronze aluminum windows, can therefore be considered its most original feature.

Continuing in the vein of pre-fabricated concrete, Arab Consultants' design of the Fisheries Headquarters in 1976 was one of the first buildings in Kuwait constructed entirely of pre-cast concrete exterior panels. The use of concrete on the facade was a choice that reflected a desire for durability, and an awareness of thermal issues – namely an intention to reduce glare and solar gain. In the late 1960s, a factory was established to manufacture prefabricated concrete in Kuwait, making the panels a more cost-effective solution by cutting shipping and import costs.

Other projects from Arab Consultants that are worth noting is their design of the Kuwait Finance House. A stepped sectional *V* was inverted to a downward Pyramid in the building's entry vestibule. The design was a collaboration between the Arab Consultants and Spanish Eulalia Marques and George Braun, through a competition they jointly won in 1981. In this building, we can see the convergence of several of Arab Consultants' design motifs. The *muqarnas* were re-explored, the tripartite facade was re-articulated and so was the use of an overhanging top four stories, supported by overdramatised columns to create shading for the glazed facade of the building. Unlike his other buildings, where the overhang occurred on all four facades or on symmetrical facades, the overhang of Kuwait Finance House was on just two facades touching each other, creating below them a deep shaded niche. This niche faded down, with the pyramidal *muqarna* that melts onto the street to create an urban plaza, announcing the main entrance to the building. The building was not oriented parallel to the street but rather on an exact diagonal, to allow the leftover four triangulated quadrants to be used as urban outdoor plazas, each articulating different access and entrance ways for women, men, and private employees. The other facades of the building had no openings, again emphasising a consistent respect for thermal issues.

The Kuwait Finance House is the most post-modern in Arab Consultant's portfolio, in which diverse architectural styles meet and collide on the exterior. Meanwhile, the interiors are dressed in Islamic 'Gulf clip-on' decorations. Perhaps this was the result of their collaboration with foreign architects for a competition of this scale or just the natural evolution of their work and a sign of the time. The Arab Consultants continue to work prolifically in the country as their designs dot the urban landscape of Kuwait's downtown, Salmiya and can even be found as far as Abu Halifa.

fachadas ligeras

EDIFICIO COMERCIAL EN SHARQ (KUWAIT)
Dr. Arqto. D. Mohamed Said Aboul Monein

8. Advertisement in *Architécti*
magazine, n. 11/12, 1991. © *Architécti*.

Architecture is a machine that contains many opposing elements: light and dark, memory and forgetfulness, permanence and evanescence. Throughout this research which relied in part on primary sources and interviews with the descendants of the architects studied, the question of preservation of both their drawings and their built work was ever-present. If lucky, the archives of their work are preserved and located in libraries around the world. Otherwise, like a missing appendix or tonsils, Kuwait's architectural archives are as imperceptibly lost as the architects that faded quickly in and out of its urban stage. The richness of the city's building process is somehow separated from the current state of oblivion regarding its built heritage, with a deep hairline crack. The demolishing of Al-Andalus, Al-Firdous, and Al-Hamra cinemas, all to make way for new malls in the early 2000s, is one of the many examples of this lack of awareness and devaluation of the importance of these Egyptian architects' foundational contributions to the city. This sentiment is echoed in Cairo, where if anything, their work at home is barely recognised, while their influence abroad is virtually unknown.

Through the snapshots presented in this research from different moments in Kuwait's architectural history, I attempted to construct an observational scaffolding in which their story was set. The role of Egyptian architects in the shaping of Kuwait's early built environment was part of a deeply embedded and tightly woven relationship between the two countries. As I attempted to demonstrate, the contribution of Egyptians in the early development of Kuwait took the form of two roles: that of the commissioner and that of the architect and builder. In addition to these two roles, Egyptians gave direction to the regional discourse of architecture through their pioneering production of magazines, printed material, hosting of architectural congresses as well as influence of the architectural educational trajectory of forthcoming generations in Kuwait.

Post-Nasser and Sadat, Egypt's political and cultural sphere of influence in the region gradually began to shrink. Meanwhile, the Gulf countries, including Kuwait, became richer, and started to spread their own investments and culture beyond their borders. It is important to read the past and present urban developments of Cairo and Kuwait in juxtaposition with the evolution of their political and economic contexts, bringing the two views together like two images in a stereoscope. As a result of regional shifts, the dynamics eventually reversed between Egypt and Kuwait in the field of urbanism and architecture. Today, the Gulf is shaping Cairo via its economic influence, its developers and ideas of suburban modernity.[50] This research thus represents a small chapter of a complex story that continues to the present. •

50. Developers like Emirati Emaar and Qatari Diar are building residential compounds and towers both in Cairo and on Egypt's North Coast. Meanwhile, Kuwaiti investors, for example, own more than thirty percent of the land in the contested central triangle of Bulaq in downtown Cairo.

My Professional Experience in Kuwait 1980 1986

ISMAIL I. RIFAAT

1. Front cover of tourists' and business visitors' guide to Kuwait; "Welcome to Kuwait – A Tourist Publication," edited by E. Geargeoura, Beirut Printing Press, n. 291, November, 1975.

I came to Kuwait from the USA in 1980 and returned to the US in 1986. I worked in four positions during my six years stay in Kuwait, each of which was enjoyable and professionally rewarding. This article describes the work I was involved in, and illustrates the exciting conditions that prevailed in the practice of planning and architecture in Kuwait at the time.

I went to Kuwait to assume the position of Head of the Office of Physical Planning at the Kuwait Institute for Scientific Research (KISR). I managed the office and acted as the owner's representative with outside consultants. Work on several major projects was underway during my tenure. Most notably, KISR's main facilities and laboratories project which were being designed by The Architects Collaborative in Boston (TAC). I followed up on the design with TAC and their London-based engineering sub consultant, Ove Arup, until the project was approved by KISR. Dr. Adnan Shehab El-Din was Director General of KISR at the time.

I worked at KISR until the end of 1981 and enjoyed my work there. After completing my assignment, I went on to practice as an architect and planner in the private sector. At the time, I was eager to return to my career as a designer, rather than manage the work of other professionals, which was mainly my assignment at KISR.

My experience at KISR revealed an admirable Kuwaiti attitude not found in many other Arab countries, namely, respect and appreciation of local and Arab talent. KISR in particular, was established to attract local and Arab scientists from around the world to conduct scientific research and development in Kuwait. My following experience as a consultant in the private sector also confirmed this unique Kuwaiti

attitude. All three major projects that I was next involved in were awarded to local firms.

Another unique and commendable Kuwaiti strategy that I recognised early on was the government's commitment to commission comprehensive national planning studies for urban development. Such plans were first called "Master Plans," then "Structure Plans," and more recently "Strategic Development Plans." Since pertinent conditions tend to change over time, such planning studies are envisioned to be iterated over five year intervals. I am aware of only a few countries in the world that systematically attempt to adhere to this planning ideal the way in which Kuwait has done over many decades.

The national studies rely on rigorous planning methodologies to estimate population growth and to quantify sundry facets of development that eventually will be needed to fulfill the needs of future populations, including residential development, commercial and public services, road transportation, and utilities infrastructure systems. The studies then conceive spatial configurations to accommodate these needs. The results of the government's strategy to adhere to such a rational planning approach are reflected in the ring and radial configuration of the road system in Kuwait city. The construction of ring roads, and grade separations at their intersections with radials, was in progress when I lived in Kuwait. The establishment of a hierarchy of attraction nodes at the city, district, neighbourhood, and local community levels is also an important part of rational planning. These centres are intended to provide a variety of services as close as possible to where they are needed in an effort to reduce travel, and, thus, contain pressure on transportation systems.

In fact, my next assignments after leaving KISR generally came from national planning considerations that were in force in the late 1970s and early 1980s.

The National plans rarely covered detailed urban design issues such as the creation of vistas, land marks, and open pedestrian urban space. Such considerations were left to the designers of the major projects outlined in the national plans. Therefore, urban design was an important aspect of the large projects that I was involved in.

This approach, however, especially in the predominantly automobile-oriented society of Kuwait, appeared at the time to have resulted in a capital city being somewhat less-exciting than other international urban centres. I did not have an occasion to visit Kuwait after leaving in 1986, and do not know how the city has evolved since then.

The Sulaibkhat District Centre

Client: The Kuwait Municipality
Consultant: UNITEC
Project Director
January 1982 – March 1983

After completing my work at KISR I accepted an invitation from the local architectural firm UNITEC – then-owned by the late Dr. Yusef Shuhaiber – to lead a team that was engaged in the design of the Sulaibikhat District Centre Project. The project was conceived in the context of the comprehensive national plan. Kuwait Municipality, under the leadership of the late Mr. Hamid Shuaib, was the client. Mr. Shuaib, an architect, also headed Pan-Arab Consulting Engineers (Pace), a prominent consulting firm in Kuwait. Also underway were designs of other nationally planned district centres by local and international firms.

The brief for the development of the roughly 475 acre site was clearly articulated by the client based on national planning considerations. The site was slated to accommodate district level facilities, a residential housing subdivision, a park and ride facility providing 2,200 parking spaces, and two covered sports arenas one for 5,000 spectators and another for 10,000. Two large sites were to be reserved for future government use.

The site was traversed diagonally by a utilities corridor, including large six metre diameter pipes carrying brackish water to the city. Prior to my assuming the position of Project Director, the UNITEC team was considering rerouting these pipes to clear the site for development, with cost considerations being a concern. My first decision after joining the team was to avoid rerouting, and to plan the site while keeping the utilities corridor in place, in order to save costs that could then be used towards the implementation of the project.

The U.S. firm Wilbur Smith and Associates were transportation and infrastructure consultants. They sent two engineers who participated with the team at these phases of the

2. Plan of "Proposed long-term urban strategy" in *A Plan for Kuwait*, Colin Buchanan & Partners, 1972.

design that required their input; these included the quantification of parking requirements both at grade and in parking garages, the design of six parking garages in the project, and most importantly, ensuring appropriate vehicular access to the site from the adjacent highways and road system.

In addition to planning and land-use allocation, our assignment included urban and architectural design of roughly fifty distinct building projects. Building design was required to be completed to design development level; i.e. covering preliminary architectural, as well as preliminary structural, mechanical, electrical, and plumbing engineering design. The plan below depicts our design of the district centre. The course of the main pedestrian spine of the district centre ran uninterrupted over a bus station, through the housing subdivision, and led to an existing park.

The district centre's public facilities included a district mosque and a local mosque, a post office, a police station, social services offices, and municipality offices. Commercial facilities included a traditional souq and a traditional food market, a supermarket and a hypermarket, as well as rental retail and office space. Cultural services included a central library, a major theatre, and two small cinemas. These uses were served by adequate surface parking as well as four parking garages; two for 1,200, and two for 900 spaces each. The project included a gasoline station and a bus station. The design of the bus station is noteworthy in the way it provided access to the main pedestrian spine of the project without crossing vehicular traffic. A large office compound with a parking garage was located on a separate site. A bachelors' housing compound was added as we proceeded with the design, because current developments at the time suggested the need for it.

The Municipality brief required the conception of a thematic architectural vocabulary to be expressed in all the components of the project. This was achieved in consultation with the client. Although many trends nowadays promote diversity of visual expression – which often leads to a discordant conglomerations of 'iconic' buildings – I feel there is still merit in harmonious and contextual design efforts.

The design of the project was behind schedule when I joined UNITEC. In an effort to catch up, we decided to establish a project-specific office, away from the daily activities of the main office, dedicated to making progress on the work.

The UNITEC team, under my guidance, included one planner, four young architects, four draftsmen, and a secretary; building engineering design input was provided from the main office. We regularly worked long hours seven days a week. We shared meals, and thoroughly enjoyed working together.

We felt confident of our capabilities, and took a brief reprieve from our main task to submit an entry to the international competition to design the Headquarters of the Arab League of Nations which was envisaged to be located in Tunis. Our design was favorably acknowledged by the competition organisers.

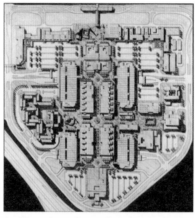

3. Site plan of the Sulaibikhat District Centre, UNITEC, 1982–83.

4. Studies of the architectural vocabulary. The Sulaibikhat District Centre, UNITEC 1982–83.

After a little over a year of hard work under my guidance, UNITEC submitted two reports to the Kuwait Municipality. One report addressed planning and urban design considerations, which covered design options, evaluation, and selection of a preferred scheme for the overall design of the project. The other report covered the architectural design of the building components of the project. Both reports were approved by the client.

The Google map of Kuwait does not reflect the footprint of the project. Thus, it seems that the project was not implemented as designed. The two projects that I was involved in next, however, were both constructed.

The Kuwait Conference Centre

Client: The Ministry of Public Works
A joint venture between KEO, Pace, and SSH
Project Manager of SSH's aspects of work
April 1983 – April 1984

The nature of my assignment in this project was different from the role I played in the Sulaibikhat District Centre Project; albeit, here too, the work had to be performed under tremendous time pressure.

His Highness the Emir Sheikh Jaber Al-Sabah invited the Organisation of the Islamic Conference to hold its meeting of 1986 in Kuwait. Thus, suitable conference facilities and accommodations for heads of states needed to be constructed quickly. Accordingly, the project had to be fast-tracked; i.e. unlike the traditional method of starting construction after the completion of construction documents, design and construction had to be performed in parallel. This approach places substantial pressure on both designers and building contractors.

KEO played the role of Construction Manager (CM) entrusted with coordinating the work of both designers and contractors. Pace designed the Conference Centre facilities, and SSH had the responsibility of site planning and designing 108 luxury apartment residences for 108 heads of state and accompanying prime ministers. My role was primarily to manage in-house efforts, rather than engaging in actual architectural design; although as I will recount, on several occasions, I had to help with the design efforts under pressure.

It was decided that all buildings be clad in granite. The amount of granite needed, 80,000 square metres, illustrates the size and importance of the project. The granite cladding contract was so substantial that it had to be awarded to three quarries, two in Italy, and one in Japan. The CM sent representatives to the three quarries to visually inspect and approve mock-ups of the cladding.

The inception of Computer Aided Design and Drafting (CADD) overseas prompted SSH management to subcontract the design of the residences to the UK firm of Michael Cassidy. Although an understandable decision due to the repetitive nature of apartment design which lends itself to CADD production, this decision had ominous consequences on the work.

Firstly, CADD had not been perfected at the time. I recall receiving messages such as: "Our computers are down; we are unable to complete our work as scheduled." Also, at the time, weekends were Thursdays and Fridays in Kuwait, and Saturdays and Sundays in the UK, leaving three working days only for direct communication, which led to us working weekends in Kuwait. Without internet at the time, communication was only possible by phone or fax. In addition, Mr. Sabah Abi-Hanna, the managing partner of SSH, insisted, for obvious professional liability reasons, that all correspondence with other consultants be in writing.

The fast-track nature of the project predicated continuous timely decisions from the designers. I recall how KEO project managers used to call on a daily basis requesting updated drawings. I was caught between them and the responses of our UK sub-consultants mentioned above. Furthermore, fast-tracking also required speedy decisions from the client to maintain progress on the project. To achieve that, the project team in Kuwait arranged for weekly meetings with the Minister of Public Works. On one occasion the Minister pointed out that the areas of the residences have to be reduced. I conveyed the Minister's decision to the UK team. Their response was that altering the design at this stage would not be possible. I had to get to the drafting board, modify the design as directed by the Minister, and in writing, direct the UK team to comply.

To his credit, Cassidy pointed out that since many of the heads of states are likely to be whisked to the Conference Centre by helicopter, the roofs of buildings should not be cluttered with mechanical equipment; he referred to the roofs as reflecting the fifth "elevations" of buildings. This led the Kuwait team to conceive a central mechanical/electrical plant and a substantive underground tunnel system to distribute utilities to all buildings on site. I was involved in this exercise, including the conception of the earth-concealed central plant.

An incident that I clearly recall relates to visiting the site at the early stages of the project. Huge earth moving machines were preparing the site for construction, and KEO representatives pressed me to establish finished floor elevations for some of the buildings. Although design was underway, I had, under pressure, to make an informed decision about finished floor elevations which, fortunately, proved to be correct.

In general, my experience as project manager for the Conference Centre with SSH was professionally challenging, and considerably demanding at the personal level. Having completed my one year contract with SSH, I was approached by KEC to direct their joint venture with Kuwait Architectural Consultants (KAC) to design Sector C2 of the NHA's Coastal Housing project. I accepted their offer.

The Coastal Development Project, Sector C2

Client: The National Housing Authority (NHA)
A joint venture of KEC, and Kuwait Architectural Consultants (KAC)
Project Director
May 1984 – September 1986

The Coastal Development Project comprised nine sectors, or neighbourhoods, each intended to accommodate approximately 10,000 Kuwaiti nationals. The design of five of these sectors was awarded to local firms, and the NHA was to design the remaining four sectors.

The site of Sector C2 is approximately five-hundred acres. The program of development included 1,270 housing lots. We planned the housing lots around three community centres each providing a local

5. Aerial view of Al-Qurain neighbourhood built between 1986–1996. © Centre for Research and Studies on Kuwait.

mosque, a kindergarten, and local shops. Neighbourhood facilities included two elementary and two primary schools, for boys and girls, one secondary school for girls, a neighbourhood mosque, and a neighbourhood park. We were able to cluster a large number of the dwelling units around central courts which could be used as playgrounds and open meeting places for the residents as depicted in the site plans below.

It is noteworthy that our scheme provided pedestrian access from each of the local community centres to the neighbourhood park and the neighbourhood mosque. The mosque is accessed from the park through a courtyard – *sahn* – thus providing a peaceful transition to the mosque.

Our assignment included site planning, urban design, and architectural design of all public buildings, as well as six prototypes of detached houses. Each prototype reflected a different arrangement of the typical house program, comprising a *diwaniyya*, living and dining, kitchen, four bedrooms, and adeq-

uate bathrooms. Some prototypes included an outhouse which is favored by some Kuwaiti families. The houses were designed in three levels connected with a staircase leading to the roof which is often used for outdoor activities.

Construction documents were to be prepared for all the components of the project, including roads, utilities infrastructure, and buildings. The work was produced at the KAC's office, which had adequate space to accommodate the roughly fifty professionals and draftsmen needed to complete the task. A subcontract for the design of roads and utilities infrastructure was awarded to an Arab-owned consultancy in Athens. Their engineers visited as needed. Production of the site plan was entrusted to a local, recently established CADD specialised firm. To attain the accuracy of the coordinates of roads and plots to three decimal points as required by the NHA, the site had to be drawn on a concave surface reflecting the Earth's curvature. Later on, another local CADD specialised firm was also retained to assist in the production of the construction drawings of two schools in the project.

6. Master Plan of the Coastal Development Project Sector C2 by KEC and KAC, 1986.

Commercial-Civic Core   قلب المركز التجاري   Cultural and Entertainment Plaza   ساحة المنشآت الثقافية والترفيهية

7. The Sulaibikhat District Centre, UNITEC, 1982–1983.

An appropriate architectural vocabulary derived from local vernacular was developed and expressed throughout the project as directed by the client.

For the purposes of the project, I joined the Kuwaiti Engineers Society, and was licensed to practice in Kuwait at the time. The construction documents included roughly 3,000 drawings. The required number of copies of the drawings, specifications, and bills of quantities were delivered by truck loads to the NHA, which used them in tendering for construction bids.

During my long professional career of more than fifty years, I was involved in a leadership position in numerous substantial projects around the world. For example, before I came to Kuwait, the firm in which I served as chairman prepared a master plan for a new town for 100,000 inhabitants in Egypt; the project emanated from a regional study by my friend and colleague Dr. Abdallah Attia. Later, after leaving Kuwait, I was involved as a sub-consultant in the preparation of the Structure Plan for the emirate of Dubai, and following that, in the strategic plan for the development of Al-Riyadh. I also participated in several major international competitions, and had the occasion to serve on two UN assignments one in Libya, and another in Qatar. My experience in Libya is particularly relevant.

The Libyan government had announced that it intended to privatise the housing sector, which was completely entrusted to the government at the time. The UN sent me to assess this proposition, shortly before the imposition of UN sanctions on Libya. Upon arriving in Tripoli, I learned that the government had previously abolished all rights to private ownership of lands and properties. The answer to the question of how it could be at all possible to privatise the housing sector turned out to be beyond my technical urban planning expertise. I cite this episode to highlight the difference between the astute actions of the Kuwaiti leadership, compared to some other Middle Eastern countries.

Without any doubt, the fondest memories of my professional experience relate to my work in Kuwait. The conditions and excitement that I experienced in the fields of planning and architecture in Kuwait were never quite matched later in my career. My enchantment about my work in Kuwait, prompted me to invite my son Adel after graduating from architecture school, and my daughter Mona after getting her degree in landscape architecture to come to Kuwait to participate in the exhilarating work underway in the country. Adel worked with me over one summer on the Sulaibikhat District Centre before returning to the U.S. to obtain his master's degree. Mona worked with Pace for a while before the family returned to the US in late 1986. •

Mobilities of Architecture in the Global Cold War: From Socialist Poland to Kuwait and Back

ŁUKASZ STANEK

1. Neil Parkyn, "Kuwait Revisited," *Middle East Construction* (hereafter *MEC*) (September 1983): 39.

2. Stephen Gardiner and Ian Cook, *Kuwait: The Making of a City* (Harlow: Longman, 1983); Lawrence Vale, *Architecture, Power, and National Identity* (New Haven, CT: Yale University Press, 1992), 248–78; Udo Kultermann, *Contemporary Architecture in the Arab States: Renaissance of a Region* (New York: McGraw-Hill, 1999), 167–78. Here and in what follows, unless otherwise specified, the dates indicate the construction year of the building in question.

3. For a rare notice, see Kultermann, *Contemporary Architecture*, 173–75; see also: Łukasz Stanek, "Second World's Architecture and Planning in the Third World," *The Journal of Architecture*, v. 17, n. 3 (2012): 299–307; Łukasz Stanek, "Miastoprojekt Goes Abroad: The Transfer of Architectural Labour from Socialist Poland to Iraq (1958–1989)," *The Journal of Architecture* 17.3 (2012): 361–386; Łukasz Stanek, *Postmodernism Is Almost All Right: Polish Architecture after Socialist Globalization* (Warsaw: Fundacja Bęc Zmiana, 2012).

4. Donald McNeill, *The Global Architect: Firms, Fame and Urban Form* (London and New York: Routledge, 2009); see also: Murray Fraser and Nasser Golzari, eds., *Architecture and Globalisation in the Persian Gulf Region* (Farnham, Surrey: Ashgate, 2013); Yasser Elsheshtawy, ed., *The Evolving Arab City: Tradition, Modernity and Urban Development* (London and New York: Routledge, 2008); Yasser Elsheshtawy, *Dubai: Behind an Urban Spectacle* (New York: Routledge, 2010).

5. McNeill, *Global Architect*, 1.

6. Ibid.

7. Steven Ward, "Re-examining the International Diffusion of Planning," in *Critical Readings in Planning Theory*, eds., S. Fainstein and A. Scott (Chichester: Wiley-Blackwell, 2012), 479–98; see also: Fraser and Golzari, *Architecture and Globalisation*; Łukasz Stanek, "Architects from Socialist Countries in Ghana (1957–1967): Modern Architecture and Mondialisation," *Journal of the Society of Architectural Historians*, v. 74, n. 4 (2015): 416–442.

Introduction

A visitor to Kuwait City in 1983 described it as a "showplace for the world's architectural prima donnas."[1] The landscape of the city was indeed shaped by architects of international renown, with Arne Jacobsen's Central Bank of Kuwait (1976), the Airport by Kenzo Tange (1979), the National Assembly Building by Jørn Utzon (1984), followed by structures designed by Rifat Chadirji, Arthur Erickson, Hassan Fathy, Mohamed Makiya, Reima and Raili Pietilä, The Architects Collaborative (TAC), and Skidmore, Owings and Merrill (SOM).[2] Yet behind what appears to be an exemplification of familiar modalities of architectural globalisation, including the emerging star system, boutique architects, and large corporate design offices, complemented by a small group of esteemed specialists in 'Arab' architecture, the production of space in Kuwait in the late 1970s and 1980s was defined by yet another actor: architects from socialist countries including Bulgaria, Czechoslovakia, Hungary, Poland, and Yugoslavia.[3] This article will discuss their work with a particular focus on a group of Polish architects, mostly from Wrocław, who left for Kuwait by the late 1970s after a decade of successful professional work in socialist Poland. They were employed by Kuwaiti design offices and, together with other expatriate professionals, they contributed to a change in the townscape of the city state by designing and supervising construction of the first generation of high rises, and of housing neighbourhoods, commercial buildings and public-use buildings. Architects from socialist countries working in Kuwait and elsewhere hardly fit the familiar image of architectural globalisation that juxtaposes an architectural elite shaping urban icons to the cultural practices of migrant workers associated with "globalisation from below;" and yet they were crucial, if rarely accounted for, agents of globalisation of architectural practice.[4]

The Gulf has become a favourite example of such processes and, in *The Global Architect*, Donald McNeill describes the "rapid intensification" of architects' travel, when "territorial boundaries that had kept most architects tied to a small set of national markets no longer make much sense for design firms capable of operating in the dynamic economies of the Gulf and China."[5] McNeill sees these processes as a consequence, or a facet, of the globalisation of capitalism, which accelerated after 1989 when "the geopolitical fixities of the Cold War softened up to create new markets in East and Central Europe."[6]

By contrast, this article shows that, far from being a "new market" opened to the globalisation of architectural practice after the fall of the Soviet Bloc, socialist countries played an important role in the global mobility of architectural services in the 1970s and 1980s. Consequently, this mobility is not to be understood as "Americanisation" or "Westernisation"; neither can it be explained with the unilateral scheme of "diffusion" of architectural and planning knowledge from metropolitan centres.[7] It appears, rather, as multidirectional, both in the sense of competition and collaboration among professionals coming to Kuwait from around the world, and in the sense that the Wrocław architects, while in Kuwait, learned at least as much as they brought with them. This knowledge proved an asset for those who returned to Wrocław after 1989 and the end of socialism in Poland.

The work of architects from socialist countries in the Gulf, more generally, was conditioned upon and contributed to the emergence of a global market of architectural resources which, besides labour, included building materials and technologies, discourses and images, most often combined on the ground with resources from local and regional networks. But the insistence on the global, rather than *transnational*, character of the exchanges discussed in this article stems also from its larger context. The present article is a part of a research project focused on what I have identified elsewhere as architecture's "mondialisation,"[8] that is to say the emergence of architecture as a worldwide techno-scientific phenomenon after WWII from within competing visions of global cooperation and solidarity. Socialist internationalism and the Non-Aligned Movement were among such visions which programmatically took the world as a dimension of practice and imagination in the context of the Global Cold War.[9] They became crucial frameworks for the recruitment of architects and planners from Eastern Europe since the late 1950s, hired for contracts abroad.[10]

Within this larger research project, the focus in what follows on a spectrum of actors and practices in Kuwait in the late 1970s and 1980s allows historicising of the mobilities of architectural resources in the economic, cultural and techno-political conditions of the final two decades of the Cold War. The work of the Wrocław architects will be shown as dependent on the institutional framework created by socialist Poland at a time when the authorities in Warsaw were putting increased stress on the economic benefits of labour export and on securing employment for large groups of intellectual workers of big state companies, and as waning ideas of "socialist internationalism" were being paid lip service at best. This shift was paralleled by a change in architectural terms. The previous generation of Polish architects can be seen as agents of the mondialisation of modernism, orientating their work abroad in large part according to the principles of the Congrès International d'Architecture Moderne (CIAM). However adapted and modified. The Wrocław architects in Kuwait, though, responded to a pervasive disenchantment with these principles that was felt as much in the Gulf as in socialist Eastern Europe.

The response to such disenchantment had been articulated in the work of the Wrocław architects before they travelled abroad, and this will be accounted for in the first part of this article, together with a review of the institutional conditions of their employment in Kuwait. The second part will show how their work in Poland reverberated with the critique of post-oil urbanisation in the Gulf and with the shift in international architectural culture associated with postmodernism. Their designs in Kuwait responded to this new climate of opinion, characterised by a turn to what were perceived as 'local,' 'traditional' or 'familiar' forms and ways of use, and often at odds with the social reality of the rapidly urbanising Gulf. These tensions will be discussed in the third part of this article by focusing on the ways the Wrocław architects re-imagined the relationship between the pedestrian and the car in Kuwait. Rather than following authors who discuss architecture as a "mediation" between (global) technology and (local) culture,[11] however, this

8. The concept of mondialisation was developed by Henri Lefebvre and Jean-Luc Nancy, see Stanek, "Architects from Socialist Countries."

9. Ibid., for the concept of the Global Cold War, see Odd Arne Westad, *The Global Cold War: Third World Interventions and the Making of Our Times* (Cambridge: Cambridge University Press, 2005).

10. Stanek, "Architects from Socialist Countries."

11. Yasser Mahgoub, "Globalization and the Built Environment in Kuwait," *Habitat International*, v. 28, n. 5 (2004): 505–519.

1. Kozanów Estate competition model, A. Bohdanowicz, R. Daczkowski, E. Lach, and K. Wiśniowski, 1974. © K. Wiśniowski archive.

part will show that techno-scientific expert systems (technologies of prefabrication, managerial and logistical schemes, Computer Aided Design software, or CAD) facilitated an engagement with the specific 'context' of the Gulf. The article's final section will show how these expert systems, characterised by Science and Technology Studies (STS) scholars in terms of their capacity for de-territorialisation and re-territorialisation,[12] found a pendant in the intersubjective "profile" of architects from socialist countries working abroad.

From Socialist Poland to Kuwait

In simpler terms, this is a story about a group of friends. Andrzej Bohdanowicz, Ryszard Daczkowski, Wojciech Jarząbek, Edward Lach, Krzysztof Wiśnowski, and many other protagonists of this study graduated from the architectural school of Wrocław Polytechnic in the late 1960s. Some of them were invited to join the Chair of History of Urbanism at the Institute of History of Architecture, Art and Technology,[13] where their research addressed questions of regional architecture. Composing various teams, they worked together on numerous competition projects, some of which they won. One of these was the competition for a section of the City Centre Housing Estate in Łódź (1969), which became a flagship project of the regime of Edward Gierek, first secretary of the Polish Communist Party from 1970 to 1980. Among other projects reflecting Gierek's modernisation effort were competitions for city centres and new housing districts, in particular the Kozanów neighbourhood in Wrocław, a project that received first prize won in 1974, designed by Bohdanowicz, Daczkowski, Lach, and Wiśniowski.[14]

In spite of this success, these architects became disillusioned with the conditions of work in Poland, which was characterised by the submission of architecture to the apparatus of the Party and the state-controlled building industry, the domination of planning over architecture, and the increasingly apparent economic and political crisis of the 1970s. Their competition entry for Kozanów is a case in point. Breaking with the "real existing modernism"[15] of undifferentiated, homogenous apartment blocks being constructed in Poland since the early 1960s, Kozanów was designed as a "small city within a big city." Their design was a topographically sensitive composition of diverse housing typologies, linked by a cluster of low pavilions with social facilities. In spite of the fact that the project won the first prize in a national competition, it was rejected by the Ministry of Construction, which did not accept the flexible prefabrication system proposed by the architects. As one of them recalled, "I had to go back to designing the very same apartment blocks that, we were told during our studies, don't work."[16]

In this context, the invitation to Kuwait, mediated by a Palestinian alumnus of Wrocław Polytechnic, was a welcomed change. The first group to come to Kuwait, in 1976, included Lach and Daczkowski, who were employed in the Gulf Engineering Office (GEO), and later co-opted Jan Matkowski and Mieszko Niedźwiecki. Wiśniowski and Bohdanowicz were employed in 1977 by the office Shiber Consultants, headed by Victor Shiber, brother of the renowned Palestinian architect and urban planner Saba George Shiber who worked in Kuwait from 1960 until his death in 1968.[17] In 1978, Jan Urbanowicz, Jacek Chryniewicz and Jarząbek replaced Wiśniowski and Bohdanowicz in Shiber's office, where they cooperated with the Industrial & Engineering Consulting Office (INCO). INCO's director, Mohammad Al-Sanan,

12. Stephen J. Collier and Aihwa Ong, "Global Assemblages, Anthropological Problems," in *Global Assemblages: Technology, Politics, and Ethics as Anthropological Problems*, ed. Collier and Ong (Malden, MA: Blackwell, 2005), 3–21; Andrew Barry, "Technological Zones," *European Journal of Social Theory*, v. 9, n. 2 (2006): 239–253.

13. They included Krzysztof Wiśnowski, Andrzej Bohdanowicz, and Ryszard Daczkowski.

14. *Krzysztof Wiśniowski, Anna Wiśniowska, Magdalena Wiśniowska, Jan Wiśniowski: 1969–2006* (Wrocław: Muzeum Architektury, 2006).

15. Łukasz Stanek, ed., *Team 10 East: Revisionist Architecture in Real Existing Modernism* (Warsaw: Museum of Modern Art/Chicago, IL: University of Chicago Press, 2014).

16. Interview with Edward Lach, Wrocław, April 2011.

17. Joe Nasr, "Saba Shiber, 'Mr. Arab Planner'. Parcours professionnel d'un urbaniste au Moyen-Orient," *Géocarrefour*, v. 80, n. 3 (2005): 197–206; Saba George Shiber, *The Kuwait Urbanization* (Kuwait: Government Printing Press, 1964).

recalls the group's successful competition entries for Site C of the Sabah Al-Salem district (designed in 1977, constructed in 1982) and for the Kuwaiti National Theatre (designed in 1978, unrealised).[18]

The competitions that were won allowed them to legalise their employment in the Gulf. They signed contracts with Polservice, the central agency of foreign trade in socialist Poland, which mediated contracts of labour export. Over the course of the 1970s, the Polish authorities increasingly foregrounded the mercantile interest in export of intellectual labour which generated the foreign currency needed to finance the Gierek regime's modernisation efforts and, later, to pay off its debts.[19] Such tripartite contracts between foreign commissioners, professionals and mediating institutions were typical for architects from socialist countries employed abroad, including Czechoslovak and Yugoslav architects working in Kuwait.[20] Polish architects coming to Kuwait recommended others, including their wives and partners: Danuta Bohdanowicz, Zdzisława Daczkowska, Elżbieta Niedźwiecka, Rudolf and Ewa Staniek, Anna Wiśniowska and Marian Żabiński. Architects from other Polish cities were arriving as well, including Janusz Krawecki, who was invited by his former student at the School of Architecture of Kraków University of Technology, and Włodzimierz Gleń of the Kraków state office Miastoprojekt, whose extensive experience in Baghdad proved very useful in the Gulf.[21] Krawecki and Gleń contributed to the first high-rise buildings in Kuwait.[22] These architects found employment in various Kuwaiti offices: INCO, SSH, the SOOR Engineering Bureau, the Arabi Engineer Office, the Kuwait Engineering Office (later the Kuwait Engineering Group, or KEG) and GEO (later Gulf Consult).[23] The professional links with Poland were rarely severed and Jarząbek, for example, sent plans for the church of St. Mary Queen of Peace in Wrocław-Popowice (1994) from Kuwait, the details of which resemble those of the Al-Othman Centre he co-designed in Hawally (with Lach for KEG, 1995). After the declaration of martial law in Poland (1981) most of them decided not to return and the monthly fee imposed on them by Polservice (up to 50 per cent of their salaries, as Bohdanowicz recalls, paid in cash to the Polservice representative in Kuwait) was one more incentive to break with the state socialist system.[24]

Labour conditions for the Wrocław architects in Kuwait on Polservice contracts were different from those of Western 'consultants' in the Gulf, such as Constantinos Doxiadis or Michel Ecochard, and from employees of large state-socialist companies working in the region, such as Energoprojekt of Yugoslavia or Bulgaria's Technoexportstroy. The daily routine of the Polish architects was characterised by their intense engagements with clients and contractors, and direct supervision of the building sites, where many details were drawn when needed.[25] They cooperated with Kuwaiti professionals, mainly educated in the United Kingdom and the United States, with professionals from the region (Egyptian, Iraqi, Lebanese, Palestinian), as well as with architects and engineers from India and Pakistan. Exchanges were intense with British professionals in Kuwait, specialists in the architecture of schools, hospitals, and housing since the period of the protectorate, as were exchanges with offices from the United States.[26] The latter were based on financial links between the United States and Kuwait and often resulted from joint-venture agreements between Kuwaiti and foreign firms; such agreements were increasingly required for larger projects by the authorities and private clients alike.[27]

18. Interview with Krzysztof Wiśniowski, Kuwait City, January 12, 2014; interview with Mohammad Al-Sanan, Kuwait City, January 13, 2014. The design for the National Theatre by Bohdanowicz and Wiśniowski was a finalist, together with that by Denis Lasdun.

19. See also, Stanek, "Miastoprojekt."

20. Interview with Stojan and Mirjana Maksimović, Nahant, MA, September 14, 2014.

21. See the following personal dossiers in SARP Archive, Warsaw: 279, 351, 353, 363, 480, 533, 983, 1091, 1138, and 1218.

22. They included the Al-Fintas towers (Gleń, J. Damija and N. Fatteh for Arabi Engineer Office, 1984) and the Al-Qibliya tower (Krawecki for Gulf Consult, 1988), SARP dossier 1091; Janusz Krawecki archive, Kraków.

23. See also, Jacek Wozniak, *Contemporary Architecture in Kuwait* (Kuwait: Jack-Art, 2003), 282–293.

24. Interview with Andrzej Bohdanowicz, Kuwait City, January 15, 2014.

25. Interview with Krzysztof Wiśniowski.

26. Tanis Hinchcliffe, "British Architects in the Gulf, 1950–1980," in *Architecture and Globalisation in the Persian Gulf Region*, 23–36.

27. Interview with Janusz Krawecki, March 2014.

28. The team working for Archicentre in Kuwait included Mirjana Maksimović, Sonja Živković, Branislav Jovin, Jovan Katarnic and Radomir Mihajlović; See, Zoran Manević, *Stojan Maksimović: Stvaralaštvo* (Belgrade: Centar VAM, 2006), 76–78.

29. Email exchange with Alexander Gjurič, March 2014.

30. "Naselje 23 dvojne kuče za rentu šeika Duaj Ibrahim al-Sabaha u Kuvajtu," "Šest vila za Mr. Youset al Shaye u Kuvajtu," "Kuče za izdavanje Mr. Abdulatif Al Touenija u Kuvajtu," *Architektura Urbanizam* 58 (1969): 46–47; Ljiljana Bakić, *Anatomija B&B arhitekture* (Belgrade: Ljiljana Bakić, 2012).

31. The designers were Tibor Hübner, Attila Emődy and László Szabados; "KÖZTI Középülettervező Vállalat" (no date), KÖZTI Archive, Budapest; Attila Emődy archive, Budapest; "Coastal Strip Development Project," private archive of Kazimierz Bajer, Kraków.

32. Stanka Dundakova archive, Sofia; Dimitar Andreychin archive, Sofia.

33. "Building and Construction Industry. Kuwait Times Special Supplement," *Kuwait Times*, August 31, 1980, 5–10.

34. Ibid.; Peter Kilner and Jonathan Wallace, *The Gulf Handbook* (London: Trade & Travel Publications, 1979), v. 3, 360; Renata Holod and Darl Rastorfer, eds, *Architecture and Community: Building in the Islamic World Today* (Aga Khan Award for Architecture, 1983), 252.

35. M. Kwiecień, "Trudny eksport usług budowlanych," Rynki Zagraniczne, 31 (1986): 6.

36. "Kuwait Is an Open Market," *MEC*, n. 4 (1983): 15.

37. Michael S. Casey, *The History of Kuwait* (Westport, CT.: Greenwood Press, 2007).

38. "East Bloc Managers Fail to Keep Up with Trends," *Kuwait Times*, April 4, 1982, 12; interview with Wiśniowski. On Cold War division of intellectual labour in architecture, see Stanek, "Architects from Socialist Countries."

Architects from other socialist countries contributed to this cosmopolitan character of Kuwait. The designer of the Sava Centar in Belgrade, Stojan Maksimović, was invited by the Kuwaiti government to participate in the competition for the Conference Centre at Bayan Park, which he won in 1980 (the realised project, however, has little to do with the design which he prepared together with the Kuwaiti office Archicentre).[28] In cooperation with Czech architect Alexander Gjurič, Archicentre won the international competition for the Amiri Diwan, the offices of the Emir, prominently located next to the Seif Palace.[29] But it was the Yugoslav construction firm Energoprojekt that became the pioneer in establishing contacts with Kuwait; as early as the 1960s, Ljiljana Bakić had designed a number of private villas and public facilities.[30] The Hungarian office KÖZTI followed, with designs for housing neighbourhoods and mosques within the Coastal Strip Development Project, the urban design of which was delivered by Miastoprojekt-Kraków from Poland.[31] Bulgarprojekt of Sofia designed the slaughterhouse in Kuwait and bid for other projects, including the Arab Cities Organisation Building; the latter was not constructed, in contrast to several buildings in the UAE designed by Bulgarprojekt.[32]

State companies from socialist countries operated in Kuwait within a highly competitive market, divided between South Korean, Indian and Pakistani contractors (receiving commissions for which cheap labour provided competitive advantage) and Japanese, European, and American firms, who were increasingly joined by Kuwaiti and Saudi contractors (competing for technically challenging projects).[33] Companies from socialist countries were part of the latter segment, either individually or as subcontractors. Some of these were highly visible commissions: Yugoslavia's Union Inženjering constructed the Kuwait Towers (1977), the icon of modern Kuwait; Energoprojekt was responsible for the Ministries Complex (1981) and the military hospital (1987); and Strojexport and Armabeton of Czechoslovakia contributed to the construction of the Water Towers (1977).[34] The planetarium for Kuwait was supplied by the GDR's Carl Zeiss of Jena (1986), and the steel sections of the new telecommunication tower (1993) were provided by Poland's Mostostal-Zabrze, which in the 1980s counted Kuwait as one of its main clients.[35]

In a 1983 interview, the Kuwaiti ambassador to the United States, Sheikh Saud Nasser Al-Sabah, complemented Yugoslav companies and explained to a US journalist: "You have to understand [that] Kuwait is a completely open market, no political consideration is given as far as the tender is concerned."[36]

This attitude followed the attempts of Kuwaiti diplomats to secure the *neutrality* of their country within Cold War geopolitics in the Middle East: Kuwait maintained close relations with the West while accepting Soviet military assistance and securing its economic interests as a founding member of OPEC.[37]

On this "open market," the relatively modest fees of architects from Eastern Europe were used as bargaining leverage by mediators such as Polservice. However, even after the Wrocław architects decided to break with Polservice and stay in Kuwait on their own, their salaries remained lower than those of Western experts. This showed the persistence of Cold War cultural hierarchies in the Gulf, reinforced by reports in the local press about the inferior quality of technology from socialist countries and their outdated managerial models.[38]

Beyond Post-Oil
Urbanisation

"Upon my first landing in Kuwait, I saw a forest of cranes and I decided to stay," recalled Lach.[39] However, as another observer put it, this construction boom was taking place "among parked cars [and] the ruins of what remains of Kuwait's stock of single-storey courtyard family houses".[40] The Kuwait that confronted the architects from Wrocław was the result of three decades of rapid urbanisation, financed by the state's oil revenues, and defined by state policy of land acquisition and resettlement.[41] The first master plan of Kuwait by the British planners Minoprio, Spencely and Macfarlane, in 1951, had envisaged a transformation of what was then a settlement of courtyard houses into a commercial and business city centre, surrounded by new residential suburbs linked by a system of radial and ring roads. While much of the urban fabric of Kuwait was erased, only a few urban projects were realised, and the next master plan, commissioned in 1968 from the British consultants Buchanan and Partners, took this condition as its starting point. Revised in 1977 and endorsed by the Municipal Council, this plan suggested a linear development following the coast, consisting of housing neighbourhoods with new centres, and the construction of two new towns in the south and the north.[42] A specialist on car traffic in cities, Buchanan suggested a renewal of the city centre by assigning specific areas to commercial uses and civic and government programmes, filling the gap in the urban fabric and laying out pedestrian zones.[43] This plan defined the development of Kuwait from the late 1970s until the Iraqi invasion in 1990, and formed the framework for architectural practices of this period.

The architects from Wrocław, during their work in the Gulf, were exposed to and contributed to a critical rethinking of the boom-era urban development in Kuwait. Falling oil prices, the disruptive effect of the Iran-Iraq War and the crash in 1982 of the Souq Al-Manakh, the unofficial stock exchange, contributed to a more reflexive climate of opinion. Prefigured by some forewarnings by Saba George Shiber from the mid-1960s,[44] calls abounded over the course of the next decade to preserve the little that was left of the old Kuwait.[45] The 1981 revision of the master plan declared the Behbehani compound, the American Mission, the traditional suq and part of the Sharq frontage as conservation areas. The Al-Ghanim Dasman, the Naif Palace and all historical mosques were to be preserved.[46] The architect Ahmad Al-Ansari suggested that plazas in the Green Belt be used for the display of Kuwaiti traditions and folklore,[47] in line with the broad definition of heritage promoted by the National Museum, itself designed by Ecochard and opened in 1983. The Kuwaiti architect Ghazi Sultan supervised the first renovation of a traditional building that was pursued by the municipality: the Old Kuwait Courts (1987).[48] Fathy, the Egyptian architect of international renown, designed the Beit Al-Reihan house praised in the Saudi architectural journal *Albenaa (Construction)* as following "the pattern of Arabian palaces which observe the Arabian Kuwaiti environment characteristics."[49] Similarly, the project for senior housing in Sharq by Jarząbek and Lach referenced the scale, disposition, sequence of spaces, materials and details of the disappearing courtyard houses in this area, photographs of which were included in all presentation drawings.[50]

The unbuilt Jarząbek and Lach design fed into the general critique of post-oil urbanisation in the Gulf press, both popular and professional, which debunked 'modern architecture' and lamented that the city-state was

39. Interview with Lach. Op cit.

40. Parkyn, "Kuwait Revisited," 42.

41. Asseel Al-Ragam, "The Destruction of Modernist Heritage: The Myth of al-Sawaber," *Journal of Architectural Education*, v. 67, n. 2 (2013): 243–52; Farah Al-Nakib, "Kuwait's Modern Spectacle: Oil Wealth and the Making of a New Capital City, 1950–90," *Comparative Studies of South Asia, Africa and the Middle East*, v. 33, n. 1 (2013): 7–25.

42. Gardiner, *Kuwait, The Making of a City.*

43. Ministry of Transport (UK), *Traffic in Towns* (London: Penguin, 1964); Shankland/Cox Partnership, "Master Plan of Kuwait: City Centre," Library of Congress, Geography and Map Reading Room, Washington, DC, G7604.K9G45 1977.S5.

44. Shiber, *Kuwait Urbanization.*

45. "The Changing Suq," *MEC*, n. 11 (1982): 14.

46. "A Master Plan to Reshape the City Centre," Kuwait Times, November 8, 1981, 19.

47. "Purposive Architecture for the Urban Development of Kuwait," *Kuwait Times*, May 10, 1978, 5.

48. "An Architect from Kuwait," *Albenaa*, v. 7, n. 38 (1987/1988): 10–11.

49. "Kuwait, Beit al-Reihan," *Albenaa*, v. 8, n. 43 (1988): 10–11, 24–29.

50. Edward Lach archive, Wrocław.

2. Senior Citizens Housing, W. Jarząbek and E. Lach, 1970s. © E. Lach Archive.

51. Jim Antoniou, "The Challenge of Islamic Architecture," *MEC*, n. 10 (1979): 16–17.

52. Ahmed Farid Moustapha, "Islamic Values in Contemporary Urbanism (1)," *Albenaa*,v. 7, n. 41 (1988): 18–24, 26–33.

53. "Islamic Architecture and Modernism," *Albenaa*, v. 5, n. 26 (1985/1986): 69–73.

54. "Kuwait's Huge Housing Plans," *Kuwait Times*, March 23, 1978, 7; "Building and Construction Industry."

55. Nezar AlSayyad, Cities and Caliphs: On the Genesis of Arab Muslim Urbanism (New York: Greenwood Press, 1991).

56. For bibliography, see Stanek, "Second World's Architecture"

57. Kahtan Al-Madfai, "Elements of Heritage," *MEC*, n. 5 (1980): 58–59.

58. Moustapha, "Islamic Values"; Ahmed Farid Moustapha, "Islamic Values in Contemporary Urbanism (2)," *Albenaa*, v. 7, n. 42 (1988): 14–19, 16–23; Christa Udschi, "International Symposium on Islamic Architecture and Urbanism," *Albenaa*, v. 2, n. 10 (1981): 2–6.

59. "A Future for the Past," *MEC*, n. 10 (1985): 31–33.

60. Charles Jencks, *The Language of Post-Modern Architecture* (New York: Rizzoli, 1977); Huda Al-Bahar, "Contemporary Kuwaiti Houses," *Mimar* 15 (January–March 1985): 63–72.

becoming "a dumping ground for alien architectural landmarks."[51] Hence, commentators writing in *Albenaa* targeted forms that they considered to be alien to the Gulf: apartment blocks with oversized spaces between them (similar to the theory of Le Corbusier), private villas with large spaces around them, the car-oriented city and the gridiron plan.[52] The critique included the analysis of the courtyard house as a flexible and multi-purpose space, opposed to the reductive understanding of the division and separation of functions imputed to the CIAM tradition.[53] This shift in opinion sometimes happened very quickly: if in 1978 the Al-Sawaber project by Arthur Erikson in Kuwait City was praised by the daily press as "modernistic, breaking with the stereotyped, impersonal, rectangular blocks of bricks," already in 1980 the project was criticised as not allowing for privacy, and hence against Islamic tradition.[54]

Debates about 'Islamic,' 'Arab,' and 'Muslim' architecture and urban design took place in a number of conferences in the Gulf countries over the course of the 1980s. During these events, the widespread demand for operative guidelines for design practices was confronted by scholars through a discussion of the constructivist character of such concepts, often based on the extrapolation of specific urban forms, which only slowly shed orientalist fantasies and Western-centred theories of culture and urbanisation.[55] Published in journals in Arabic and in English, and hence accessible to expatriate architects, most of these voices differed little from the discourse of a modernism "adapted" to local conditions, which had proliferated since WWII in colonial "tropical" modernism and its postcolonial mutations.[56] But new themes were emerging as well. Besides the widely argued (if rarely realised) postulates of accounting for specific local conditions in terms of climate, social structures, customs, and local materials and technologies, the debates introduced architectural form as a self-sustained condition and not a 'result' of other factors. The Iraqi architect Kahtan Al-Madfai, for example, argued for a continuation of traditional forms, which he catalogued as either monumental or domestic.[57] Another example is the discussion of the *mashrabiya* which stressed its synthetic character in the way it serves multiple functions: anchoring the building in a visual tradition, regulating climatic conditions, negotiating the relationship between public and private, and linking the building to local economies, craftsmanship, and materials. Some authors engaged in a speculative enterprise of translating the laws and values of the *Shari'ah* into architectural and urban-planning principles, while others explicitly opposed the association between architecture that is constantly evolving, and religion, immutable and eternal.[58]

Some of these debates resonated with international discussions on postmodernism, to which architects from socialist countries who were working in Kuwait gained easy access by means of journals, exhibitions, and newly constructed buildings. For example, in 1985 the journal *Middle East Construction* published Basil Al-Bayati's designs of a mosque in the form of an oversized open book and of a telecommunication tower shaped as a gigantic palm tree.[59] These designs could have been included in any of the postmodernism manifestos which Charles Jencks had been publishing for a decade, and which were reflected by authors writing in Kuwait since that time.[60] Jarząbek, by reading *The Architectural Review* in Kuwait, discovered the work of James Stirling, his ferryman to postmodern architecture, which then reverberated not only in his Kuwaiti designs, but also in those he drew in Poland upon his return in the 1990s. Professionals in the region followed the development of Baghdad closely as it was led by Chadirji under Saddam Hussein with the participation of Denise Scott Brown, Robert Venturi, Ricardo Bofill and Erickson: a "laboratory of postmodernism" where new urban typologies were tested.[61]

Beyond academic and professional discussions, the dissatisfaction with post-oil urban development in Kuwait was shared by inhabitants of state-subsidised housing, interviewed for the first time in the mid-1970s by the National Housing Authority (NHA). With the aim of guaranteeing every Kuwaiti citizen an accommodation, the NHA divided housing into two categories: Low Income Group (LIG) and Average Income Group (AIG); their dimensions were often generous and, for example, in the Messila neighbourhood, LIG housing was built on lots of 300 sq. metres, and AIG housing on lots of 500 sq. metres.[62] These housing areas were realised by the NHA, together with mosques, shopping malls, and schools, for which Mieczysław Rychlicki and Daczkowska delivered type designs in the early 1980s (for Gulf Consult).[63] The NHA interviews conveyed the uneasiness with the typologies that had until then been applied by the housing authority, ultimately deemed foreign and unsuitable. Instead, the inhabitants expressed preference for one-storey courtyard houses that included the *diwaniyya* (semi-public/semi-private room for male visitors), accessible from both inside and outside the dwelling unit, usable roof space, and a paved courtyard with an area for plants.[64]

Reference to an often-unspecified 'Islamic tradition' was becoming a standard requirement by the 1970s in governmental commissions in the Gulf, and foreign designers needed to comply.[65] The London-based office Fitzroy Robinson Partnership designed banks in Dubai, Abu Dhabi, and Muscat in a generic modern idiom, for example, but its design for the Ministry of Foreign Affairs in Muscat was given a "vernacular appearance."[66] Similarly, the design of the Kuwait Law Courts by Basil Spence Partnership evolved in order to accommodate stylistic recommendations and the sequence of its seven facade variants shows a transformation from the abstract grid of the competition project into a display of "familiar elements of Islamic geometry and decoration."[67]

Yet it was precisely such a 'cosmetic' application of ornamental motifs on the facade that was debunked by the most notable architects from the region.[68] Their differing design positions notwithstanding, Chadirji, Makiya, Sultan, and Abdel Wahed El Wakil agreed in their search for a tectonic facade and a more *organic* connection between the skin and the structure. Examples included Chadirji's housing project in Hawally (1968), Makiya's Grand Mosque in Kuwait City (1985)[69] and, less known, the integration between the plan and the facade in the Al-Mazidi building in Fintas, designed by Bohdanowicz (1982, demolished). The plan of the building was based on an eight-point star; in the words of the designer, "an Arab geometry," the *gestalt* of which appeared only in the pronounced balcony of the penthouse, otherwise resulting in an abstract checkerboard of bright stone and tinted glass.[70]

Negotiating Urban Typologies

What this overview shows is a sentiment, shared by many among Kuwaiti elites, professionals, academics, journalists, and inhabitants that urbanisation patterns of the previous two decades needed to be left behind.

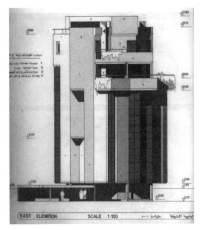

3. Elevation drawing of Al-Mazidi Building in Fintas by A. Bohdanowicz, 1982. © A. Bohdanowicz Archive.

61. "Urban Renaissance in Baghdad," *Albenaa* v. 4, n. 21–22 (1985): 76–88; Stanek, "Miastoprojekt."

62. "A Road Network Sized for the Products of Detroit," *Construction Today – Middle East* 3 (1979): 30; National Housing Authority (NHA, Kuwait), *National Housing Programme* (London: Buchanan, 1976), 5 vols.

63. SARP Archive, dossier 1138.

64. "Household Interviews," *National Housing Programme*, v. 4.

65. "Sunshine and the Rule of Law: Kuwaiti Law Courts Scheme," *Building Design* (June 1980): 24; see also: Nezar AlSayyad, "From Modernism to Globalization: The Middle East in Context," in *Modernism and the Middle East: Architecture and Politics in the Twentieth Century*, eds. Sandy Isenstadt and Kishwar Rizvi (Seattle, WA: University of Washington Press, 2008), 255–263.

66. "Calling the Tune," *MEC*, n. 8 (1985): 20–21.

67. "Sunshine and the Rule of Law," 25.

68. Al-Bahar, "Contemporary Kuwaiti Houses."

69. "Islamic Architecture and Modernism." Op cit.

70. Andrzej Bohdanowicz archive, Kuwait City.

4. General plan of Site C in Sabah
Al-Salem, A. Bohdanowicz, W. Jarząbek,
K. Wiśniowski for Shiber Consult/INCO,
1982. © Wiśniowski Archive.

The Wrocław architects projected into this sentiment their own uneasiness with post-war urban designs in Poland, as it had been expressed in projects such as Kozanów. Yet this overview also shows that the concomitant demands for a more 'contextual' design differed widely in motivations and references, and that calls for a 'local,' 'traditional,' or 'familiar' environment in the Gulf, more often than not, were either going in incommensurable directions or left unspecified. The architects from Wrocław responded with a variety of proposals and, in what follows, these will be reviewed by focusing on urban typologies that negotiated the relationship between the pedestrian and the car in Kuwait. This focus will allow a bringing together of questions of technology, lifestyle and rhythms of everyday life, and will also demonstrate that this 'contextual' turn at times foregrounded tensions within the processes of space production in the Gulf, rather than assuaging them.

Pedestrians and cars were at the centre of one of the first designs in Kuwait by the architects from Wrocław: the competition entry for Site C in the Sabah Al-Salem district, submitted in 1977. This community of 60,000 people, combining LIG and AIG housing, was designed as a part of the linear-urbanisation scheme proposed by the Buchanan plan. Sabah Al-Salem was one of the biggest districts planned in Kuwait in the 1970s, organised in neighbourhoods of c.3000 housing units with social facilities, further divided into 'sites' of 300 to 500 housing units.[71]

After the competition was won by Bohdanowicz, Jarząbek, and Wiśniowski for Shiber Consultants, it was developed together with INCO and realised in 1982. The design comprised sand bricks and cement blocks for walls, with ceilings and staircases in reinforced concrete poured on site, and

71. "Housing the Arab Population," *MEC*, n. 1 (1983): 27–34; "A Road Network," 30–31.

after several years it was retrofitted with elevators. The competition brief by the NHA included requests for an 'Arab design' and floor plans that sustained traditional customs, and the designers responded with an interpretation of Kuwaiti courtyard typology. This typology, they argued, allowed secure privacy, enhanced by a split-level disposition, with the day area below and the night area above.[72] The day area included two larger rooms, one of which could be separated from the rest of the apartment and used as a *diwaniyya*, while the night area could be used as a living room for the entire family. This differentiation of privacy in the apartment followed the recommendations of the NHA, as did the possibility of transforming the terrace into an additional bedroom.[73] The ground floor apartments were extended by a small garden or patio, separated from the public space by a wall.

Another key attempt to respond to the "local tradition" was, in the words of the architects, the careful design of external spaces, topography, and greenery. In contrast to other neighbourhoods in Sabah Al-Salem and the AIG al-Khiran district (Bohdanowicz, R. Singh and Wiśniowski for INCO, 1988), Site C was furnished with a network of pedestrian-only pathways. Inspired by the urban fabric of Sharq, these pathways linked the houses to the local community centre with its mosque, kindergarten, and shops, situated diagonally across the neighbourhood. Perpendicular to the pedestrian paths, a grid of roads was introduced for vehicle traffic, with parking spaces shaded by the overhangs resulting from the split-level section of the apartments.[74]

The relationship between the pedestrian and the car had been recognised in Kuwait since the 1960s not only as a problem of urban planning and technology, but also as an architectural challenge. This recognition was, for instance, the starting point for a 1968 brief of the studies of urban development of Kuwait City, commissioned by Leslie Martin from BBPR, Candillis-Josic-Woods, Reima Pietilä, and Alison and Peter Smithson.[75] A typology that took hold was a reinterpretation of the souq, combining garages, shops, offices, and cafes, shops, offices, and cafes, and equipped with up-to-date air-conditioning systems, elevators, and telecommunications facilities. Developing the typology of the souqs constructed since the 1960s along Fahad Al-Salam street, the Souq Al-Kuwait (SOM with SSH, 1975) was divided by a double atrium, and the Souq Al-Wataniya (TAC with Pace, 1979) included a "village" of duplex courtyard houses on the roof.[76] Architects of the Wrocław group designed the Souq Dawliyah, combining a multi-storey parking garage with an atrium and an office block (Daczkowski and Lach for GEO, 1978), and imagined as a nodal point within the new pedestrian zones of the master plan for Kuwait City.[77]

The tense relationship between the pedestrian and the car was captured in the design of the Al-Othman Centre, a commercial and residential complex in Hawally. The centre consists of three floors of shopping and office areas, twin ten-floor residential towers and a multi-storey car park for 350 vehicles. The foundations were ready before the Iraqi invasion, but the building was not finished until 1995, four years after liberation. The department store comprised a number of small shops located around a narrow central atrium with escalators. The building is located at a major intersection of Al-Othman and Ibn-Khaldoun streets, and its arcaded entrances are located on the corners of the allotment. Yet in spite of the arcades, the building is introverted: the shops on the ground floor were designed not as opening directly to the streets, but rather to a passage

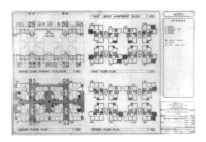

5. First floor plan of Site C in Sabah Al-Salem, A. Bohdanowicz, W. Jarząbek, K. Wiśniowski for Shiber Consult/ INCO, 1982.
© K. Wiśniowski archive.

6. Souq Dawliyah during construction, Daczkowski and E. Lach for GEO, 1978.
© E. Lach Archive.

72. "Interview with Wiśniowski." Op cit.

73. "Household Interviews." Op cit.

74. Krzysztof Wiśniowski archive, Kuwait City.

75. Alison Smithson, "Proposals for Restructuring Kuwait," *Architectural Review* (September 1974): 179–190.

76. Sara Saragoça Soares, "Modernization or Change?," *YourAOK Pages* (Summer 2013): 53–59.

77. SARP Archive, dossier 480.

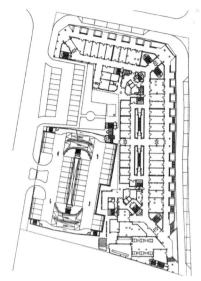

7. Ground floor plan of Al-Othman Centre, Hawally, W. Jarząbek and E. Lach for KEG, 1995.© E. Lach Archive.

78. Lach archive, Wrocław.

79. Abdulrasool A. Al-Moosa, "Kuwait: Changing Environment in a Geographical Perspective," *British Society for Middle Eastern Studies: Bulletin* 11.1 (1984): 45–57; Farah Al-Nakib, "The Bidoon and the City: A Historical Account of the Politics of Exclusion in Kuwait," *Al Manakh 2*, ed. Rem Koolhaas et al. (Amsterdam: Stichting Archis, 2010), 384–87.

80. For an overview of the history and typologies of Kuwaiti housing, see Al-Ragam, "The Destruction of Modernist Heritage."

81. Interview with Wiśniowski.

82. Bruce G. Hutchinson and Galal M. Said, "Spatial Differentiation, Transport Demands and Transport Model Design in Kuwait," *Transport Reviews: A Transnational Transdisciplinary Journal* 10.2 (1990): 91–110.

83. Farah Al-Nakib, "Public Space and Public Protest in Kuwait, 1938–2012," *City: Analysis of Urban Trends, Culture, Theory, Policy, Action*, v. 18, n. 6 (2014): 723–34.

shielded from the streets by a set of kiosks with stairs between them so as to accommodate the slope of Ibn-Khaldoun street.[78] While these kiosks were eliminated in the realised building, the stairs were built according to the first design – narrow, sparsely distributed – and at odds with the image of the arcade. The long stretches from the street entrances to the atrium contrast with the short connection between the atrium and the car park at the point where the two buildings, designed on skewed construction grids, touch each other.

A similar hiatus between an image of urban space and its ways of use can be seen in three apartment buildings constructed in Salmiya in 1978, according to the design by Bohdanowicz for Shiber Consultants. They are distinguished among the neighbouring structures by a careful sequence of transitional spaces sandwiched between the apartment buildings and the streets. However, these shared spaces are hardly maintained, nor are the streets nearby, which often have no sidewalks. This poor level of maintenance reflects the fact that immigrants to whom these buildings are rented out have few instruments for putting pressure on the authorities and landlords. According to the 1980 census, more than fifty-nine percent of the population in Kuwait and three-quarters of the labour force consisted of immigrants, which reflected both the skilled occupations and the semi- and unskilled occupations. At the same time, only citizens were entitled to housing provisions. As a result, housing districts in Kuwait have been divided into low-density villas, inhabited by citizens and set along landscaped avenues, and areas inhabited by Bidoun (stateless people) and immigrants, with these areas ranging from upper-grade apartments for better paid professionals, to workers' apartment blocks, overpopulated and surrounded by poorly maintained streets.[79] While Kuwaitis expected the government to provide welfare services, non-citizens could, at best, associate in district neighbourhood councils in order to coordinate self-help and to petition the government.[80]

The design of spaces with an appearance at odds with their uses cannot be explained by the allegedly formalist approach of the Wrocław architects, since the authorities explicitly demanded such spaces. A case in point is the Al-Baloush bus station, near Ahmad Al-Jaber street, resulting from a competition won by INCO (Leopold Chyczewski, Wiśniowska and Wiśniowski, 1986). After the competition, the Kuwait Public Transport Company changed the programme and replaced the commercial spaces the architects had proposed with publicly accessible spaces with no commercial use.[81] Yet the programme of a bus station implied that the building was to be frequented mainly by low-income, non-Kuwaiti residents, the primary users of public transportation in Kuwait.[82] In spite of the station's multiple gestures towards public space – pronounced eaves, two open-entrance pavilions, and the basilica section of the main hall – it could not have become a space where people of different backgrounds meet, as it was unable to fill the gap of such spaces left in a city centre that had been severely depleted during the process of post-oil urbanisation.[83]

These examples show that the Wrocław architects responded to the climate of opinion in Kuwait in the 1980s by re-imagining the pre-oil urban fabric (Sabah Al-Salem), by alluding to images acculturated in the Middle East by colonial urbanism (Al-Othman Centre, the Baloush bus station), or by reinterpreting the 1960s souq (Souq Dawliyah). These buildings engaged the voices in Kuwait that demanded putting an end to the architectural and planning patterns of the two post-oil decades, patterns widely considered to

8. Port Authority Shuwaikh, A. Bohdanowicz, K. Wiśniowski, Kuwait, 1984. © Dar al-Athar al-Islamiyyah, Nelson Garrido, 2015.

be alien and alienating. However, it was against the background of these more familiar images that the 'other within' appeared: the migrant, the non-citizen, the Bidoun. This is particularly visible in the Port Complex in Shuwaikh, another competition project that was won by Bohdanowicz and Wiśniowski for INCO (1984), one in which the designers wanted to see their scheme as being inspired by the courtyard-house typology in the region. When visiting today, in spite of the sophisticated landscape of stairs and ramps, the only pedestrians one meets around the Port Complex building are immigrant blue-collar workers trying to catch a minibus. They must wait for it on the artificially watered lawn next to the expressway, as there is no other place a bus can stop without disturbing the traffic of the private cars of white-collar employees.

Technologies of Context

The projects of the Wrocław group that are discussed above might appear to be a confirmation of the familiar narrative of architecture's role as a cultural "mediator" of modern technology, as postulated by a variety of post-war architectural idioms, from "tropical architecture" to "critical regionalism."[84] The technologies of the car, the escalator, the elevator, the highway, and prefabricated construction systems appear to be integrated into floor plans inspired by courtyard houses, arranged according to morphologies derived from familiar urbanisation patterns, and covered by details abstracted from pre-oil monuments in Kuwait. In the final part of this this article, however, it will be argued that several of these imported expert

84. Jane Drew and Maxwell Fry, *Tropical Architecture in the Humid Zone* (New York, Reinhold: 1956); Kenneth Frampton, "Towards a Critical Regionalism: Six Points for an Architecture of Resistance," in *The Anti-aesthetic: Essays on Postmodern Culture*, ed. Hal Foster (Port Townsend, WA: Bay Press, 1983), 16–30.

systems themselves facilitated the re-contextualisation of Kuwaiti architecture – and that these technologies found their subjective pendant in the portable, shared "profile" of the Wrocław architects.

Much of the disappointment with 1950s and 1960s buildings in Kuwait stemmed from the rapid pace of their deterioration, and this concerned, in particular, the one material most strongly associated with the Modern Movement: reinforced concrete. While most buildings in Kuwait were less than twenty to thirty years old, concrete structures quickly deteriorated in the hot, humid, dust-laden climate of the Gulf. Expatriate architects were accused of specifying building materials that often proved unsuitable, especially in light of the fact that maintenance protocols were often not adhered to.[85] A 1987 study estimated the life expectancy of a concrete building in the Gulf to be ten to fifteen years (in comparison with sixty to eighty years in less trying environments). This was soon challenged, and another study extended this span to twenty-seven years, which was hardly an optimistic estimation either, and meant that buildings constructed during the boom years would need to be demolished by the end of the century.[86] The oil boom brought about rising costs of land, construction and rents, followed by the shift among main investors in real estate from individuals to developers and governmental agencies.

This shift contributed to the professionalisation of the building industry and to tighter supervision. Yet the fast pace of construction during the boom period had an adverse impact on the quality of construction.[87] Private investors and government agencies introduced a number of control measures and encouraged the use of prevention techniques (coated rebar, dense concrete, and pulverised fuel ash as an alternative to cement, anti-chloride surface coating, and prefabricated cladding with protective finishing for facades).[88] This was supported by the emerging Kuwaiti and Saudi building industries, which were increasingly able to supply materials produced with foreign licences that had been adapted to the requirements of the local market.[89] These adaptations included protective measures against the climate and also accounted for aesthetic proclivities by means of ornamental rubber moulding for prefabricated concrete elements, and with cladding elements with openings in the shape of ogee arches.

More generally, the shift beyond the townscape of post-oil urbanisation in Kuwait was facilitated by innovations in the building industry. These included the organisation of building sites, and over the course of the 1970s the NHA argued against large housing projects, which proved to be too difficult to manage. The construction site of the Sabah Al-Salem neighbourhood proved to be a case in point in October 1980, when 3,500 workers went on strike because their employer, the National Construction Company, owned by the Pakistani government, had not paid their wages for two and a half months. This was a consequence of the company's inability to accommodate rising prices of building materials, which had been underestimated in the tender documentation submitted two years earlier.[90] The NHA proposed that no single contractor was to be given more than 500 units to build and opted for increasing the share of contracts going to locally registered joint ventures. While the main aim was to support local contractors (in order to divert profits back to the country, to provide more efficient procedures of capacity control and risk management and to enhance the knowledge and expertise of local firms)[91] this regulation brought to an end the large, uniform housing projects of the 1960s and early 1970s.

85. "Facing Facts," *MEC*, n. 3/4 (1987): 19–20.

86. "As Solid as Concrete?" *MEC*, n. 4–5 (1987): 20–21.

87. "Building Maintenance in Kuwait," *MEC*, n. 1 (1980): 51–53.

88. "As Solid as Concrete?" Op cit.

89. "Innovation: Computer Screen Printing," *MEC*, n. 2 (1986): 17.

90. Simon Dunkley, "Housing Project Runs into Difficulties," *MEC*, n. 12 (1980): 11.

91. "Ambitious Housing Projects Keep the Market Buoyant," *Kuwait Times*, November 8, 1981.

During the same period, the NHA introduced the requirement of computerisation of the design and construction process. The aim was the acceleration of information flow between all actors involved, facilitation of communication between them, and ensuring their accountability.[92] For many Western firms, in particular from the United States and the United Kingdom, the Middle East became one of the first places to develop computer-aided design (CAD) on a commercial scale. CAD was particularly useful for managing commissions within the "design and build" procedure that was increasingly favoured in the Middle East, when contractors were expected to submit design proposals together with building cost estimates.[93] For example, CAD was used in Kuwait by John S. Bonnington, the designer of the Stock Exchange (1984) and by Arup, the designer of the Salhia Complex (1979). Representatives of the latter stressed the necessity of CAD for exceptionally fast-moving contract programmes, and the use of dynamic databases allowed for a quick response time to contract programme updates and forecasts.[94]

Salah Salama, the head engineer of KEG, recalled that the General Drafting System (GDS) was bought by the office in the early 1980s for the working drawings of the Fintas Centre project in the Fintas area, because of its size, complexity, and the particularly short timing of the commission.[95] For this project, the conceptual design was delivered by Erickson and the execution drawings were worked on by a number of architects from Wrocław employed by KEG. In the wake of the unrealised Fintas Centre, CAD technology was used in other KEG projects,[96] including the Audit Bureau, designed by Jarząbek and Lach before the invasion, and then completed in 1996. The building is located at Ahmed Al-Jaber street in the heart of Kuwait City and includes office spaces, a conference hall, a library, an emergency shelter, and parking for 650 cars. Within the narrative sensitivity developed in their Kuwaiti projects, Jarząbek and Lach took the punched computing card as a direct inspiration for the facade, combining this with complex, ornamental *mashrabiyyas*, themselves drawn in CAD. The technology was also used in the design of the Al-Othman Centre, which, as with the Audit Bureau, was only finished after the Iraqi invasion. The designer argued that the building's careful details, including the decorative geometry of the tiles, would not have been possible without CAD, and they appear exceptional within the decline of building expertise in Kuwait during the 1990s.[97]

In this way, the implementation of CAD and other technologies in Kuwait through the 1980s displays the processes of de-territorialisation and re-territorialisation of expert systems across diverse social and cultural situations, which have been described by STS scholars in studies on global knowledge transfer. Accordingly, the Kuwaiti offices which implemented CAD in order to cooperate with Western architects and construction firms could be seen as "technological zones," discussed by Andrew Barry as sites where differences between technical practices, procedures, and forms are reduced and common standards are established.[98] Similarly, the implementation of computerised management systems at construction sites in Kuwait could be analysed as unstable "global assemblages," as studied by Stephen J. Collier and Aihwa Ong, in which impersonal forms of techno-science are assimilated and contested within specific, situated arrangements.[99] Barry, Collier, and Ong stress that such "technological zones" and "global assemblages" forge a separation between "global/Western" and "local" regimes (political, economic, social, and ethical). By contrast, I argue that several of the expert systems discussed above bridged this separation and

9. CAD rendering of Audit Bureau Headquarters Building, W. Jarząbek, E. Lach for KEG, 1996. © W. Jarząbek Archive.

92. Ibid.

93. "Design and Build," *MEC*, n. 5 (1984): 29; "Number One for Jubail," *MEC*, n. 5 (1985): 21–23; "Dynamic Management," *MEC*, n. 4 (1986): 32–33.

94. John A. Davison,"Computer Aids in Modern Architectural Practice," *Albenaa*, v. 2, n. 9 (1981): 52–54; "Salhia Complex Kuwait," *Arup Journal* (July 1979): 2–5.

95. Interview with Salah Salama, Kuwait City, January 2014.

96. KEG Archive, Kuwait City.

97. Interview with Wojciech Jarząbek.Op cit.

98. Bary, "Technological Zones." Op cit.

99. Collier and Ong. "Global Assemblages." Op cit.

facilitated a 'contextual' response, in line with the new architectural climate of opinion in Kuwait in the 1980s. In particular, the prefabricated systems and CAD software accommodated the demand for a visual environment into which collective identities could be projected. This shift, from the self-assigned mediation between 'technology' and 'context' (as postulated by various regionalisms, "critical" and otherwise) towards their conflation in what can be called "technologies of context," testified to a reshuffling of architectural culture in the Gulf, to which architects from Wrocław contributed.

At the same time, their professional approach displayed a similar dynamic of de-territorialisation and re-territorialisation. Their generational experience of disenchantment with post-war modern architecture in Poland, as well as the specific interest in architectural history shared by many of them, was an important resource for their practice in Kuwait. At least equally important for their employers, however, was a set of more generic attitudes: flexibility, professional ambition, the willingness and ability to learn and to implement innovations, whether in architectural culture, building technology or construction management.[100] These attitudes were delineated in a collective "profile" of "specialists abroad" as specified by Polservice in a 1972 publication.[101] Polservice stipulated the advantages of Polish specialists by their professional qualifications, efficiency and dedication, an ability to adapt to the environment, the "selfless" transfer of know-how to local staff and good knowledge of languages, while it explicitly prohibited their employees from "getting involved in political or religious debates" in the host countries.[102] In Polservice's recruitment procedures during the final decades of the Cold War, a general profile such as this took precedence over specific experience with post-war reconstruction, such as the state-led rebuilding of Warsaw or the construction of new towns, which had legitimised earlier Polish master plans for cities in Algeria, Libya, Syria, and Iraq.[103] Aspects of this profile had been provided by the typically Central European training of the Wrocław architects, straddling engineering, architecture and urban planning, which was valued in Kuwaiti offices, often headed by civil engineers – all the more so as it came with a modest price tag.[104] Such training furnished them with a broad set of portable rather than localised skills which were advantageous within the expanding global market of architectural services: a market which Polservice and state companies from other socialist countries as this article demonstrates, not only took advantage of, but also helped to define.[105]

Afterword:
From Kuwait to Poland

The 1990 Iraqi invasion resulted in the destruction of many buildings in Kuwait, and also in the closure of several Kuwaiti architectural offices including Archicentre, and in foreign professionals leaving, some of whom moved to Dubai and Abu Dhabi in the years that followed.[106] The invasion coincided with the end of socialism in Eastern Europe, and most architects of the Wrocław group who were leaving Kuwait decided to return to Poland. Upon their arrivals there, they became known by the nickname "Kuwaitis," and they helped shape the urban landscape of post-socialist Wrocław. Jarząbek used CAD technology, for example, which he had previously utilised in the Audit Bureau and Al-Othman Centre projects, to design the Solpol department store (1993), the first in the Wrocław city centre after 1989. Lach

100. *Krzysztof Wiśniowski*; Bohdanowicz archive; Andrzej Wyżykowski, "Zagraniczna twórczość architektoniczna Janusza Kraweckiego" (The architectural oeuvre of Janusz Krawecki abroad), *Kwartalnik architektury i urbanistyki* XLI, n. 3–4 (1996): 339–42.

101. Stanisław Grzywnowicz and Jerzy Kiedrzyński, *Prawa i obowiązki specjalisty* (Rights and duties of an expert), (Warszawa: Wydawnictwa UW, 1972), 26, 49–50.

102. Stanisław Grzywnowicz and Jerzy Kiedrzyński, *Prawa i obowiązki specjalisty*. Op cit.

103. Stanek, "Miastoprojekt;" Łukasz Stanek, "PRL™ Export Architecture and Urbanism from Socialist Poland," *Piktogram. Talking Pictures Magazine* 15 (2011): 1–54.

104. Interview with Al-Sanan. Op cit.

105. See also: Donna C. Mehos, Suzanne M. Moon, "The Uses of Portability: Circulating Experts in the Technopolitics of Cold War and Decolonization," in *Entangled Geographies: Empire and Technopolitics in the Global Cold War*, ed. Gabrielle Hecht (Cambridge, MA: MIT Press, 2011), 43–74.

106. Muhannad A. Albaqshi, "The Social Production of Space: Kuwait's Spatial History" (PhD diss., IIT, 2010); Yasser Mahgoub, "Kuwait: Learning from a Globalized City," in Elsheshtawy, *The Evolving Arab City*, 170.

was responsible for the Dominikańska department store alongside the medieval town (1999), among other projects.[107] In 1994, when the construction of the church in Popowice was completed, the cardinal who consecrated the building associated its interior with Islamic architecture – and went on to jokingly thank Jarząbek for designing "such a beautiful mosque."[108]

Beyond anecdotal references, the experience of working in the Gulf, the Middle East and North Africa in the 1980s was a decisive career step that prepared architects from Poland and other then-socialist countries for practising architecture after the political transformations. They distinguished themselves by their professional knowledge and familiarity with programmes with which architects that had remained practising in state socialism had little experience, such as underground car parks, middle-class housing, office parks, shopping malls, and modern department stores.[109] They benefited from the experience with current building processes, from CAD through construction technologies and advanced materials, the organisation of the office and the construction site, to contacts with international developers and construction firms. No less important was the acquaintance with postmodernism, embraced by investors and the public alike. While postmodern tendencies were present in Polish architecture since the 1970s, it was only after the end of socialism that they were turned into a new mainstream, facilitated by imported programmes, materials, building technologies, and capital. Yet while boosting individual careers, the work on 'export' contracts often came with a sympathetic association with developers and construction firms, reinforced by the experience of a 'public' deemed too fragmented and contingent to become an obligation for an architectural project, and an architectural culture valorising the detachment of architectural images from broader processes of space production. These experiences dovetailed with the new professional habitus in 1990s Eastern Europe, which linked the conditions of labour of Polish architects back in the Middle East with those in post-socialist Poland. •

This article is an excerpt of Łukasz Stanek, "Mobilities of Architecture in the Global Cold War: From Socialist Poland to Kuwait and Back," *International Journal of Islamic Architecture*, v. 4, n. 2 (2015), 365–98.

107. Stanek, *Postmodernism.*

108. Ibid., 73.

109. See also Stanek, *Postmodernism.*

Stig Egnell

An experienced planner, Stig Egnell has a master's degree in architecture from Chalmers University in Sweden (1960). After 1960, Egnell incorporated VBB/SWECO, where he developed his practice until 1987, carrying out several projects in the region, including the University of Al-Ain in the UAE, and the water towers in Kuwait and Jeddah, Saudi Arabia.
In Kuwait he was also involved in the Master Plan for Rumaithiya neighbourhood (1962–64), the low income housing scheme for Rumaithiya between 1964–65 (with pre-fabricated units from Ohlsson and Skarne's AB), and the Coastal Strip Development Plan for Sulaibikhat from 1982–85. From 1981 he was the Vice-President of SWECO, Head of the Urban Planning Department and a Member of VBB's board.

Ricardo Camacho conducted this interview via email in September 2015.

Ricardo Camacho: *Mr. Egnell, can you tell us a bit about your involvement with VBB/SWECO?*

Stig Egnell: The architectural projects carried out with VBB/SWECO include, among others: The university in Al-Ain, UAE, the Ericsson telecommunications plant in São José dos Campos, Brazil, the Water Towers in Kuwait, Jeddah, and other locations in Sweden.
Examples of international planning projects are: Rumaithiya residential area and the Coastal Strip development area in Kuwait, Bafuloto tourism development project in Gambia, Okuhida recreational area in Japan, and San Agustin recreational housing area in Gran Canaria. The many planning projects in Sweden include a regional plan for the Sundsvall area, master plans for Kalmar and Piteå, detailed master plans for Ekerö and Mariefred, and a detailed plan for Berghem residential area in Järfälla.

RC: *Considering your previous experience at VBB, can you confirm whether or not you have a deep knowledge of Kuwait, considering the projects you refer to while at VBB between 1960 and 1987?*

SE: I was involved in various projects in Kuwait between 1962 and 1985, working for the Swedish international consultantancy VBB, today renamed SWECO. My tasks included two main planning projects: From 1962–64, a detailed plan for Rumaithiya area for some 17,500 inhabitants, [and] between 1982–85 a development plan for the coastal strip area for 1.5 million inhabitants.

RC: *Can you explain your involvement in the project for the water towers? It is still confusing to understand the role of certain intervenients, such as Sune Lindström, Energoprojeckt, or even Buckminster Fuller Company, who developed the structural design of the Kuwait Towers' spheres.*

SE: I participated in the design team for the Kuwait Towers and for several groups of mushroom water towers in various areas of Kuwait from 1967–68. The towers were given Aga Khan´s award for architecture in 1980. In addition, I designed an administrative building and several pumping stations for Kuwait water works.

RC: *How were these projects developed and where were they produced?*

SE: VBB at one time had a branch office in Kuwait. The planning and design work, however, was carried out in Sweden.

RC: *Can you tell us more about the role of Saba Shiber in Rumaithiya and the importance of contemporary interventions in Kuwait, such as Dorsh and other English consultants in developing the neighbourhood unit, or even the projects developed by Doxiadis and Miastoprojekt in Iraq?*

SE: I forgot to mention an interesting commission for the Swedish construction company Ohlsson & Skarne's AB and its local partner in 1964. I designed layouts for four types of one-family houses, to be built from prefabricated concrete elements. The houses were supposed to be built in groups (e.g. in the Rumaithiya area) and with proper consideration for the local climate and social conditions. •

Hisham Munir

Hisham Munir (1930–) is an architect with a B.Arch from the American University of Beirut and the University of Texas, Austin, and holds an M.Arch from the University of Southern California. He established, in association with Medhat Ali Madhloom, the Hisham Munir and Associates practice after returning back to Iraq in 1957. As Head of the Technical Section 3 of the Ministry of Public Works in Baghdad he oversaw some of the key governmental works such as the Civic Centre (W. M. Dudok, 1957) and the University (TAC, 1957). Among the first professors of the Baghdad faculty of architecture he was active in establishing the post-graduate program and in 1966 presented at the Iraq Engineers Scientific Conference an article entitled "Environment and Urban Design." Following the official roles in the Civic Centre and University the firm developed new plans for the Civic Centre (1971) and the Medical City (1973–77). In the mid-1970s the firm was especially active with the accomplishment of the Iraqi Reinsurance Company (1976) and the Agricultural Complex (1975) in Baghdad and the competition entry for the Anwaar Al-Sabah Complex in Kuwait (1976). Following Ahmad Hassan Al-Bakr's fall from power and up to end to Iran-Iraq War, the firm served the regime's optimism, being in charge of several projects including the collaboration with Roger Butler & Burgan Associates and Whiting Associates for the development of the Medical City up to completion in 1983, the Ministries of Higher Education, Oil, Interior and Trade head-office towers, the Social Security and the Baghdad Mayor Office. This period culminates with the collaboration with Khalid Al-Rahaal and Marcello D'Olivo for the 'Unknown Soldier Monument' and the Kuwait Embassy building (1979–84). The departure of several key collaborators in the office such as Bob Khewro (left in 1980 for Pace) and Hisham N. Ashkouri (left in 1986) together with the fall of the regime led eventually to the closing of the firm. Today, Munir operates from as the Munir Group.

Ricardo Camacho conducted this interview via email between October 2015 and May 2016.

Hisham Munir: I left home [Iraq] in 2003 because of the [George W] Bush war and have never been back because of bad security. Although I was asked by the mayor of Baghdad for a conference to be held in the city, I checked with them about security and it was not enough so I refused. My office like many others was robbed or burned and destroyed.
I have few documents left in my house and the Aga Khan are trying to find way to bring them for my archives which they want to keep.

RC: *In previous exchange, you have mentioned some relation with Gulbenkian Foundation, is this related to the Stadium or to the Modern Art Centre in Baghdad?*

HM: I also notice you mention Algarve. I was in Lisbon with drawings to meet Gulbenkian Foundation group to finance some projects in Baghdad which they did. A beautiful city with some interesting Arabian landmarks.

RC: *When did you came to Kuwait for the first time and when did you established the first work relation with the country?*

HM: I recall there were two Iraqis that shared in developing Kuwait at early dates. One I only recall his last name Al-Sa'dy, a British-educated married to a Scottish lady. His younger brother worked as lawyer in our office named Aziz Al-Sa'dy. The other I think Al-Ghanim from Basra. In the early sixties when I was visiting Kuwait I met Al-Sa'dy, and his family are friends of ours, he said that Kuwait has interest in sponsoring/financing, a housing scheme for Yemen. He asked me if I would prepare the design so we can go visit Yemen. I was ready but needed more information about the area. But after a while the project was cancelled for some reason. He kept working for Kuwait. We kept contact for a while. It will be interesting if you can trace the story of these people and their service to Kuwait.

RC: *Do you confirm that Mr.Sami Al-Bader from Kuwait collaborated with you? After he went to TEST Kuwait. I'm always wondering about his impact in this country as an extension of the work done in Baghdad with you.*

HM: I had an Iraqi draftsman who was good and smart. He was first left-leaning and would spend days sleeping in our office to avoid security which I permitted him so, believing in freedom of individual thinking. His name was Sami Al-Bader. His family was from Basra. Many of them became Kuwaiti citizens. So he moved to Kuwait and became citizen. He wanted to study architecture in the United States and asked me to make him a recommendation which I did and he completed his degree and opened his own office in Kuwait (TEST). He kept in contact which I was very happy to help. You can check about his work. You may also inquire by phone to Shakir Al-Bader who is his senior relative or his son Ramzy.

RC: *As local consultant your firm was involved in many of TAC works in Iraq including the University of Baghdad and University of Mosul Master Plan (1966), and the Sheraton Hotels in Baghdad and Basra (1981). Can you elaborate on this.*

HM: Our office worked with The Architects Collaborative (TAC) headed by Walter Gropius for thirty years, ending in 1990 when the boycott was put on Iraq. For Baghdad University I was consultant on the project, all their projects in Iraq were joint ventures. I was also helping in Kuwait to provide them information and engineers to work with them, also in UAE for the Cultural Centre and Saudi Arabia Al-Khobar complex.

RC: *Regarding the competition entry for Anwaar Al-Sabah complex, can you explain to us how that project was introduced to you and if there is any relation with TAC or their local affiliation Pace?*

HM: Further contact in Kuwait was with Kuwait Engineers Office owned by Faisal Sultan and Fawzi M. Al-Saleh, the president of Musaad Al-Saleh & Sons contracting company. I recall being invited to join in a competition to design a complex of apartment on a large site next to the Hilton Hotel and overlooking the sea. The land was owned by Mr. Fawzi's family. I believe maybe five offices join and we won second prize, I do not know the actual design they implemented.

RC: *Can you tell a bit more about the project for the Kuwait Embassy building (1979–84). Actually the building is now under renovation works led by Pace from Kuwait.*

HM: Yes, our office was selected, after interviews with other Iraqi offices, to design the Kuwait Embassy and the Ambassador's Residence in Baghdad. The selection was conducted by Kuwait Real Estate Investment Consortium (KREIC) who were entrusted to design and build embassies on behalf of the Ministry of Foreign Affairs. The project was completed and I was invited to the Ambassador's Residence for the inauguration. Unfortunately, the unwise war of which we have no involvement with (us being a private firm), took place in 1990. However, KREIC did not pay us the last payment due which was $120,000.00. •

Ala Hason

Ala Hason is an Iraqi architect who worked in Kuwait from 1981–90. Hason lives in Abu Dhabi, UAE, and is Vice President and Director for the MENA Region at HKS, Inc. – an American international architecture firm headquartered in Dallas, Texas, founded in 1939 by Harwood K. Smith. Between 1994 and 2009 he was principal at Gensler. He graduated in Architecture from Ain Shams University (1975–80). As junior architect at Archicenter Kuwait between 1981–83 he was involved in Phase 1 of the Bayan Conference Centre, the Social Medical Centre in Sulaibikhat, the Iraqi Embassy in Kuwait, the Al-Mulla Residential Complex and two villas – one for the Bukhamseen family and the other for architect Abdullah Qabazard. As senior architect at Pace (1986–90), Hason participated in the following projects: Bayan Conference Centre – Phase 2, the Gulf Investment Corporation, Kuwait University Administration Building, Kuwait University Campus facility renovation, Kuwait University Student Dining Hall, Ports Department Mosque, Al-Mulla Group Headquarters Building, Abdullah Al-Ahmad Street Development, the Commercial Bank of Kuwait's new offices, in joint venture with SOM, Souq Al-Tujjar (Merchants Market), Al-Andalus Cinema Master Plan in Hawally, the Court complexes of Al-Jahra and Al-Farwania and the Bahrain Exhibition Centre (Phase II) in Manama, Bahrain.

Ricardo Camacho conducted this interview via email in August 2015.

Ala Hason: Hello Ricardo: Just to clarify, I am originally from Iraq. I was born in Baghdad, but left when I was ten years old. I was always fascinated by the old civilisation in Iraq (Mesopotamia), in Babylon, and later the pyramids and Islamic architecture in Egypt also amazed me. After graduating from Ain Shams University, I went to Kuwait and worked with Mr. Qabazard at his Archicenter architectural firm for three years, from 1981–1983. After that I went to the United States, where I took my master's degree in architecture, with a minor in landscape architecture, from 1984–86. Following my graduation from North Carolina State University, I went back to Kuwait and worked with the late Hamid Shuaib at Pace from 1986–1990. I was in the United States on vacation when Iraq occupied Kuwait and I never went back.

RC: *What influenced your decision to enroll at Ain Shams University?*

AH: Ain Shams University was known at the time to have a stronger program than Cairo University.

RC: *What were the main qualities of the university back then?*

AH: The architectural school was one of the best in Egypt. The majority of the teaching staff were from École des Beaux-Arts (the French School), with fewer instructors from the architecture program at ETH Zurich-Swiss Federal Institute of Technology. The studio projects work was amazing. We worked long days and many nights to meet deadlines. One of the great aspects of the program was the mentoring of freshmen by seniors, and in return the freshmen assisted senior students with the drafting and rendering of their projects. It was also a tradition of the school for the entire senior class to go by train to Luxor and Aswan with their instructors before their final projects.

RC: *Was the work of Kuwaiti Medhat Mohamed Al-Abd, Ain Shams Alumni from 1959, known at Ain Shams University and discussed? I'm not sure if he ever taught there, but did you meet him at any point?*

AH: I did not meet Mr. Abd.

RC: *How important were the influences of Sayyed Karim and Hassan Fathy during your time at Ain Shams University?*

AH: I was fascinated and inspired by Hassan Fathy's architectural principles. He lectured at Ain Shams, and I was fortunate enough to meet him. We had a studio based on his principals of vernacular architecture.

RC: *How relevant was the education you received at Ain Shams University to your professional practice?*

AH: It gave me a foundational understanding of the fundamentals of architecture (theory, history, drawings, design, and presentation), as well as a strong foundation in technical aspects (structural, materials, construction documents).

RC: *Were you interested in the regional context back then?*

AH: Yes, this was very natural, but our education was also oriented towards the Modern Movement and 'International style.'

RC: *Were you aware of the work of other colleagues in Kuwait, Iraq, Lebanon or even Morocco?*

AH: Not really. There was no Internet at the time. Our only sources of information were the French, German, and British architectural magazines we had access to in Cairo, Egypt.

RC: *Straight after graduation you joined Mr. Qabazard's office in Kuwait. Were the works of other Egyptian architects influential for you back then – such as Sayyed Karim, Mahmoud Riad, Omar Azzam, General Ramzy Omar, George Habib Al-Hag and Michel Habib Al-Hag, or even Hassan Fathy.*

AH: Not really. When I worked at Archicenter for Mr. Qabazard, the office was under the influence of the late Mohamed Makiya – an Iraqi architect who worked with the office as a consultant while he was completing the Kuwait Grand Mosque. In the office we were also inspired by architects like Rifat Chadirji, Hisham Munir, and others.

RC: *How did you get the opportunity to work in Kuwait?*

AH: After my graduation from Ain Shams University, I wanted to go to Iraq, but the Iran-Iraq War started in 1980, so I went to Kuwait with the hope of going back to Iraq when the war was over.

RC: *During this period architect Abdullah Qabazard was leading the design and implementation of the Ministries Complex in Kuwait, with the support of Archicenter; Did you follow the building project and construction experience?*

AH: The Ministries Complex was one of the great examples of modern architecture. It respected the local climate and provided a sustainable approach to open spaces in the hot climate of the Gulf region.

RC: *What was the feeling like in the city when you came to Kuwait, particularly the architectural scene?*

AH: Architecture was experiencing a boom. Kuwait was the shining star in the Gulf, like Dubai today, before the stock market crash in the 1980s.

RC: *Did any building or architectural practices catch your attention back then? If yes, can you elaborate?*

AH: We were pushing the boundaries of true modern architecture with a vernacular flavour that respects the cultural values of the region. Clients wanted unique designs that represented their values and prestige in Kuwait. We worked on the design of many fancy villas with indoor squash courts, indoor swimming pools, spas, elevators, etc.

RC: *Can you describe the environment at Qabazard's office and the key elements there at the time?*

AH: It was an exciting environment for a young graduate like me. It was a true design studio (there were no computers then). We used to draw and sketch by hand and used colours for rendering and presentation. We worked with senior designers from Czechoslovakia, such as the former professors at Baghdad University, Václav Bašta and Jan Čejka, but also Alexander Gjuric, Radim Bohacek, Jovan Katarnic and Yvona Bohackova and others, I'm not sure of their names), along with many other architects from Yugoslavia (Adela and Sonja Zivkowic – I don't remember their full names), and others from Iraq, Pakistan and Egypt. It was an exciting mix of senior and young architects working along side structural and MEP engineers. It was a very collaborative environment. We felt like a family then. Mr. Qabazard invited us to social events at his house and his father's beach house.

RC: *Regarding the Bayan Palace Conference Centre project, can you describe your role, the role of Mr. Qabazard and later Pace. How was the joint venture with SSH and other consultants managed? What was the role of the Bosnian architect Stojan Maksimovic and his Yugoslavian team?*

AH: Mr. Qabazard originally won the competition (1980) to design the Kuwait Convention Centre (Bayan Palace Conference Centre), with Maksimovic's office in Yugoslavia. I heard that Maksimovic designed the Belgrade Convention Centre (Sava Centar built between 1975–79), which the Kuwaiti client really liked. Maksimovic sent around twelve architects from his team to be stationed with Mr. Qabazard in Kuwait for eighteen months to complete the design. When Kuwait won the honor to host the non-aligned countries' summit, there was not enough time to build the Archicentre and Stojan Maksimovic design. This led to the creation of a design consortium between Archicenter, Pace and SSH, which became known as the Bayan Palace Phase 1. I left Archicenter by the end of 1983, before this joint team started work on the new design.

RC: *After the first experience in Kuwait (1981–83), as a fresh graduate from the United States, what influenced your move to Pace in 1986?*

AH: I always respected Pace and the quality of their work. After my return from the US, I met Hamid Shuaib and he hired me as a senior architect.

RC: *Can you describe the company structure and the key personnel at the time? Did you meet Hamid Shuaib on a personal level? Can you describe his role in the office and his thoughts on some of the office projects?*

AH: Hamid Shuaib was a father figure and master, not only for the architects at Pace, but for all Kuwaiti architects. He was well respected by clients and colleagues everywhere in Kuwait. His soft-spoken wisdom, and his artistic and thoughtful vision were amazing. You couldn't help but love and respect him. Pace was going through financial problems after the crisis in Kuwait in the eighties, but there were a few exciting projects and opportunities that attracted many of us to work hard to revive it. There were many young Middle Eastern architects with western education from the United States and, Austria for example, and others. These young practitioners were determined to raise the Pace flag again. We won a few design competitions that lifted our moral and gave us the confidence to work harder.

RC: *Can you describe the Merchants Market proposal for Mubarakiya?*

AH: Souq Al-Tujjar was next to the old souq. I'm not sure if they demolished it? It was the original place for all the Kuwaiti merchants near the Ameri area (towards Seif palace). It was designed similarly to old souqs.

RC: *The Social Medical Centre in Sulaibikhat is a building surveyed under the first volume of "Modern Architecture Kuwait," in which we had a special interest mainly regarding the design process, and how the site strategy and material condition of the building became decisive elements. Can you tell us more about this project?*

AH: I am not sure if the one you are referring to is the same one we designed when I was at Archicenter.

RC: *Was the war the main motivation for your departure? What memories do you have of this time, and what expectations did you have of your career back then?*

AH: I was on vacation in the United States with my wife when Iraq occupied Kuwait. It was a disaster and came as a surprise to all of us. We lost everything in Kuwait and we had to start over again in the United States.

We just won the contract for the Gulf Investments Corporation, Al-Mulla Headquarters building and the Abdullah Al-Ahmed street competition. And we were working on Bayan Palace Phase II, along with the requalification works at Kuwait University Campus, including the Administration and Library buildings, the Amrit Resort in Syria and many other exciting projects.

I recently worked with Pace on the Kuwait Judicial Courts Complex at Al-Farwaniya and Al-Jahra when I was at Fentress Architects in Denver, Colorado (both projects are under construction now). •

Saad Al-Zubaidi

Saad Al-Zubaidi earned a degree in architecture from Baghdad University in 1967, and a master's degree in Tropical Studies from the Architectural Association in 1971. He began practising at Iraq Consult (IQC) as a student in 1965 until 1973. From 1982 to 1999, he lectured regularly at the University of Baghdad. Al-Zubaidi developed his career as designer and architect until 1987, when he established the IDRISI Centre for project management and supervision. After the war he became a leading figure in the reconstruction effort in Kuwait, assuming the direction of the National Centre for Construction's laboratories and becoming Technical Director of the Minister of Housing and Construction.

Ricardo Camacho conducted this interview via email in July 2015.

RC: *Mr. Zubaidi, considering your previous experience at Iraq Consult (IQC), can you confirm your involvement in Kuwait projects between 1968 and 1973?*

Saad Al-Zubaidi: In answering your enquiry on the subject, I state the following: (i) Prior to working at IQC as an architect (68–73), I completed an internship as a part-time student architect (1965–1968); (ii) I was a team member at IQC design studio in Baghdad, headed by Mr. Rifat Chadirji, a world-renowned architect, and senior team member Maath Alousi, a well-known architect in the region. (iii) The list below includes some of the projects IQC worked on in Kuwait during this period: Kuwait National Assembly (international competition); the four Kuwait Sport Clubs (Kuwait Sporting, Al-Qadsiya, plus two others) which were constructed; two medium-rise housing compounds with communal facilities which were also built: Al-Qabas newspaper editorial and printing facilities (also constructed), the cinema in Hawally (which was finally built under Pace), and Al-Hamad villa (the private residence for the Kuwaiti ambassador to Iraq).

RC: *I recognise the project list you gave in your reply, with the exception of Hawally Cinema. At that time there was one main cinema in Hawally – Al-Andalus (one of the housing complexes by IQC for Mr. Al-Hassawi was in front of it). However, there is a cinema for Al-Jahra that I suspect was designed by IQC. Do you remember any other projects you may have been involved in during this period in Kuwait?*

SZ: Additionally, and during my work as House of Design (HoD) at the National Centre for Architectural Consultancy (NCEAC), between 1973–1987, I worked on the design of the Iraqi Embassy in Kuwait, implemented in collaboration with their local office (Archicenter).

Saad Al-Zubaidi interview and reference in a series of articles by Nicolai Ouroussoff for the Los Angeles Times, published between December 14 and 16, 2003.

[Baghdad] used to have all these streets running perpendicular to the river. It allowed the breeze to flow into the neighbourhoods. Rashid Street is cut parallel to the river. But the unity is very powerful. The arcades worked climatically. It was the heart of the city until the 1970s.

For these people, heritage was linked to poverty. The traditional houses and alleyways, the sleeping on the roof – they were not proud of it. It was a question of identity. People wanted something new. •

Abdulaziz Sultan

Abdulaziz Sultan, received a bachelor's in Engineering Science from the University of Michigan, Ann Arbor, USA, in 1963 and immediately joined the Ministry of Public Works where he stayed for four years. In 1971, received the PhD from the same university and joined his brother, Faisal Sultan at KEO (Kuwait Engineers Office) where he is president since 1992. In KEO he had management positions throughout the 1970s and 1980s being involved in many of the projects developed by the firm in those decades.

Ricardo Camacho conducted this interview in Kuwait in February 2016.

RC: *I start by asking about your motivations to pursue civil engineering studies?*

Abdulaziz Sultan: Oh well it's a good question. To tell you the truth, neither do I (laughs). Alright. Well, of course I grew in the old Kuwait City that I deeply regret that was demolished. And I deeply regret that the wall of Kuwait was demolished. Both were down when I wasn't here. The civil advisor from the United Nations – UNDP I think – who was there, a planning advisor. He resigned once the decision was made – a government–made decision to demolish the city of Kuwait.

RC: *Who was this?*

AS: Sami, I think Sami Abdel Baqi.

RC: *But this was before you right?*

AS: Yes, I worked for almost four years at MPW (Ministry of Public Works). My boss of design section was Mr. Fox, a German. And he is the one who designed most of the schools you see in Kuwait now, with the two floors, I think.

RC: *Those with a the exposed structure.*

AS: Yeah that's right. Okay, he designed all these. That was where I was working with him.

I know a first pre-stressed building that we produced was the Gulf Bank. The building was very iconic at the time. We used precast concrete in a very heavy way.

But I was telling you about some the details, let me tell you a detail I thought was very funny at the time after I got my PhD I was called by then the State Secretary. So I sat down and he asked me a funny question, he said "Why [do] we have this problem of dusting in Kuwait? What can we do about it?" I say in my head, I say my God I haven't read this anywhere, maybe I missed it. I said to him "I really don't know, I have nothing to use for that," he said "What we should do [is], install showers all over Kuwait, very high showers, and when there's a dusty storm we turn them on."

RC: *What was the first project you were involved in when you came back to work with KEO in 1971?*

AS: Kuwait Industrial Company, there was a competition and was done by two Japanese architects working for KEO, they were brothers and one then went back to Japan and became a professor at Osaka University.

RC: *How was the relation between Ghazi Sultan and KEO, was he part of KEO?*

AS: No. Well, Ghazi had an office inside KEO, but he didn't have an office there formally. And then we had all the engineering disciplines at the time. And Ghazi of course wanted somebody to manage his projects. So, Ghazi did the architecture, he was in charge of it, KEO did the engineering.

RC: *But when you say Ghazi did the architecture, like he had his own staff hired by him?*

AS: No, no, it was KEO staff. Ghazi did certain projects that went signed as Ghazi.

RC: *For instance Zahra Complex in Salem Al-Mubarak street?*

AS: No, Zahra Complex wasn't done by Ghazi. Ghazi did the renovation of the old Municipality on Fahad Al-Salem street. The relation with Ghazi was very straightforward, he did his projects, he had his own fees, we had our own fees, and once accepted he did the architecture.

RC: *But did Ghazi had any office outside KEO.*

AS: Not that I know, no. Ghazi didn't want to bother with managing offices.

I remember Anwaar Al-Sabah Phase II, that was a competition he won. There were five local offices, I don't remember who exactly, but I'm sure Pace wasn't, because Hamid Shuaib was on the jury.

RC: *Not far from there, Souq Al-Mutaheda and Al-Massaleh were special projects developed at KEO, the brief required precast elements assembled at site.*

AS: You mean the parking garages? Oh, well they wanted something very fast, I know that. We did design two parking garages, and all the structural elements they're… using the same system, precast system.

RC: *Do you think this building had an impact, because all the other parking structures being developed by Pace or by SSH didn't have such restriction.*

As far as I saw in the brief, there was a specific requirement for the precast. So, I thought that at a certain point KEO gained some expertise and recognition as the local office that could better deal with that condition, no?

AS: You are applying really a Western approach to things, it doesn't work like that in Kuwait. It doesn't. Okay, this is not a fisher's market. You know I was Chairman of a Bank for four years – oh you know that…

RC: *Gulf Bank?*

AS: Okay. This market is not everything, in the sense is nobody comes to you because you're good. But when they get in trouble… they come to you.

RC: *But, we were talking about the car parks, the garages… there you worked with Bonnington.*

AS: Jack Bonnington.

RC: *Yes, and also for the Stock Exchange Market.*

AS: Yes. But the relation, I think, started before.

RC: He was working with Sir Basil Spence.

AS: Yeah, and then he separated. They created his own office, and my brother then was in charge of KEO, and he developed some friendship with him, they were friends.

RC: Can we clarify what you said regarding Zahra Complex not designed by Ghazi, so it was designed by whom?

AS: Zahra Complex was I think designed by Basel Hassan. Iraqi architect, or American-Iraqi.

RC: Hassan. But he was with TAC, no?

AS: He was with KEO. He was the Head of Design then. He was with TAC before.

RC: The process of the waterfront. Because it's also like something where it's unclear, again, what was the role of each party involved?

AS: I think Sasaki was invited to that, it was a design competition. Sasaki won that competition in association with Ghazi and KEO. But Sasaki did the master plan, total process... Ghazi of course worked with them on the master plan and did all the buildings and KEO did all the engineering.

RC: And the Dasman Complex in the former Dana Roundabout, Sharq.

AS: It wasn't done by Ghazi. That was done by an Iraqi architect who used to be with KEO, his name is John Aziz. He immigrated to the United States.

RC: Sorry, but how did these two entities, 'Ghazi Sultan, Architect' and KEO developed parallel practices along the years, here inside the office?

AS: I mean, Ghazi he had his clients...he was coming everyday, normal.

RC: And did Ghazi ever advise KEO on the selection of an international consultant?

AS: Not as far as I know, no...

Look, With true respect to architects but not the best managers. Okay, because...I had this when George Candilis was doing the Aisha Al Salem (United Centre Housing Project, 1971–1975). They used to send us architecture drawings sometimes this much, sometimes that way, sometimes this way. So I was in the car with him one time, I said "Look George, I mean we do – I mean this is very confusing for us, you have twenty-five sizes for drawings. How you organise your work?" He looked at me, he said "If I organise my work, I can't be creative." He said "I must..." so, okay.

RC: That's always a good answer!

AS: He concluded by saying 'I must be creative.' Architects are not very disciplined when it comes to management. At KEO, we were totally private sector. After the bank crisis, the financial crisis of 1981–82, we had to diversify our clients, and work for the government. For that, we came up with a strategic plan based on two major decisions. I remember very vividly: to diversify our market and our services. It really worked out.

RC: Interesting, that's something that Pace and SSH tried to do at a later stage.

AS: It's too late for them to do anything now. That was 1985.

RC: But, regarding your relation with architecture? We have discussed KEO's relation with different designers such as Ghazi and Candilis ...

AS: No, no, a lot of different architects, there was my brother Faisal. Candilis was one among others, such as Jack Bonnington, and there was the Swiss architect, Alfred Roth, who designed some prototype schools for Khaled Al-Essa. He did some work with us too. He loved the tents, he loved to sit there. •

Souq Brutal: Kuwait's Modernity and the New Souqs

SARA SARAGOÇA SOARES

In the mid-twentieth century, the re-construction of cities through large highway networks and stand-alone buildings was commonly perceived as a way to modernise and renew the post-war enterprise. In joint efforts, governments, contractors, architects, and planners claimed for the rejection of the old town leading to the demolition of large extensions of old towns that were consequently replaced by large-scale building facilities. In the Middle East, following the discovery of oil, the western presence in many territories generated similar urban processes, and was used as tool to legitimate development policies of newly independent nations.

Kuwait, as the first and most extreme case of post-oil modernisation, contextualises the challenges of a nation-building project that was as much embraced by its ruler as it was imposed by others.

Under the Master Plan of 1952 by British planners Minoprio, Spencely, and MacFarlane, road networks and new neighbourhood units were rigidly planned and implemented outside the city wall. The old cohesive settlement was radically abandoned and transformed into a business district. Up until the 1970s, the desired Modern Kuwait failed to integrate the older city, lacking a clear urban identity and a civic sense of belonging. The city rapidly became dominated by an *affluent individualism* among citizens and city officials, who devoted their efforts to the erection of modern monuments as diverse as their authors, requiring architectural and urban strategies.

The idea of self-contained units was encouraged in an attempt to recover a lost city and meet the needs of a new society. The initiative resulted in multiple modern souqs scattered all across Kuwait City. By their size and volume, these exuberant concrete buildings rapidly became a dominant feature of the cityscape, projecting a hegemonic image of modernity. Today, both local and foreign scholars have labelled them *brutalist*.

During recent years, these structures, almost forgotten by the native population, have suffered gradual deterioration and the challenge of conservation. Confronted with the current processes of urban development from Dubai and Qatar's twinkling trends, these souqs have started to be modified, but face the risk of demolition in the near future if the mass destruction of modernist buildings – taking place since 2003 – do not stop.

Within the framework of a localisation policy that has fostered feelings of patriotism and nationalism over the last decade, politicians, scholars, and even architecture and planning practitioners have labelled these structures "foreign" and implicitly distinct from local history and building traditions. Only very recently, under narratives of nation building through memory and identity, has an emerging community of young, well-educated artists and professionals from varied sectors of society started to give these buildings 'archaeological status' for preservation.

Based on the recognition of Kuwait City as a valid case study in the debate and discussion on the adaptive re-use of modern heritage, this paper aims to re-evaluate the achievements and failures of Kuwait's modernisation through the rich repository of multi-use, self-contained units, exploring their response to the desired modern city and its implications on the local community.

1. Aerial view of Kuwait City, 2015.
© Dar al-Athar al-Islamiyyah, Nelson Garrido, 2015.

Modernity
in the Middle East

Most Arab countries, including the most conservative, experienced deep political and social changes in the 1930s and 1970s that have had a huge and rapid impact on the ways that territories, particularly major cities, are perceived. Independence from European countries, the exodus of Palestinians,[1] and fundamentally the discovery of oil, resulted in unpredictable urban growth.

In many cases there was no historical continuity, but rather a radical disruption to the norm, with extreme effect in Kuwait. The desire for a modern life within an Islamic society and the rapid increase in population that accompanied the oil boom presented challenges for the organisation of the city.

In response to multiple patriotic aspirations, architecture and planning are called upon to reflect nationalistic identities that could sustain the formation of new independent states. This generated hundreds of new buildings and city plans by a generation of architects trained in the 1930s in connection to local council boards. Many of them were then in the final stages of their lives, and their pupils, Arab architects and planners trained in European and American schools, or at the American universities of Beirut and Cairo. All of them contributed to the implementation of large-scale national projects, such as parliament and ministry buildings, central banks,

1. The first big exodus took place in 1948, the year the state of Israel was formed, known as the *Yawm an-Nakbah*: the day of the catastrophe, that led to an emigration hump of 900,000 Palestinian Arabs, according to a 1952 United Nations Commission for Palestine report. The Six Day War (1967) caused a new migratory wave of 325,000 Palestinians. There was a sudden increase in population in the host countries, spurring major changes to the physical condition of their cities, and in some cases, refugee camps have been gradually transformed into uncontrolled, fixed residential areas.

2. Poster from *Engineering and Architecture in the 21st Century*, Riyadh Al-Nakib, Kuwait, 1978.
© Riyadh Al-Nakib.

2. Sandy Isenstadt and Kishwar Rizvi, "Modern Architecture and the Middle East: The Burden of Representation," in *Modernism and the Middle East, Architecture and politics in the twenty century* (Seattle: University of Washington Press, 2008), 4.

3. "Kuwait: the fabulous Sheikdom," *Life Magazine*, v. 46, n. 9 (1959): 57.

4. Michael N. Barnett, "Sovereignty, Nationalism, and Regional Order in the Arab States System," *International Organisation*, v. 49, n. 3 (1995): 497.

5. Muhannad Albaqshi, "The social production of space, Kuwait Spatial History" (PhD diss., College of the Illinois Institute of Technology, 2010).

6. Farah Al-Nakib, "Kuwait's Modern Era Between Memory and Forgetting," *Acquiring Modernity*, ed. Noura Alsager (Kuwait: National Council for Culture, Arts and Letters, 2014), 7.

7. Sara Saragoça Soares, "Man of Kuwait, Other Modernities," *Acquiring Modernity*, ed. Noura Alsager (Kuwait: National Council for Culture, Arts and Letters, 2014), 17–19.

schools and universities, hospitals, stadiums, social housing, and urban plans, producing an entire regional stock of modernist buildings, and prompting the global architectural concept of Brutalism. "With such attention to its deep traditions and rapid modernisation, the Middle East has emerged as a rich setting for the study of modern architecture."[2]

In Kuwait there was a violent clash with the twentieth century.[3] The development process that transformed a humble coastal town into a rich modern country was based on massive urban transformation, supported by a welfare state that linked the material and political interests of citizens to the state.[4] This "social production of space"[5] enabled Kuwait's modernisation to take place at breakneck speed, and can be analysed in three phases: The British protectorate period, independence, and nation-state building. Words such as *nahda* (awakening), *taqaddum* (progress), and *almustaqbal* (the future), became popularly used by both state and society.[6]

This complex process of Kuwait's nation building has presented several challenges and dilemmas: The absence of qualified local technicians paved the way for foreign actors, external perspectives and globalising trends.

No attention was given along the way to the old city and loss of heritage. The inhabitants of the small-walled coastal town welcomed profound physical transformation without really understanding the process of construction of the new city. Such change was viewed as a symbol of progress and as being synonymous with a comfortable life. It was strongly supported by welfare subsidies that, in a very short time, created hundreds of Kuwaiti millionaires.

Without fully realising it, a new "Man of Kuwait" was born, challenging traditions and beliefs in typologies that have led to new limits for individuality and privacy.[7]

Kuwait's Modernisation, the Discovery of Oil and British Influence

In just 40 years, Kuwait was able to redefine itself through a radical urban transformation, with the medieval city being rapidly demolished and replaced by a new town. This is not the result of social or cultural evolution, but is a reflection of urban assumptions that were defended in Europe after WWII. This period, commonly known as *Al-Asr Al-Thahaby* (the Golden Era), brought Kuwait years of prosperity resulting from an intense modernisation program that will repurpose a new capital city-state in a few years, as well as a new political and social hierarchy. With the discovery of oil in 1938, the port economy that was once fundamental to the country's subsistence disappeared dramatically. Maritime activities such as boat construction and pearl diving and trade were erased by the exclusive production and export of oil. With the first export of oil in 1946, taking advantage of favorable international conditions after the end of WWII, newcomer Sheikh Abdallah Al-Salem Al-Sabah (r. 1950 to 1965) assumed full control of the country's finances, formerly the responsibility of the town's merchants, and stressed a plan for an ambitious nation that would make Kuwait unique among other Gulf countries: a new physical capital city, implemented parallel to a social welfare system.

The Kuwaiti leader's ambition for a modern city, commissioned to the British Political Agency in 1951, was then grounded on the successful experience of the Ahmadi oil town, built between 1947–51. Planners and planning advisors for the British resident minister were influential in KOC building program and master plan guidelines, commissioned in 1947 to Wilson Mason & Partners.[8] Back then the references to Abadan in Iran was a stronger precedent, as well the West Africa's[9] post-colonial projects developed by British architects Maxwell Fry and Jane Drew,[10] and Alfred Alcock.[11] The experiences of Wilson in the post-WWI colonial planning enterprise, from New Delhi to Abadan,[12] and Garden City to architecture in the tropics and self-build experimentalism, provided a comprehensive approach to Ahmadi's building program implementation, with distinguished interventions from Fry and Drew.[13]

Under strong British presence in the territory, the process of envisioning Kuwait's new capital city and its first and decisive Master Plan arose under the influence of the principles of the New Town,[14] led by British planners Minoprio, Spencely, and Macfarlane (MSM). Under a *tabula rasa* condition, the 1952 Master Plan laid out a city separated into functioning districts, embedded onto a modern road system of concentric rings in an East-West direction, recalling the concepts behind Ebenezer Howard's Garden City and Social City (1902). In 1957, traffic congestion dictated the demolition of the *soor*,[15] replaced by the green belt and fulfilling another criterion of the Garden City.

The medieval courtyard house was quickly replaced by a large suburban detached villa implemented in the designated neighbourhood unit, on the outskirts of the city. The plan initially covered eight district units for 6,000 people each, located between the first and third ring roads, in a total area larger than the old city. This successful relocation process, without major social objections, was only possible due to a concept of the welfare city-state that generated huge income for Kuwaiti families. A first distribution of oil-wealth was done through a Land Acquisition Policy, whereby private land within the walled city was nationalised at prices much above their actual value. Along with the housing units, priority was given to the water system, energy supply, and the port.[16] By 1953, Richard Costain (Middle East) Co. Ltd.,[17] one of the "Big Five,"[18] accomplished the important first desalination plant, designed by English architect Bernard Frankland Dark.

An intensive program of constructing hospitals and schools took place concurrently. Education turned out to be one of the priorities of the Kuwaiti ruler. The first schools were commissioned to WWII veteran Philip Oliver George Wakeham and his partner Anthony Charles Tripe, who were commissioned with several secondary schools and nurseries.

John R. Harris, a young English architect, got his first overseas appointment in 1952, with the design of the Kuwait Research Laboratories – pioneer in the Middle East for testing materials according to local physical conditions.[19] In 1953, he was awarded the design of the New State Hospital in Doha, and shortly after returned to Kuwait to design the Sulaibikhat Hospital, also known as the Women's Hospital (1954–1964). At this stage, the design was strongly linked to climatic conditions and the precepts of Tropical Architecture promoted at the Architectural Association by Maxwell Fry and Jane Drew.

Most of the buildings were not yet equipped with air conditioning, so it was common to see double-layered facades, shaded roofs and walkways, pre-cast concrete grills and sun-screens in response to the climate. The repetition of standard, prefabricated concrete elements served during the 1950s to implement and distribute nationwide hospital buildings, sports and schools facilities, solving issues of time and local resources.

8. Reem Alissa, "The Oil Town of Ahmadi since 1946: From Colonial Town to Nostalgic City," *Comparative Studies of South Asia, Africa and the Middle East*, v. 33, n. 1 (2003), 41–58.

9. Collective name for the former British colony, now the independent countries of Gambia, Sierra Leone, Ghana, and Nigeria.

10. The British couple Edwin Maxwell Fry (1899–1987) and Jane Beverly Drew (1911–1996), pioneers of the 'style' modern tropical, specialised in large-scale planning projects for tropical countries in Africa and the Middle East, as well in Chandigarh, India. Co-authors of the publications, *Village Housing in the Tropics* (1947), *and, Tropical Architecture in the Humid Zone* (1956). Iain Jackson and Jessica Holland, *The Architecture of Edwin Maxwell Fry and Jane Drew: Twentieth Century Architecture, Pioneer Modernism and the Tropics* (Surrey and Burlington: Ashgate, 2014).

11. British architect Alfred Edward Savige Alcock (1902–1991), pioneer in developing self-build villages in Kumasi, Ghana 1936–45. The "experimental village" album was very well-known among the British architectural and planning community working overseas.

12. Wilson Mason & Partners, British architecture and planning office was founded in 1926 after winning an important commission to design the colonial company town Abadan in Iran. Mark Crinson, "Abadan: Planning and Architecture Under the Anglo-Iranian Oil Company," *Planning Perspectives*, v. 12, n. 3 (1997).

13. Jane Drew's autobiography mentions the authorship and construction of Ahmadi General Hospital, housing, clinics, and social amenities (1949–1951). Also, in 1950, while preparing Chandigarh selected documents, Maxwell Fry refers to Ahmadi buildings as nearly completed.
Jane Drew, "Fragments of Jane Drew's Autobiography and relating documents, 1983," RIBA Archive, F&D/25/1. Maxwell Fry, "Maxwell Fry, Full Autobiography, 1985," RIBA Archive, F&D/20/2.

14. The New Town Act of 1946 was the new urban agenda in the UK post-WWII, aiming to reconstruct London's satellite cities, and according to the guidelines of the 1902 publication, "Garden Cities of To-Morrow" of Ebenezer Howard. The British architectural firm of Minoprio and Spencely and Macfarlane (MSM), founded in 1928, was involved in this movement with the towns of Chelmsford, Crawly and Worcester.

15. Mud wall.

16. Colonel Amps, in 1953, in a lecture at The Royal Central Asian Society, reveals Kuwait as a new country with hundreds of works in progress simultaneously, reporting the presence of eighteen boats patiently waiting their turn to dock at the port. The English Colonel Leon Williams Amps was a civil

Reclaiming the Arab Identity: Urban Strategy and Context

engineer and director of the Gulf Engineering Company.
L.W. Amps, "Kuwait Town development," *Journal of the Royal Central Asian Society*, v. 40, n. 3–4 (1953): 234–40.

17. Richard Costain (Middle East) Co. Ltd., a subsidiary of Costain Group, arrived in Kuwait in 1952 in partnership with the newly established Gulf Engineering Company of Abdallah Saleh Al-Mulla (2nd Secretary of State from 1932 to 55). Richard Costain was a pioneer in the development of urban blocks, such as Dolphin Sq. (1935) in London, at that time the largest collective housing building with 600 apartments; Well-known also by its industrial infrastructure of reinforced concrete silos in particular the Tyne (1937) in Newcastle, considered the highest silo in the world, and designed by Oscar Faber; During WWII created the famous Mulberry floating concrete port, a logistics platform in the English Channel after "D-Day" and the Normandy Invasion. The company know-how and manufacturing processes were fundamental during the early years of Kuwait's modernisation.

18. The Big Five were five British construction firms that monopolised the market in the early years of Kuwait's development: Richard Costain Limited; D.C. and William Press; John Howard; Taylor Woodrow; and Holland, Hannen, and Cubitts.
Rula Sadik, "Nation-Building and Housing Policy: A Comparative Analysis of Urban Housing Development in Kuwait, Jordan, and Lebanon" (PhD diss., University of California at Berkley, 1996), 225.

19. Anthony Edwin James Morris, *John R. Harris Architects* (Hurtwood press Ltd, 1984), 8.

20. Ali Gholoum Ali Rais, *Kuwait in Postcards* (Kuwait: Center for Research and Studies on Kuwait, 2009), 539.

21. Saba George Shiber (1923–1968) was an Arab Palestinian planner with American citizenship who worked particularly in Lebanon and Kuwait. He developed his studies and works around the built environment of Arab cities. He was considered "Arab of the year" in 1963 by the magazine Middle East Business Digest, who called him "Mr. Arab Planner."

22. *The Kuwait Urbanization*, is Shiber most famous publication. In 650 pages he makes a deep analysis about Kuwait City's urban development, with harsh comments on Western practices, reinforcing a preconceived idea that post-oil architecture does not reflect local culture but rather Western civilisation.

23. Saba George Shiber, *The Kuwait Urbanization* (Kuwait: Kuwait Government Printing Press, 1964), 158.

24. Ibid., 167.

The country was experiencing profound physical change, but without a clear strategy and mostly in the city centre, where only Fahad Al-Salem street was completely paved by 1960. Colourful postcards, conceived in the style of French boulevard images, showed the world a modern and busy commercial avenue, concealing, in fact, a chaotic and scattered city.[20]

The Development Board, established in 1951 to manage the implementation of the Master Plan, was inefficient, and criticism surrounding the opportunism and self-interest of British practice began to emerge. An anti-Western sentiment was reinforced as pan-Arabism developed in the region, spurred by Egyptian President Gamal Abdel Nasser.

Amid this turbulent period, Kuwait saw the increased arrival of numerous engineers, architects, and planners from Arab countries in the late 1950s after the Suez Canal Crisis. Palestinians, Jordanians, and Egyptians started to work in state departments. Egyptian architect Sayyed Karim was tasked with designing various cinemas, along with Lebanese architect Kamal Shair, who signed his first major contract for a power plant building, which helped drive his newly formed office Dar Al-Handasah into the scene. In this context, Arab urban planner Saba George Shiber[21] arrived in Kuwait in 1960, taking up a position as the government's architectural and city planning adviser, first in the Public Works Department and then at the Development Board and Municipality. In addition, national sovereignty in 1961 spurred greater confidence and the involvement of local people in the decision-making process.

In 1960, all projects and plans in progress or under construction were suspended. Only the international architectural competition for the Kuwait National Museum went ahead and was won by French architect Michael Ecochard. With Shiber in charge, architecture experienced a running battle between modernity and tradition, in which there was an appropriation of local forms and materials in an effort to enhance a sense of local identity in response to the new status of a modern, independent Arab nation.

As noted in his famous publication *The Kuwait Urbanization*,[22] he proposed a new strategy for the city centre – the Central Business District (CBD). This urban redevelopment outlined eleven areas for "community-wide higher education and research institutions, hotels, showrooms, offices, parking and, a rare spectacle [...] by landscaping through which consolidated pedestrian shopping centres and pedestrian walkways [...]."[23] No residential areas were designated in this plan, contributing dramatically to the future of a city without local inhabitants.

The design process and construction of these areas, characterised mostly by private demand, was conducted under tight Municipality supervision. Several buildings were raised under a policy of "architectural control," achieving a unified design in the CBD. Even the multi-owner three-parcel units, commissioned to different architects, were encouraged to agree on a unified design.[24] Shiber's influence was apparent in the design of all these buildings, which sought a uniform language between Islamic decorative motifs and geometry of polygons framed by reinforced concrete.

After the implementation of Areas 1, 2 and 3, and following "Mr. Arab Planner" design criteria, Al-Mirgab Area 9 followed the template of a conventional type of bazaar, in which multiple buildings that could be traced the old *qaysariyas*, were built like a long, covered street at double height, becoming the famous tissues markets. The majority of these areas emerged in the post-Shiber phase, between the 1970s and 1980s, diverging from the original concept of a controlled design process.

With the CBD development, the old city increasingly disappeared in a process that was far from clear. Certain areas were already demolished and rebuilt three times before they reached full stabilisation.[25]

The first decade of modernisation was coming to an end, marked by rational planning and an obsession with modernity that shattered the old town in a rapid development project that proved to be unstable and poorly defined. Saba George Shiber left Kuwait in 1964 and by the following year the country started experiencing a particularly new and vibrant period.

3. Model of CBD Area 3 in Kuwait City, Saba George Shiber, 1961.
© *The Kuwait Urbanization.*

Back to the West and a New Era of Nation-Building

The first generation of Kuwaitis educated abroad started to return to the country, bringing with them new ways of thinking and practicing. All this excitement was translated into an era full of cultural events, including the first national short film *Al-Asifah*, the opening of the Sultan Gallery in 1969,[26] and the inauguration of Kuwait University in 1966 (former girls' secondary school designed by German architect Rambald von Steinbüchel-Rheinwall).

The spirit of pan-Arabism was shaken by the twin failures of the 1960s: the end of the United Arab Republic (UAR) in 1961, and the 1967 Arab-Israeli War, which led Nasser to give up his dream and also to the rise of the status quo-oriented Gulf States.[27]

This was all reflected in the practice of architecture, as the first local architects who had studied abroad with government-sponsored scholarships returned, opening their own offices and leading public institutions, which also led to the foundation of the Kuwait Society of Engineers in 1962. Two architects, Ghazi Sultan and Hamid Shuaib, were largely responsible for a Western focus, contradicting the ideals previously defended by Saba George Shiber.

According to Shuaib:

4. Hamid Shuaib, Kuwait City, 1971.
© *Al Kuwaiti.*

> Building was sporadic – a bit here, a bit there – Shiber did his best, but it was a muddle. The MSM Master Plan was eventually completed – space was filled up to the Fourth Ring Road, but only by additions made by the Ministry of Public Works' planning staff. There was no follow-up of the Master Plan, because there was no notion of how to proceed on from it.[28]

Shuaib, who graduated from the University of Liverpool, established the Pan-Arab Consulting Engineers (Pace) in 1968, and, together with SSH, Gulf Consultants and the Kuwait Engineering Office (KEO), was among the first architecture firms in Kuwait.[29] Shuaib, in the Municipality since 1965, created the Town Planning Department in an attempt to establish criteria for city development, which generated the first stage of the Municipality Development Plan in 1967.

The Kuwaiti architect requested the collaboration of various foreign experts through Omar Azzam, the United Nations' representative of Middle Eastern affairs, among whowere requested were Colin Buchanan and his partner Alan McCulloch. In a return to the recent past, these English planners were commissioned with executing the second master plan for the country in 1968. The "Plan for Kuwait" was a national plan for both urban and rural

25. Stephen Gardiner, *Kuwait the Making of a City* (Harlow: Longman, 1983).

26. The Sultan Gallery was founded in Kuwait in 1969 by the siblings Ghazi and Najat Sultan, supporting and publicising contemporary Arab art.

27. Barnett, "Sovereignty," 488.

28. Gardiner, *Kuwait, The Making of a City*, 56.

29. The Pan-Arab Consulting Engineers (Pace) was founded by Kuwaitis Hamid Shuaib and Sabah Al-Rayes and the Palestinian-American Charles Haddad. Today is still one of the largest architecture and engineering offices in the region, directed by Tarek Shuaib, son of Hamid Shuaib. SSH was the first Kuwait office, founded by the Lebanese architect Sabah Abi-Hanna in 1961, and later joined by Salem Al-Marzouq. The Kuwait Engineering Office (KEO) was founded in 1964 by Faisal and Abdul Aziz Sultan. Gulf Consultant was created in 1967 by Hamad Alghanim.

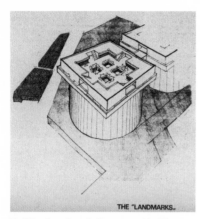

THE "LANDMARKS."

5. "The Landmarks" proposal in *The Future Development of the old city of Kuwait*, BBPR, 1969.
© Kuwait Municipal Archive.

30. Colin Buchanan and Partners, *A Plan for Kuwait* (1972).

31. "Mat-building can be said to epitomise the anonymous collective; where the functions come to enrich the fabric, and the individual gains new freedom of action through a new shuffled order, based on interconnection, closely knit patterns of association and possibilities for growth, diminution and change" (Smithsons, 1974).

32. See "Proposals For Restructuring Kuwait," *Architectural Review* (September 1974): 178–190.

33. Roberto Fabbri, Sara Saragoça Soares, Ricardo Camacho, *Modern Architecture Kuwait 1949–1989* (Zurich: Niggli, 2016), 134.

34. Received the Aga Khan Award for Architecture in 1980.

areas. Certain guidelines were taken into consideration for the first time, such as the estimated population growth, employment, and traffic. Also, the comprehensive master plan outlined three strategic schemes: a long-term urban strategy for the whole country known as The National Physical plan, a short-term master plan referred to as The Plan for Kuwait Town, and an action area-detailed plan to tackle urgent needs.[30]

Meanwhile, an advisory committee, composed of Leslie Martin, Franco Albini, and Azzam, together with Shuaib, was responsible for selecting the teams of architects to develop a strategic plan for Kuwait Town. It came down to a choice between British architects Alison and Peter Smithson, French architects Candilis–Josic–Woods, Reima and Raili Pietilä from Finland, and the Italians, Belgiojoso, Peressutti, and Rogers (BBPR). With the exception of BBPR, all of them were an active part of a group of young architects known as TEAM X.

The 1969 Urban Form Studies for the Old City and its "demonstration areas," provided an opportunity to rethink the city centre, introducing concepts such as the *mat building*,[31] *the mega-structure, self-contained unit, habitat units*, and urban preservation.[32] None of these proposals progressed further, but they led to further opportunities for some of the stakeholders, such as the Ministry of Foreign Affairs, which was commissioned to the Pietilä couple, amid the logic of a new global approach drawing boundaries and connections between modernity and the local culture. Indeed, architects started to advocate practices that held a sense of place.

Iraqi architect Rifat Chadirji personally advocated for modernist concepts in his time at the Iraq Development Board (IDB), which put him in direct contact with Walter Gropius and Le Corbusier. Chadirji's motivations for his Al-Hassawi Residential Complexes (1968–1973) in Kuwait, via Iraq Consult, were clearly influenced by a regionalised architecture that preserved a sense of place.[33]

Also, the launch of large public buildings in the late 1960s revealed a new sensitive design process recognising context and traditional forms, with the reinterpretation of vernacular elements, such as doors, tiles, fountains, domes, minarets, and the *mashrabiya*.

The National Assembly (1968–1982) by Jørn Utzon, and the important water network system of the Water Towers (1965–1976) and Kuwait Towers (1965–1977), by the Swedish Sune Lindström representing VBB and Danish architect Malene Bjørn,[34] soon became state symbols and successful examples of modernisation processes, in opposition to the Central Bank (1966–1976), by Arne Jacobsen, which was profoundly changed only nine years after its completion.

Although the second master plan was never part of an official state policy, the following decade of the 1970s was one of prosperity and progress, supported by large oil revenues. Benefiting from the 1973 Organisation of Arab Petroleum Exporting Countries (OAPEC) oil embargo and the full nationalisation of the Kuwait Oil Company in 1975, Kuwait City thrived by building on the 1952 Master Plan.

The main government buildings in Kuwait projected the notion of a modern country designed by the best architects. In addition, public-private partnerships and several private initiatives produced large-scale and multi-program building typologies, exposing local firms not only to European architectural practices, but moreover to large corporate architecture and engineering firms that emerged in North America after WWII.

Before the 1970s, few American firms were involved in Middle Eastern construction. There were isolated exceptions in Manama, Bahrain, where Marcel Breuer Associates designed the Regency Hotel, and in Iraq, when the country experienced an extensive modernisation program under the Iraq Development Board, established in 1955.[35] Frank Lloyd Wright was invited to design the never-built Opera House, and Walter Gropius – with The Architects Collaborative (TAC) – to conceive the new university campus for Baghdad, in what would be their first experience in the Middle East.[36] There was an increase in American influence due to the commissions promoted both by Arabian American Oil Company (Aramco) and the US Army Corps of Engineers. Aramco had already been deeply involved in Saudi Arabia since the 1930s, when several oil enclaves were built in the desert for workers and their families, such as Dhahran, Dammam, and Al-Khobar. American design influence was also apparent in international hotel chains: TAC designed the InterContinental Hotel in Sharjah, and William Pereira the Sheraton Hotel in Doha.[37] By that time, the more active firms were Candill, Rowlett, Scott (CRS) – mostly in Saudi Arabia – Skidmore, Owings & Merril (SOM), and TAC.[38] These US firms, with experience in expensive, major projects, brought a different approach from the European firms – usually more focus on public social architecture – and knowledge of new materials.

With the oil embargo and it's devastating impact on the American economy, American architects started to branch out in the region, pursuing ambitious state-led development programs, such as international airports and military and governmental complexes, but also contracts from private clients, such as banking towers, hotels, and commercial centres, "nothing but the best."[39]

Concrete was the preferred material, where pre-cast concrete proved to be more effective in large-scale projects. Not only was it more suitable for the Middle Eastern climate, it also enabled quality control prior to its application, reducing the construction problems of poor hand-skilled labour. Concrete was no longer regarded as just "concrete."[40]

The New Souqs:
Modernity and Community
in a Self-Contained Unit

The consolidation of urban and architectural values was understood mainly by Kuwait's rulers as an essential vehicle for preserving social cohesion, attributing and distributing land, and reinventing ancient typologies, like the souq.

An assortment of new multi-purpose mega structures was prominent in shaping new architectural approaches and replacing an urban life that has since been lost to the new suburbs of the neighbourhood units. Under a typology of self-contained units, these brutalist large-scale buildings were expressions of new concrete construction methods – "[...] An urbanism in which functionally compatible buildings, like the components of a tea set, would acquire a kind of neutrality and family likeness with the space between them becoming the collective of the spaces that each of the buildings carries with it," as Smithons said.[41]

The geographic, cultural and institutional terrain in Kuwait, in which the Smithsons were operating from 1968 to 1972, together with three other teams, was complex and shifting. The "old city is vanishing, but development by modern buildings has not replaced this with anything that can yet mark

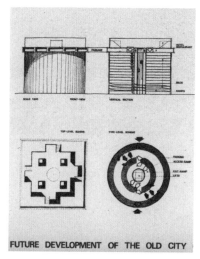

6. "The Landmarks" proposal in *The Future Development of the old city of Kuwait*, BBPR, 1969.
© Kuwait Municipal Archive.

35. "American architects' broad based involvement," *Middle East Construction* (September 1980): 75.

36. Political instability with the Iraqi revolution (1958–1963) cancelled many of IDB's projects. The university town, despite being one of the exceptions, suffered delays and changes to its implementation. With the death of Gropius in 1969, the project continued during the 1970s and 1980s with TAC and Iraqi architect Hisham Munir, although just a few buildings followed the initial designs of Gropius. Magnus Bernhardsson, "Vision of Iraq, Modernizing the Past in 1950s Baghdad," in *Modernism and the Middle East* (Seattle, London: University of Washington Press, 2008), 81–93.

37. "American architects' broad based involvement," 78.

38. Ibid 76.

39. Neil Parkyn, "Kuwait Revisited," *Middle East Construction* (September 1983): 39–42.

40. Tony Morris, "Precast concrete's Middle East Future," *Middle East Architectural Design* (May/June1979), 19.

41. Reyner Banham, "The New Brutalism," *Architectural Review* (December 1955): 355–361.

7. Areal view of Kuwait City with Souq Al-Kuwait, 1970s.
© Saudi Aramco World /SAWDIA, Tor Eigeland.

42. Alison Smithson, "Proposals for Restructuring Kuwait," *Architectural Review* (September 1974): 179.

43. See "Kuwait: The Smithsons' Scheme," *Architectural Review* (September 1974): 183–190.

44. Studio Architetti BBPR, *The Future Development of the Old City of Kuwait,* report submitted to Ministry of Planning, Kuwait, 1969, 4.3.

45. Souq Al-Kuwait; Souq Al-Kabeer; Souq Al-Safat; Souq Al-Manakh; Souq Al-Wataniya; Souq Al-Watiya. For more, see Fabbri, Saragoça, and Camacho, *Modern Architecture Kuwait,* 220–235.

46. Edward O. Nilsson (TAC principal architect for Souq Al-Wataniya), personal archive.

47. Public-private partnerships – a private entity receives a concession from the public sector to develop and operate a certain facility.

48. Interview with Edward O. Nilsson, Kuwait, May 2016.

the new City of Kuwait as a great capital city."[42] Smithsons' demonstration proposal utilised a low-mat building system, supported by "stations," and complemented by "interchangeable cell units" suitable for several functions.[43] Also, in the BBPR proposal, the Italian architects considered "The Landmarks" as volumetric structures with a multi-programmatic use. They were supposed also to act as town observation and motoring points, where users would leave the cars and gain access to a city with large pedestrian areas.[44] Both projects were never built, but were fundamental to show an appropriate building form, and as a guideline to gauge how people would use the space, which lead to the construction of the Kuwait's new souqs from 1973 to 1979.[45] The first, Souq Al-Kuwait (1973–76), in CBD Area 8, was initially designed by BBPR and follows the CBD land classification as per the Final Report on the CBD General Development Plan. This plan produced by BBPR, organised the downtown in a categorisation of building uses that became the determining input for the emergence of this new city typology. The multi-level zoning plan brought different uses to one building, proposing pedestrian-oriented activities at the ground level, and office or residential uses at upper floors.[46]

Under the first Build-Operate-Transfer (BOT),[47] the Souq Al-Kuwait was delivered to Kuwait Real Estate Company, which replaced BBPR with SSH and SOM, adapting the initial project without the residential program. This souq is marked by an outer ramp, flying sinuously above the urban space that leads to the semi-open car park with surprising city views. Different entrances at the commercial ground level establish a relationship with the adjacent old Mubarakiya souq, functioning almost as its extension. Souq Al-Kuwait was developed in parallel with Souq Al-Kabeer, of similar image and program, located in commercial Area 11.

The municipality proceeded with the BOT development methodology, as it proved to be successful, encouraging the idea of self-contained units as a good solution, occupying large portions of empty land within a multi-function programmatic use, and thus reviving the city centre by fulfilling the aspirations of the modern Kuwaiti population.

TAC, now without Gropius, who died in 1969, started what would be its long nationwide practice with the commission of the Kuwait Fund for Arab Economic Development (KFAED) building, in joint venture with the local Pace office. Souq Al-Safat (1973–75) was the first of the four souqs completed by the firm, and its successful acceptance confirmed TAC as one of the most prominent architectural offices practicing in the country, which lead to TAC's Kuwait branch in 1976. Carefully placed into Shiber's well-established Area 9, this sand-blast concrete unit was divided into two volumes, one for commercial purposes and the other for offices spaces. At the street level, pedestrians were invited in through permeable arcades within a regular metric. Inside, double-height spacious lobbies worked as large gathering and distribution areas.

The initial design sketches for Souq Al-Manakh (1973–75) took in consideration the proximity of the old souq and a station for a monorail line, a never built structure that was intended to connect the car park with otherparts of the CBD.[48] Its final volumetric mass was dotted by angular stair towers in the corners, arched openings at the street level and arched windows on the top floor, symbolically representing medieval fortifications. Inside, the two commercial floors were occupied by countless small offices, giving this souq an unusual office environment.

These mega structures of sandblasted raw concrete stand as the new urban renaissance, "because its design was not about the individual, it was about multitude."[49] Working as a contained unit, they were to function as the new city shelters, where it was possible to buy daily goods, park the car, work, or even to live, as in Souq Al-Wataniya.

Completed in 1979, Souq Al-Wataniya differed from the others by its "Arab settlement" on the rooftop. TAC principal, Edward Nilsson, decided to give a different architectural expression to these duplex apartments. Shaped as a village, they were grouped on a 4.40m module around pedestrian walk ways, and communal courtyards with gardens and fountains, expanding the urban experience to the roof of the demolished town. This attempt to reflect the vernacular spatial organisation on top of a compact concrete solid is indicative of TAC's best use of *beton brut* in shaping new opportunities through recognition of Kuwait's genius loci. The remaining floors contained parking space for 1000 cars and small shops, providing for the needs of the community in a self-sufficient contained unit and reflecting the BBPR's multi-level zoning plan desire to repopulate the city centre.[50] National Real Estate Co. (NREC) was also responsible for the development of Souq Al-Watiya (1974–79). TAC and Pace developed a scheme together that was never realised. Souq Al-Watiya today has a similar program, but a different design, and due to its location is still one of the most popular souqs within the foreign community. TAC souqs made use of the capabilities of reinforced concrete, with large concrete panels shaped by arches with small vertical openings, in contrast to large horizontal gaps. Environmental graphic design, created by TAC's graphics department,[51] was also an essential part of the design process, providing new opportunities for the large-scale interior patios covered with skylights.

According to Charles Gibson:

> Many architects of the time, including some at TAC who designed those large mixed-use projects for Kuwait were into 'brutalist' structures with a lot of exposed concrete. I think the principals designers realised that something more was needed to soften and humanise all of this concrete. So I believe TAC's architects considered signage and banners to be not just decoration or 'window dressing,' but an integral and necessary part of the architecture. Certainly, we at TAC Graphics held this view.[52]

In the exterior design of Al-Muttaheda and Al-Masseel souqs by British architect John Bonnington, is possible to identify its repetitive prefabricated elements, highlighted by a sequence of binary pairs: opened/closed, outside/inside, sunlight/shadow, revealing unexpected views from the inside. Intentionally designed in a precast concrete system, these projects acted as an experimental study for a new precasting factory set by the client in Kuwait in partnership with the German company Thosti AG.[53]

In all of these city units one could recognise an uncommon mixed-use typology, uniquely combining car parking, retail, services and housing.

Several modern architectural elements, such as access ramps, stair towers, lifts and a moving staircase, together with the ancestral concepts of the multi-functional *khans* and *wakalas*,[54] were noticeable in the interior courtyards at double and triple heights. These types of fortresses emerged amid the non-consolidated modern city fabric as seemingly isolated solid objects, established profound levels of interdependency with their surroundings and became an essential part of the town structure.

8. Souq Al-Manakh, TAC, Kuwait City, 1973–75.
© Aga Khan Visual Archive AKVA, MIT Documentation Center, TAC.

49. Cristopher Beanland, "Concrete buildings: Brutalist beauty," *The Independent*, January 19, 2014.

50. At this point there were more attempts to return Kuwaitis to the urban centre. In 1977, Arthur Erickson presented, at the request of the National Housing Authority, the Al-Sawber Housing Complex, a mega-residential project with 900 apartment units, of which only 500 were built. The goal was not achieved, and the complex came to be rented to low-income immigrants. At present, it is being reacquired by the state, which will lead to its total demolition.

51. TAC Graphics department joined TAC Interiors and TAC Landscape as co-equal collaborative resources within the organisation. "The field of environmental graphic design was just beginning to be recognised as a discipline that related to, but was distinct from, traditional graphic design. In this field, TAC was a leader, along with just a few other large American architecture firms like CRS in Texas, in integrating the design of architectural signage as an in-house capability that was equal in status with the more traditional departments of landscape architecture and interior design." Interview with Charles Gibson via email in February 2016.

52. Charles Gibson worked for TAC Graphics department from 1976 to 1979 in Cambridge, Massachusetts. His work with TAC, which he considered as an "once-in-a-lifetime" design opportunity, focuses on architectural banners and murals design for some of the souqs in Kuwait city. Interview with Charles Gibson via email in February 2016.

53. Morris, "Precast concrete's Middle East Future," 25.

54. Regional souqs made for travel merchants. They were closed-markets open to an inner courtyard with shops on the ground floor and a hotel on the upper floors.

9. Interior lobby of Souq Al-Wataniya in Kuwait City, TAC, 1974–79. © Charles Gibson Private Archive, TAC Graphics.

10. Signs of indigenous animals used in floor patterns, door medallions, banners, and exterior signs in Souq Al-Safat and Souq Al-Manakh, 1973–75. © Charles Gibson Private Archive, TAC Graphics.

55. Saragoça, "Man of Kuwait, Other Modernities," 17–19.

56. Souq Al-Manakh stock market was a market separated from the official one, considered the third-largest in the world by early 1980s. Mohamed Ramady, *Political, Economic and Financial Country Risk: Analysis of the Gulf Cooperation Council* (London: Springer, 2014), 100.

57. John Frazer, "Aladdin's Lamp of Middle East: Kuwait," *National Geographic*, v. 135, n. 5 (1969): 636–67.

To a certain extent, it might even be said, given the typology and the way they were enclosed and concentrated in the interior of the city, that this was a compact Islamic city, closed off to the desert and the dry and hot climate. In such a harsh environment, the eight colossal playgrounds, with a unique building program, generated the most successful public space, providing shelter for the first "Man of Kuwait," who had become, first and foremost, a shopper.[55]

The relevance of a public, self-contained, multi-program unit in the configuration of a modern society, built at the peak of the country's economic apotheosis during the post-oil embargo, represented the wealth of Kuwaitis who had a comfortable physical lifestyle, leisure time, and surplus cash to spend. In 1982, the crash of the nonofficial stock market in the Souq Al-Manakh bankrupted Kuwait's financial institutions and prompted a recession that rippled through society, preventing new real estate investments.[56] This situation was aggravated by the Iraqi invasion in the summer of 1990. After this period, the next decade was full of uncertainty.

Preservation and Society in Conflict

During this revolutionary process of nation formation no one seemed to realise the extent of the physical extinction of the old city, or at least no major concerns were raised. The blending of old and new was more a conception of ideals, as the Undersecretary of Ministry of Foreign Affairs Rashid Alrashid said in 1969:

> What we wish to preserve first is our religion, then our hospitality, then our family relationships [...] Then, the simplicity of simple men and the respect of the younger for the older. Finally, our individualism [...].
> We hope all these will remain.[57]

It was only after the 2003 Iraq invasion by US and British troops, which led to the death of Saddam Hussein in 2006, that building construction began to flourish once again, and with it the mass demolition of the post-oil buildings. Demolition became part of the daily life of the city, rapidly reshaping the urban landscape, encouraged by increasing floor area ratios that enabled the construction of skyscrapers, making the city more anonymous and incohesive.

Major state buildings that were hardly hit during the invasion began a fast recovery process and adopted a patriotic nature without architectural preservationist motivations. Thus, the vast majority of buildings underwent profound changes, with the introduction of new elements and materials, at a time when *alucobond* was being massively introduced as coating material. At the same time, the remaining pre-oil buildings started to be protected from demolition, fomented by a nostalgia that emerged after the 1990 Iraqi invasion, such as the Old Amiri Hospital or the Sheikh Khaz'al Palace, which did not avoid natural deterioration due to lack of intervention.

The brutalist units of the mid 1970s were able to keep up the pace, with no major exterior interventions. Inside, the simplicity of rationality from another time was compromised by rebuilding work since liberation.

After having been virtually abandoned by the native population, in favour of other commercial developments, the new users' status as "urban refugees" – formed of a large expat community – brought new life to these

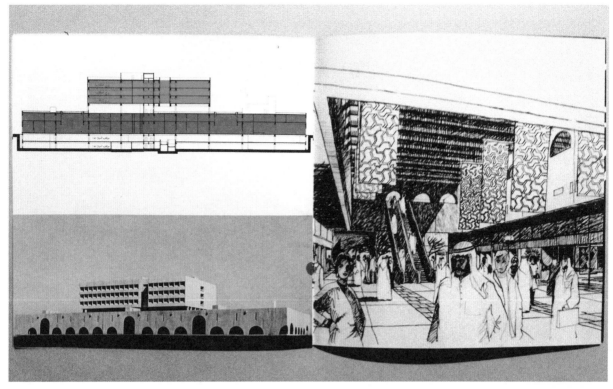

11. Brochure for Souq Al-Safat, TAC, 1973–75.
© Edward O. Nilsson Private Archive.

large human platforms, as they brought with them their culture, habits, motivations and frustrated hopes. The souqs of today accommodate thousands of parking spaces and hundreds of shops, reflecting the many cultural and social contrasts and influences of Kuwaiti society that have long been brought to the country by continuous mass migration, showing how architecture has been able to respond to changes. Souq Al-Wataniya lost its residential function and is now a big Indian bazaar, while Souq Al-Muttheda supplies a large Filipino community.

Although low-income foreign communities revived these mega-structures by reappropriating the souqs to their needs, they were also the reason for scrapping them, as is happening now in Al-Sawber Residential Complex, designed by Arthur Erickson in 1977.[58] The increase in social segregation, has emphasised the dichotomy of the indigenous vs. the foreign, leading directly to associations of a space that is not worth it, not good enough. Indeed, the post-oil, non-governmental city buildings are mostly occupied by non-Kuwaitis, which added to a poor technical performance of materials and systems, and, together with the absence of maintenance, have relegated them to demolition. Nevertheless, the scale and construction method of the new souqs has given them a solid and unshakable image, challenging the opportunity for their replacement.

The joint-venture agreements between public and local real estate companies, based on BOT contracts of limited duration, has also protected these buildings from major changes. However, recently, new BOT agreements are promoting renovation processes that may include dramatic changes to the integrity of these buildings.[59] In order to make them more modern and commercially attractive, beautification programs have begun to

58. See Arthur Erickson, "The Sawaber Project Development Study," for National Housing Authority – Kuwait, 1977.

59. On the web page of Aqarat, officially Kuwait Real Estate Company: "Aqarat is proud to have been able to secure a ten-year extension on its existing BOT government contacts for Souq Al-Kuwait. As part of the agreement with the government, Aqarat will commence a multi-phased renovation of the building. The renovation of the property will be all encompassing and will include both aesthetic and core disciplines." Accessed on January 26, 2016, http://www.aqarat.com.kw/properties-kuwait-other-projects-souk-al-kuwait.html

SOUK AL WATANIYA
Kuwait City, Kuwait
Presentation Model

12. Presentation model of Souq
Al-Wataniya, TAC, 1974–79.
© Edward O. Nilsson Private Archive.

be implemented, in particular with the replacement of what are considered to be old elements, such as doors, windows, and lighting, and by exterior concrete painting.

Maintenance is a rare exercise, as concepts of preservation and the adaptive reuse of existing buildings are non-existent in a country where exceptional economic circumstances drove a society for mass consumption, quickly dropping anything considered to be outmoded. This ephemeral way to handle *things* is also what disconnects Kuwait from physical values of space, as the Smithsons state: "Arab cities are full of buildings started and never finished, and finished and then abandoned, for it would seem the Arabs are more spontaneous, less worldly than the east or west."[60]

The unfortunate association that made brutalism widely unpopular does not apply here, since Kuwait's buildings are not consciously recognised as such, but more as simply old, large infrastructures, without architectural significance.

Kuwait does not have basic legislative control, nor listed buildings or any kind of conservation industry.[61] The lack of interest shown by public and private building patrons, or by the population in general, has been confounded by very strong profit-driven activity, with general contractors

60. The Alison and Peter Smithson Archive, Frances Loeb Library, Special Collections, Graduate School of Design, Harvard University, Folder BC000.

61. "Princely Decree No.11 of 1960, Law of Antiquities" is the single document drawn up for the protection of antiquities. The content is abstract and limited, and has no law enforcement.

dominating the future of the city. Herein lays a very clear enfeeblement of Kuwait, where in this *business* as *usual* environment, keeping existing buildings is not a good deal.

In addition to what Australian architect Susan Mcdonald summarises in "Reconciling authenticity with repair: Philosophical difficulties for modern buildings,"[62] a lack of objective knowledge in Kuwait to define criteria for protection, the legal gap due to lack of government support, and the lack of implementation of projects are also chronic difficulties that have remained as rampant today as they have been in the past.

Only in 2012 was post-oil architecture historicised and curated on a consistent basis, with the first participation at the 13th International Architecture Exhibition of la Biennale di Venezia, which included the first international conference "Modern Kuwait." In 2014, the Kuwait Towers, or *Abraj Al-Kuwait*, became part of UNESCO's tentative list for the first inscription of a twentieth-century building in the Arab Gulf region.[63]

Even though this attempt is more indicative of a political exercise rather than a cultural priority, it represents a huge step forward in the recognition of modern architecture as part of Kuwait's cultural heritage.

Since 2014, *Madeenah's* city tours have recalled memories through informed guided walking, and, in the spring of 2016 the first survey and systematic analysis of Kuwait's modern buildings was launched through an exhibition and publication entitled: *Modern Architecture Kuwait 1949–1989*.[64]

All these projects identify and recognise Kuwait's post-oil buildings as being of historical significance in relation to an evident Arab identity that emerged at a very specific time and within a very specific context.

With the demolition of the old city, Kuwait could prove to be the perfect ground to protect the modern architecture of the twentieth century, commonly referred to as the 'old buildings.' To demystify the pejorative sense of the word "old" in a society that was formed with terminology like *hadith* (new or modern), and challenging the co-habitation between multiple communities, only an adaptive reuse, dictated by the existing condition and by innovative programs can give a unique, and maybe the last, opportunity to such buildings. Brutalist buildings were built to be solid, reliable, permanent, and most off all they were meant to be public, using the same principles that guided Kuwait to modernity. •

62. Susan Macdonald, "Conserving 'carbuncles' Dilemmas of conservation in practice: an overview of current English Heritage research and advice," in *Structure and Style, Conserving 20th Century Buildings* (London: E & FN SPON, 1997), 207.

63. See more in http://whc.unesco.org/en/tentativelists/5933/

64. Fabbri, Saragoça, and Camacho, *Modern Architecture Kuwait.*

Edward Nilsson

Edward Nilsson graduated with a B.Arch. from The Cooper Union, an M.Arch. from Harvard University Graduate School of Design, and an MBA from Babson College, and has taught architectural history and case-study seminars at Boston Architectural College. In the mid-1970s Nilsson served as project architect at The Architects Collaborative (TAC) for Souq Al-Manakh (Area 5 of the Central Business District), and then as Principal Design and Project Architect for Souq Al-Wataniya (Area 10C).

Ricardo Camacho conducted this interview in the United States, during April 2016.

Ricardo Camacho: *Incredible pictures! Is this the monorail here on the side of Souq Al-Manakh? [pointing at pictures of sketches from TAC projects in Kuwait that Nilsson collected for this interview]*

Edward Nilsson: Yes, the monorail was designed to go through Souq Al-Manakh and link to other car parks in the Central Business District (CBD), but the system was never built. These large projects, initially thought of as utilitarian parking garages, were also an integral part of Kuwait's urban design plan, as proposed by BBPR in 1973 (Zoning Plan from April 1973). These were meant to be multi-use buildings that contributed to the streetscape, with souqs at the ground level and offices or housing on the upper levels of the buildings in the CBD.

RC: *So when did the program evolve from parking garages to these large, multi purpose buildings?*

EN: It was part of the BBPR urban design plan from the beginning. The idea of a multi-level zoning plan makes sense. The top level of the building has views and light – good for offices or housing, and the pedestrian traffic at grade level supports the shops in the arcade. Such a plan can provide continuity by horizontally connecting sites of similar use, thereby making the city more discernable. The initial sketches for Souq Al-Wataniya (Area 10) layered its various uses once the number of cars was estimated. However, there was concern that this new type of building needed a more traditional form. Applying arches to the building, similar to Souq Al-Manakh (Area 5) and Souq Al-Safat (Area 9) at first seemed merely decorative, especially for those who graduated from architecture school in the 1960s and 1970s. Then we started making study models and noticed how the arched form, if used properly, could add something positively to the project.

RC: *Was that search for the "traditional form" a request from the client or your response to the site context, considering the large perimeter of the building and the interaction with the immediate surroundings, particularly in the first two souqs?*

EN: This is something that may have been communicated from the client: "See if you can add something to give it more local character."

RC: *But the surface... the materiality of the building.*

EN: The exterior of the building is bush-hammered concrete. It was based on the Kuwait Fund's (KFAED) building, which was completed just before the car parks.

RC: *But wasn't the material condition of the building also part of this search for "traditional form," or was it purely a maintenance issue?*

EN: It was an issue of maintenance, aesthetics and also function, as the heavy concrete skin would absorb heat during the day and release it at night. It was also compatible with the cast-in-place concrete girders and the Freyssinet pre-cast framing system, which was very appropriate for a parking garage with eighteen-twenty-metre column-free spaces.

The Freyssinet system was probably suggested by the Municipality or the structural engineer, Souza & True. For the cast-in-place concrete, it was necessary to have a specialised consultant design the concrete mix, because one could not use the local sand as it was. The US firm Concrete Associates Inc. was brought in to help with the specifications. Souq Al-Wataniya is a mixture of structural systems. In addition to the concrete system, it also contains steel beams for framing the roofs of the residential units.

The initial construction bids for Area 10C came in higher than expected, even though the feasibility study projected a twelve percent return, possibly even as high as twenty-five percent. The project stalled for some time, and it wasn't clear if it would proceed or not. The Korean contractor Hang Yang submitted an acceptable bid proposal, partly, I understood, because their labour rates were subsidised, as young men could substitute work for military duty. Obviously there were many local workers involved as well.

We were doing this when the SOM garage collapsed.

RC: *Yes, Souq Al-Kabeer.*

EN: That was a tragedy.

RC: *Were these SOM garages already being built when you started Souq Al-Manakh and the design for Al-Wataniya? There was Souq Al-Kuwait, which was self-standing on an empty and demolished landscape, and Souq Al-Kabeer filling the interior of a modern urban block. Were these moments important for the design development of the TAC garages?*

EN: The other car parks were not known to us back in Cambridge. Other than traditional Kuwaiti buildings in the area, we were only focused on the given program.

RC: *Were you aware of Saba Shiber's studies on "Kuwait Urbanization?" Were there any other references?*

EN: That's an excellent resource, but unfortunately it wasn't known to us at the time.

I read up on Kuwait, and we visited in July 1974 to deliver the drawings for Area 5 and 9 and to begin research work for Souq Al-Wataniya (Area 10) and Souq Al-Watiya (Area 15), including a tour of the city and a visit to the pre-cast concrete facility. We met with the Fire Department and Municipality to discuss which building code to use. The BOCA Code (Building Officials Code Administrators International) was selected. It was the code we were most familiar with.

RC: *But in 1974 there was a Building Code in Kuwait and Pace had it translated into English. Didn't they provide you with it?*

EN: The choice of which code to use was left up to us.

RC: *So, the interference of Pace in the project was reduced?*

EN: The design work was largely TAC, Souza & True, structural engineers and Shooshanian Engineering Associates, HVAC, plumbing and electrical engineers. However, Pace was involved in translating our specifications into a local book of tender format and providing and coordinating electrical requirements with the Municipality.

Regarding coordination, I would add that the building needed to be a certain size to accommodate the number of cars, but it didn't fit the given plot boundaries. It also needed more shops around the edges. The planning modules were 2.80 metres for the parking garage, 3.30 metres for the shops and 4.40 metres for the housing units above. The different levels didn't quite line up, resulting in the need for an additional five metres. The building plot was lengthened a bit during this phase, as there were no accurate plot surveys available from the client or the Municipality.

RC: *Wait, so there were no site plans or plot configuration?*

EN: The plot plans given to us were schematic and without detailed dimensions. To make the car allocation and related shopping and houses spaces work, and the fact that this part of the city was all government-owned land, the site could accommodate minor adjustments to the lot boundaries.

But the program was clear – 1000 cars – that was non-negotiable and the required number.

RC: *Do you have any idea about who designed the building program? Who discussed the program with you?*

EN: The contract was between the National Real Estate Company and TAC/Pace. Every project with a non-Kuwaiti consultant was required to partner with a local firm. [He reads the consultancy contract.] In the contract it says: "The purpose of this study is to find the most functional and economic solution for each car park [...] data analysis of traffic patterns, space utilisation, and customer parking habits. An estimate of supply and demand [...] a functional layout plan for the most modern and economic car park and commercial floor, which should show general parking, traffic patterns, interior ramp system, stairs, elevators, etc."

RC: *The program doesn't mention housing [he reads the contract]. Wasn't it considered from day one?*

EN: Yes, from day one it was a different program from the other three car parks [He refers to Al-Manakh, Al-Safat and Al-Watiya].

RC: *Charles Haddad told me that Roland Kluver might have had some impact on this program. Can you confirm this?*

EN: I was given the program from the feasibility study and contract, and also referred to the 1973 BBPR urban design plan for the Central Business District.

RC: *Were you there during the expansion of the Kuwait Fund?*

EN: Yes, the second phase of the Kuwait Fund, also by TAC, was just starting up then.

RC: *Had Souq Al-Safat (Area 9) been developed by then?*

EN: It was on a parallel track to Area 5. They were designed together with a similar program, however, Area 5 required 500 cars and Area 9 was to have 900 cars.

RC: *Were you working in the same office?*

EN: Yes, we worked out of the Cambridge annex office, a few streets from TAC's main office. There were about fifteen to twenty people working on Souq Al-Wataniya from beginning to end.

RC: *The building perimeter sections in Areas 9 and 10 are similar in typology, but in Area 5 there is a different use of arches, and an exceptional edge. The structure and layout of the corner towers in Souq Al-Manakh is similar to the Kuwait Fund tower's lateral cores. The geometric resolution of the staircase is identical.*

EN: Yes, Area 5 was based on TAC associate Basil Hassan's initial sketch proposal. He designed the elevations, the concept for the large ground floor arches, the smaller arches on the top floor and the diagonal corner towers.

RC: *And this internal covered court yard? Are all these elements locally referenced?*

EN: Yes, the courtyard houses were certainly an inspiration ... especially for Souq Al-Wataniya.

RC: *When the construction of this building started [Souq Al-Manakh], there were many others under construction, right? Souq Al-Kuwait, the ABK, the Gulf Bank and the CBK headquarters. There was another tiny building designed by Pace (Abdulaziz Al-Duaij Offices) What was the relation between your project and this wider context?*

EN: My view is that TAC was working mostly in the context of the first Kuwait Fund Building and TAC's other buildings in the Middle East.

RC: *Was there no concern during the [Area 5] process with establishing any kind of context-specific design? Was the process at TAC more focused on reproducibility and self-referencing?*

EN: For Area 5, the main context was the nearby Old Souq and the three banks adjacent to the site. The available lot was an irregularly shaped space in-between. The garage function required a standardised system based on a pre-cast beam framing system. The reason for the unique corner angle was the site boundary – we needed the most standard building possible for that irregularly shaped site.

RC: *The main constraint was the efficiency of the parking spots. I'm insisting on this point, because there is still a romantic conception that Souq Al-Manakh was designed according to the surrounding context and later influenced the other garages.*

EN: Well, I can't speak for Basil. He would know better than I whether these corner towers have any relation to the context of the original canopies, or whether there were images of what was there before.

My task was to carry the concept through to the final design and meet the client's schedule for bidding and construction.

RC: *Correct. Regarding materials, you told me that the concrete was taken from the Kuwait Fund building. However, the introduction of tiles, which weren't present in the Kuwait Fund building, is very refined here.*

EN: The interior was developed with assistance from the TAC Graphic Design department. We specified the German tile Buchtal, using their green palette.

RC: *Did the decision to use the tile on these surfaces come from the interior design of the building, or was it suggested by the graphic design department?*

EN: The form was prepared by the graphic designer. There were several departments at TAC: architecture, interior design, graphics, landscaping, etc. The interior department may have suggested the tiles, but the graphic designers chose the actual type and colours.

RC: *We discussed the projects with Charles Gibson, who was a graphic designer in the department. He worked in Souq Al-Safat I think. Apparently he spent about two years following these garage projects, particularly as they were closer to completion. Was there a concern that the buildings were too austere and not animated enough, or commercially friendly? Were the tiles part of that strategy?*

EN: Yes, and in Area 10 banners were also added. Harish Patel was the lead graphic designer then.

RC: *Exactly. These banners, inspired by the Sadu rugs, brought a very specific imagery to the buildings. Were the banners temporary installations, or were they conceived to remain there?*

EN: Yes, and some of the banners had a motif on them based on hand-held mathematical calculators that were popular at the time.

RC: *Considering the reference to the Kuwait Fund building, was there any common conception of the interiors that also inspired the Souq buildings? Apart from the building's volume, there is an impressive sensibility for the human scale and user behavior. The 'wayfinding,' and the graphic design in general, are extremely precise in their mediation between languages and codes. In Souq Al-Wataniya, the sectional relation on the upper floors – between parking experience, street, garden and the individual units – is extremely familiar.*

EN: I had not seen the interior of the Kuwait Fund Building at that time. TAC had very talented graphic designers, who were familiar with tile murals and 'wayfinding systems,' such as those used in hospitals. They helped the projects tremendously. I'm glad that was appreciated in the Kuwait projects.

RC: *Definitely, it had a big impact on the whole culture of building design in Kuwait. These were totally absent, even from the garages SOM was working on [Souqs Al-Kuwait and Al-Kabeer]. TAC's buildings are still particular in this regard, and their influence in projects such as Al-Nugra in Hawally, or Al-Muthana in the city centre, are obvious. Signage and 'wayfinding' only became a subject in the architectural scope for public and private contracts after the completion of the TAC souqs.*

EN: The graphic design tenders, such as Areas 5 and 9, were conducted separately on the completion of the projects.

RC: *As I mentioned before, in Souq Al-Wataniya, another exceptional moment is the section experience. The method of getting to one's car on the fourth floor, and having direct contact with the street outside is something that's very unusual.*

EN: You mean the openness of the fourth floor?

RC: *The openness of the fourth floor, but also the fact that you can park your car, walk a few steps, and there you are, in one of the streets walking home.*

EN: Yes, the layout allowed for parking close to the designated apartments.

RC: *The building section of the two top floors is not something obvious. Can you tell us more about the motivations behind it? It could have been done in so many different ways.*

EN: In the preliminary design phase, the apartments are all on one level, and only at one end of the building. When the study model was prepared, not the presentation model, we realised the interior apartments didn't have as good a view. Raising the apartments in the interior of the plan up one level allowed the parking underneath to continue around in a loop, and then exit back down again. Going from preliminary design concept to final design was a simple decision once you saw the model.

RC: *There was a more picturesque reading, before it was flat, now you get the hill town – that's what's so impressive about it when you're there, it's much more, it doesn't look like the concept for a mat – it looks like a very traditional town because of the lift. It makes for a more complex silhouette.*

EN: There are four types of units, all with courtyards: A two-bedroom unit, a three-bedroom unit (some with added mezzanines), four special corner units to make the transition, and four two-storey units adjacent to the corner units. Once the middle section is raised up one level, there are privacy issues with the lower units around the perimeter. Teak trellis beams were added across each courtyard to block sight lines, and also for shading.

RC: *The incorporation of the residential component in the program is the key parameter for this discussion. According to Ibrahim Al-Shaheen, who became Director of the Public Authority for Housing Welfare and was a student of Louis Kahn in Pennsylvania, when he returned to Kuwait in 1973, the planning agenda at the Municipality was to implement housing back in the city centre.*
A few years earlier (1969–71), the study on housing that Georges Candilis developed for Sharq was an important model or reference point for Sawaber residential development, which was commissioned to Arthur Erickson by the Housing [Welfare] Authority. The Authority's programs were very specific and precise in terms of ratio and typology.
Souq al-Wataniya also became an important reference, mainly for those district centre tenders launched in 1977, where a similar building program was referred to as a "self-contained" unit. In response, you can find some of these projects, by Northern European firms, which were very close to Souq Al-Wataniya, not only in terms of imagery, but particularly in the way the residential units were organised along the looping street.

EN: Even though this wasn't finished until 1978, the housing units were for rent or sale. The street we thought could also be a running track. In addition to each unit's private courtyard, there was also a public courtyard for the community on the upper level. People could choose to be in a private courtyard or semi-public courtyard.

RC: *Were these semi-public spaces an attempt to simulate public urban areas, such as real squares and streets?*

EN: We tried to make it as habitable as possible, given the environmental challenge. We were told it cost US$600 a year to water a tree at that time, so we wanted to provide a shaded space and foliage, so that one would want to live there. The upper terrace design was by the TAC's landscaping department, who did a very nice job of the fountains, plants, and trellises in order to make it a destination point, and brought light to the shopping courtyard below via skylights. Interestingly, the bridge was the owner's suggestion – NRC. He said he didn't want people to feel like they were going through a shopping centre to get to their apartments, so he requested a separate entrance. So here we have a lobby at the base of the stair/elevator tower.

RC: *Wow, so this area with the shed roofs at the base of the tower, where a restaurant operated for many years, was not a commercial space? Was this lobby meant for guests coming from the street, or was it a main entrance to the residential section, either from the street or from the basement car park?*

EN: This was an elevator lobby. It was meant to be a nicely appointed lobby, a reception space with a doorman that one could drive up to. It was a space for people coming to visit. Half the parking, 500 spaces, is on the two levels below grade – sixteen feet into the water table. The basement mat is over a metre thick, because of the uplift from the ground-water pressure. Tenants or visitors can park on the lower levels via the ramp, then access an elevator lobby from the lower level up to the bridge and cross over to the apartments. I understand that many apartments also were soon converted to offices.

RC: *Great. Also, it's incredible how tower and bridge can bring back the link to the Old City, not only as a formal element but also the experience and relation of views.*

EN: Yes, scale-wise it connects to the pre-oil Old City. Wasn't there a garden next to it?

RC: *There isn't one today. If there was a park, someone removed it. The only elements that relate to this tower are the mosques and a garage designed by Jack Bonnington, in association with KEO for United Realty Company (Souq Al-Masseel).*

EN: Right, but isn't there a park there? [pointing at the picture.] I always thought this photo was unfinished. Was it ever completed?

RC: *Actually, it's incredible how similar it is to those in London – the Trellick Tower or the Balfron tower, designed by Ernö Goldfinger during the 1960s.*

EN: I am unfamiliar with those projects. But the tower was an add-on, and it has three elements: the stair tower, the elevator, and the mechanical exhaust shaft – to circulate air at the basement garage levels. The curved form of the exhaust duct and the angled roofs of the lobby relate to the slanted roofs and arched windows of the apartments.

RC: *Here you have more pictures.*

EN: Oh, it looks very different... the arches... we initially didn't want to use the arch form... obviously influenced by Moshe Safdie's 'Habitat 67' (Montreal, Canada) and Louis Kahn's library (Phillips Exeter Academy Library, New Hampshire, US)... so there was a lot of debate about whether the walls would meet in the corner, or opening the corners and making the walls appear thin, plain... just after the 'Habitat 67' housing project and about the same time as the Exeter Library was being designed. The latter also had a large circular concrete motif in the interior skylit courtyard and angled spaces above the roof parapet, amid an otherwise Cartesian facade. The arch form at the ground floor of Al-Wataniya wasn't structural, so we wanted to make clear that it was seen accordingly. We might have used the Gropius' image of the University of Baghdad arch, which has a gap in the middle, creating two cantilevers to 'disarm' the arch, adding narrow slit openings above the facade arches, which was preferred.

RC: *Did you follow construction until the end?*

EN: I was involved in the design, administration of construction, shop drawings, etc. back in Cambridge. I haven't seen the completed building.

RC: *Wow! You have to, it's an incredible building. Until the Invasion in 1990 it was one of the most popular buildings in the city. So it was actually one of the first buildings to be renovated right after the invasion.*

EN: The principal structural engineer, Terry Louderback of Souza & True, who was also responsible for the Kuwait Fund tower (KFAED) and Al-Sawaber, went there after the invasion to help with the structural repair, costing up to eight million dollars, or so I heard. I have seen photographs of what it looked like during the war, and understand there were eight gasoline fires inside, but it seems to have successfully returned to normal.

RC: *During the design, or even during construction, was there any pressure to convert the residential units into office spaces? According to some former coworkers at the NREC, during the construction of the building, they realised that housing would never be feasible, considering the low value of rent. They also confirmed that the Municipality never approved the building's residential component.*

EN: But, isn't that in the plan? As I refer to earlier, residential is mentioned as one of the three components of TAC's feasibility study for NREC (shops, housing and car park), and was also part of the BBPR urban design plan. When you look at the plan [BBPR Zoning Plan for the CBD from 1973], you can see different functions at different levels. Obviously there was the intention to include housing.

RC: *Correct. Another relevant subject are the individual courtyards. Were they part of an initial vision for these apartments? When we were talking about Souq Al-Manakh you pointed out the reference for the traditional courtyards.*

EN: These courtyards are inspired by the traditional courtyard housing type in the region. In addition to privacy, another purpose of the courtyard is to trap cooler evening air, so that during the day, one can open the doors and the cold air comes in. When we talked with the fire protection consultant engineers, they said, if you open up the roof for smoke from fires, the air would come down instead of going up, because of temperature gradients that are opposite to those of cold climates.

In Souq Al-Manakh, the courtyard was meant to bring light in to the shopping level. Similarly, in Al-Wataniya, the sky-lit shopping courtyard was designed to transform the space, to make it more pleasant. The courtyards in the souqs are gathering spaces and also a gesture towards traditional Arabic courtyard houses.

RC: *But the [roof level] courtyard here is also an extension of the public common area that runs vertically through the shopping, car park, and residential segments, which is very interesting. Placing the courtyard between the units, and facilitating circulation through the streets, amplified the air-cooling effect.*

EN: We wanted to utilise traditional motifs by using the courtyard form in the souq, in the apartments themselves, and on the upper terrace level. The entryway into the courtyard ... these are individual homes and they could be totally isolated if wanted. The semi-common area could become central, depending on the activities chosen by the community.

RC: *Were these dwelling duplex units the result of mass modeling, or something trying to build on the idea of a vertical floor plan that is more stable and gives you more of a feeling of a house, somehow? Also, it's interesting that you were able to do it not only in the vertical but horizontal plan. Actually, looking now at the early designs [looks at the drawings of early stages of the project], I really understand how this happened. I had a different idea.*

EN: That's a good analogy, making it more visual. The work I've done in New England was often multi-storey spaces; my own house is like that. But I think this idea of variety, and not a monolithic form, is important.
TAC's Church Park Apartments (1973) on Massachusetts Avenue in Boston has a monolithic volume, which is appropriate to the streetscape. Al-Wataniya had to be something different – with housing, it needed to be more expressive of the individual units. The first scheme had a similar exploration of vertical height.

RC: *From the drawings you get the impression that the car park at the bottom is embedded in the top residential structure. And it looks as though you had the idea of stacking everything on top of the other – you had the car park higher on one side, and then you just built on top of it, as you said?*

EN: The layering is an important organising principle. The parking level above the souq and below the apartments, which is completely open on all four sides, isolates the residential level, giving an impression that it could fly off the building like a carpet to the pre-oil era housing that once occupied the site.

RC: *There is a building culture these souqs brought that is close to what Reynar Banham defined as "Megastructure," but much more successful than any of those. I mean, it's strange that these garages in Kuwait, achieved much more of the 'megastructure' agenda than Banham's cases.*

EN: I think there was a culture at TAC that tried not to impose Western models ... we were aware of bringing Western technology and advanced mechanical systems that had to be durable, that could be maintained, and service the building for a long period of time. The new technology needed to be balanced by traditional features.

RC: *This is so sophisticated. It was very unpredictable in terms of what happened in Kuwait. When we look at the SOM buildings, it's not clear what happened. I personally don't understand that this was designed by SOM in 1974 [points at Souq Al-Kuwait pictures].*

EN: It could be Chicago; it could be anywhere.

RC: *SOM drawings for the souqs were signed and stamped by a Paris branch. There was actually an SOM branch in Paris for two years that was working on several US Embassy buildings in Germany, and on a large scheme in Paris. However, I'm assuming the BBPR plan was influential – it seems like those buildings are exactly the diagram of the three different zoning levels.*

You mentioned before that Souq al-Wataniya was built with the Freyssinet system, right? But neither the building, nor the drawings carry this pre-cast imagery that is opposite to Jack Bonnington's garages (Souqs Al-Masseel and Al-Muttaheda), where the assembly joint is present everywhere.

EN: Yes, there is a lot of British influence there. In Al-Wataniya, the girders are cast in place, but all the beams are pre-cast, pre-stressed I-beams, doubled up to carry the block walls in the housing. The pre-cast panel spans between the beams, with a 5 cm top layer above it.

RC: *Here you can look at what I said earlier regarding the cores of the KFAED tower – the staircase and elevator cores are very similar to those in Souq Al-Manakh.*

EN: Yes, this is the later building [looking at KFAED tower]. That was a game changer for TAC [pointing at KFAED's first building].

RC: *Here [looking at the pages of "Modern Architecture Kuwait, 1949–1989"] are some of the buildings Pace started working on after the construction of the souqs. There was an immense amount of work during those years [late 1970s]. Here you have another, from Pace, the Gold Souq ... the imagery here is very close to TAC's souqs, no?*

EN: This is Area 5, too?

RC: *This is close to Area 5.*

EN: I mean conceptually. It is very nicely done.
So much changed so quickly [looking at pictures from different buildings in Kuwait]. It's amazing. I didn't realise how much was going on. This really paints a picture of how vast the scale of the work that was going on.

RC: *I don't know many cities in the world where this concentration of building activity and diversity took place. Here you have this one...*

EN: And Al-Essa [he reads in one of the vol.1 pages] was the one that built Area 5 (Souq Al-Manakh).

RC: *Al-Essa was the brother of the Minister of Public Works, who was later the owner of the pre-cast company.*

EN: How was the invasion, because ... all of our experience was pre-invasion? We don't know what impact it had ... I saw pictures of some of the buildings, but, were the old souqs preserved?

RC: *They were rebuilt. They are still a very strong attraction. You might be interested to go there, no?*

EN: I'd love to. •

Edward Nilsson accepted the invitation and travelled to Kuwait in May 2016, almost forty years after the completion of Souq Al-Wataniya. He had the chance to visit his building for the first time, which was, despite the post-war changes, fully functional and occupied with people and activities.

Nilsson presented his original project during one of the architectural debates, which were part of the book launch of the first volume of Modern Architecture Kuwait 1949–1989.

Speculations:
U.S. Architects and Modernisation in Kuwait

MICHAEL KUBO

Within a few short years after the start of the global spike in crude oil prices after 1973, a raft of journal articles in the United States had begun to speculate in earnest about the new opportunities for architects to build in the expanding economies of the Middle Eastern Gulf states. Written in the manner of apprehensive but enticing field guides to the region, such articles sought to outline the opportunities, risks, and intricate protocols that Western architects would have to negotiate if they hoped to chase the specter of petroleum-fueled development and the tempting yet often precarious finance economies to which it gave rise. Governmental complexes, vast military cities, new towns for oil workers, international airports, banking towers, commercial centres, and luxury hotels were among the vast array of commissions on offer for foreign firms able to navigate this new market, financed by a spectrum of public and private clients made wealthy by national oil revenues. In *Architectural Record*, Charles Hoyt wrote of the "oil-rich Middle East [...] the new frontier for professional services," and asked with both anticipation and unease: "is this the new client?"[1] In *Fortune*, Walter McQuade warned that "for the eager American construction men involved, there are rich rewards to be earned, but there are also immense difficulties."[2] *National Geographic* offered a guide to Gulf countries that were riding "a magic carpet of petrodollars [...] to undreamed-of prosperity and influence," and wondered: "Who are those oil-rich Arabs, and what are they doing with all that money?"[3]

What these articles chronicled above all were the speculative dimensions – potentially lucrative yet risky – of this desire by Western architects to enter the global market for architectural commissions in the Gulf. Reaching its peak between the oil embargo that followed the Arab-Israeli war of October 1973 and the series of intertwined political and economic events that marked the end of the Gulf construction boom after 1982, the heaviest presence of U.S. firms in the Gulf states paralleled both the spike in crude oil prices and the corresponding recession in the United States and Europe in this decade. This desire, thus, formed a natural corollary to the desperation of many Western architects to escape the increasingly precarious conditions of practice in their own countries, on the opposite side of the revised formulas of oil and capital exchange that had so enriched the Gulf states. In this way the involvement of U.S. architects in the Gulf acted as a hinge between the collapsing space of Western building practice and the coveted but also economically risky territories of the Middle East, where these firms hoped to chase those same sources of wealth that had been suddenly evacuated from architectural commissions at home.

The notion of *speculation* provides a useful framework for understanding the cultural and economic forces that governed both sides of this equation. The term alludes, on the one hand, to the processes of speculating for oil reserves, which had generated the national wealth of the

1. Charles Hoyt, "The Oil-Rich Mideast: The new frontier for professional services?" *Architectural Record* (June 1975): 101.

2. Walter McQuade, "The Arabian Building Boom is Making Construction History," *Fortune* (September 1976): 112.

3. John J. Putman, "The Arab World, Inc.," *National Geographic* (October 1975): 494.

Gulf states so precipitously after WWII. On the other, it refers to the global mechanisms of financial speculation that were erected on top of this oil revenue, which included the creation of new state and parastatal institutions in the Gulf from banks and investment companies to international aid organisations, as well as private companies like the engineering and construction conglomerates that would prove crucial in mediating the relationship between foreign firms and local projects. In this exchange, the search by U.S. architects for commissions in the Gulf constituted a related form of financial speculation, a process that often carried significant levels of professional risk as much as potential benefits.

Speculation carried additional meaning in the context of Kuwait, among the first and most extreme examples of large-scale urban transformation in the Gulf states following the master planning and demolition of much of the existing centre of Kuwait City after 1952. Here, it resonates with the idea of *spectacle*, which historian Farah Al-Nakib has posited as a by-product of Kuwait's extended modernisation by the 1980s. Exploring the ideological construct of *Al-Nahda* (the awakening) as the main driver of the processes of modernisation in Kuwait after 1950, Al-Nakib argues that beyond the government's attempts to plan a functional city centre through the demolition of the existing fabric, development in Kuwait was driven by the desire to create the urban spectacle of "a cityscape that would serve as the definitive symbol and visual reflection of Kuwait's newfound modernity."[4] These ambitions were emblematised early in Kuwait's modernisation by the Fahad al-Salem Street development after 1957 and later by the iconic Kuwait Towers (Sune and Joe Lindström of VBB and Malene Björn of Björn & Björn Design, 1965–1977). At the same time, the term resonates with the contemporaneous sense of Kuwait as a speculum, or mirror, for the changes taking place in architectural practice in the West. Forming the obverse of the corporate images of an abstract finance economy based on the distant specter of "oil" that circulated in the U.S. in this period, there lay the parallel conviction among visitors to the Gulf that in its urban spectacle, "Kuwait today is like a mirror of all that is totally modern in the western world."[5]

Architectural historians on both sides of this equation have continued to pass over these relationships as no more than "an exemplification of familiar modalities of architectural globalisation, including the emerging star system, boutique architects and large corporate design offices," as if such phenomena were unworthy of analysis.[6] Yet it is precisely in the relationship between the changing economy of Western architectural practise and the deep involvement of foreign architects with the processes of modernisation in Kuwait and other Gulf states that the evolution of more anonymous, corporate architectural practices can be traced. Just as modern architecture and urbanism in the Gulf cannot be understood without accounting for the sustained role of U.S. architects after the 1960s, so too the conditions of practice for U.S. architecture firms in these decades cannot be described without exploring the fundamental consequences of their engagement with the oil economy.

Kuwait Funds

Among the Gulf states, Kuwait played an early and outsized role in constructing these new global processes of exchange. The nation had been among the first Gulf states to fully nationalise its oil industry, with its rapid takeover of financial control of the Kuwait Oil Company (begun as a

4. Farah Al-Nakib, "Kuwait's Modern Spectacle: Oil Wealth and the Making of a New Capital City, 1950–90," *Comparative Studies of South Asia, Africa and the Middle East*, v. 33, n. 1 (2013): 9.

5. Stephen Gardiner, *Kuwait, The Making of a City* (Harlow: Longman, 1983), 31. On the late modern mirror-glass buildings through which "the fetishism of 'oil' as pure liquidity, pure circulation" was reified and abstracted in the West in this period, see Reinhold Martin, "Materiality: Mirrors," in *Utopia's Ghost: Architecture and Postmodernism, Again* (Minneapolis: University of Minnesota Press: 2010), 93–122.

6. Łukasz Stanek, "Mobilities of Architecture in the Global Cold War: From Socialist Poland to Kuwait and Back," *International Journal of Islamic Architecture*, v. 4, n. 2 (2015): 366.

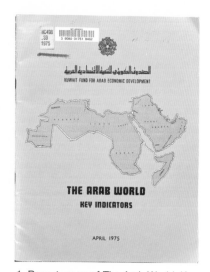

1. Report cover of *The Arab World, Key Indicators*, by the Kuwait Fund for Arab Economic Development, 1976.
© KFAED.

7. Robert Stephens, *The Arabs' New Frontier* (Boulder, CO: Westview Press, 1976), 38.

8. *The Kuwait Fund for Arab Economic Development,* promotional pamphlet (The Kuwait Fund for Arab Economic Development, June 1964).

9. Stephens, *Arabs' New Frontier*, 33.

10. See "Town Planning in Kuwait," *Architectural Design* (October 1953): 272–273. On the Land Acquisition Policy (LAP) of 1951 and its consequences, see Suhair A. Al-Mosully, *Revitalising Kuwait's Empty City Center* (PhD Diss., Massachusetts Institute of Technology, 1992) and Asseel Al-Ragam, "The Destruction of Modernist Heritage: The Myth of al-Sawaber," *Journal of Architectural Education*, v. 67, n. 2 (2013): 243–252.

joint-venture between the American-owned Gulf Oil Corporation and the British-owned Anglo-Iranian Oil Company) – first negotiating 60 percent ownership in 1974 and then full ownership the following year – providing a model that was quickly exploited in Saudi Arabia, Iraq, Qatar, and Abu Dhabi.[7]

At the time, Kuwait was the third-largest oil producer in the Gulf after Saudi Arabia and Iran and the sixth-largest in the world, extraordinary figures given its relatively minute size. Moreover, Kuwait provided a home for the entity directly responsible for the 1973 embargo and the ensuing price shocks that launched the "second" oil boom after World War II: the Organisation of Arab Petroleum Exporting Countries (OAPEC), established in 1968 with Kuwait, Saudi Arabia, and Libya as its founding members.

Even more crucially for its regional importance, both the state's inability to absorb the enormous quantities of oil revenue and the desire to ensure its protection among the Arab states (particularly relative to the territorial claims of Iraq) led the Kuwaiti government to establish an unprecedented framework for lending international aid for development projects in the Arab world, the Kuwait Fund for Arab Economic Development (KFAED), immediately after achieving independence in 1961.

Western observers of the Kuwait Fund in the 1970s reflected on the institution's uniquely "Arab character" and the remarkable success of its lending model in the Arab world as compared to traditional Western sources of development aid such as the World Bank. Within three years of its establishment, the list of Arab countries in which large-scale development initiatives backed by the Kuwait Fund were in progress or soon to be underway included Jordan, Egypt (then part of the United Arab Republic), Tunisia, Algeria, and Morocco, with projects ranging from irrigation and agricultural development to electrical power plants, mining, and tourist infrastructure.[8]

In the twelve years prior to the 1973 embargo, Kuwait was the world's largest donor of aid relative to GDP and the seventh-largest overall after the United States, the Soviet Union, Britain, Germany, Japan, and France, the traditional Cold War sources of international aid. An astonishing fifteen to twenty percent of the country's national budget was given to foreign aid projects in these years. The result of this framework was that "it was the small Gulf oil state of Kuwait which was the first to make a more serious effort to use oil money constructively in the Arab world."[9]

Yet the most immediately visible impacts of Kuwait's newfound wealth were at home. Within a few years of the discovery of the Burgan oil field in 1938 and its exploitation in earnest after WWII, the state embarked on an ambitious program of urban clearance and development beginning in the 1950s that would fundamentally alter the structure of the city centre. The key mechanism for these efforts was a state policy of land acquisition and resettlement that enabled the almost complete demolition of the old town as specified in the first master plan for Kuwait, prepared in 1952 by the British town planning firm of Minoprio, Spencely, and Macfarlane (MSM).[10] The ensuing landscape of multi-lane streets and vacant urban parcels – many left empty for decades due to the extreme land values that resulted from their initial purchase at artificially inflated prices – provided the ground for the construction of a vast array of governmental, institutional, and commercial projects through which the state sought to reconfigure the spatial and economic bases of a modern Kuwait on the world stage.

The role of foreign architects in creating this image of modernity was crucial. By the time of the second boom in oil prices in the 1970s, the city centre of Kuwait had become the territory of what Łukasz Stanek has described as "a global market of architectural resources which, besides labour, included building materials and technologies, discourses and images [...] most often combined on the ground with resources from local and regional networks."[11] For many observers of the steady influx of foreign architects to Kuwait, "the famous names that were appointed to build as a consequence" of the city's modernisation constituted "a veritable Who's Who of the international giants, all candidates for the front cover of *TIME* magazine. Nothing but the best."[12] Such commentary was typically reserved for the major civic icons of Kuwait's development, a list that included Michel Ecochard's National Museum of Kuwait (1960–1983), Arne Jacobsen's Central Bank of Kuwait (1966–1976), Kenzo Tange's Kuwait International Airport (1967–1970), Jørn Utzon's National Parliament (1972–1982), Reima and Reilli Pietilä's Seif Palace Complex (1973–1983), and Arthur Erickson's Al-Sawaber Housing (1976–1989, though Erickson's office was only involved until 1977). So too the roster of foreign luminaries encompassed the largely Team 10-affiliated group of architects invited after 1968 to submit visionary large-scale proposals for the city centre, including the Pietiläs, Alison and Peter Smithson, BBPR, and Candilis–Josic–Woods.[13] Largely in the background of these discussions were more anonymous, large-scale practices like The Architects Collaborative and Skidmore, Owings & Merrill, as well as the heavy presence of professional architects from socialist European countries including Poland, Bulgaria, Czechoslovakia, Hungary, Romania, Yugoslavia, and Greece.[14]

In assessing the work of these international architects in Kuwait, contemporary Western critics combined astonishment at the sheer scale of the country's urban transformation with persistent misgivings about the ability of such "star" designers to contribute meaningfully to these processes of modernisation. Neil Parkyn, a British architect in Kuwait who returned in 1983 to assess the city's development after a five-year absence, admitted that "given the firm clues and themes there for the taking – strong light, privacy and formality, waterfront sites in some cases, abundant resources, competent contractors – some of the stars turned in their standard home performance, airfreighted to Kuwait Bay." ("Not," he was quick to venture, "that this was always inappropriate").[15] Others reflected on the speed and impact of urban change, reflecting on the ways in which "For good or ill [oil] has brought enormous material and moral changes to Kuwait, transforming it in little more than a decade from a quiet traditional desert town into a kind of Arab Los Angeles, spreading its highways and suburbs over the surrounding desert to take in the daily flow of its scores of thousands of big American cars."[16] Such statements seemed to confirm the fears of architects like Parkyn that Kuwait's construction boom had become nothing more than a "showcase for the world's architectural prima donnas."[17]

Yet the office that best exemplified the imbrication of U.S. architects with Kuwait's large-scale urban transformation was in many ways far more anonymous than the signature architects whose buildings provided a ready image of spectacle for both Western and Kuwaiti critiques. This was The Architects Collaborative (TAC), the team-based practice established in 1945 in Cambridge, Massachusetts by seven young architects along with the German émigré Walter Gropius. TAC's heavy presence in Kuwait began in

11. Łukasz Stanek, "Mobilities of Architecture in the Global Cold War", 366. Stanek describes this complex as part of broader processes of "mondialisation," a term taken after Henri Lefebvre to refer to "the emergence of architecture as a worldwide techno-scientific phenomenon after World War II from within competing visions of global cooperation and solidarity."

12. Neil Parkyn, "Kuwait Revisited," *Middle East Construction* (September 1983): 40.

13. See "Proposals For Restructuring Kuwait" and "Kuwait: The Smithsons' Scheme," *Architectural Review* (September 1974): 178–190.

14. An account of the socialist architects working in Kuwait in this period is given in Stanek, "Mobilities of Architecture in the Global Cold War: From Socialist Poland to Kuwait and Back."

15. Parkyn, "Kuwait Revisited," 40.

16. Stephens, *Arabs' New Frontier,* 39.

17. Parkyn, "Kuwait Revisited," 39.

2. First phase of Kuwait Fund for Arab Economic Development, Kuwait City, 1974. © Pace Archive.

1968 with the commission to design the headquarters of the Kuwait Fund for Arab Economic Development, a project gained after a diplomatic trip by partner Louis McMillen to seek work in the Gulf states as an extension of the firm's ongoing involvement with the University of Baghdad in Iraq after 1957.[18]

The inauguration of the first Kuwait Fund building in 1974 began a period of thirty years of sustained work in Kuwait for TAC, so much so that the firm opened a dedicated branch office there in 1976 (the only international office run by the firm until its bankruptcy in 1995, aside from the one it had begun in Rome in 1959 to conduct work on the University of Baghdad project). TAC's dozens of projects in Kuwait over these decades included a series of commercial developments for the Kuwait Investment Company combining ground-floor souqs with parking, offices, and housing (1973–9), the Kuwait Institute for Scientific Research (1979–1983), the Kuwait News Agency (1981–7), the Kuwait Foundation for the Advancement of Sciences (1982–6), and the Public Authority for Civil Information (1986–1992). This involvement in the Gulf reaped benefits in other countries in the Middle East as well, including numerous projects in Saudi Arabia, the United Arab Emirates, Iraq, and Jordan. While the bulk of the articles directed to U.S. architects in the 1970s reflected the palpable anxiety for those unfamiliar with the Middle East about how to access this market and negotiate its risks, the situation was clearly different for firms like TAC that had already been working in the region for two decades at the time of the oil embargo.

Concrete was the material of choice in nearly all of these buildings. Indeed, precast and poured-in place concrete became the preferred materials for the vast array of large-scale commissions designed by U.S. firms in the Gulf States between the 1950s and the 1980s. Perhaps no

18. Interview with Sabah Al-Rayes, May 29, 2013. Ironically, one of the initial motives for the Kuwait Fund's aid program to Arab countries had been to bolster international support for Kuwait in the face of territorial claims by Iraq under General Abd Al-Karim Qasim, whose rise to power following the coup of July 14, 1958 had spelled the demise of nearly all of the cultural projects by international architects commissioned under the pro-U.S. Hashemite monarchy of Faisal II, with the notable exception of the University of Baghdad.

construction material better embodied the relationship between large-scale architecture firms in the United States and the expanding economies of the Middle East. A synthetic material formed by the chemical interaction of ingredients produced through varying technical means, concrete hardened the complex exchanges among Western architectural specifications, transnational material networks, local construction firms, and on-site labor through which the building economy of the Gulf states took shape in these decades.

The resulting buildings were often seen by local architects as modern as much for their technical proficiency and material refinement as for any stylistic or architectural expression. A significant element of these transactions was the changing signification of concrete as a 'local' material, one in which foreign technics and on-the ground material and labour were synthesised. In Saudi Arabia, Caudill, Rowlett & Scott (CRS), the architects of the University of Petroleum and Minerals in Dhahran (1964–1982) – among the earliest large-scale projects by U.S. architects for Gulf clients after the University of Baghdad and Minoru Yamasaki's Civic Air Terminal in Dhahran (1958–1961) – had found that "in Saudi Arabia even the sand does not behave the same as sand elsewhere [...] wind-blown desert sand loses its sharp, irregular edges and does not bond well."[19] Instead sand had to be obtained from the seashore and mixed with local limestone and cement to produce sufficient hardness. Yet for CRS the resulting composite still constituted 'a Saudi product' despite its reliance on Western protocols of sourcing and assembly, one that was "sand-blasted to expose aggregate and matrix, colour compatible with the *jebel* site."[20] In this way, in contrast to purely import materials like steel, concrete directly materialised the transnational mixture of expertise and matter at play in these buildings, literally hardening these flows into the image of a 'local' architectural expression.

A crucial element in the work of U.S. firms in Kuwait was the presence of consulting firms, large engineering and construction conglomerates that acted as mediators of foreign technical expertise and construction details with on-the-ground protocols. This differed from the situation in Saudi Arabia, for example, where much of the contractual and logistical work of U.S. firms was enabled by para-statal multinational clients like the Arabian-American Oil Company (Aramco) or more directly through Western proxies like Bechtel and the U.S. Army Corps of Engineers.[21] Key to TAC's proficiency in the Gulf was their sustained collaboration with Pan-Arab Consulting Engineers (Pace), the consultant for nearly all of the firm's projects in Kuwait as well as those of other large U.S. firms, notably Skidmore, Owings & Merrill (SOM). As with TAC and Pace, foreign and local firms frequently operated together through joint-venture agreements, a way of satisfying the governmental regulation that foreign firms were required to work with Kuwaiti consultants for all construction projects in the country.[22] Pace's close association with TAC also began with the Kuwait Fund headquarters, one of the earliest projects taken on by the firm after its establishment in 1968.[23] Indeed, the growth of this relationship was crucial for Pace's emergence to become one of the largest consultants in the Gulf, as its founding members later credited their acquisition of drawing standards and design protocols in the first years of the office directly to their work with TAC.[24] Conversely, it was largely through the close relationship with such consulting firms that TAC grew into one of the largest architectural practices in the U.S. these decades, sustained by dozens of large-scale projects, both iconic and anonymous, in Kuwait.

19. Jonathan King and Peter Langdon, eds., *The CRS Team and the Business of Architecture* (College Station, TX: Texas A&M University Press, 2002), 143.

20. Charles E. Lawrence, *Saudi Search* (Houston: CRSS Research, 1986), 9.

21. On Aramco, see Robert Vitalis, *America's Kingdom: Mythmaking on the Saudi Oil Frontier* (Stanford, CA: Stanford University Press, 2007) and the various area guides for foreign workers published by the company, such as *Aramco Handbook: Oil and the Middle East* (Dhahran, Saudi Arabia: Aramco, 1968). On the role of the U.S. Army Corps of Engineers in Saudi Arabia, see Robert P. Grathwol and Donita M. Moorhus, *Bricks, Sand, and Marble: U.S. Army Corps of Engineers Construction in the Mediterranean and the Middle East 1947–1991* (Washington, D.C.: Center of Military History and Corps of Engineers, United States Army, 2009). On Bechtel in the Middle East up to 1958, see *Bechtel in Arab Lands, A Fifteenth-Year Review of Engineering and Construction Projects* (San Francisco: Bechtel Corporation, 1958).

22. For example, the requirement for foreign firms to involve a local consulting office with the design and supervision of works in Kuwait was specified in a letter from Sabah Al-Rayes of Pace to Louis A. McMillen of TAC regarding the contractual agreement for the Area 5 and 9 commercial parking garages (the Souq Al-Manakh and Souq Al-Safat), sent between June 14 and August 22, 1975. A draft of the joint-venture agreement between TAC and Pace for the Area 5 and 9 garages is dated August 26, 1975. Courtesy of Pace Archives. SSH, one of the largest consultants in Kuwait, claims that the requirement for foreign firms to work with local consultants after 1973 was the result of lobbying by partner Salem Al-Marzouq, a U.S.-educated civil engineer then in the Ministry of Public Works and a member of the National Assembly. Rod Sweet, ed., *SSH Design: The First 50 Years* (Kuwait: Al-Khat printing Press, 2011), 47.

23. The project number given to the Kuwait Fund project by Pace was 68006, with the first two digits indicating the year of the commission, which also indicates that this was the sixth project ever taken on by the firm in the year of its founding.

24. Interviews with Tarek Shuaib, current head of Pace and son of founding partner Hamid Shuaib (August 1, 2012), and founding partners Sabah Al-Rayes (May 29, 2013) and Charles Haddad (May 30, 2013).

3. Offices of the Pan-Arab Consulting Engineers (Pace) in Hawally, Kuwait. © Pace Archive.

25. Putman, "Arab World," 523.

26. "Some Aspects of the Oil Controversy: An Arab Interpretation," lecture given by al Hamad at the Industrial Development Bank of Japan in Tokyo, May 8–9, 1975. The lecture was published as *Some Aspects of the Oil Controversy: An Arab Interpretation* (The Kuwait Fund for Arab Economic Development, May 1975).

27. Stephens, *Arabs' New Frontier*, 65.

28. In 1985 Al-Hamad moved on to become director of Arab Fund for Social and Economic Development, an inter-governmental aid body created in 1974 as an expansion of the Kuwait Fund's country-specific purview to sponsor cooperative projects of multinational scope. There he extended his role as a sophisticated architectural patron with the creation of the exceptionally lavish Arab Organisations Headquarters Building, inaugurated in 1994 with TAC partner Louis McMillen as architectural consultant. In addition to headquarters of the Arab Fund, the building Inter-Arab Investment Guarantee Corporation (created with the help of the Kuwait Fund in 1974 to guarantee loans to Arab corporations against non-commercial risks), the Arab Maritime Petroleum Transport Company, and the global headquarters of OAPEC, the multinational agency that organised the global oil embargo in response to the Middle East war in October 1973.

29. Gardiner, *Kuwait, The Making of a City*, 137. Robert Stephens, a British visitor studying the Kuwait Fund's institutional structure a few years after its opening, noted that while some of its employees had apparently held "misgivings for fear that it might lose something of the compact intimate atmosphere" of its previous offices on the outskirts of the city, the new headquarters ensured that "through imaginative architectural design and the determination of the staff, much of this atmosphere has been preserved in the new building while gaining in space, comfort and modern equipment." Stephens, *Arabs' New Frontier*, 57.

It is no coincidence that TAC's arrival in Kuwait came via an entity whose creation reflected a sophisticated philosophy of the relationship between Western technologies, local resources, and modernisation efforts in the Arab world. The Director-General of the Kuwait Fund, Abdulatif Al-Hamad, spoke of the reciprocal relations of dependence among the Arab countries, in which Kuwait's need for territorial protection and its lack of natural resources could be remedied through the lending of developmental aid to foment support within the region: "We are a small country and rely on our neighbours for almost everything – food, teachers, labor. In turn we share with them what we have, money."[25] Abroad, Al-Hamad lectured audiences in the so-called 'First World' about the Arab perspective on the changing equations of trade that had enabled the creation of institutions like the Kuwait Fund and their role in revising the traditionally exploitative relationship of the Western powers to the oil-producing Gulf states:

> For years our countries lived literally at the periphery of the world, too weak and too poor to protest against the management of national wealth by foreign private interests, against the low price of oil, against the rapid exhaustion of our reserves, against the draining away of export receipts, and the alienation of the whole oil sector from the national economy. History and the conjunction of several favorable factors began to change all this in the late sixties. We began to recover sovereignty over our national resources, to analyse the different aspects of the world oil markets, to accumulate knowledge, and this led finally to what we refer to sometimes as the oil revolution.[26]

Instead of this unilateral model of resource exploitation, the conception and   operation of the Kuwait Fund "envisaged a triangular cooperation between the technologically advanced oil-consuming countries, the oil producers with surplus funds, and the developing countries seeking to industrialise and modernise themselves. Oil money and Western technology would together transform the economies and societies of the Third World, including the Arab countries."[27]

The construction of the Kuwait Fund's own headquarters made these triangular relationships explicit, involving a large U.S. architecture firm, a technologically sophisticated local consultant, and a client empowered to provide both an expressive and a functional symbol of the new role of oil revenue in reshaping the modern Arab states.[28] The building consisted of square rings of offices suspended around an enclosed central courtyard, held by an outer ring of piers under an overhanging roof. This parti had appeared in earlier international civic buildings by TAC, first at the U.S. Embassy in Athens, Greece (1956) and later in the library at the University of Tunis School of Law (1962), developed for the United States Agency for International Development (USAID). What was new at the Kuwait Fund was the ziggurat-like stepping of the office floors and the simplified, monolithic character of its massing, with deep piers of sandblasted concrete merging into a solid upper floor punctuated by an irregular pattern of vertical slit-windows. Stephen Gardiner, the author of perhaps the sole book-length survey of Kuwait's modern architecture in these years, praised the stepping back of these platforms "to reveal the entire contents of the building – its space, contents, structure, materials." Contrasting the building's openness with the introversion of Jacobsen's Bank, which he likened to "the closed, heavily guarded world of finance," he related the Kuwait Fund building, in turn, to the international mission of its client, as a headquarters dedicated to "cultural exchange, education, discussion, ideas."[29] For Gardiner, its meticulous

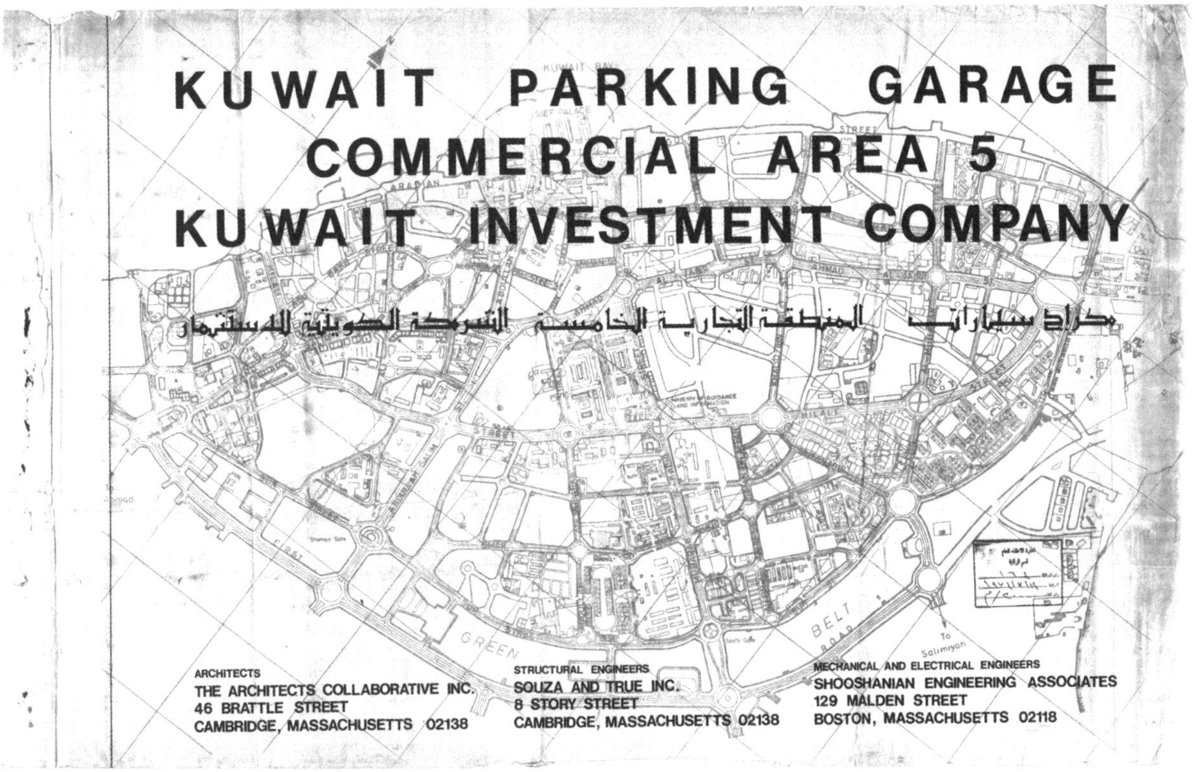

KUWAIT PARKING GARAGE
COMMERCIAL AREA 5
KUWAIT INVESTMENT COMPANY

مكراچ سيارات المنطقة التجارية الخامسة الشركة الكويتية للاستثمار

ARCHITECTS
THE ARCHITECTS COLLABORATIVE INC.
46 BRATTLE STREET
CAMBRIDGE, MASSACHUSETTS 02138

STRUCTURAL ENGINEERS
SOUZA AND TRUE INC.
8 STORY STREET
CAMBRIDGE, MASSACHUSETTS 02138

MECHANICAL AND ELECTRICAL ENGINEERS
SHOOSHANIAN ENGINEERING ASSOCIATES
129 MALDEN STREET
BOSTON, MASSACHUSETTS 02118

4. Drawing set cover for Souq Al-Manakh, TAC, July 1974. © Kuwait Municipal Archive.

sand-blasted concrete and stone reflected a sumptuous headquarters in which "the outstanding excellence of the detail depends largely on the clear expression of materials – the simplicity with which weighty components like beams and columns are put together, and the candour with which the granite aggregate of the concrete is displayed."[30] Many of these details became signature elements of TAC and Pace's projects in Kuwait and throughout the Gulf, particularly its patterning of recessed slit-windows topped with circular arches, set within sheer concrete surfaces.

Tower and Souq

To the extent that specific architectural types can be identified with Kuwaiti modernisation after the 1970s, two stand out as a particular legacy of the U.S. firms that participated in the construction of the city centre. One was the office tower, emblematic of both the proliferating array of new financial institutions that dominated Kuwait's urban landscape and the cargo-cult of technological culture offered by corporate U.S. firms.[31] The Kuwait Fund was among the first of these, adding a concrete office tower by TAC adjacent to its main headquarters, completed after 1981, that betrayed the influence of Araldo Cossutta and I.M. Pei & Partners's administrative tower for the Christian Science Center in Boston, Massachusetts (1964–1973).[32]

Three other new financial entities – the Bank of Kuwait and the Middle East, the Industrial Bank of Kuwait, and the Kuwait Real Estate Bank – came together to develop the Joint Banking Centre, a complex of three prismatic towers designed by SOM with Pace (1976–1982). Among the U.S. firms that became major players in the Gulf, SOM's presence in earnest began relatively late with the design of the Hajj Terminal in Jeddah, Saudi

30. Gardiner, *Kuwait, The Making of a City*, 137–138.

31. On the concept of architectural "cargo-cult" and the emblematic role of SOM office towers in signifying "nearness to the fountain of technological culture," see Peter Smithson, "The fine and the folk: An essay on McKim, Mead and White and the American tradition," *Architectural Design* (August 1965): 394.

32. On the Christian Science Center, see Mark Pasnik, Michael Kubo, and Chris Grimley, ed., *Heroic: Concrete Architecture and the New Boston* (New York: Monacelli Press, 2015). The master plan for the Christian Science Center included TAC's Church Park Apartments (1967–1973), directly across from Cossutta and Pei's complex.

Arabia (1975–1982), a project that promptly led to prominent commissions for banking towers in Saudi Arabia, Kuwait, and Bahrain.[33] In these towers, attention to the harsh desert climate and an interest in uninterrupted mass led the firm to develop an aesthetic of what might be described as "Gulf monoliths," simple geometrical solids whose power derives from an alternation of sheer blank surfaces in stone or concrete with overscaled, often deeply recessed openings. This series reached its peak in the hermetic National Commercial Bank (1977–1983) in Jeddah, Saudi Arabia, a window-less triangular volume with offices facing onto interior courts revealed on the exterior by three immense openings on its otherwise blank facades.[34]

The Joint Banking Centre project was won by invited competition in 1976 over entries by TAC, Philip Johnson, and Kenzo Tange, though the scheme was subsequently redesigned by SOM. Its three banks are articulated as an offset composition of triangulated slabs, each occupying roughly one half of a square in plan, with the other half occupied by skylit banking halls at the base of each tower. The two short sides of each tower exposed to direct sunlight are windowless, with office windows subsumed into the long face of each tower, bracketed by monolithic stair cores. The result was a "striking abstract composition of solids in the sunshine, supported by immaculate detailing. No attempt at 'Arabic' forms or a false vernacular; a precise, telling statement to which nothing can be added or taken away."[35] Outwardly expressive of the unity of Kuwait's banking industry, the external uniformity of the three towers gives way to customised interiors particular to each bank, chosen among a remarkable twelve alternative schemes developed by SOM for the three banking halls (six options were developed for the executive floors). The result was a complex "considered the first 'world class' series of office towers in the third generation of Kuwait's post-World War II building programs," not least for an interior "palette of materials of enormous richness which this project demonstrates in such superbly sumptuous style."[36] This sense of luxury was amplified to an extreme at the Al-Ahli Bank (1979–1988), where stone-clad semi-circular cores flank spanning office floors whose decor befits the relatively more ostentatious character of a privately held, rather than state-affiliated, bank.

The other building type that marked Kuwait's development in the 1970s was less iconic, yet far more consequential in its impact on the structure of the city centre. These were the modern 'souqs,' multistory structures built as infrastructural anchors for the large urban mega-blocks designated as urban 'areas,' each one divided into smaller parcels for development. Referred to as souqs on account of their enclosed shopping areas – and regarded as evolutions of the enclosed linear souqs planned under Saba George Shiber in the 1960s – in reality these were commercial parking garages, new hybrids of lower-level commercial spaces, multistory parking garages, and upper-level offices and/or housing. As they developed in the 1970s, these new amalgams reflected the particular real-estate economics that resulted from the rapid demolition of Kuwait's city centre in the 1950s and its interrelated products: artificially inflated land values, large empty spaces overrun with cars, and the urgent need to alleviate traffic congestion.

The Land Acquisition Policy of 1951 had provided the key mechanism by which the state was able to rapidly clear nearly the entirety of the old town centre of its existing fabric of courtyard houses and narrow streets to make way for an ambitious modernisation program of new roads

33. Among the U.S. firms with the heaviest presence in the Middle East by the 1970s, the earliest arrivals were TAC (the University of Baghdad, begun 1957), Minoru Yamasaki & Associates (the Civic Air Terminal in Dhahran, begun 1958), Brown Daltas (the Palace of Princess Fatemah in Tehran, begun around 1962), and CRS (the University of Petroleum and Minerals in Dhahran, begun 1964). Later arrivals included Leo A Daly (the Saudi Arabian National Guard Headquarters in Riyadh, begun 1973) and HOK (the King Saud University in Riyadh, begun 1975 in a consortium with CRS and three other foreign firms). SOM's first commission in the Gulf may have been an office building for Aramco in Dhahran (1962), though little about the project is known. A timeline of these and other projects by U.S. firms in the Middle East is given in Eva Franch i Gilabert, Michael Kubo, Ana Miljacki, and Ashley Schafer, ed., *OfficeUS Atlas* (Zurich: Lars Müller, 2015), 750–53.

34. Aybars Asci, the senior designer for SOM's Al-Hamra Firdous Tower in Kuwait (2011), has described the current firm's awareness of this Gulf aesthetic of monolithic forms and its explicit interest in reviving this lineage in their design for the al Hamra tower. See his recent talk at the *Export Agendas* symposium at Northeastern University, Boston, February 25, 2015.

35. Parkyn, "Kuwait Revisited," 40.

36. Maeve Slavin, "Blue Chip Banking," *Interiors* (November 1984): 130, 141.

5. Model of Joint Banking Center, SOM, Kuwait City, 1976–1983.
© Pace Archive.

streets to make way for an ambitious modernisation program of new roads and public buildings. Under this scheme, land was purchased from property-owning families within the old town walls (itself demolished to form the green belt that defined the new city centre) at deliberately inflated rates, reputedly up to ten times above market value, as an expedient way both to distribute oil revenue and to bring development areas rapidly under state control. These families were then given corresponding plots by lottery and interest-free loans (originally 70,000 Kuwaiti dinars for the first to move after 1952) to build homes outside of the green belt, generally as single-family villas rather than traditional urban courtyard houses.[37] The consequence of this policy was that land values in the city centre remained permanently raised to such artificial levels that that many parcels remained undeveloped for decades, as "land speculation became a much more lucrative venture than construction for the private sector."[38] Combined with the extreme congestion that followed the opening of car traffic through the old centre (among the main drivers of the MSM Master Plan),the result was an urban landscape of multilane roads and half-empty mega-blocks, overrun with parked cars.

37. Al-Ragam, "The Destruction of Modernist Heritage," 245.

38. Al-Nakib, "Kuwait's Modern Spectacle," 13.

6. Souq Al-Wataniya, TAC jointly with
Pace, Kuwait City, 1974–79.
© Aga Khan Visual Archive (AKVA), MIT
Documentation Center, TAC.

Faced with the urgency of combating these choking conditions of traffic congestion, the state sought to incentivise private developers to build public infrastructure on land that would otherwise remain empty for speculation. The solution was a decision to sponsor the construction of forty commercial parking garages for 1000 cars each within the green belt, a decision Gardiner criticised as "hardly a recommendation for planners of experience."[39] Such structures had already been predicted in the studies for the city centre submitted by BBPR to the Municipality in 1969, which called for a series of sixty-metre "landmarks" that would provide observation points and recreation areas, "supplied by large autosilos" below.[40] The mechanism for inducing private developers to build parking (on which little profit could be made) was a "build–operate–transfer" (BOT) arrangement in which sites were bid to developers to build commercial structures on twenty-five year leases before transferring their operation to the government, with twenty-five percent of their space allotted to profit-generating uses, i.e., rental offices and ground-floor souqs. So ubiquitous were the garages built over the next decade that for Western visitors like Parkyn, by the early 1980s they had "come to represent, in a surprisingly short space of time, almost a 'traditional' Kuwaiti building form – small shopping units for rental grouped around an internal public concourse, topped by parking levels and office floors."[41]

Foreign firms played a crucial role in realising this new infrastructural type. One of the new financial institutions created in the wake of the oil boom, the Kuwait Investment Company (KIC), commissioned Pace and TAC to design two of these parking garages, Souq Al-Safat and Souq Al-Manakh, in

39. Gardiner, *Kuwait, The Making of a City*, 42. The locations of these garages as built are recorded in a map by the State of Kuwait Ministry of Public Works, Roads Administration, Kuwait City, ca. 1980s. Courtesy MIT Dome.

40. Studio Architetti BBPR, *The Future Development of the Old City of Kuwait,* report submitted to Ministry of Planning, Kuwait, 1969, 4.3.

41. Parkyn, "Kuwait Revisited," 40.

1973. The following year, another of these new institutions, the National Real Estate Company (NREC), commissioned Pace and TAC to design Souq Al-Wataniya and Souq Al-Watiya, the latter of which was eventually completed to an alternative design scheme. Local consultants SSH designed two others with SOM, Souq Al-Kuwait and Souq Al-Kabeer (1973–6). Others were completed in conjunction with British firms (Souq Al-Muttaheda and Souq Al-Masseel, Jack Bonnington Partnership with KEO, 1973–1979) or by expatriate Polish architects (Souq Dawliyah, Ryszard Daczkowski and Edward Lach for Gulf Engineering Office, completed 1978). These projects occasionally laid bare the intersection of differing demands and technical abilities between local and foreign firms, as when the concrete frame of the Souq Al-Kuwait collapsed while under construction (killing laborers who slept on the building's open-air floor slabs at night), a failure rumored to have been caused by the contractor's overzealous desire to increase the speed of construction.[42]

The BBPR study had envisioned an extensive "connecting framework" of elevated passages that would connect these and other buildings via "moving stairways, conveyor belts, and air-conditioned spaces" throughout the old city centre between the Seif Palace and Safat Square.[43] By the early 1970s this scheme had been translated into a proposed monorail ringing the city centre along roughly the same route, which would have connected Souq Al-Manakh, Souq Al-Kuwait, Souq Al-Safat, and Souq Al-Wataniya, among other buildings.[44] No such elevated connections, however, were built. The result was a patchwork of urban interiors surrounded by empty spaces, tenuously connected to the existing network of souqs that had been extended under Shiber.

Visitors seemed ambivalent about the impact of these new structures on the city. Parkyn, for example, could claim that via "the new multifunction souq superblocks [...] it is now possible to traverse considerable sections of the downtown area *without* stepping onto the sunbaked sand or fragmentary pavements remaining from the First, or was it the Second, Great Surge of urban renewal in the '60s and '70s," while at the same time warning that "their proliferation and presumed success raises interesting issues not resolved in a city which still thinks in terms of single site development [...] At present they stand in isolation, having no 'back' or 'front,' often no planned linkage to the next one."[45] Seen as suffering from the same lack of urban cohesion that marked the city's more iconic "monuments-to-be," Parkyn wrote that as of 1983, most of the souqs were still free-standing "among parked cars, the ruins of what remains of Kuwait's stock of single-storey courtyard family houses and the dusty walk-ups from the 1950s building boom [...] they float like giant and beautifully constructed space stations in a sea of sand, although this sand is apparently some of the most expensive real estate in the world, on paper at least."[46] The most extreme example of the type was the Souq Al-Wataniya (1974–1979), in which a mat of courtyard housing on the top floor provided a surreal afterimage of the traditional structure of the city centre prior to 1952, now floating above the infrastructural blocks which had replaced it.

Yet it was another souq designed by TAC, the Souq Al-Manakh, that unwittingly became the decisive site – if not the symbol – of the speculative building economy and its hazards at the end of the boom in crude oil prices. Less exceptional than the Souq Al-Wataniya in its mix of functions, the building was organised with five levels of parking and top-floor offices above a

42. Interview with Sabah Al-Rayes, May 29, 2013.

43. BBPR, *The Future Development of the Old City of Kuwait*, 4.1, 4.2.

44. The southwest portion of the Souq Al-Manakh was originally designed to accommodate a future monorail stop on the first parking level above the ground floor and mezzanine, a feature indicated in the drawing set as of September 1974. See drawing sheet A6, "Plan – Level 5 (Showing Future Monorail) 100 Cars," dated September 6, 1974. Courtesy Pace Archives.

45. Parkyn, "Kuwait Revisited," 40.

46. Ibid., 42. Among these isolated "monuments-to-be," Parkyn identified Utzon's National Assembly (1972–1982), Mohamed Makiya's Kuwait State Mosque (1977–1981), and John S. Bonnington Partnership and KEO's Kuwait Stock Exchange (1978–1986).

commercial ground floor and mezzanine and two levels of parking below ground. A seemingly innocuous request for TAC to redesign the first underground parking level to accommodate offices for the Kuwait Stock Exchange in 1978 marked the moment when the Souq Al-Manakh became the place in which the real risks of the Kuwaiti finance economy would ultimately manifest themselves in force.[47] Within a year the Souq had become the site of a vast unregulated market for speculating on foreign companies that were prohibited from being traded on the official stock exchange, open to Kuwaiti citizens only and restricted to government bonds and securities on entities registered in Kuwait. The vast majority of these "companies" existed on paper only, fictional entities registered abroad by Kuwaitis in other Gulf states (particularly the Emirates) solely for the purpose of trading on the Souq Al-Manakh exchange. By early 1982 storefront offices on the ground floor of the souq were selling to traders for up to $50 million, and the government worried about the potential collapse of a black market that operated almost exclusively on post-dated checks and held more total investment than Kuwait's annual revenue from oil.[48] The stock bubble finally burst in August of that year, by which time it had ballooned to absorb some $94 billion in excess speculation.[49]

The sudden collapse of the Souq Al-Manakh exchange was among the most dramatic of the events that spelled the end of the boom in construction by U.S. architects working in the Gulf after 1983. The crash caused a fifty percent decline in construction in Kuwait within the year, an immediate and heavy blow to foreign firms that had overcommitted to work in the country. The ripple effects of the Souq Al-Manakh combined with the economic impacts of the Iranian Revolution, the beginning of OPEC price quotas on oil production in 1982, and the Iran-Iraq War to reveal the underlying volatility of financial and architectural speculation that dictated the rise and fall of U.S. firms in the Gulf. Many of the same offices that had grown in size through the 1970s primarily due to work in the region now suffered the negative consequences of this involvement following the decline in crude oil prices.

For example, these events were among those that precipitated the end for TAC, slowly but inevitably, after 1983. Office memos registered the slow process by which the firm laid off waves of staff and tried unsuccessfully to shift its practice back to domestic work in the U.S, unable to recoup its assets and suffering from the end of the construction boom in Kuwait and other Gulf countries.[50] Within a year TAC had reduced from 390 employees to 220 and kept declining, eventually down to fifty and then to a handful by the 1990s. A final blow for the firm came with the Iraqi invasion of Kuwait in August 1990 and the ensuing Persian Gulf War, when some $2 million in payment for TAC's ongoing work in Iraq were frozen. The firm ultimately filed for bankruptcy in April 1995, just before the next wave of petroleum-fueled development by U.S. architects in the Gulf, now in the United Arab Emirates, Qatar, Bahrain, and other inheritors of the speculative economy of oil. •

47. Invoice from Moncef Eladhari (TAC) to Hamad Al-Bahar (Kuwait Investment Company) for "conversion of level two parking floor in the Area 5 Commercial and Parking Building to office use for the Kuwait Stock Exchange and Associated Functions," December 18, 1978. Courtesy Pace Archives.

48. "Kuwait's Bustling Stock Souq," The New York Times, April 5, 1982, D1.

49. Ihsan A. Hijazi, "Kuwait in Bailout Effort After Market Collapses," The New York Times, December 20, 1982: 29, 32; Paul Lewis, "Kuwait's Market Bailout," The New York Times, February 18, 1983, D1, D7.

50. See "Points Discussed With Bank of Boston," TAC office memorandum, July 18, 1983; letter from John C. Harkness to all members of TAC, September 28. 1983; "Future Commitments in Iraq," TAC office memorandum from John Hayes to board of directors, November 28, 1983. Courtesy MIT Museum.

Sabah Abi-Hanna

Sabah Abi-Hanna (1938–) received a bachelor's degree in architectural engineering from the American University of Beirut (AUB) in 1959, one year after his first experience in Kuwait as an intern at the Department of Public Works. Upon completing his degree, Abi-Hanna returned to Kuwait, where he worked at the Planning Division of the Department of Public Works, and was later transferred to Kuwait Municipality. During this period, Abi-Hanna was involved in building inspection and construction license approvals. Soon he established his own practice, in which his early commissions were confined to domestic projects such as private homes and low-rise residential buildings, including Khaled Al-Zaid Al-Khaled neighbourhood on Baghdad street Maidan Hawally (1965). In 1968 he was commissioned to design the residential complex Loulou'a Al-Marzouq (1968–1971) and Messilah Beach Hotel (1970–74), which opened up opportunities for work overseas, including the Sharjah Carlton Hotel in the UAE. In 1972, with Salem Al-Marzouq joining the firm, Abi-Hanna's practice was expanded into a partnership – Salem Al-Marzouq and Sabah Abi-Hanna (SSH).

Ricardo Camacho conducted two interviews with Sabah Abi-Hanna in both Lebanon and Kuwait, between September and December 2015. The interviews have been combined and edited for length and clarity.

Ricardo Camacho: *You received your degree during a period when AUB architectural engineering training was primarily influenced by the European models of the Ecole Polytechnique, and later the Bauhaus. The affluence of opportunities to build, especially in Beirut, produced an emerging community of architects more interested in imagery rather than the principles of functionalism and rationalism which opened ground for individualism and selfesteem among the most well known architects, especially in their roles as practitioners and professors. On the contrary Prof. Assem Salam had a holistic vision of the practice in general and Beirut in particular. He was involved in different roles and responsibilities, such as the implementation of building codes, laws and regulations, and the preservation of Beirut's urban fabric.*

Being one of your professors, how influential was Prof. Assem Salam in contributing to your understating of architecture, practice, and disciplinary interests?

Sabah Abi-Hanna: The two people who had an influence on me were Professors Assem Salam and Raymond Ghosn. Did you research the building Dean Ghosn designed for Kuwait Oil Company (KOC) in Ahmadi?

RC: *The KOC building, yes. It was called the General Oil Affairs Office in Ahmadi. It later became the Governorate of Ahmadi offices and Municipality building today. Its construction was initiated in 1957 and it was completed in 1958.*

SAH: It was completed in 1958, which means I came in and it was there. I know who built it also, the CCC's (Consolidated Contractors Co. or CONCO). The Chairman, the late Said Khoury apparently appointed Prof. Raymond Ghosn to do the design.

RC: *The other personality is Michel Ecochard. Were you familiar with his work in Lebanon?*

SAH: Michel Ecochard came to Lebanon in the 1950s, and had a lot of impact and input on master plans for cities and the whole of Lebanon. Unfortunately, most of what he planned was never implemented, and what remains has been transformed by the continuous revisions to the master plans he developed.

RC: *Did you visit any specific buildings during your early travels to Japan and Asia Minor after school?*

SAH: My first trip overseas was to Sydney, Australia. That was in the early 1960s. The most significant professional impact on me from that trip was the Sydney Opera House, designed by Utzon, which was under construction. I was fascinated by the turmoil and political dialogue surrounding it. On my way back, I stopped in Manila, the Philippines, before taking a flight to Tokyo. I was so young, in my early twenties. I later visited Japan a couple of times in relation to work in Kuwait during the 1980s, when we were supervising and designing Bayan Palace.

As far as architecture is concerned, Kenzo Tange was famous during the design and construction of Kuwait's airport. We had also a collaboration with the Jordanian architect, Jafar Tukan. I knew him from AUB. He was one or two years younger than me, and he used to have such a beautiful voice. He sang Nat King Cole songs, if you know old songs. We kept in touch, and he was involved with Kenzo Tange when he designed the university in Amman [Yarmouk University].

On another note, we also employed an American architect, in the late 1980s I think, who was a former associate of TAC (The Architects Collaborative). His name was Ralph Montgomery. Before we employed him, he worked for Jafar Tukan in Amman, Jordan. Ralph was one of our good architects. He did things by the book, and he was disciplined and well-organised when he ran a design project. He reminded me of Prof. Raymond Ghosn. He did everything very neatly, his reports were written very nicely.

RC: *That was when?*

SAH: That was in the late 1980s, I think, before the invasion. I'm starting to remember that maybe he was with us before, but definitely he had a lot to do with us during the 1990s, after the Liberation. We co-won the competition for the cultural centre (Sheikh Jaber Al-Ahmad Cultural Centre) – the same one that is now under construction, but with a totally different program. Back then, our proposal was for a monumental building structure and a large plaza.

At the time I came to Kuwait, the Lebanese architectural presence was represented by the firm Dar Al-Handasah, and their senior architect Robert Wakim. But I think the majority of the buildings in Fahad Al-Salem street were designed by Egyptian architects. I mentioned some already: Mahmoud Talaat was one, and before him Sayyed Karim, who designed the predominant building on Jahra Gate (the Thunayan Al-Ghanim building), and there was also a very good friend, architect Mohamed Sharara.

RC: *To conclude the connection with Lebanon – When you completed your degree at AUB, Niemeyer's project in Tripoli was under construction.*

SAH: My memory of the Rashid Karami Expo Centre is of Oscar Niemeyer, who gave us a lecture at the time in the Bechtel building lecture room at AUB. It had a very steep seating arrangement. He placed the butter paper on the board and he sketched [draws while talking] one of the buildings for Brasilia (the Planalto Palace, 1958). He was explaining to us how they designed Brasilia. He came to AUB to lecture in the late 1950s.

RC: *Another not frequently discussed theme in the region is that of the pan-Arab diaspora during the late 1950s. When discussing architecture, Beirut stands out as an incubator and a relevant experimental platform for developments elsewhere in the region.*

SAH: Yes, but of course Beirut is a very old city compared to Gulf cities, and therefore it exported experience in design and construction. Most of the contracting and consulting companies working in Kuwait in the 1960s were established by either Lebanese or Egyptians, I think.

RC: *Did you join the village welfare service during your studies? AUB's summer course, which sent architecture and engineering students to villages either in Syria or Lebanon to support low-income communities or areas affected by natural catastrophes?*

SAH: I had two summer experiences in Lebanon. The first one was during my first year when we were sent to the countryside to be introduced to topographical survey. The second time, there was an earthquake in Lebanon, and an organisation called Ta'meer [re-construction] was established – headed by the late Contracting and Trading Co. (CAT) establishing partner Emil Bustani. Professor Ghosn helped me join this organisation.

RC: *I remember Mounir Khatib. Do you know him?*

SAH: He established the Associate Consulting Engineers (ACE). Mounir Tahir Khatib used to teach civil engineering at AUB and he taught me. I was taught by a number of professors at AUB, but they didn't have the same influence as Raymond Ghosn and Assem Salam, who were our daily tutors.

Khatib got a lot of Lebanese professional involvement, because he became head of the Order of Engineers and Architects (OEA) in Lebanon for some time, so did Assem Salam and Dr. Khalil Maalouf who became a good friend through family connections and we stayed in touch. He was also a professor at AUB and one of the main partners who established ACE.

RC: *Were you by then aware of the ambition for a pan-Arab future? Were you inspired by the spirit of an Arab union?*

SAH: I'll tell you about a Lebanese politician who had a vision for the future – Maurice Gemayel. He was a lawyer and a member of the Parliament. I'm sure if you spoke to any Lebanese citizen they would mention him. He had a vision beyond just the professional. I was friend of his brother who lived in Kuwait, and he was a regular visitor so we used to meet often. During that time, in the late 1960s, early 1970s, when I was still on my own, he spoke to me of his vision for water supply in Lebanon, and about an Arab motorway [the pan-Arab motorway from Beirut to the Gulf].

RC: *The idea of infrastructure.*

SAH: While I was struggling Lebanese architect trying to build something in Kuwait, he advised me not to compete with Western architectural firms. "Don't be ashamed to go to the West, get them to help you, get them to do things for you as consultants, learn from them, and then start relying less and less on them over time," he said. That's what happened with SSH.

He said it to me when we were once in our village, Hamat, in Lebanon. We have a sort of mountain plateau overlooking the Mediterranean, and we sat on our balcony and he said, looking towards the horizon and the sea: "What you need to do is manage experts … when you design, you need engineers, planners, and architects, but you also need economists, doctors, and environmental specialists."

He really had a vision for the future.

RC: *You mentioned before that you and Dar Al-Handasah were some of the Lebanese practices in Kuwait during the early 1960s.*

However, aside from practice, you also had intriguing personalities, such as Sami Abdel Baqi, who credits himself with bringing many architects from Lebanon to Kuwait.

SAH: That's an interesting question. I am one of those that came to Kuwait because of his brother, Fouad Abdel Baqi. Sami was also there at the time, designing and supervising the Municipality buildings complex. Fouad was assigned as the man in charge of the Department of Public Works. At that time, I knew three or four of the Lebanese engineers that had contracts with the Department or were employed by the Department because of him. And I know that in our group from AUB there were five or six of us who interned at the Department of Public Works, and Fouad was the one who brought us to Kuwait.

My cousin was also working at the time on the Municipality building, under the supervision of Sami Abdel Baqi. They were still concreting the raft foundations, and, in my experience, that was the first time I saw a heavy-duty concreting job. They had the vibrators whizzing across the raft area. They were pouring concrete in large quantities during the night. Naturally, at that time, Sami's name was quite popular because of that particular job.

RC: *It's interesting for us to look at the small moments that influenced the growing Levantine diaspora in the Gulf.*

SAH: Apart from the Lebanese and Egyptian architects there was a Palestinian architect – Said Breik who had an office with a Lebanese engineer – Ibrahim Monaimeny.

At that time, the important roles were assigned through the government; the private sector wasn't as influential.

RC: *You mentioned Saba Shiber. There was also his brother, Victor, right?*

SAH: I don't know who came first. I think they were two different people. Saba came as a planning advisor to Kuwait Municipality and had a specific role, which he did well. Victor was a freelancer; he had more freedom and was very well known among the Lebanese community. Saba's role was more theory-based. His large green book [Recent Arab City Growth] is still what every architect in Kuwait wants to have a copy of.

He implemented many ideas, such as the Anwaar Al-Sabah Complex and others, of which some have now been demolished and redeveloped as high-rises. I remember he designed them free-hand. That street [Fahad Al-Salem street], was there for fifty years, those were my fifty years. When you walked, you walked under the colonnades of Saba Shiber.

RC: *One of the things we always question is if all these buildings were designed by the Municipality, whether there were any building codes and regulations, or even if the so well-known 'facade regulation' for Fahad Al-Salem and Mubarak Al-Kabeer streets really existed.*

SAH: Regarding the one building I designed for the Textile Association in Area 9 of the CBD [Central Business District], the design criteria used by the Municipality was a blueprint from another building.

At the time there were some Indian architects working with me, and we explored the architectural treatment of internal and external facade elements – I don't remember changing the dimensions of the commercial atrium. I don't think we changed any master plan, the number of floors, or the area. All of this was…

RC: *Under Saba Shiber's guidance?*

SAH: Yes because it took place at the same time as Fahad Al-Salem street was being developed. Definitely all of them had the same general blueprint criteria, in terms of sections and the plan.

RC: *You talk about blueprints. Were these collected from the municipality?*

SAH: It's how one complies with regulation. Remember in Kuwait at the time we were practicing in the late 1950s and early 1960s. The building and zoning code were part of a small A5 booklet that was 20 pages.

RC: *Wow. Where can we find this booklet today?*

SAH: I don't know if I have one in my archives. I doubt it. Did I mention that I stayed for less than a year at the Municipality after we moved, and my main job was building permits? I don't know how else the instructions were conveyed at that time, because even if it was through word of mouth, it was very good because everybody complied.

RC: *It's been difficult to find documentation regarding Saba Shiber's 'design control' guidelines, particularly those for Fahad Al-Salem and Mubarak Al-Kabeer street facades. Where these also blueprints, or were they a written set of rules and regulations?*

SAH: I don't know. If you talk about facades and the use of colour, for example, in the Anwaar Al-Sabah complex, what you find is the personal interpretation of a particular designer. The general instructions that were issued by the Planning Department, by Saba Shiber, were line drawings, nothing more. Mainly dimensions in terms of a plan and sections. And you can see they were 100 percent complied with. All of Fahad Al-Salem street, maybe with the exception of some differences at the roof level, but nothing more. I think you can give him credit for this, God bless his soul. At that time, Kuwait was just emerging as a desert development. There were concerns about the weather, sun, dust, and so on, and he [Shiber] responded to this with the Fahad Al-Salem concept and with the CBD areas, particularly the textile souqs, and *qaissareyas*. The *qaissareyas*, for example, again, were a weather-related solution. Air conditioning was very limited, if present at all, and I don't know if the orientation of the buildings and the study went as deep as to allow for better circulation of air. But, other than that, they were a very basic response to climate.

RC: *There were strong typological decisions in these new qaissareyas. It wasn't just a translation of the old souqs, or the projection of environmental constraints, the scheme evolved from something. The Municipality blueprints were architectural design projects. Still, it's strange how Shiber could develop these regulations with no design process.*

SAH: Now I'm thinking, it's the first time I've thought about it. I think what he developed was his own translation of the old souq idea. For associations like the Textile Association to build their own buildings and make them recognisable as such... also by marking these with doors and entrances.

And the fact that he introduced the basement as a shopping arcade by solving the vertical circulation issues and its relation to the outdoors.

RC: *Do you remember if that was in the guidelines, for example construction ratios?*

SAH: They didn't need them, because the plan and sections were already there.

RC: *So the different zones – footprint and sections – were pre-defined?*

SAH: Yes, when you mentioned the sections, I remembered one Egyptian engineer who survived a few decades, his name was Mashhoor – there were two Mashhoors, one was a consultant, Abdel-Raouf Mashoor, they were two brothers I think. One of them was the designer of one of those textile blocks.

RC: *Did you mention Mahmoud Talaat?*

SAH: No, I mentioned Abdel-Raouf Mashhoor. Mahmoud Talaat was an architect who worked for Sayyed Karim, and later on his own.

RC: *Moving a bit deeper into your practice, you mentioned before that your first works were private commissions, mainly houses. I imagine projects like the White Palace on the Fourth Ring Road, which was built by CAT from what we know, could have been designed by you?*

SAH: The White Palace? You are right. I think CAT built it during the 1950s, but I had a very small involvement with it when I started working on my own. There were a few Lebanese engineers who were older than me, but we were still friends. They saw a young architect and wanted to help. I started with a small job for Ahmadiah [Contracting and Trading Co.]. They were doing renovations for the Palace, including, I think, the first floor. I didn't even have an office, I was sitting in one of my friend's offices on the Gulf Road.

Other than working for contracting companies, I was part of a team of designers. Naturally, because the office was small for the first ten to fifteen years, most of my jobs were private sector buildings, apartment buildings. They later became commercial office buildings, but very few. My relationship was not just with contractors, it was also influenced by my nature – I was liked by them, I don't know. Also there were some Kuwaiti families who had good relationships with me, they just picked me up, and then I got a series of assignments with their friends and neighbours.

RC: *It's interesting that we discussed the White Palace, with other large houses built during those early years, such as the palace in Surra, designed by Farmer and Dark [for Sheikh Jaber Al-Ali Al-Sabah], you can see a strong relationship between client and architect.*

In many circumstances, these dynamics generated schemes that were not as disciplined and well-ordered as the White Palace, but rather became extremely complex in terms of building programs, typology and facades, ornament, and materials. These other large domestic developments brought together local material culture and traditions, something between a vernacular imaginary and the ambition to become 'luxurious' beyond the common.

The White House is a pragmatic building in typology, program and the relationship to the site and its surroundings, as a whole. Definitely, a modern building.

SAH: I would expect that from CAT at the time. CAT and CCC, even Ahmadiah buildings, were function-oriented. These were straightforward buildings to construct, I would say. I don't think they were looking for architectural landmarks, that wasn't their vision.

RC: But the White Palace is a very sensitive gesture, with a curved footprint that is raised from the ground. It's not the obvious building to design.

SAH: At the time that the White Palace was built, there was nothing else around it. The entire district was flat.

RC: Other projects you have mentioned are the National Bank of Kuwait (NBK) branches and some particular commissions for Kuwait Public Transportation Co. (KPTC). Can you tell us more about these projects?

SAH: The main buildings of KPTC in Shuwaikh and Mirqab, were not designed by us. Mirqab was developed by an expat firm that also designed the main bus terminal. I don't remember well, but it could have been designed by Design Construction Group (DCG). However, in that building, one of the three or four shops fronts we developed for NBK, on the left side of the building. I want to take two sheets of paper and sketch something for you.

RC: Back to the KPTC bus stops.

SAH: Yes, I'm going to do the sketch for you. It was extremely basic. It was a main, simple structure, and the roof was something like this [draws while talking], and the waiting and ticket area, which also had a small refreshment area, was like this. It was a multi-disciplined structural design. The cantilever was about two to three metres. This was the first big job, but it was very basic. My contract with KPTC was for a long-term relationship, and we lived with it for many years.

RC: And the Loulou'a Al-Marzouq commission? How did that happen? It was an innovative project, way beyond the conventional building typology that was being developed at the time, but also extremely clear in the way the site was positioned towards the Ras-Al-Salmiya context.

SAH: We have photographs that show the massive project itself and how the other buildings were houses that have been demolished. God bless his soul, Mr. Khaled Al-Marzouq was a very audacious developer. We worked with him for about fifteen years, and during most of it he was very assertive. He wanted to innovate beyond the traditional, to innovate in the design interpretation of regulations and building codes. It was successful, and was an example for other investors who followed in his steps.

In Loulou'a Al-Marzouq, the client was the agent, interfering and challenging the building height and volume, the introduction of commercial units on the ground level and below the residential block, but also introducing the possibility of using duplex units. The client also expanded the shops along the perimeter of the building, which was not the common interpretation of the codes for residential complexes. The client was able to introduce a small supermarket at the front, which was additional to the building footprint and construction ratio. As a developer, he had foresight about the site. He knew the site next door [south] was public property, so, if we were going to build on this side [north of the public property], we should have an open U-shape footprint [open to the south] and all the facades facing northwards, to the sea, and the low skyline east and west. I'm sure he had foresight with that.

RC: Was the Messilah Beach Resort project developed at the same time?

SAH: Same time, give or take a year.

RC: At the time, these two projects created strong alternative life patterns. The concept of providing a new lifestyle for a permanent resident and a holiday or weekend experience...these were definitely the commissions for two of the most important projects at the time, which radically changed the expat community, but also the urban dynamics across the southeast expansion of the city. These are a few of the projects that changed the patterns of life in modern Kuwait.

SAH: Yes, if you look now at the Messilah Beach location, at that time, it was away from the city. Salmiya had started becoming a city. Messila was out in the desert, even though it was on the beach. During the initial stages of the design, Mr. Mubarak Al-Hassawi, God bless his soul, agreed to develop a concept based on the repetition of small chalet units. He was the one who did it, and it became a landmark that was hidden from the main roads and public areas. Here I can confirm that there was less involvement from the client in the design process and decision-making. He did want the sort of courtyards, and so on, but not in the way we designed it. Here, the project was entirely generated within our team..

RC: Impressive. How did the client react to the principle of an exposed cement block resort with bungalows confined in hexagonal prisms?

SAH: Let's say it was a concept that evolved between my personal early interpretation of an environmentally controlled concept and the owner's trust in our capability to pursue his own vision for Kuwait further.

RC: Completely. Mr. Al-Hassawi was very aware of and encouraging of the architect's role. The residential and mixed-use complexes developed in the late 1960s for Salmiya and Hawally with Pace and Iraq Consult are an example of that.

SAH: Yes he did. To me, the relationships with clients were the best way to promote and expose my work. In Messilah, Mr. Al-Hassawi trusted our design competence, but also my personal judgment, my own capacity to relate to others, the way I deal with people.

But you know, suddenly, the scale of the operation changed. We started associating with international consultants, for example, on projects such as the car park buildings [Souq Al-Kuwait and Souq Al-Kabeer], and not this instant reaction to being commissioned and starting the design immediately with the client.

RC: Actually, these car park buildings, apart from other repercussions, brought new technologies and eventually a new relationship between the design process and construction. For example, the massive use of pre-fabricated components, the structural solutions for foundations, and simply the access for motorised vehicles up a few levels from the ground.

SAH: You will be astonished, here I am going to introduce another person who had a substantial impact on our design process – the contractor. For instance, it was the contractor who suggested the fiber dome for Sheikha Badriya Mosque. The pre-cast panels we used on Salem Al-Mubarak street, in the North and South Salmiya buildings. On the Al-Bahar building, and in the case of this one [refers to North Salmiya building on a picture], in the original design, we had three towers on top of them, and eventually you could find a fourth, because there is one in the intersection between these two.

The upper shopping arcade facade resulted from a dialogue with the contractor himself, who offered to move ahead with a solution using concrete. He was a hilarious character, a good friend. He did this one and this one [points at different pictures of the Salem Al-Mubarak street commercial galleries], and he loved it when I told him thank you very much, it is beautiful concrete, exposed concrete. It was a constructive relationship. From the beginning, he would assure me that he could do it and implement certain details, even if they would become different from what we had originally specified. This all emerged because we were a small office. I was sitting with contractors, trading ideas, and so on.

RC: *Incredible, this is the kind of honesty in the relationship between architect and builder that you can't see these days. But you just mentioned something very interesting regarding the high-rise proposals for the Salmiya concourse area [North Salmiya building]. Are you referring to this round tower [points at an old picture of the Al-Salam building] behind? Was this part of the project?*

SAH: No, Mahmoud Talaat was the architect, I think. Now I remember he was the architect of the famous residential tower with the circular plan in Salmiya.

RC: *Between the South and the North project [Salmiya buildings], I do remember that you mentioned earlier the proposal for a gate.*

SAH: That was back at the beginning, on the south side [at the end of the Fourth Ring Road and Qatar street].

RC: *Was the project commissioned to you during 1970–71?*

SAH: Yes.

RC: *Was that area, now referred to as 'Old Salmiya,' a commercial strip by that time?*

SAH: The areas in-between were all residential, until the application for new buildings. At the beginning here [points at plan for the TEST district centre proposal for Salmiya concourse], on the other side, we also got two buildings that were allowed to be for commercial use.

RC: *It's again an incredible project. Once more, you have the developer who has the foresight to develop the beginning and end of a street that was to become the most dynamic commercial strip in the country. Was this something you developed with the client?*

SAH: You are teasing me, assuming that I had a major influence on the master plan for Salmiya. I may have. The thing is that, after we were given permission for commercial use above the ground floor, others followed. It was permitted for the whole street. Afterwards, I think Pace designed a project for a mixed-use complex here [points at the plan for Salem Al-Mubarak street].

RC: *The Al-Anjari Complex?*

SAH: Yes, it's white cement, and was built right after we built ours. It was a natural development for the street, filling the gap between the North and South buildings, making the street a continuous commercial front.

I do remember the way decisions were taken at the time. There was no master plan or specific building regulations for the area. From the fire brigade building here [Salmiya on the

Fourth Ring Road], there was a traffic light, then our buildings here [North Salmiya building], and then they just kept going.

The street [Salem Al-Mubarak] was the subject of ongoing rumours, promises, and expectations at the time, not just for years, but for decades. Every time we used to hear somebody saying this was going to go all the way until it reached the Gulf street on the other side, which eventually happened.

But the way it developed was, year after year, through landowners and developers. One of these developers was Mr. Khaled Al-Essa [former Minister of Public Works]. He was the owner of one of the buildings we worked on, the Spring Continental.

RC: *Was this building the Essa Al-Saleh Commercial Galleria? Was it originally named the Spring Continental? Was it a hotel?*

SAH: Yes, there was a small hotel on top. It was residential, but later, it was converted into a hotel. The building was not meant to be commercial on the upper levels. There was commercial space only on the ground floors, including the basement and mezzanine levels. It was the client himself who came up with that idea.

RC: *This movement below ground, creating the lower commercial square, was it meant to increase commercial space and the value of the building, or to protect the central outdoor area from the street?*

SAH: Not to protect it. The client was mainly motivated to increase the commercial potential.

RC: *Correct. Another project I would like to discuss with you is the Rehab Complex in Hawally, developed by URC (United Realty Co.).*

SAH: At that time, during the early 1970s, my partner Salem Al-Marzouq was still a Member of Parliament. And it was almost taken for granted that all the URC work, which was a public fund, would be assigned to others. However, for some reason, the chairman of the URC commissioned us to do the job, and we started designing it. We started by making the most out of the commercial podium up to the first floor.

Here I may claim a very personal influence on the design, because sometimes when you have a team, others bring ideas and you continue them. But this building is a reflection of my influence.

RC: *This building is definitely worth more attention. However, it's not even portrayed SSH's "The First 50 Years" book. The building is intriguing, and far from ordinary in terms of architecture. The scale of the building is uncommon – the bottom was cantilevered, lifting the podium from the street level, the facade system is geometric, and a succession of vertical concrete louvers control the opening position and dimensions... and so many other features in the way the building is developed that are of interest. Apart from this, I can imagine the resolution of the floor level typologies and building sections. Unfortunately, we have no access to the building plans, or the apartment units above.*

SAH: It's a continuation of the office discipline culture. At the time, many of the people who drafted the design drawings were draftsmen not architects. And we used the discipline of preparing a design development, and so on. But there were some relevant additions and inputs into this culture. Since I started practicing during the early 1960s, our major references, design-wise, moved from Dar Al-Handasah, through DCG, to SOM later on. All these were part of a background of architectural references that were relevant in the architecture we conceived. I do agree with you, that this culture can be better understood through Al-Rehab Complex, in the non-alignment of the facade's columns, which define this sort of pixelated negative between the exposed surface of the outer facade, and the recessed surfaces for balconies in the shade.

However, I would like to mention that it was not my habit to watch over the shoulders of the draftsman to make sure they designed the way I wanted. This was an office culture acquired over decades. The job was commissioned in the late 1970s, it was purely an SSH job.

RC: *Interesting, so this project came right after the completion of the car parks [Souqs Al-Kuwait and Al-Kabeer]?*

SAH: Yes, yes after... and there was another project being developed in parallel – the Fahaheel Towers.

RC: *Now I understand the relationship, and where this culture came from. I can see the effects on these residential or mixed-use complexes and the car park buildings.*

SAH: I see what you mean, but there is no influence. By the way, I myself had some good design architects who were Lebanese...I don't remember who the architect was. For instance, for this building [Fahaheel Towers], we had a Yugoslav architect called Thomas Kraljević.

Kraljević moved from SSH during the late 1970s, early 1980s, and started working full time with Khaled Al-Marzouq, the developer of Loulou'a Al-Marzouq.

RC: *His wife was also an architect, right?*

SAH: She worked for us as well for some years – Milica. They were very young; they got married in the late 1960s. But they didn't have anything to do with the projects that were under construction then. Maybe he helped on this job. There are some buildings where I know for sure he was part of the concept design team.

RC: *Can you tell us about the motivations of Al-Rehab Complex, in terms of program and typology? Was it supposed to be a mixed-use building? Were the units meant for sale or to rent?*

SAH: I remember Al-Rehab before it became a URC project. It used to be a neighbourhood complex of small buildings for the Al-Sabah family, part of HH Sheikh Sabah Al-Ahmad's compound. I remember the details of the inside, but it was like that [draws a sketch of the old building's arcade]. And that of course at the time was when Hawally was still coming up.

Selling at the time was not an issue. Usually, when you develop high-density, tall apartment buildings like this one, they are for expats. The only project that was being built for Kuwaitis was the Arthur Erickson project [Al-Sawaber] in Mirqab/Sharq. Other than that, nothing was to be offered to Kuwaitis [in Kuwait, only nationals can buy property]. You wouldn't be surprised to see a young Kuwaiti couple here [Loulou'a Al-Marzouq], and you live with your wife and your mother next door. That became the case.

The alternative to long leases or selling is something that just recently started being developed. The only developer that was doing long leases by then was Mr. Khaled Al-Marzouq, with the individual houses by the Gulf road in Salmiya.

RC: *But was that also a strategy for Loulou'a Al-Marzouq?*

SAH: Yes, I think it was. And, actually, it was one of the attractions for some Kuwaitis who began taking apartments there, introducing Kuwaiti citizens to living in an apartment building and sharing the complex with other foreign tenants.

RC: *But, during the design process and while researching and developing the residential typologies, who were they for?*

SAH: I think it was on a case-by-case basis. It was even thought through at a later stage, and was not part of the design process.

RC: *But what were your references in terms of user experience? I imagine that designing an apartment for an expatriate family was substantially different than designing for a Kuwaiti family.*

SAH: Most of the buildings we built that had rental apartments were designed mainly on our own initiative. I lived in an apartment in Salmiya, across from the traffic intersection of the Sheikha Badriya Mosque. There were two apartment buildings with green sand-lime bricks. I designed those.

The apartments had split levels. I had the apartment on the ground with the garden and half the level above. The parking was underneath, and then there was another apartment, and another apartment. These typologies were derived from my own personal initiative. That was primarily for the developer's family and friends. When they asked us to do something for them, all we did was the outline, as per the zoning, and what went inside was all my design.

RC: *But, for instance, the concept of a split-level typology emerged as a design strategy to respond to a specific problem, opportunity, or even concrete requirements, such as the need for privacy or division of a program.*

SAH: Yes, privacy. You have one door, you don't have a landing with too many doors. And the other motivation was to avoid corridors. I developed these typologies for the first time in 1964–65 on Baghdad street for huge complex – Al-Khaled apartments. We didn't have someone like Mr. Khaled Al-Marzouq there. We developed the typologies by ourselves for the client's family members.

RC: *That is again an exceptional project. Al-Khaled Complex is the most abstract of these projects. The residential units are among the few experimental attempts to reinvent the 'Arab villa' in Kuwait.*

Apart from the building's typological innovation, its position in the plan [different from the street grid] generates a specific urban landscape, where relations between parts [buildings and streets] are controlled through the recessed ground floor of these and the facade screens above. The visibility between public and private realms, avoiding the use of any conventional windows or balconies, is impressive in this project. But was the master plan already in place? And the small retail compound in the middle, with the water tower?

SAH: No, I don't remember if the streets were already there. We had nothing to do with the retail plaza, so maybe the streets were already there.

RC: *The mode in which these residential buildings are distributed builds its own, autonomous reference system over the street grid. This sort of free plan, where the space between buildings is not linked to the street alignment or layout, was not very common in Kuwait during this period. In Al-Khaled Complex, there is always* the tentative idea to release the ground plan and allow public permeability from Baghdad street to the neighbourhood. Also the way in which the access to the house, parking, and footprint are organised rejects the prospect of a fence.

The residences are completely resting on common ground, and the street layout of the neighbourhood complex is reduced to accessibility, unlike in other parts of the city, where the street is the element that regulates and mediates the public and private.

In addition, the entrance to the building reveals an intentional perception of scale, given the free and open ground floor plan that was lowered for economic reasons, but also increases shade and protection, while the entrance and core of the building are set towards the middle of the floor plan.

SAH: I remember also that the predominant colour was grey, the dark grey sand-lime bricks, which are present across all the buildings. Then we developed the bricks in texture and colour, but I can't recall how exactly. We never set on a panel and discussed colour. Regarding the facades, what led us in that direction was mainly the privacy of the split-level, and the layout inside was very comfortable for that size of apartments.

You're talking to me about all these things and I'm trying to remember how we went around design control. I know we had one or two team members who were manually drafting at the time. And I used to have a partner designer from MPW, but other than that, I'm wondering about people like Frank Lloyd Wright. How did they do buildings? I'm sure they didn't go into every detail themselves.

RC: *I imagine at that time, but you know better than me, that you managed your design process from the moment the project was commissioned. What were your first steps? How did you manage meetings with clients? Were these workshops with the clients, or just meetings where you went alone? Did these clients come to your office?*

SAH: We couldn't enjoy time to plan in most cases. When I was alone in the first years, and we were mainly designing houses, I did visit my clients at their places. And very often I went to lunch and then the discussion continued. The market itself was new. The only material I was courageous enough to use was the sand-lime bricks, nobody else used them. At that time, the only people who used them were government departments for low-income housing, and they didn't want to relate these buildings to low-income people. But I did it because I believed in it. That same brick was used in the four villas I supervised at the seaside.

RC: *Those villas at the end of Salem Al-Mubarak street? Close to Gulf road?*

SAH: Yes, I know the villas you're referring to. But I didn't design them. It was the DCG partner, Gordon?

RC: *Gordon Brown.*

SAH: Yes. The owners came to me – the family, the father, and the three brothers wanted me to supervise them and I did. But when I supervised them, of course, I was very involved in the construction details, because the buildings were not planned by a contractor, they brought a subcontractor in for concrete, etc. These same clients had another site with an elongated facade, which I designed for them – a long residential building on Baghdad street, also using a sand-lime brick facade.

Anyway, all of this is beautiful. •

العدد ٢٦٥ – ١٦ يوليو ١٩٧٤ – ٢٦ جمادى ثانى ١٣٩٤

The Role of Franco Albini in Kuwait

CLAUDIA CAGNESCHI AND ENRICO MAMBELLI

An introductory study based on the architect's archival documentation

Translated by: Valerie Fontana Shulman and Francesca Gordini

The following essay is the result of research based on the study of letters and archival material from the Albini Foundation, and additional information collected from an interview with Marco Albini, Franco's son, who was also involved in the firm during its collaboration with Kuwaiti planning authorities.

Franco Albini and the Middle East

Throughout his career, Franco Albini created works of architecture known for their profound relationship to their surrounding environment, the result of rigorous project methods that sought to understand and re-interpret traditional elements within their contexts. He stayed true to the principles typical of the Modern Movement, of which he played a part.

With this in mind, Albini's experience in the Middle East, first in Kuwait and later in Saudi Arabia, were opportunities for exploring the geography, architecture, and culture of these places, which led to useful analysis that underpinned his guidelines for future local projects in the Middle East.[1]

Between 1974 and 1978 the architectural firm founded by Albini, in partnership with architects Franca Helg and Antonio Piva, worked on a beautification project of Qasr Al-Hokm, in downtown Riyadh, the capital city of Saudi Arabia. The task that Albini's architectural firm was contracted to complete in this area followed the instructions outlined in a former comprehensive master plan for the entire city, prepared by architect Constantinos Doxiadis. This Master Plan defined Qasr Al-Hokm as the 'action area' for redevelopment, with a program based on commercial exchange and transportation, which would transform the city into a cultural hub.

In studying Qasr Al-Hokm and finding new buildings alongside historical buildings, like Al-Murabba Mosque, Qasr Al-Hokm Palace and Masmak Fortress, Albini's firm saw

1. Cover of *A Plan for Kuwait*, Colin Buchanan and Partners, Kuwait, 1972. © Kuwait Municipal Archive.

the need to modify some of the area guidelines previously proposed by Constantinos A. Doxiadis. Contrary to the Greek architect's vision of a vertical city, Albini aimed to build "aesthetic continuity"[2] integrated with the surrounding urban fabric that would not only respect the horizontal pattern typical of Arab cities, but would create a more unified whole.

Franco Albini and Kuwait City: his Role in the Advisory Group

In 1965, Dr. Omar Azzam, acting as consultant for Riyadh's local administration, was called, together with Mr. Mahmoud Riad, to revise and refine the urban development plan currently in place for Kuwait City. They formed a team of consultants in charge of supervising all the analysis, research, and planning work for the local environment. Dr. Azzam proposed the involvement of two architects on the project, Leslie Martin and Franco Albini, with whom he had previously worked in Saudi Arabia and Lisbon (architectural competition for the Calouste Gulbenkian Museum, 1958).

In 1969, during some preliminary meetings held in London, the advisory group discussed and developed several hypotheses for the redevelopment of Kuwait City, which were subsequently implemented by the local administration and incorporated as guidelines in the new master plan. Additionally, the advisory group was called to evaluate several new projects for Kuwait City.

The local government requested, revised and expanded regulations for the old city, including new infrastructures, new satellite cities, 'residential quarters' and cultural centres, such as the new university, the National Museum and the new National Assembly.

At the Albini Foundation Archives, a folder simply labeled "Kuwait" contains extensive notes

on Franco Albini's works and experience that further clarify his role within the group.

The archived material consists, for the most part, of correspondence between Albini, Martin and Azzam, showing their work as supervisors in different countries overseas, but always in close collaboration. The frequent exchange of letters allowed each member to actively participate in the collective supervision of the works in progress. The group typically met three to four times per year, usually in London, to generate ideas and discuss the projects. They were often corresponding with Hamid Shuaib, the representative of the Kuwaiti government. Shuaib subsequently founded, in partnership with three other partners, one of the country's major architectural and urban planning firms, the Pan-Arab Consulting Engineers (Pace). Another clear fact that emerges from the correspondence is that Martin held an important role as intermediary between the Kuwaiti government, the advisory group, and various international designers involved in ongoing transformation works in the city. Martin in fact designed many letters addressed to various recipients, copies of which were sent to Albini.

On the other hand, Franco Albini's role in the advisory group was mainly to supervise and critically analyse the design work on the ground and to coordinate each project in Kuwait within the context of a wider plan. Furthermore, he was appointed to review the design of the new museum, according to the master plan drawn up by Colin Buchanan and Partners (more detailed information to follow).

Lastly, through Albini's inputs, the advisory group became an active agent of the modern way to conceive architecture in Kuwait. Albini was in contact with each design

group invited to participate in the architectural competitions organised by Kuwait Municipality, to the point that we can speculate as to his direct role in the selection of the participants. In his letter exchanges, Leslie Martin often referred to him as the primary reference for the foreign teams during this period.

In 1968, Colin Buchanan, a design professional who had previously served with Martin on the Planning Ministry of London, was nominated as lead planner of Kuwait City. Buchanan and his partners completed a study on the current status of Kuwait, including economic and social analysis, and the study outlined their proposal for reorganising and improving the city for high-quality growth.

Buchanan's work, which was similar to the work of Doxiadis in Riyadh, helped the advisory group to single out action areas within their master plan for Kuwait that called for specific interventions and distinct functions or zones in these urban areas. Further development of these action areas became an essential part of the master plan of the advisory group, which aimed to reintroduce a renewed Kuwait in the Gulf.

The Architectural Competition for the Parliament Building and the New Museum Building

During the years of collaboration with the advisory group, Franco Albini oversaw many projects, including the establishment of the city's new university, and two other significant buildings: the Kuwait National Museum and the New Parliament building, all of which had to satisfy the vision for grand cultural centres, as outlined in Buchanan's Master Plan.

As a norm, every major project to be developed in the city was sent to the advisory board for review and evaluation. Moreover, the government relied on the advisory group to launch a series of international competitions for the design of major public buildings, such as the National Museum, the Parliament and a new university headquarters. The advisory group was involved in drafting the competition brief, shortlisting the candidates and evaluating the submissions.

The competition for the National Museum project dates back to the early 1960s, and the French architect Michel Ecochard was awarded first prize. However, the building was not fully realised until the early 1980s. Therefore, in the early 1970s, the advisory group was called to comment on the old museum project and to contribute with a new definition of the functional program and with new guidelines that could align this with the frameworks of the second Master Plan for the city.

The local municipality added a new consultant to the existing team: Mr. George Henri Rivière, in some of his early writing, referenced the comparison notes that Albini had provided during his work reviewing an earlier design for the museum. There was a large building mass concept in the initial design for the museum: a centralised complex to serve the entire city. Upon reviewing Albini's notes, Rivière modified the design concept in order to create a "system of museums,"[3] whereby smaller individual buildings would be distributed throughout the city. This new design solution fit the museum program within the urban fabric and nestled the spaces within their local contexts. In the following years, this museum concept was further refined by Rivière and ultimately built as a multi-functional series of "cultural containers." The museum took the form of four separate pavilions shaping a central courtyard.

In the 1970s, according to initial correspondence between members of the advisory group and Kuwait Municipality, four internationally renowned architectural firms were invited to compete for the new Parliament building.

The advisory group members were in charge of the competition and selecting the firms writing the draft proposal for the National Assembly building. They also selected the winning proposal. Albini, as indicated in a letter from Martin to Shuaib in June 1970, was directly involved in this process.

The advisory group initially invited seven designers to submit portfolios in order to narrow a shortlist down to four competitors, outlined by the government. These four firms would then proceed to the next phase: providing a preliminary design proposal for the National Assembly building, which would meet the programmatic design criteria and follow the "Master Plan for the Old City" by Colin Buchanan and Partners.

Among the invited designers were some of the greatest proponents of modern architecture: Jørn Utzon (who won the competition); Ignazio Gardella; Balkrishna Doshi; Spence, Bonnington & Collins; Rifad Chadirji; Mohammed Ramzi Omar, as well as a design consortium made up of five local consultants.

Another letter in the advisory group's correspondence, dated June 1970, reports that Albini was the one to send the final draft of the competition to the representatives of the Kuwaiti government, just before their scheduled meeting in London. Noted in Albini's cover letter, was the building program for the competition and focus area in the city. Among the competition documents that the advisory group provided were general plans of the area, a site plan outlining locations of prominent existing buildings and aerial photographs.

Albini also highlighted a key theme that would provide a basis for the design of the National Assembly building. His "new concept of an Arab city"[4] was centred on the relationship between the existing city's urban fabric and the site in which the new building would be placed, as well as the relationship between that specific building's site and its immediate surroundings. Eventually the proposals would have to also follow the guidelines in Buchanan's Master Plan.

The winning project that met Albini's vision was submitted by Jørn Utzon, who described his design as functionally derivative of the typical Arab bazaar. Utzon's idea consisted of a series of modular cubes positioned along a central spine: a long corridor that connected different programmatic spaces in a sequence. This structural form, presented as the next evolution of the traditional 'souq structure,' allowed for incremental future expansion and took into account the historical features of an Arab city. These modular forms created an alternating rhythm of solids and voids along a major north west – south east axis. This central artery connected the commercial harbour to the main 'open hall' square: a vast, covered plaza for public gatherings.

In selecting this winning design, Albini shows his "attention to urban form"[5] that seeks coherence in the whole design of the city. Similarly, Albini's business partner, Franca Helg, wrote several notes on other projects developed for the city of Riyadh that also makes a clear case for the importance of considering the local context of places when working to redevelop existing urban patterns. This approach to design became a constant in Albini's career, beyond his role as member of the advisory group. The centrepiece of his work was how design must appreciate and enhance the existing historical features of the Arab city – both its character and its structural form.

Interview with Marco Albini, Franco Albini's son.

Claudia Cagneschi and Enrico Mambelli conducted this interview in April 2015.

How did Franco Albini get involved with the Advisory Group? Could you better explain his relationship with Leslie Martin?

Kuwait Government decided to form the advisory group, made up of Leslie Martin, Omar Azzam and architect Belgiojoso in Italy. The Advisory Group was overseen by the Local Municipality, therefore all the meetings were to take place in Kuwait. I only attended those meetings between 1972 and 1973 and Franco was brought into the picture by Martin, after having worked with him on previous projects.

What was Albini's role in the advisory group?

The advisory group, as I still remember it, used to work in a very homogeneous way. All its members had established very solid relationships and didn't face any managerial issues. It was thanks to Omar Azzam [consultant for both the Kuwaiti Municipality and Saudi Arabia's Municipality] that Albini got involved in Saudi Arabia.

What was Franco's work process in the advisory group? How well do you think he got to know and truly understand Kuwait's territory?

The advisory group worked most substantially between 1970 and 1974. I think they met three to four times a year, and I have reason to believe their knowledge of the local geography was very limited, with the exception of the case study for Kuwait City.

How did he establish his relationship with Kuwaiti personalities, such as Ghazi Sultan and Hamid Shuaib?

I truly can't say much about this topic. I only remember Hamid Shuaib. I simply remember that Kuwaiti governement officials were very knowledgeable people with calm personalities and a strong ability to listen and relate to the advisory group. Everyone seemed satisfied with the relationship.

As an advisory group member, Albini was called to revise Colin Buchanan's Master Plan, which also involved the Italian group BBPR. What was Franco's role in this process? What was his relationship with the BBPR group?

Buchanan's project consisted of a generic master plan indicating different areas, one of which was assigned to BBPR. There wasn't much of a relationship with BBPR, most of the contacts and reviews were conducted through discussions with Leslie Martin, who also acted as a key manager of the work.

With the exception of Franca Helg, who else at Albini's firm was involved in this project?

No one. Franca Helg also never actively participated in the advisory group meetings. I was the only one who took part in a couple of meetings between 1972 and 1973.

Was Franco Albini ever involved in any other project in Saudi Arabia besides the one in Riyadh? Where does his interest in Middle Eastern countries come from?

After the project in Kuwait, I participated in the development of projects for Riyadh and Jeddah. Riyadh's historical district was to be renovated and new projects for its administrative centre were to be designed. This possibility arose thanks to connections with Leslie Martin and Omar Azzam – they were both already working in Saudi Arabia. Leslie Martin had designed Al-Taif's Government Centre; Omar Azzam was a consultant for Riyadh Municipality and had indicated that Franco Albini would be the architect to renovate Masmak [a tower made of mud, located in a historical position]. The project was initially supposed to become a museum, but grew in scope over time, three buildings were designed and built: one served the local municipality and the police, one was for the King, and the last one was a mosque. The total area for the project was close to 800x800 metres. •

1. Francesco Tentori, "Riyadh," *Lotus International*, n. 18 (March 1978): 105.

2. Ibid., 106.

3. George-Henri Rivière, *Musées du Koweït*, Preliminar Report, December 1969.

4. Franco Albini, "Parliament House Competition," Draft for the programm of the competition, May 15, 1970. Fondazione Franco Albini, Milano.

5. Franco Albini and Franca Helg, "Some note on the mail road system of the old city of Kuwait," 1970.

Prototyping Spaces for Education
Pedagogy, School Planning, Standardisation, and Prefabrication in Kuwait's Drive to Modernity

ROBERTO FABBRI

Since the beginning of the nation's journey to modernisation, Kuwait has paid particular attention to free public education for its citizens, and has consistently invested in school buildings and educational facilities.

With a population growth that reached an unprecedented peak in the 1960s and 1970s of 140 per cent, the need for educational institutions triggered the construction of an extraordinary number of schools, which, given their number, size, and distribution, contributed largely to the urban landscape of the modern city. The extent of this can be seen in public spending for education in the early 1980s – the third largest allocation in the national budget after defense and electricity and water.[1]

Over thirty years, the school construction program also largely contributed to change and improving building techniques in the country. The general lack of local skilled labour and quality materials forced architects, developers, and authorities to completely rethink the design process in terms of cost and time, paving the way for a shift to industrialisation, standardisation, and prefabrication.

The Land Acquisition policy of 1951[2] that acquired the majority of private plots in the old city, followed by the First Master Plan zoning strategy for the new residential neighbourhoods (1951–2), allocated substantial plots for public and communal facilities at the centre of each neighbourhood. These plots eventually provided the land required for a large number of educational structures. The Master Plan explains:

> Schools should be sited among the houses which they serve and away from main roads, so children do not have to cross roads on their way between home and to school. The schools should, wherever possible, have their playing fields nearby. More schools will be required, particularly in the undeveloped parts of the town, and sites are suggested in the Plan. Two existing schools are situated in areas now being commercialised near the waterfront. These are not good localities for children on account of traffic dangers and shortage of space for playgrounds. Their sites would be better redeveloped commercially, and other sites for these schools chosen in the residential areas [sic].[3]

Kuwait's Early Didactic Structures

Formal education in Kuwait dates back to 1912. The Mubarakiya School was founded at the initiative of local merchants, and served until 1931, when the pearl diving industry declined and with it the merchants' revenues that were sustaining the school.

Meanwhile, other schools opened, such as Al-Ahmadiya (1921) and Al-Sa'ada (1922), while the first courses in English were taught – reportedly for a very restricted group of pupils – at the American Missionary Hospital, mostly for the doctors' dependents. The situation changed radically in 1936

1. John Whelan, ed., *Kuwait: a MEED practical guide* (London: Middle East Economical Digest, 1985), 103.

2. The Land Acquisition policy was initiated by the Kuwaiti government in 1951. It involved the government's purchase of property and land at artificially inflated prices, in order to achieve political, economic and social ends. The land acquisition was justified in general by the "public interest," without any further specifications. The policy was later reinforced by the promulgation of Law no. 33/1964. Ghanim Al-Najjar, "Decision-making process in Kuwait: The land acquisition policy as a case study" (PhD Diss., University of Exeter, 1984).

3. Minoprio, Spencely and P. W. Macfarlane, *Plan for the town of Kuwait. Report to His Highness Shaikh Abdullah Assalim Assubah, C.I.E, The Amir of Kuwait* (1951), 17.

with the establishment of the Council for Education by Sheikh Abdallah Al-Jaber Al-Sabah, and in the same year girls education was also implemented. The majority of teachers at the time were imported from Palestine and other Arab countries, but in the early 1940s, Kuwait was able to employ the first native teacher, Mariam bin Abdulmalik Al-Saleh.[4]

In 1954, Kuwait had forty-one operational schools, and the following year "two leading Arab educationalists" were invited to assess the current condition and lay the base and curricula for a modern educational system subdivided into three phases: primary, intermediate, and secondary.[5] Meanwhile, the British architectural firm Tripe and Wakeham was appointed by the ruler of Kuwait to design and build a series of 'western standard' educational facilities based on the requirements drafted by the Council of Education, still led by Sheikh Abdallah Al-Jaber. The projects were ready by September 1952 and the firm established an office in town to supervise the construction. The program was ambitious: one technical college for 750 students, including dorms, dining areas, laboratories, and workshops; three elementary schools of eighteen classrooms each (Salah Al-Din, Shamiya and Al-Siddiq); five nurseries for 105 students (Jahra, Shamiya, Tariq, Muhallab, and Magwa). In addition to this, the architects were commissioned to design a central kitchen to cater for 10,000 meals a day.[6]

The design principle followed by Tripe and Wakeham was essentially based on balancing the solar exposure of the building. Despite differing plans, all the buildings were designed one-room thick to enhance cross ventilation. The principal spaces were northeast oriented, with balconies and cantilevers south-easterly, often protected by louvres and screens. The real challenge the architects faced was on the construction site: not many local suitable materials existed and those that were imported were in limited supply. Moreover, the designers expressed concern as to how the lack of skilled labour might affect construction. The solution came from the standardisation of concrete elements, such as floor panels, beams, and column sizes, all implemented by a regular three-metre grid and from the use of *Amara* brick, locally available, for panel walling.[7]

At the same time, Emile Bustani's CAT was building a large secondary school complex in Shuwaikh, identified by the First Masterplan as the Educational Zone. This complex for 1,400 students, including technical laboratories, boarding facilities, and a stadium, was triumphantly celebrated in the local press as, "probably unequalled anywhere in the word."[8]

All these buildings were operational by the mid-50s, but despite the government's efforts to reach international educational standards, it seems foreign visitors were not impressed by the didactic plan behind the erection of school facilities. R.L. Banks, who visited Kuwait in 1955, noted:

> A large number of well-designed, beautifully finished schools of all grades have been built, and a central kitchen to provide meals for all school children. There is also a big technical college. But all this has been done without any clear idea of where the children are to come from, who is to teach them and what opportunities Kuwait will be able to provide for them when they leave school.[9]

Despite some criticism, the government continued the development plan, reaching, in the following decade, higher levels of student enrolment in comparison to other Arab countries. At the First Regional Conference of the Ministers of Education of Arab States, organised by UNESCO in Beirut in 1960, the need for educational planning in Arab countries was declared

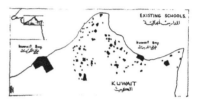

1. Distribution of schools in Kuwait by Saba George Shiber, 1964. © *The Kuwait Urbanization.*

4. *100 Years History of Education in Kuwait* (Kuwait: NCCAL, 2013).

5. The Ministry of Information and Guidance of Kuwait, *Kuwait Today. A Welfare State* (Nairobi: Quality Publication LTD, undated), 103.

6. Notes on new schools. Programme Undertaken by Messrs. Tripe and Wakeham for H.H. the Ruler of Kuwait, August 1954.

7. Raglan Square, ed., "Schools at Kuwait," *Architectural Design* (March 1957): 94.

8. The Ministry of Information and Guidance of Kuwait, *Kuwait Today*, 109.

9. R. L. Banks, "A Note on a Visit to Kuwait," *The Town Planning Review*, v. 26, n. 1 (1955): 48–50.

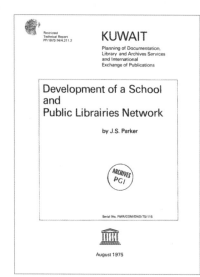

Restricted
Technical Report
PP/1973-74/4.211.2

KUWAIT

Planning of Documentation,
Library and Archives Services
and International
Exchange of Publications

Development of a School and Public Librairies Network

by J.S. Parker

(ARCHIVES PGI)

Serial No. FMR/COM/DND/75/115

August 1975

2. UNESCO report from J. S. Parker, Kuwait, 1975.

10. UNESCO, *Report on the Educational Needs of the Arab States* (Paris: UNESCO, 1960), 14.

11. M. N. Raafat, Kuwait. Educational Guidance and Examination System (February–May 1966) (Paris: UNESCO, 1966); C. K. Capon, *Kuwait Advisory Mission for the Institutional Development and Construction of Kuwait University* (September–October 1966) (Paris: UNESCO, 1966); J. Deeb, *Kuwait. Primary Teacher Training* (October 1965–January 1966) (Paris: UNESCO, 1966); R. Elias, *Kuwait. L'Education Technique* (UNESCO, 1967); W.R.Lee, The Teaching of English in Kuwait (UNESCO, 1966); F.B. El Sayel, *The Project of the Experimental Centre for Adult Education and Community Development* (UNESCO, 1966); J.S. Parker, *Development of a School and Public Library Network* (UNESCO, 1975); Taher A. Razik, *State of Kuwait. An Appraisal of Educational Structure* (UNESCO, 1981); Rolf Strahle, *Planning School Buildings* (UNESCO, 1981); State of Kuwait and ICOM, *Kuwait National Museum: Assessment of the Technical Assistance and Plan of Action* (Paris: UNESCO, 1981).

12. "The Statistic Abstract, 1964. Central Statistics Office, The Planning Board Publication," *The Kuwait Urbanization,* Appendix 16, Saba George Shiber (Kuwait Government Printing Press,1964), 556–57.

13. International Bureau of Education and UNESCO, *International Yearbook of Education,* v. XXIX, 1967, 250.

14. Barron, Donald G., *Kuwait. The Design of Schools and Related Problems* (Paris: UNESCO, 1967), 10.

urgent, and Kuwait was among the few to have built on plans and achieved some satisfactory results.[10] Kuwait had joined UNESCO in the same year. In 1961, the country declared its independence from the British Protectorate, and in 1962, with the establishment of the new nation-state departments, the Council for Education formally became the Ministry of Education (MOE). Evidently the emerging Gulf state was able to attract the attention of the international agency towards its educational system and school building programs, as documented by the 12 UNESCO missions organised in Kuwait from the 1960s to the early 1980s, two of which also involved technical support for the creation of the Kuwait National Museum. The scope of the missions ranged from primary teacher training, to adult education, to technical education, to visual education, to English language teaching, to the establishment of the university and the development of school and public library networks.[11] Two missions in particular addressed the problem of educational facilities from an architectural point of view.

100 Modern Schools to Educate Modern Kuwaitis

Donald G. Barron, an Associate Member of the Town Planning Institute in the UK, visited Kuwait for four weeks in late November 1966. He was able to meet with members of the government, administrators, educationalists, headmasters, and teachers, while inspecting a number of school facilities and recognising the vigorous efforts in place. His report gives an insight into the overall plan envisioned by the MOE, with the technical support of the Ministry of Public Works (MPW) and the Planning Board for the construction of 100 new school buildings in the following five years. In fact, the number of students enrolled in the public educational system went from 34,000 in 1959 to nearly 70,000 in 1964, putting the MOE under enormous pressure and in need of a large number of new classrooms.[12]

This trend was also reinforced by the introduction of a law regarding compulsory education, adopted in September 1966, which made eight years of school attendance obligatory. Education was free at all levels, and pupils were provided with textbooks, clothes, school supplies, and meals.[13]

With this challenging program already approved, Barron expressed his concern regarding the quality of the school facilities he visited, most of which, in his opinion, contradicted true educational modern values: they didn't utilise space efficiently, were not economically efficient in terms of the construction process, and lacked a "human touch." He speculated as to how this could be improved in future construction plans. He attributed the current condition of schools to the fact that "[…] architects and educationalists need time to convert educational concepts with [sic.] effective school buildings, but in Kuwait the paramount problem has been to build quickly."[14]

He, therefore, proposed the establishment of a Research and Development Team, involving the UNESCO resident educationalist, an architect and UNESCO expert in school design and one or two officials from the MOE and MPW. The objective was to establish essential standards and guidelines for the future design of schools. In addition, since the current projects stemmed from the client's brief and were not based on proper studies into the requirements for schools in the country, it was envisaged that the team would be tasked with advising and assisting in the preparation of briefs for the impending school building program.

Moreover, the team would be tasked with studying four key technical aspects: the introduction of air-conditioning as a possible tool to reduce room heights and achieve more compact buildings, lessening the overall cost of construction, the use of industrialised building techniques, such as prefabrication – a more economically sustainable approach to a five-year construction plan, the establishment of construction cost standards based on the ratio of pupil per square metre, in order to help the government develop a more accurate budget plan, and finally the technical aspects of design, such as sun control, insulation and acoustic needs, anthropometric standard, furniture, and fire regulations.

Barron's last recommendation was to implement all these studies and guidelines by creating four model schools, one for each grade, to be designed and built as soon as possible and to serve as prototypes for the rest of the construction program.

Spaces for Education as a Global Priority

One year before Barron's report another expert was appointed by UNESCO to conduct an assessment of the condition of school buildings in Kuwait: Alfred Roth, at that time professor at ETH Zurich, arrived in Kuwait in October 1965.

As one of the leading architects on the international scene with thorough experience in school design, Roth was a prominent candidate to represent UNESCO on this mission. After collaborating on the designs for schools with the Municipality of Zurich, and publishing extensively on education facilities, he was appointed head of the Commission of Study for School Construction of the International Union of Architects (UIA) in 1951. For UIA Roth developed a report titled, "L'École et ses Problèmes; Première Rapport de la Commission des Constructions Scolaires de l'UIA à la demande de l'UNESCO," in 1955. He was appointed a member of the Committee for Education of the BSA[15] from 1952 to 1956, in 1953, he organised a symposium on school buildings with the International Committee for Open-Air Schools and the Swiss Foundation, and in 1957 he led the *Conférénce Internationale pour l'Instruction Publique* in Genève, with the participation of education ministries from 70 countries.

Roth based his work on the pedagogical principles and studies of Johann Heinrich Pestalozzi (1746–1827), who saw education in schools as a continuation and extension of parental education at home. As a result, the classrooms and schools were to be rethought with the same sense of security and intimacy as the family environment. Pestalozzi considered both the natural and built environments part of every child's learning experience, and consequently affirmed, in contrast with other contemporary pedagogists, that education should have taken place within society and not in isolation from it.

In 1950, Roth published *Das Neue Schulhaus/the New School/la Nouvelle École*, a book deeply rooted and grounded in Pestalozzi's pedagogical approach. It was the first comparative study on recent school buildings and a practical manual on the planning and design of educational facilities. The book's intention was to demonstrate how the school building should have been considered one of the pivotal elements in modern town planning strategies, in direct emotional and practical connection with housing and

3. *L'Architecture d'Aujourd'Hui*, n. 34, March 1951.

15. Bund Schweizer Architekten. Association of the Swiss Architects.

landscaping. The book addresses the subject at the urban scale, at the architectural scale and at the human scale, defining the single component of furniture to be anthropometrically appropriate to the dimension of the students. scale, through the architectural scale to the single component of furniture, detailed to be anthropometrically appropriate to the dimension of the students. School design was a compelling matter in the architectonical debate of post-war Europe, due to a growing population of scholarly age. Consequently, the author collected, as a reference, a number of informative examples in the second half of the volume. These case studies demonstrated features things such as orientation, flexible distribution, a sun protection system, a double-sided illumination and effective cross ventilation, ensuring the best possible environment for study. Some of them also portrayed the implementation of prefabricated elements to achieve construction quality and reduce cost and time. Others represented solutions in harsh climates, for example in North Africa, like the Primary School of Longchamp in Casablanca, by Moroccan architect Elie Azagury.[16]

The *New School* was widely disseminated among practitioners and experts in school design, and Roth also curated an exhibition in 1953 in Zurich, showcasing most of the school buildings collected in the book. The latter not only became a practical reference for architects, but also cemented, with the second and third editions in 1957 and 1966, the figure of Alfred Roth as a leading expert in school building design.

One of the main and most common criticisms of the roles and achievements of western designers invited to work in states like Kuwait lies in the assumption they were unprepared to 'perform' in completely different contexts, away from their usual, comfortable environments. Most of them are commonly said to have relied only on their technical knowledge and their status with clients and local authorities, imposing abstract visions in complete disregard of the local background and framework.[17]

On the contrary, by examining the architectural literature published between the 1950s and 1960s, it seems the discourse around the new frontiers of modern architecture, especially in upcoming states, was at the centre of the international debate. Among other possible examples, the April–May 1963 issue of *L'Architecture d'Aujourd'Hui*, which was entirely dedicated to the school buildings and universities and promoted by René Maheu, director general of UNESCO, showed how the focus was on numerous buildings in developing countries, such as Tunisia, Morocco, Madagascar, Lebanon, and Ivory Coast.[18] Not to mention the UNESCO's effort to establish research centres for school buildings, especially in Asia, Africa, and Latin America.[19]

When Alfred Roth touched ground in Kuwait's old airport in Mugwa, October of 1965, he might not have been fully informed of every aspect of Kuwait's specific situation, and this is the reason why the visit was arranged, but we may assume that he had all the theoretical knowhow and practical experience to face the complex challenges of his mission.

The School Buildings of Kuwait: an Assessment and a Plan

The scope of Roth's travel is clear from the title of his report: "The School Buildings of Kuwait. An appraisal of the existing educational facilities with regards to the future school building program."

16. Alfred Roth, *Das Neue Schulhaus/The New Schoolhouse/La Nouvelle Ecole* (Zurich: Girsberger 1950).

17. Muhannad A Albaqshi, "The Social Production of Space: Kuwait's Spacial History" (PhD diss., Illinois Institute of Technology, 2010), 135–140.

18. *Constructions scolaires et universitaires*, *L'Architecture d'Aujoud'Hui*, n. 107 (April–May 1963).

19. *L'UNESCO et Les Constructions Scolaires* (Paris: UNESCO, 1963), 4–5.

Roth met with officials from the MPW, the MOE, the Municipal Council and with Ahmad Al-Duaij, director of the Planning Board. Then he visited six schools: three kindergartens, one intermediate and two secondary. Each school was assessed precisely and recorded in the mission report. None of the kindergartens visited met his expectations, with the exception of Tariq, built by Tripe and Wakeham a decade before. The following assessment focused on Shuwaikh Boys Secondary School, the *jewel* of Kuwait's school facilities. Roth praised the quality of the overall design, however he openly disapproved of the building's "monumentality," which he considered to be inappropriate according to his pedagogic principles, and the small fenestrations, clearly reduced in size for better control of sunlight, which he hailed insufficient for natural illumination of the classrooms. On the other hand, he appreciated the practical and functional design approach to the Girls Intermediate School in Qortuba, a project developed in-house by the construction section of the Planning Board of the MPW, and labelled as "Standard Secondary School Type." This typology, which was reiterated in large numbers in several neighbourhoods in the country until the late 1970s, is characterised by a clear constructive structure, a concrete frame envelope, rigid but clearly efficient enough in Roth's eyes. Despite several design errors, which Roth accurately noted and were mostly related to distribution, size and how the internal spaces related to each other, Roth perceived the standard schools to have the correct approach to local needs and saw them as an opportunity, with a few adjustments, to achieve a first rapid phase of improvement. The last visit focused on Khaldiya Secondary School, recently completed following the design of the Austrian architect Rambald von Steinbüchel-Rheinwall. Roth's criticism was particularly severe in this case. He dismissed the general layout, which was extremely widespread, pointing out the excessive use of land and uneconomic planning, the functional inadequacy and waste of inner spaces. He also criticised what he called the "unforgivable" negligence of local climatic conditions, addressed only with the use of expensive metal louvres and internal curtains, and disapproved of the architectural design, which he labelled as "superficial" and whimsical, far away from the principles that – in his words – should motivate contemporary design. In other words, not an example to be followed for future construction plans.[20]

Roth's mission was not organised to assess and expose the condition of Kuwaiti schools, but to identify issues and address them with proactive strategies. The schools he was able to visit denoted a general lack of identification of the correct typology that was adequate for the local climate and not cost efficient. The excessive use of glass did not correspond with the correct standard of illumination, or sufficiently protect against radiation and glare from the sun. An absence of study into the correct classroom sizes and proportion, in relation to general distribution and overall layout, resulted in a large waste of inner space, which also complicated the performance of the building in severe weather conditions. In response to all this, Roth's proposal, supported by data and schemes, started by differentiating schools by size, number of classrooms and number of storeys, according to different grades. It went on to identify the correct dimensions and proportions for a single class unit and a possible aggregative system that was cost-efficient and flexible for future needs. In alignment with Pestalozzi's vision, Roth expressed how the "the classroom should be like a living room," stressing the need to include landscaping as an essential part of the overall

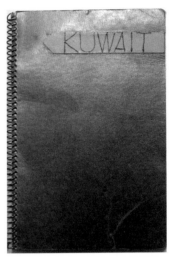

4. Notebook belonging to Alfred Roth, entitled *Kuwait*, 1977.
© ETH – gta Archiv.

20. For detailed descriptions of all these buildings see Roberto Fabbri, Sara Saragoça Soares, and Ricardo Camacho , *Modern Architecture Kuwait 1949–1989* (Zurich: Niggli, 2016), 40–45; 54–57; 126–27.

design, as well as furniture design and equipment supply. Finally, he recognised climate control as a pivotal theme for any future construction, which he recommended should be addressed not only with the implementation of modern technologies, such as air conditioning and brises-soleil, but with the adoption of a typology, an enclosed layout revolving around the courtyard, which was a well-known traditional solution in the local environment.

The proposal was concluded with two projects: firstly, a revised version of the Standard School type, with detailed new plans and a different internal distribution in harmony with the concrete envelope of the MPW's original projects; secondly, a concept design for a new school type hinged on an inner courtyard.[21]

From Planning to Prototyping

The Kuwaiti government proved very receptive to both Roth and Barron's suggestions, and in the second half of the 1960s, a coordinated effort between MOE and MPW made possible a wide ranging and complete new approach to the five-year construction plan. The necessity for a number of new schools in the short-term was addressed, in many cases, by adopting the revised plan for the Standard Schools. Meanwhile, Roth was appointed to develop a series of prototype schools for different grades, based on the fieldwork and data collection of educationalists from the School Study Commission of the MOE. At the same time, the MPW, led by Khalid Al-Essa, explored the possibility of creating industries for prefabricated structures in Kuwait, and agreed with the MOE to establish a technical training program for engineers and architects from the ministries in school design and construction, as per Barron's suggestion.

This is not an isolated case in the Kuwaiti urban history of the mid-1960s. After a decade of focusing on infrastructure, commonly through disjointed efforts, resulting in good architectures but a fragmented urban landscape, the local authorities endorsed a more coordinated approach to shaping the city, relying on the expertise of a large number of renowned international architects. The peak of this new vision was the appointment in 1968 of Candilis, Pietilä, BBPR and the Smithsons to design the new 'urban form' for Kuwait City centre, under the guidance of the triumvirate Leslie Martin, Franco Albini, and Omar Azzam, while Buchanan was developing the Second Master Plan. However the same vision can be seen in the competitions launched for the Sports Centre, which involved calibres like Kenzo Tange, Frei Otto, Pier Luigi Nervi, Felix Candela, or for the National Assembly, with Jørn Utzon, B.V. Doshi, Sir Basel Spence, and Rifat Chadirji. And again in the vast plans for social hosing, involving Dar Al-Handasah, Luigi Moretti, and Jafar Tukan, among several others. Under the sheikhdom of Sabah Al-Salem Al-Sabah, Kuwait opened the door to urban experimentation, and architects like Alfred Roth saw fertile ground to convert advisory missions into tangible achievements.

From his office in Leonhardstrasse, Roth developed a series of studies, plans and proposals for school prototypes, in coordination with the local consultant, Kuwait Engineering Office (KEO). Roth travelled frequently to Kuwait to coordinate the School Study Commission, which was in charge of research and data collection in support of the prototype design. A substantial questionnaire was prepared with personnel from the MPW and sent to headmasters, teachers and, educationalists involved in didactic

21. Alfred Roth, *The School Buildings of Kuwait. An appraisal of the existing educational facilities with regards to the future school building program*, 1965. ETH – gta Archiv, Zurich.

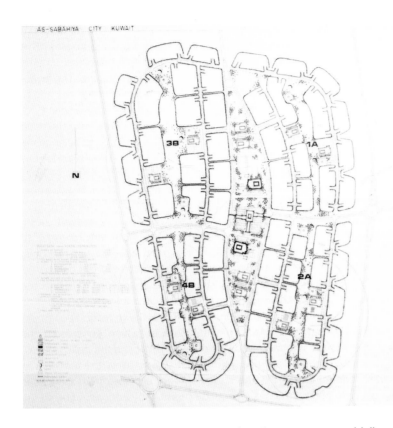

AS-SABAHIYA CITY KUWAIT

N

5. School distribution plan for
Al-Sabahiya, Alfred Roth, 1970.
© ETH – gta Archiv.

activities in the country, in order to gather the necessary guidelines and
technical information. Between 1967 and 1969, the design of new prototypes
for kinderdgarten, primary, intermediate, and secondary schools was
developed, reviewed by the MOE and the MPW, integrated with the results of
the Schools Study Commission's fieldwork and finally presented to the
authority to receive approval and be assigned a location for construction.[22]

The first result of this work was the appointment, in 1970, to assist
Colin Buchanan in with assigning proper locations for all school facilities,
within the zoning-plan of the new neighbourhood of Sabahiya, 30km south of
Kuwait City. Roth allocated fifteen schools in the neighbourhoods, according
to the grade and to the distance from the residential areas. He revised the
plot sizes and their connection with communal facilities, and identified the
proper typologies based on the prototypes he had just developed for the
MOE. In this project in particular, he emphasised the importance of the
"modular design" of the prototypes as a prerequisite to implement the use of
prefabricated elements and rationalised building methods.[23]

Two
Model Schools

In 1967 Roth received a formal commission to design and build the
first two model schools, an important step in progression from planning to
tangible examples. The assigned plot for the first one was in the residential
district of Rumaithiya, which was under intense development in the late
1960s. Rumaithiya had a quite a different shape to the other residential areas,
which were commonly planned as chessboards of eight squares for housing,
with a ninth square plot in the centre to allocate public and commercial buildings. In this case, the land was subdivided into thirteen sub-units (blocks),

22. Alfred Roth, *Consolidation of results
received from the school directors on the
questionnaire prepared by M.P.W. for the
improvement of educational building,
undated*. ETH – gta Archiv, Zurich.

23. Alfred Roth, *As-Sabahiya City Kuwait.
Master Plan. Report on the distribution of
schools, 1970*. ETH – gta Archiv, Zurich.

aligned on a central spine, the main road. Each block had, at its centre, a large plot allocated to schools at walking distances from the houses. This plan was designed in 1962 by VBB,[24] following a precise hierarchical scheme to place pedestrians at the centre of the distribution of functions. The layout was conceived to avoid intersections between streets and walkways, and to distribute the schools in order to achieve maximum convenience for commuting on foot and by car. At the same time, parks, squares and recreational facilities were proposed to be sufficient in number to balance the residential populations – close to nurseries and primary schools, and interlaced with the walkway grid. The town plan was not implemented as initially envisioned, particularly with regards to the clear differentiation between car circulation and green pedestrian paths, which was based on different ground levels that were visible in the project's perspective sketches. Nevertheless, Rumaithiya in 1967 seemed to represent the perfect environment to materialise the principles of a mutual relationship between housing, schools, and landscaping that Roth had theorised in his book fifteen years earlier.

The assignment was for an intermediate school for girls and the scheme was clear from the beginning: a large planted internal courtyard as the central functional and distributional core for all the didactic spaces. An 'introverted' building, protected from the outside, which considered the lessons learned from the tradition of the caravanserais and the patio houses. In the plan, the ground floor was 'porous' enough to allow the teachers to have visual control of the children during outdoor activities from the rooms surrounding the courtyard. This was made possible by concentrating all the services and staircases at the four corners. The first floor was entirely dedicated to the classrooms served by the internal balcony. Particular care was put into the design of the fenestration, to ensure enough natural illumination: the apertures in the perimetral walls were protected by concrete sun breakers, while the internal windows, overlooking the central planted court, were shaded by deep porticoes and cantilevers. On the ground floor in particular, glass bricks were introduced to reduce the glare and the visual interference between courses and outdoor activities. Since no air-conditioning system was initially planned, the concrete slabs were shaped to create a horizontal channel through the building, which could trigger natural cross ventilation.

Two separate wings, juxtaposed with the didactic court, were designed for the administration, other communal facilities (assembly hall, gym, dining, etc.), and the teachers' apartments. The aggregative system of the wings was thought to be adaptable to different plots, locations, or future expansions. Considering it was a prototype, Roth originally proposed a prefabricated construction system, though Kuwait was not ready yet to implement it. Therefore the skeleton was a white painted concrete frame, cast on site, and the walling was built with light limestones and rendered bricks. The building was operational in 1973.[25]

The second model school commissioned to Roth was a kindergarten in Monsouriya, which shared the same principles of the one in Rumaithiya. Its design was reminiscent of the *architecture scolaire pavillonaire*, diffused in Switzerland in the 1950s, but in this case the pavilions revolved around a central courtyard. The single pavilion was a cluster of three classrooms, with dedicated outdoor space and common services. The one-storey height building was created by a reiteration of the single module around an internal square court.

24. Later renowned in Kuwait for the construction of the Water Towers.

25. "Kuwait: Mädchen-Sekundarschule," *Das Werk*, v. 60, n. 11 (1973): 1358–1360.

ROBERTO FABBRI • PROTOTYPING SPACES FOR EDUCATION

6. Model of Intermediate School for Girls in Rumaithiya, Alfred Roth, 1967–1973. © ETH – gta Archiv.

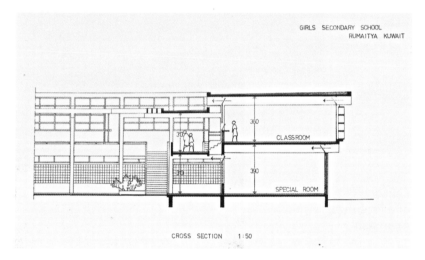

GIRLS SECONDARY SCHOOL
RUMAITYA KUWAIT

CLASSROOM

SPECIAL ROOM

CROSS SECTION   1:50

7. Cross-section of Intermediate School for Girls in Rumaithiya, Alfred Roth, 1967–1973. © ETH – gta Archiv.

The two schools are still functioning today. The clear structures of the buildings are still discernable behind some major cosmetic modifications, most of which have been carried out on other buildings of the same age in Kuwait, such as adding a new thick layer of plaster over every surface, new aluminium windows and space-frame structures over the courtyards. Also the introduction of air conditioning systems has altered the cross ventilation channels and the internal height of the spaces. Inside, the distribution layout has also been casually adapted, and low-cost decorative elements added, like gypsum columns and Moorish arches, fulfilling the apparent need for a more 'local' touch. Today it is difficult to assess how the buildings perform and meet the needs of contemporary education, because the students and teachers could not be interviewed. In general, the buildings look aged, particularly the one in Rumaithiya, which is in great need of maintenance.

However, the school principal, who didn't disguise her surprise at the interest in her "old school," openly confessed in a discussion in early 2015, her strong intention to convince the MOE to demolish the structure and finally agree to a brand new building, like in other neighbourhoods – although she didn't seem optimistic, as the entire educational system has radically changed in recent years in Kuwait, focussing on private bilingual institutions that offer international degrees to students and a higher social status to families.[26]

26. The individual has asked for her name to be withheld.

8. Courtyard construction at the
Intermediate School for Girls in
Rumaithiya, Alfred Roth, 1967–1973.
© ETH – gta Archiv.

Consequences
of a Prototype
Approach

The legacy of several decades of combined efforts from various ministries, international agencies like UNESCO, and professional consultants, can be read as having made an unprecedented contribution to Kuwait's educational needs and, at the same time, as a missed opportunity to shape the urban form of the city in a different way.

The entire construction program of school building in the 1970s and 1980s was based on the guidelines arranged by Roth, Barron and their collaborators, but the actual results differ from case to case. After the erection of the prototype in Rumaithiya, the courtyard typology proved to perform better in the Kuwaiti environment and it was adopted in every project later developed by the MOE and the MPW. In several instances, various visible details were also taken directly from the prototype, such as the concrete elements for sun protection, confirming that this construction served as a practical example for other designers. Secondly, on a similar note, we can assume that the seminars and courses organised between 1969 and 1970 to strengthen the design capacity of the MPW and the MOE, educated a group of architects and engineers who were operating in the following decade with a more accurate knowledge of the pedagogical needs in their field. Thirdly, since in the mid-1970s Kuwait was finally ready to cast prefabricated concrete elements, the majority of schools were implemented with a strategy of cost and time control, based on standardisation and prefabrication, as portrayed by Barron and developed by Roth and the School Study Commission.

Roth himself also participated actively to make this shift in construction technology possible. In 1973, he started a collaboration with Khalid Al-Essa, the former minister of Public Works, and now chair of the Industrial & Real Estate Co. (IREC). At the time, IREC intended to establish an industrial unit for precast concrete in Kuwait, and consequently, Roth developed a new series of prototype schools with the technical support of Steiger & Partners from Switzerland (Steiger system, later abandoned) and of Freyssinet from France (STUP pre-stress system) in the following years. IREC was commissioned with a large number of schools by the MPW and the Credit and Savings Bank, and, in 1978, the industrial unit was ready to build precast elements, with the Freyssinet/STUP system, and aggregate them according to Roth's standardised design. At this point IREC was capable of implementing the various school projects on its own, however, Roth continued to visit Kuwait on a yearly basis until the early 1980s, and he was able to inspect a series of erected buildings, like the Secondary School in Sabahyia, built on one of the plots he assigned ten years before to the neighbourhood layout, during his collaboration with Buchanan. During this phase, Roth also developed a colour scheme to visually differentiate the various constructions.

Over thirty years, this intense effort resulted in a better and more accurate answer to the nation's urgent needs and to clients' aspirations of new modern school facilities in a new modern city. But the rush to build, and to build in high numbers, placed the emphasis entirely on the construction strategy, and consequently the design was adjusted for and by the process. Since the urban form of Kuwait, especially in the residential districts, was made to be repetitive by the "chessboard zoning" and by the reiteration of one single housing typology – the single family house – the serial replication of school prototypes, it failed to contribute with sufficient character to the urban landscape in the making. If we consider that a similar approach was in place for schools and other public structures, such as community centres, commercial sites, clinics, etc., most of Kuwait's neighbourhoods are now showing a lack of identity and landmarks, which does not foster a sense of belonging in the population. Another crucial aspect to be considered is the fact that the schools were built inside a fenced plot. Isolated behind walls, cut off from the urban fabric and detached from the other public spaces, they could not act as landmarks, and, at the same time, could not work in synergy with the neighbourhood.

It is difficult to assess if this was a consequence of the MOE's guidelines being too restrictive, or excessively focused on the functionality of the spaces, or if the engineers at the MPW were not yet capable of implementing them with sufficient skills to originate more case-specific designs, assuming that they could have had this kind of mandate. In any case, the prototypes were mostly used as ready-made objects; rigid and fixed, to be simply reiterated as needed, without any relationship to the surrounding context.[27] As happened on many occasions during Kuwait's urbanisation process, the gap between urban planning and the architectural/human scale was not mediated and adjusted at the urban design scale. •

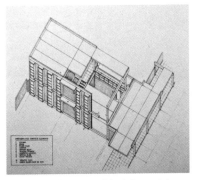

9. Typical classroom block in prototype elementary school with Freissynet-STUP prestressed system, Alfred Roth, 1971. © ETH – gta Archiv.

10. Experimentally erected prefabrication with Friessynet elements in factory, Kuwait, 1970s. © ETH – gta Archiv.

27. This aspect of monotony and repetitiveness was also noted by Rolf Strahle in his early 1980s UNESCO assessment of schools in Kuwait, which also funds a critical lack of parking areas in support of the schools, and above all, the total absence of maintenance practices. On a general note, Strahle praised the constructions quality of the buildings that were executed with prefabricated elements. Strahle, *Planning School Buildings*, 5.

ZDRAVKO BREGOVAC • KUWAIT NATIONAL MUSEUM COMPETITION ENTRY • DECEMBER 1960

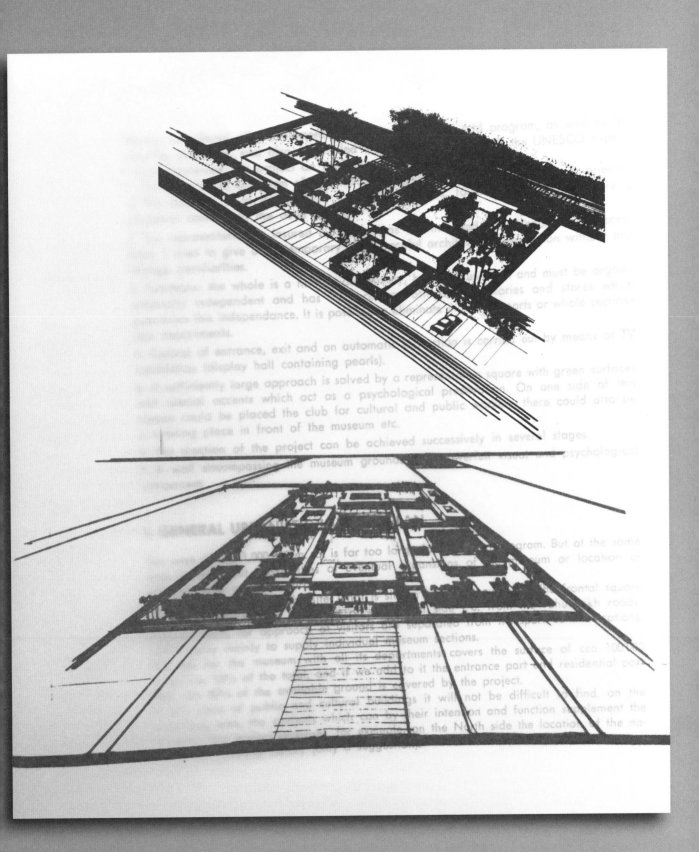

Utopian Dreams in the Making of Kuwait: From Sand and Mud to Grass and Concrete

DALAL M. ALSAYER

Kuwait, a small nation-state on the Arabian Gulf, was transformed from a small desert emirate to the a full-fledged welfare nation with the adoption of the first Kuwait Master Plan by the British firm Minoprio, Spencely, and Macfarlane (MSM) in 1951. The plan, which was loosely based on Ebenezer Howard's Garden City, called for locals to move from their mud-brick homes and workplaces within the traditional city gates to the newly established western-influenced neighbourhood units with single family detached houses beyond the First Ring Road. This move, while in essence was based on Howard's Garden City, took its physical form from the New Town Acts of post-war reconstruction. MSM idealised Howard's Garden City due to its universal approach and the increased desire to create a dignified city centre.[1] In their approach to Kuwait City, the planners implemented Howard's diagram in its entirety including the creation of both the *Garden* and *City* which were achieved through large-scale, state-led urban and social modernisation schemes. The state-led rehousing schemes used the new Master Plan as a state-subsidised mechanism of city-making: buying houses at an inflated rate to distribute the new oil wealth evenly amongst Kuwaitis. The Garden City as both a *place* and an *ideology* is at the forefront of this non-West adoption.

In the adoption of the new Master Plan, the existing urban fabric was demolished to create the elements needed to reproduce Howard's magnets: the city, the garden, and the greenbelt surrounding the city. With the newly-constructed city centre, there was a need for a garden to escape to and this is when the *mazare'e* (farms) of Al-Abdali and Al-Wafra were born. These two garden 'villages' for recreation and farming are state-subsidised to provide the much needed green and also to offer the 'counter'-city for Howard's ideas to be fully adopted. While the plan did indeed call for a spatial reconfiguration of the city, the societal structure was also greatly altered through the development of local *cooperative societies* (co-ops), which are located within the neighbourhood units. Due to the localised nature of these co-ops, they ushered a new social structure and as Robert Fishman argues: "Radical hopes for a cooperative civilisation could be fulfilled only in small communities embedded in a decentralised society."[2]

The story of Kuwait's development from a compact mud-brick town to a decentralised quasi-suburban city has predominately been told absent of its social ramifications even though MSM's 1951 Master Plan played a critical role in both the spatial and social transformations of the existing community. Their plan idealised a vision of utopia that was utilised to usher Kuwait into modernity and offer a precedent of planning in the East for "[t]he situation as a whole – the tremendous activity, the uneven advance, contrasts between the most modern and the most primitive and wealth and squalor – suggests that Kuwait is at present the most interesting of all points of contact between East and West."[3] Positioning Kuwait as an in-between opens the

1. For more see Minoprio, Spencely, and Macfarlane, *Plan for the Town of Kuwait: Report to His Highness Shaikh Abdullah Assalim Assubah, C.I.E. The Amir of Kuwait.* (Kuwait: 1951), 22. Print.

2. Robert Fishman, *Urban Utopias in the Twentieth Century: Ebenezer Howard, Frank Lloyd Wright, and Le Corbusier* (New York: Basic Books, 1977), 23–90.

3. R. L. Banks, "Notes on a Visit to Kuwait," *Town Planning Review*, v. 26, n. 1 (1955): 49.

possibility of exploring other in-betweens. This story, then, becomes about these in-betweens: primitiveness and modernity, mud and concrete, sand and grass, and utopia as an imagined place and a non-place.

The British Legacy and Middle Eastern Oil

With both the Ottoman Empire expansion into the Middle East and the British's desire to expand into the region, allegiances were formed between Great Britain and countries in the Middle East. Kuwait, in particular, signed the Anglo-Kuwaiti Treaty of 1899 in which the then Sheikh of Kuwait, Mubarak Al-Sabah, approached British officials and made Kuwait a Protectorate under the British Crown.[4]

This political move served instrumental to the British in the time leading to and following WWI. More influential, however, was the possibility and promise of petroleum in the Middle East, and specifically in the Gulf. This, in turn, increased foreign involvement which was spearheaded by the British's existing stronghold in the region and began as early as 1914. Oil treaties and concessions were signed for exploration between the Sheikhs and Anglo-American companies solidifying a much valued commodity to the British and placing these new regions on the map. In 1943, a treaty between the Sheikh of Kuwait and the Anglo-American conglomeration Gulf and British Petroleum (BP) was signed.[5] These words of the introductory paragraph of the treaty marked the start of a new era in Kuwait's history and a move towards modernisation:

> IN THE NAME OF GOD THE MERCIFUL. This is an AGREEMENT made at Kuwait on the 23rd Day of December in the year 1943 corresponding to the 16th day of Ramadhan 1353 between his Excellency Sheikh Sir Ahmad Al-Jabir As-Subah, Knight Commander of the Most Eminent Order of the Indian Empire and Companion of the Most Exalted Order of the star of India, the SHEIKH OF KUWAIT in the exercise of his powers as Ruler of Kuwait on his own behalf and in the name and the behalf of his heirs and successors in whom is or shall be vested for the time being the responsibility for the control and government of the State of Kuwait (hereinafter called "the Sheikh") and KUWAIT OIL COMPANY LIMITED, a company registered in Great Britain under the Companies Act, 1929, its successors and assigns (hereinafter called "The Company").[6]

Modernisation

Sheikh Mubarak's decision to align with the British was also a move to modernise Kuwait and connect it to both the British Empire in India and the growing metropolises of Basra and Baghdad in Iraq. While there was talk about connecting Kuwait to the Baghdad Railway therein connecting Kuwait to Europe and opening up the Gulf and India, these plans did not come to fruition. However, this desire to modernise Kuwait continued to grow with Sheikh Ahmad Al-Jaber Al-Sabah, Emir of Kuwait from 1921 until 1950, who paved the way for oil concessions and the subsequent discovery of the Burgan field which propelled Kuwait forward. It is said that finding oil in Kuwait was not as easy as it seemed:

> The search for it went on for three years before the precise location of the first site was pinpointed by an extraordinary hunch of the British Political Agent in Kuwait, Sir Harold Dickson, a person who has been deeply involved in the oil negotiations. He had had a spectacular dream in which a beautiful girl who was treated by bandits rose out of the sand near a tree he knew. Later on, as in a Grimm's fairly tale, he met an old bedouin woman who interpreted his dream to mean that the girl promised great riches for Kuwait,

4. The protection agreement gave the British more rights to the region; Sheikh Mubarak also received benefits in the form of arms and protection. Sheikh Mubarak, who rose to the throne in 1896, was instrumental in forging the Britain-Kuwait relationship and positioning Kuwait out of the Ottoman Empire's reach.

5. Anthony Sampson, *The Seven Sisters: The Great Oil Companies and the World They Shaped* (New York: The Bantam Books, 1975).

6. Stephen Gardiner, *Kuwait: The Making of a City* (Harlow: Longman, 1983), 13.

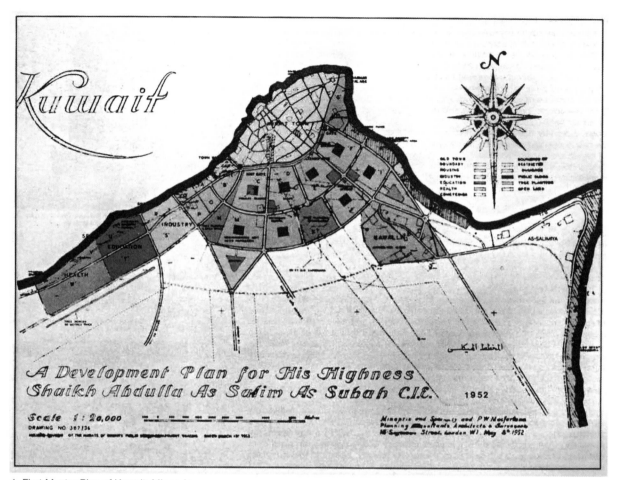

1. First Master Plan of Kuwait, Minoprio,
Spencely, and Macfarlane, 1952.
© Kuwait Municipal Archive.

but that there were dangers – the riches could bring good or bad. Second sight? Whatever it was, the dream was so vivid that Dickson persuaded the company's sceptical engineers to investigate the spot, and on the 24th of February, 1938, the company struck high pressure oil 3,672 feet down at that place, in Burgan.

Gardiner continues:

And so, at last, Kuwait's immense oil industry got underway: the figures speak for themselves – from a little under 800,000 tons exported in 1946, over 17,000,000 were exported in 1950. Kuwait's existence as a world centre of commerce began at the same time.[7]

This newfound wealth, coupled with a new, forward-looking Sheikh in 1950, Sheikh Abdullah Al-Salem Al-Sabah, catapulted Kuwait into the modern era.

The stipulations of the 1943 oil agreement preserved the little town within the walls of Kuwait[8] as a way for the Sheikh to maintain the livelihood of his citizens through fishing, boat-building, pearl diving, and foreign trade. However, due to the close-knit nature of Kuwaitis, it was hard to house foreigners who were needed for the booming country within Kuwait City. This, coupled with the location of Burgan field, led to the establishment of the oil town of Ahmadi[9] exclusively for foreign petroleum engineers and executives by "recreating a rough likeness of 'home' for themselves with

7. Ibid., 14.

8. Three walls were built around the city (1760, 1811, and 1921) containing dwellings and traditional *aswaq* (marketplaces). The walls also formed a defence mechanism around the rest of the city.

9. For more on Ahmadi see Reem Alissa, "Building for Oil: Corporate Colonialism, Nationalism and Urban Modernity in Ahmadi, 1946–1992" (PhD diss., University of California, Berkeley, 2012).

bungalows, gardens, and by planting trees."[10] Kuwaitis, who once lived in tightly packed mud brick houses with narrow alleyways nestled in the gates near the port and the sea, were now ready to live a modern life. With the steady growth of oil revenues and a dire need to redistribute this newfound wealth to the citizens, Kuwait City was destroyed and a new plan was needed.

The Planners
and the Plan

> In Britain, it is sometimes said that town planning is 50 years too late, as past rebuilding has established vested interests which have prevented the realisation of bold schemes of replanning designed to fit existing towns to modern conditions. But in Kuwait a master plan should be just in time to guide rebuilding. The Kuwaitis are untroubled by complex laws of compensation and betterment, while the buildings are mainly insubstantial and can easily be demolished to make way for improvements. Indeed, Kuwait now has the opportunity and the financial resources, under the wise guidance of the ruler, to become the best planned and most socially progressive city in the Middle East.[11]

The underlying desire for this new town was to position Kuwait on the map and steer Kuwaitis into the new era of modernisation for they have remained undereducated and underdeveloped for far too long. Sheikh Abdullah Al-Salem Al-Sabah decided it was upon him to redistribute the nation's newfound wealth equally amongst the Kuwaitis who were there in time of hardships, droughts, and famine.[12]

It is with this mindset that the *Welfare State* was born. Sheikh Abdullah Al-Salem "found it necessary to make a break with patriarchal tradition in order to administer his enormous revenue. He formed a cabinet on Western lines with a Secretary of State, and departments of Security, Justice, Health, Education, Public Works and so on."[13] One of the first moves towards building a new Kuwait was the establishment of a central authority that governed the planning, construction, and implementation of a new city which was given to the Town Planning Department under the Department of Public Works (DPW). The Political Agent at the time in Kuwait, H. G. Jakins, was directly involved in the suggestion for the hiring of a British, rather than an Arab town planner, and was instrumental in swaying the Ruler's decision to facilitate the choice of the firm. In his report on January 2, 1951 on the matter of hiring a planner, Jakins writes:

> when I visited him [Ruler of Kuwait] on December 31, the occasion seemed propitious I raised with His Highness the desirability of having a proper town plan and of appoint a British engineer on the lines of a Borough Engineer in the United Kingdom. The Ruler then said that he was engaging a Palestinian as a town engineer. […] I propose to take an early opportunity of recalling to the Ruler his undertaking to employ only British experts and to express my disappointment that he, who said that he wished the Political Agent to be his Advisor, should contemplate taking the step he proposed without consulting or informing me.[14]

While the actual selection of the Town Planner was unclear, a report made six weeks later on February 23, 1951 indicates that the firm Minoprio, Spencely, and Macfarlane was selected. "He [H.T. Kemp, London representative of the Ruler of Kuwait] has followed the advice of Mr. Beaufoy of the Ministry of Local Government and Planning and recommended that the Ruler should engage Messrs. Minoprio, Spencely and Macfarlane [as Town Planners for Kuwait]."[15] It is here that the plan for Kuwait was born.

10. Gardiner, *Kuwait, The Making of a City*, 15.

11. P.W. Macfarlane, "Town Building in Kuwait: Rebuilding a Middle East Capital," *The Times: Review of Industry*, v. 5, n. 57 (1951): 91.

12. Citizenship rights were granted based on the actual time Kuwaitis were actually in Kuwait as this was seen as the best way to reward the Kuwaitis that were there before the oil wealth.

13. Banks, "Notes on a Visit to Kuwait," 49.

14. Richard Trench, ed., *Arab Gulf Cities: Kuwait City* (Slough, UK: Archive Editions, Oxford, 1994), 545.

15. Ibid., 548–9.

The Plan:
Roads, Co-ops, Houses,
and Villages

'All we could give them,' Minoprio said, *'was what we knew.'*[16]

The new plan of 1951 was adopted and the changes to the city were underway. It is worth noting that there was both a physical plan and a social plan. While their interconnectedness is unknown, it is imperative to explore their importance.

2. A house in one of the new neighbourhood units, Kuwait, 1960s. © Kuwait Oil Company Archive.

Anthony Minoprio and Hugh Spencely were both trained in Liverpool and had adopted the New Town postwar rebuilding agenda in London and had recently completed a New Town, Crawley, making them apt planners for the new town of Kuwait. The legacy and transformation of the Garden City into that of the New Town (as a duplicable plan) was at the forefront of both the Crawley New Town and Kuwait's New Town, for "Kuwaitis must have known next to nothing of modern planning and architecture, and about the theory of New Town design, and certainly nothing at all of its origins in the Garden City."[17] While the Master Plan of Kuwait had all the elements that would constitute it as a New Town: country centre, concentric ring roads, greenbelt, self-sufficient neighbourhood units, and satellite villages, it seems that "New Town theories took possession of the scheme for the old town, with the planners regarding this as the growing centre – as the magnetic centre perhaps – of the country."[18] This city centre was, to some extent, similar to Howard's centre and Crystal Palace in that the Central Business District (CBD) was designated in the heart of the city with each CBD area providing one sector: textiles, housing, and real estate, etc. Spaces in these CBDs and the remnants of the old open-air souq (market), where local produce and imported goods were sold, were rented out to individuals on a monthly basis. This centre would also house the growing civic buildings that are needed to sustain this rapid development. Several civic buildings were

16. Gardiner, *Kuwait, The Making of a City*, 35.

17. Ibid., 22.

18. Ibid., 37.

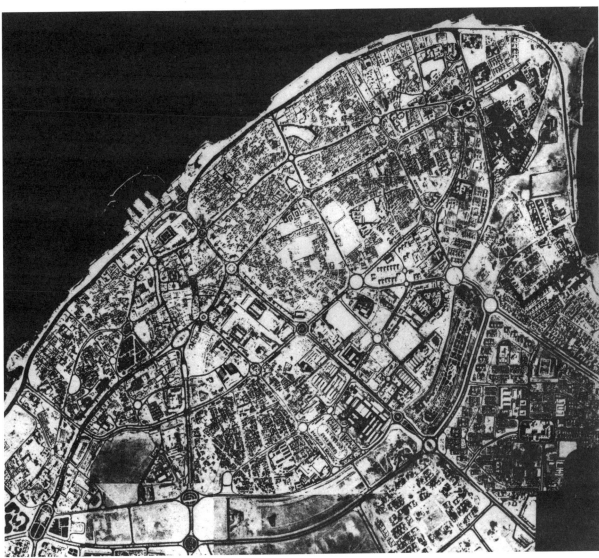

3. Aerial view of the new city, 1967.
© Kuwait Oil Company Archive.

commissioned to foreign architects to create the sought-after dignified city centre.[19] "As the new streets gradually take shape, public buildings, shops and houses will arise on their allocated sites, trees will be planted, water pipes and electric light cables laid, until all the pieces fit into their proper places and the town is complete."[20] Second to MSM's idealised city centre was the need for circulation and connectivity. Roads were crucial in the development of the New Town Plan, for in order to *really* modernise Kuwait, the car (the ultimate modern machine) had to be able to freely move in the city and that also meant that more traditional elements of the Kuwaiti city (compact walkable pattern) had to be abandoned to provide way for its new road system.

> We would emphasise the need for a system of wide roads in Kuwait. A generous width is essential because traffic is likely to go on increasing in volume as the town prosperity grows. Kuwait is destined to be one of the largest and most important towns in the Middle East and its roads, if spaciously laid out with avenues of trees and adequate car-parks can be one of its finest features. Every important town has its fine roads.[21]

19. Kuwait invited several architects to design civic buildings such as Reima Pietilä (Ministry of Foreign Affairs), Jørn Utzon (Parliament Building), Arne Jacobsen (Central Bank of Kuwait), Michel Ecochard (Kuwait National Museum), Arthur Erickson (Al-Sawaber, a Kuwait subsidised apartment block), Alfred Roth (Prototypical Schools), The Architects' Collaborative (Commercial Centres and Parking), etc.

20. Minoprio, Spencely and Macfarlane, *Plan for the Town of Kuwait: Report to His Highness Sheikh Abdullah Assalim Assubah, C.I.E. The Amir of Kuwait.* Kuwait (1951).

21. Ibid.

4. Opening day of Shamiya Co-operative
Society, 1964. © Al Kuwaiti.

The proposed esplanade width is thirty metres, which is wide enough
for one carriageway and mimics Howard's one-hundred and twenty foot
boulevards. This ushered Kuwait forward as R. L. Banks states:

> Western technicians tend to wish to introduce the tastes and the standards
> of Britain or the U.S.A. – waterborne sewage, 1,000 sq. ft. houses, dual
> carriageways, trolleybuses – and have to be slowed down by the warnings
> of economists and sociologists concerning the ability of the country to pay
> for all these things or to adjust itself quickly to all the changes they would
> bring. Usually lack of money keeps the rate of change down to a pace which
> enables the country to make the social changes and produce the technicians
> and administrators needed before Western technical methods and machines
> can be properly used. But there is one place – Kuwait – where finance
> presents no difficulty, where a small and rather isolated community has
> been able during the past few years to order almost what it liked from
> Western countries. A visit to Kuwait is, therefore, of special interest in that
> Kuwait displays in concentrated form the major and minor consequences of
> Westernisation at maximum speed.[22]

The plan called for the carving out of a road system from the existing
old mud-brick houses essentially creating a city magnet. Kuwait's final
mud-brick wall, which was built in 1935 to fend off the *Akhwan*[23] of Saudi
Arabia, marked the boundary between the city and the rest of Kuwait: with
the city being inside and new development outside. Upon his visit to Kuwait
in April 1951, Anthony Minoprio recalls that the wall was a fascinating feature
and initially wanted to keep it, but the desire to accommodate the car
triumphed that need and the wall was demolished but its gates were kept,
perhaps a constant nostalgic reminder of the past Kuwait has left. These
gates now serve as the intersection of the First Ring Road and the extending
esplanades.

It seems that the planners' intentions were to gain a foothold in the
Middle East and have the opportunity to design other Middle Eastern and
nearby cities.[24] Whether the intention was to create various self-sufficient
Garden Cities or a single Garden City in Kuwait is unclear; but, it seems
probable especially with the proximity and existing reliance of the other Gulf
cities.[25] However, their intention to create self-sufficient neighbourhood units
in Kuwait was clearly defined in their 1951 Master Plan:

> Outside the wall, the land planned for development will accommodate some
> 48,000 persons and covers an area greater that the old town inside the wall.
> Almost flat and all sand, it is being divided by main roads into eight
> communities of approximately 6,000 persons. Each will have its mosque,
> public hall, shops, site for service industry, and separate primary schools for
> boys and girls with ample room for play and games, as well as six nursery
> schools.[26]

In addition to the schools, each neighbourhood unit (or two) is
self-sufficient through its co-ops, which are in essence a central conglomeration of a large supermarket, bakery, butcher, dress-shop, police
station, bank, schools, nurseries, post office, and a network of parks. In
essence, one could live in their own neighbourhood unit without the need to
leave except to work either in the new industrial area of Shuwaikh or one of
the CBDs in Kuwait *Town*. The co-ops were state-owned but the neighbourhood dwellers had shares in the profits of the yearly revenue, which, in
turn, created an allegiance between the inhabitants themselves and the
state. Elements of Howard's social ideas were more prominent than his
physical approach in Kuwait. This can be seen from the socialist trend of
collectively owning land but also in the encouragement of private enterprises,

22. Banks, "Notes on a Visit to Kuwait,"
48–50.

23. Also spelt *Ikhwan*.

24. MSM went on to design the Baghdad in
1956, Dhaka in 1959 and Chittagong in 1962.

25. This was stated in the British
correspondences: "Minoprio said that his firm
is interested in the possibilities of Qatar and
he emphasised the necessity for making a
plan in the early stages of development."
Trench, *Arab Gulf Cities: Kuwait City*, 553.
Morever, Minoprio, Spencely, and Macfarlane
went on to develop the Master Plan for
Baghdad in 1956, never implemented.

26. P.W. Macfarlane, "Planning an Arab
Town: Kuwait on the Persian Gulf," *Journal of
the Town Planning Institute*, v. 40, n. 5 (1945):
113.

as was the case with the newly forming Kuwaiti-British partnership between construction companies. Moreover, in the need to build the city, there emerged both state-led enterprises that provided building materials such as the Woolaway Factory (now, State Housing Factory) and the privately-owned carpentry workshops, dairy factories, an iron foundry, and clothing and textile factories. Kuwait was on its way to self-sufficiency.

Housing was also an integral scheme to facilitate the success of these neighbourhood units, "[t]hree housing options were made available to the townspeople in the new suburbs, depending on income: they could obtain a plot of residential land on which to build their home, a plot in conjunction with an interest-free thirty-year loan to build, or a govern-ment-built 'limited-income group' (LIG) house."[27] This diversity offered those who are able to buy land the opportunity to do so, and for the less affluent to slowly own their house; nonetheless, this also led to later social stereotyping based on which type of house a person lived in.

MSM sought to zone the main function in the city; with the industrial zones in Shuwaikh and the commercial zones in the new town centre, they "proposed that the narrow coastal strip north of Dimna should not be built up solidly, but should provide sites for houses standing in large gardens, with an open area in the centre for access to the beach."[28] Dimna, presently known as Salmiya, was seen as a 'village' in contrast to the townships outside the wall. This creation of both a town and village does not end at this typology but extends to that of the garden.

Manufacturing the 'Garden'

Gardens in the form of parks within the neighbourhood unit and through the greenbelt surrounding the new centre were an integral part of MSM's scheme for Kuwait with the planners envisioning the greenbelt as "a park – and beyond this were the new townships."[29] However, Kuwait's harsh desert climate did not allow for the widespread of agriculture lands, parks, green spaces, and lush tree-lined avenues to completely adopt the Garden City, yet attaining that vision was at the forefront of this new construction. One of the first major works of the DPW was the electrification of Kuwait and the creation of a steady supply of fresh, potable, and irrigation water, which came in the form of desalination plants and power stations.[30] This need for a water supply was crucial to Kuwait's self-sufficiency as "fresh vegetables are flown in from Lebanon."[31] This need to grow its own food and provide a lush landscape led to the provision of *mashatel* (plant nurseries) on the, then, outskirts of the city near Shuwaikh, outside the Fourth Ring Road. These *mashatel* were designated to provide the city with trees to line the new avenues with the irrigation being provided through both the sewage and the newly erected desalination plant. The city's sewage was also hoped to serve as a fertiliser to aid in growing food and creating a green landscape.[32]

In addition to *mashatel*, the *mazare'e* were also developed far away from the city centre, such as Al-Wafra in the south near the Saudi Arabian border and Al-Abdali in the north near the Iraqi border. These *mazare'e* were initially started as experiments in sustaining agriculture and growing provisions such as date palms and vegetables. In order to encourage adopting this sedentary agricultural lifestyle and similar to Saudi Arabia's sedentarisation schemes, the *mazare'e* attracted the 'villagers' with state-subsidised funding plans for every plant that bore fruit. The government

27. Farah Al-Nakib, "Revisting Hadar and Badu in Kuwait: Citizenship, Housing, and the Construction of a Dichotomy," *International Journal of Middle Eastern Studies*, v. 46, n. 1 (2014): 15.

28. Minoprio, Spencely, and Macfarlane, *Plan for the Town of Kuwait*.

29. Gardiner, *Kuwait, The Making of a City,* 37.

30. In 1951, Farmer and Dark were commissioned by the Ruler of Kuwait to design a water desalination plant and power station in the industrial area of Shuwaikh. The station and plant were to provide electricity and drinking water from the Gulf seawater.

31. Banks, "Notes on a Visit to Kuwait,"49.

32. Saudi Arabia was successful in growing wheat, becoming the world's sixth largest producer. While Kuwait did not intend to grow wheat, there were experiments on productive landscapes. For more information on water in Saudi Arabia, see Toby Craig Jones, *Desert Kingdom: How Oil and Water Forged Modern Saudi Arabia (*Kindle. Cambridge, Massachusetts: Harvard University Press, 2010).

5. Town-dwellers at the waterfront of Kuwait City, 1950s. © Centre for Research and Studies on Kuwait.

6. Bedouins, Kuwait, 1940s. © Kuwait Oil Company Archive.

7. Expat family in Ahmadi, Kuwait, 1950s. © Kuwait Oil Company Archive.

33. Muhammad Rashid Al-Fil, Subhi AlMutawa, and Al-Takhtit Al-Zirā'ī, *Li-Mintaqat Al-Wafrah (Agricultural Planning in al-Wafra)* (Kuwait: Kuwait University – Department of Geography and Society of Kuwaiti Geographers,1983).

34. Al-Nakib, "Revisting Hadar and Badu in Kuwait," 5–30.

35. Lienhardt, Peter. *Disorientations: A Society in Flux: Kuwait in the 1950s*. Ed. Ahmed Al-Shahi (England: Ithaca 1993).

36. Farah Al-Nakib, "Revisiting Hadar and Badu in Kuwait: Citizenship, Housing, and the Construction of a Dichotomy," *International Journal of Middle Eastern Studies* 46.01 (2014): 15–6. Web. Urban and Rural Spaces.

37. One such example is the disappearance of the *housh* (courtyard) and the persistence

provided the 'villagers' with the needed infrastructure and a subsidy to maintain the agriculture.[33] While there was a constant drive to create a productive landscape, the British Political Agent (and his representative in the DPW) also called for countless surveys to test the validity of large scale agriculture and husbandry. While ideal, Kuwaitis growing their own food is a far cry from reality. Just like houses, *mazare'e* now became a status symbol, a sign you have made it and have the luxury to buy your own farm for recreation.

Constructing the Town-Village Dichotomy

In the building of the new town of Kuwait and in the state-led 1950s modernisation agenda, certain terminologies began to emerge in correspondences and reports. Whether this proliferation was a conscious decision or not remains unclear. However, these terminologies lend themselves useful in understanding the perception of Kuwait in the 1950s. Prior to the urbanisation of Kuwait, there existed two main subsets of people the *badu* (nomads) and the *hadar* (sedentary or town-dwellers). While there was no animosity between the two and the interdependent nature of the sea-based and land-based trade, the literature on these two groups suggests a make-believe struggle. Farah Al-Nakib argues that this *badu/hadar* dichotomy is the outcome of these 1950s state-building strategies linked to housing and citizenship policies; however, it can also be argued that this make-believe struggle emerged much earlier with the city walls.[34] Moreover, in addition to this social distinction amongst Kuwaitis, there is also the separation between 'Kuwaitis' and 'foreigners.' Stemming from both the strong British presence and the sheer number of migrants coming to Kuwait to work in the growing oil sector, being Kuwaiti became a new social status. This status was further instigated by the citizenship schemes that further positioned Kuwaitis above foreigners. A sociologist visiting Kuwait in the 1950s recalls that "[w]hen I suggested stopping a taxi myself and offering him [Kuwaiti] a lift, he said, 'You can take a taxi in Kuwait, but I can't'."[35] This social stigma attached to riding a taxi, coupled with their new gained "citizenship," led Kuwaitis to have preferential treatment in the recently established welfare state. The dichotomies do not end with social grouping but extend to that of architecture.

In the state-led education reform of the 1950s which pushed for the equal education of girls and boys, newly built schools were defined as being either in the 'village' or in the 'town.' This delineation did not exist in the British correspondences prior to the adoption of the Master Plan for Kuwait, schools were referred to only by name. The "village" label extends past labels in correspondences, as Al-Nakib articulates, the relocations of 1964 allowed for "city-dwellers" to relocate to the areas between the First and Fourth Ring Road while "villagers" could only relocate back into their "villages."[36] The reasons for this seem to stem from the need to maintain the existing social hierarchy and from the need to keep growth in check. While ambitious, the welfare state of the 1950s with its radical need for social equality and state-provided amenities was instrumental in the nation's modernisation agenda. Along with the Master Plan of 1951, it ignored the existing social construction of extended families, social ties, and tribal allegiances. This constructed vision of "townspeople" and "villagers" living in their separate manufactured neighbourhoods has further emphasised the social divide and created a defined social hierarchy which was facilitated by the architecture of the city.[37]

8. Fountain under construction at the waterfront in Salmiya, 1974.
© *Al Kuwaiti.*

Conclusions:
Utopian Dreams

MSM's plan for Kuwait, while admirable, has caused a dramatic social restructuring in Kuwait. The adoption of the co-ops has indeed created the cooperation Howard envisioned, as has the diversity and friendly competition instated in the souq and CBDs, but it has failed in transposing the Garden City/New Town theory in its entirety in a non-British context. This could be partially attributed to the social structure that already existed in Kuwait but was thoroughly ignored in hopes of creating the universal adoption of a utopian idea. When we have veered so far away from the planners' desires of a clear division between city and garden, can we really say that the Master Plan of 1951 was indeed adopted? Did the planners' ambition to create an idealised utopia lead their visions to remain in the domain of imagination and dreams? For "[s]uch is a brief outline of the exciting developments taking place in Kuwait; it is indeed a town planner's dream. To drive along a splendid dual carriageway [sic] road, which only a year before was a line on paper, is an experience given to few in this country!"[38] This planner's dream and the utopian vision it imposed did not succeed in its attempted manner, it instead created a new utopia where Kuwait is encountering a new state of in-between, one in which new dreams are created, ignoring the on-ground social dynamics. MSM's constructed division of 'city' and 'village' led Kuwait to become a place in which Kuwaitis became associated with the goods they consume, their social status – town versus village, *badu* versus *hadar* – and the location of their neighbourhood. Kuwait, while unaware, became a social and architectural experiment in the plans of MSM and the outcome of a utopian dream that started in the sand and mud and ended in the green grass and concrete that epitomises the Arabian Gulf. The decisions made in the coming years will define the state of Kuwait moving forward. Will it remain in this in-between balancing growth and sustaining its urban fabric? Or will it fall into the cycle of imagination and failed realities once again? •

of the *diwaniyya*, a male-only gathering place. For more on that refer to Al-Jassar, Mohammad K. "Constancy and Change in Contemporary Kuwait City: The Socio-Cultural Dimensions of The Kuwaiti Courtyard and Diwaniyya" (PhD diss., University of Wisconsin-Milwaukee, 2009).

38. Macfarlane, "Town Building in Kuwait," 113.

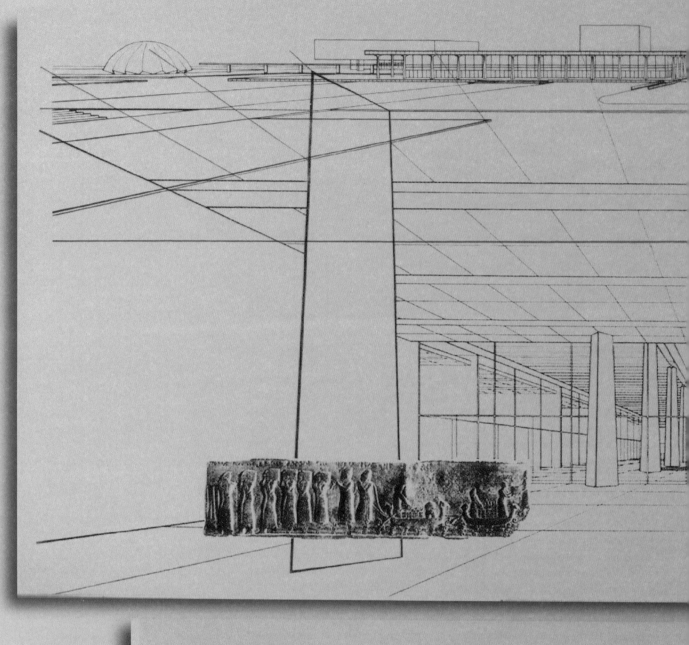

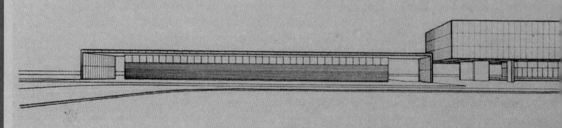

Perspectiva externa: da esquerda para a direita, volume dos edifício de escritórios, "Kuwait de Hoje e Amanhã" e planetário. Abaixo prancha apresentada: cortes do edifício "Kuwait de Hoje e de Amanhã"

External perspective: from left to right, the office building, the Department of Today's and Tomorrow Kuwait and the planetarium. Below, presented drawing: sections of the Department of Today's and Tomorrow's Kuwait.

The Evolutionary Identity:
At the Occasion of Um Qasaba
Waterfront by Doxiadis Associates

YANNIS KITANIS

Kuwait grew exponentially right after the end of WWII. A joint venture from Britain and the US became in charge of the area's oil extraction and exports as long as Kuwait was still under the British protection (1899). Its booming era lasted steadily until the early 1980s and then again later during the 1990s until today. Under the first wave of vast development, the country's prominence was reflected both in urban planning and architectural build up. In search for a new identity through modernity, big architectural names both from the West and the (Far) East were commissioned by the Kuwaiti government to be involved in the country's developmental awakening. Along with titans of architecture such as Jørn Utzon, Kenzo Tange, the Smithsons, and others, Doxiadis Associates from Greece participated in an international competition for the creation of a leisure and recreation area at the Um Qasaba coast, fifty km south of the city of Kuwait.[1] The event of this competition took place shortly after the death of Doxiadis. The entry of the Greek team was never realised. However, the correspondence and collaboration between Doxiadis himself, the local planners in the Middle East, and his associates at the office reveal a process of modernisation that encloses the idea of the evolutionary identity in terms of architectural typology, city growth, and a local ecosystem.

In Search of an Adhesive Idiom and the Rationalisation of the Traditional Practice

During the 1960s and the 1970s the leading ideology of the newly emerged schools of thought comes from the periphery of the West. The tendency of architecture to be culturally and politically detached from former colonists and deputies is the basic ingredient of what many have called Critical Regionalism. However, the idea of inventing a local idiom contains a paradox. Since antiquity, local cultures and traditions were developed and progressed through interactions as a result of trade or battle with other cultures and never formed as constructed ideologies. In the Kuwait of the 1960s and the 1970s the odor of a constructed idiom is particularly intense with the international architects interpreting the Arab tradition as a style. Rem Koolhaas in his survey of the Gulf region observes:

> The Gulf became a field of architectural experimentation where, vernacular elements, particular indigenous cooling and natural ventilation techniques, were used to renew and redefine contemporary architecture.[2]

M. Hancock during a symposium held in Kuwait in January 1969 paved the way for Critical Regionalism to begin as an inevitable discussion for the nation's cultural progress. He presented his study under the title "Architectural Conception of Buildings in Accordance with Twentieth Century Islamic-Arabic Style," where he argued that traditional Islamic-Arabic

1. "Kuwait: Um Qasaba Recreation Area." *DA Review*, v. 12, n. 96 (April 1976): 10.

2. Rem Koolhaas, "A Region in Brief" in *Al Manakh* (Dubai: Archis + AMO + C-Lab + Moutaramat, 2007), 80.

architecture developed through the climate, the local availability of materials, and the traditional way of life. He alarmingly points out that the radically increased Arab purchasing power combined with the availability of foreign skills and materials should be considered a threat for the desired case-specific architectural vocabulary.[3]

According to Hancock, the Arab World had to decide whether to submerge into other concepts or to ensure that the traditional awakening becomes compatible with modern building technologies.[4] The solution of neglecting the Arabic element and focusing on "non-representational" concepts of building technology seemed simplistic to Hancock. He urged the Kuwait Government to increase drastically through policies the quantity and quality of Arab architects. Thus, he suggested the newly built Kuwait University to launch a local School of Architecture.[5] The apparent consequence of his argument would be rehearsed with the inauguration and continuous publication of an Arab World Architectural Journal alongside the establishment of events such as nominations of architectural medals and annual seminars on contemporary architectural matters.[6] Thereby Kuwait could promote in-depth discourse in a direction that absorbs solely the creative elements of the Western thought and experience.

Doxiadis Associates, since the late 50s, had already the trust of almost every Government in the Middle East. Projects in Iraq, Lebanon, Syria, Pakistan, and Iran were designed and implemented.[7] Doxiadis's practice postulated *ekistics*, as a system and methodology for studying in depth the human settlements. According to Doxiadis, the science of Ekistcs (from the Greek word oikos meaning home) had to combine with a multidisciplinary ethos economics, culture, technique social science, and politics. Ekistics was an attempt to derive a 'theory of species' for cities in order to systematise the design process in an era of massive and rapid development. Doxiadis relied on Ekistics to be the most useful tool against the inevitable homogenisation of Modernism. As he envisioned, Ekistics would be a science prescriptive and not descriptive whose ultimate goal would be the construction of environments suitable for the human joy and satisfaction: a return to Humanism through science and knowledge.

During the period between 1957–1961, the international firm of Doxiadis collaborated with the Egyptian architect Hassan Fathy, already known for his New Gourna project – a prototype for mass housing for the rural population in the region near Luxor. Fathy joined the Doxiadis Associates directly after he was expelled from the Nasser regime and proved to be the most valuable asset for Doxiadis's expansion towards the East. As Panayota Pyla observes, although Fathy believed in the revival of traditional architecture as a form of resistance against the Western influence, the Ekistics' approach seemed palatable to him.[8]

As long as Doxiadis Associates were commissioned projects in the Middle East (Iraq and Pakistan) Hassan Fathy was assigned to be *in situ* and conduct research on annual sun movement and prevailing winds, in order to determine the optimal position of buildings and configuration of facades.[9] There, he examined traditional empirical solutions of vernacular architecture and measured their response to a variety of climatic realities. However, in terms of research Fathy did not stick solely with his immediate context. He also studied typologies from the Greek islands demonstrating that the region of the eastern Mediterranean is a broader cultural context affecting also the countries of the Middle East.[10] Fathy's conclusive report suggested that the

1. Original sticker of Um Qasaba Waterfront, Doxiadis Associates, 1975. © Contantinos Xanthopoulos Archive.

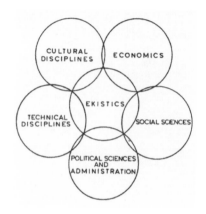

2. Diagram of "Ekistics and Development," Doxiadis Associates, 1968. © Doxiadis Associates.

3. M. Hancock," Architectural Conception of Buildings in Accordance with Twentieth Century Islamic-Arabic Style," *Symposium of Kuwait Municipality 25–29 January 1969* (Kuwait: 1969),1.

4. Ibid., 2.

5. Ibid., 9.

6. Ibid., 5.

7. "How Doxiadis is changing the face of the Middle East," *Special Report* (25 June 1958): 21.

8. Panayota Pyla, "Hassan Fathy Revisited: Postwar Discourses on Science, Development, and Vernacular Architecture." *Journal of Architectural Education*, v. 60, n. 3 (2007): 30.

9. Ibid., 31.

10. Ibid.

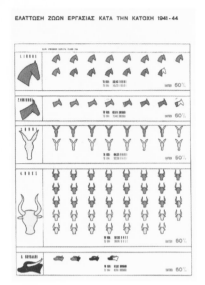

ΕΛΑΤΤΩΣΗ ΖΩΩΝ ΕΡΓΑΣΙΑΣ ΚΑΤΑ ΤΗΝ ΚΑΤΟΧΗ 1941-44

3. A presentation board depicts Greece's casualties in WWII. *The Sacrifice of Greece in WWII*, Ministry of Restoration, Athens, 1946.

traditional houses and local knowledge tested over generations through countless experiments offer solutions to the practical problems of housing, far better than those applied by contemporary international architecture. Fathy presented this as an inherent value of Ekistics' approach to the extent that it could systematise the scientific integrity of traditions. In that way searching for relationships which made habitat successful in the past seemed to be appropriate in the contemporary urbanising practice too, when dwelling had to be built much faster and in much larger quantity than ever before.

Thus, Doxiadis with the support of Fathy and through the Ekistics' milieu reckoned that tradition is not transferred through the generations as typology in the iconic way of vernacular architecture. Instead, tradition would help to rationalise the modern systems as a dosage of condensed experience added to the formula of modernism. The new idiom or otherwise the architectural identity of a nation in the same circumstance of Kuwait, according to Doxiadis, needed to learn from this. Practices from the past should enhance the contemporary building systems rather than advocating for being exotic and different.

Um Qasaba City and the Shape of Future Growth

In March 1961, Doxiadis in his letter to Dr. Saba George Shiber introduced the engagement of the Athens Technological Institute (ATI) with the research project "The City of the Future." The project was based on the analysis of problems and dynamics that shaped a great number of cities until the mid-twentieth century. As Doxiadis alluded to Dr. Shiber, the project should be based on foundations derived from the careful analysis of problems and trends of cities.[11] Thereby the Doxiadis Associates would gain a deeper and precise awareness on human settlements all over the world. Dr. Shiber, being chief consultant in urban matters in many countries around the Arab World, was probably the most relevant person in charge to provide information for the town of Kuwait in particular.

By filling up a questionnaire made by Doxiadis Associates, he could systematise all kinds of Kuwait's distinct characteristics (urban, demographic, climatic, topological, etc.).

Already by 1958, Doxiadis had founded the Athens Technological Institute, a nurturing idea since the start of his practice at the office in the early fifties. After the end of WWII, Doxiadis served as the Deputy of the Greek Ministry for the Recording of War Casualties throughout the country. His seminal work and research upon urban matters, entwined even more with his vision for the creation of meticulous databases, essential for future restoration of devastated areas. Under those terms, the Athens Technological Institute would accumulate and categorise the data acting as the supportive department of the Doxiadis Associates. In the second paragraph of ATI's declaration text, the institute's purpose was diligently stated:

> The target of the Institute is the promotion of technology and science by all means in order to contribute in the improvement of the human living. In order to achieve the above the Institute will conduct research, study the housing problems, fund schools, labs, museums and scientific societies, organise lectures and conferences, provide scholarships, publish books, magazines and articles.

11. Constantinos Doxiadis, Letter to Saba George Shiber, April 4, 1961 (TS. Doxiadis Archive, File n. 17854, Athens).

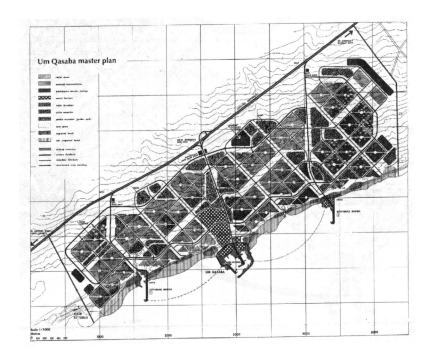

4. Um Qasaba Waterfront Master Plan, Doxiadis Associates. © *DA Review*.

Dr. Shiber's response was delayed due to being hospitalised after suffering a heart attack. In his handwritten letter, found in the Doxiadis's Archives, Dr. Shiber satirised the situation by replying that the information he was providing to Doxiadis Associates in the questionnaire would be "as sketchy as the new image of Kuwait, in its fluid city shell."[12] Frankly, the questionnaire mailed back to Doxiadis Associates is scattered and almost unanswered. However, Dr. Shiber's view on Kuwait unfolds deliberately in his gigantic volume *The Kuwait Urbanization*, published three years later and sent directly to Doxiadis Associates as an additive element to his sparse handwritten report in the form of a gift. In this book, he tirelessly advocates the human settlement and unleashes a libel against the booming urbanisation of the modern Arab World. This was in absolute alignment with Doxiadis, who eagerly condemned the speed in transition and development of cities without sophisticated reasoning in every lecture he delivered around the globe.

Dr. Shiber, as a chief planner in the state of Kuwait, documented all the characteristics of its past urbanisation as well as the ongoing urban projects and the new realities to finally conceptualise his personal opinion with a rationale similar to the practice of the ATI. The volume catalogued the attributes of Kuwait since it was a fishing village of the Persian Gulf and until it became a rapidly urbanised area after the advent of oil. Through his critical writings, Dr. Shiber criticised the geometric paper plans as they have been imposed on the desert by several foreign regional planning companies without taking into consideration the urban qualities of organic-shaped Arab towns.[13]

In a chapter entitled "Laying the Foundation Stones for the Masterplan of Kuwait," Dr. Shiber urges Kuwaitis to learn under the counter-influence from the mistakes that were recognisable in the cities of the Western World. Therefore, he quoted an article from *The New York Times* entitled "The City Spreads Outward" (October 12, 1961). In this article, it is mentioned that if New York City continues to expand in the same fashion in

5. Typology of Um Qasaba Waterfront, Doxiadis Associates, 1976. © *DA Review*.

6. Chalet cluster at Um Qasaba Waterfront, Doxiadis Associates, 1976. © Doxiadis Archive.

12. Saba George Shiber, *The Kuwait Urbanization* (Kuwait: Government Printing Press, 1964).

13. Ibid.

7. Marina facilities at Um Qasaba
Waterfront, Doxiadis Associates, 1976.
© Doxiadis Archive.

8.Chalet cluster at Um Qasaba
Waterfront, Doxiadis Associates, 1976.
© Doxiadis Archive.

14. Ibid., 254.

15. Ibid.

16. Constantinos. Doxiadis *Between Dystopia
and Utopia* (London: Faber and Faber, 1968).

17. Shiber, op cit.

18. Saba George Shiber, *Kuwait Urbanization*,
255.

19. Ibid.

the years to come, the new spread city will eventually cover an area inclusive of New York, New Jersey, and Connecticut and will result in thousands of malfunctions such as, traffic jams, congestion, high taxes, and new slum-formations.[14]

In the same wavelength, Dr. Shiber rang the bell to the Kuwaiti administration board, citing one of his past articles entitled "Kuwait: Year 2000 AD – Towards a Curvilinear City."

> A city must derive form, shape and structure as much as possible from the compulsions of geography, topography, philosophy and ecology.[15]

Dr. Shiber elaborated on the idea above, citing that contemporary cities must be defined from the climate, the adjacent nature, the inherent habits, and the cultures of the inhabitants. He supported the organic model of the Medieval or the typical old Arab city in the same abstract and almost naïve way as Doxiadis. The latter, at the occasion of one of his numerous lectures about Ekistics (London 1969), used the paradigm of Constantinople as one of the biggest cities in medieval history. "Emperor Theodosius expanded the fortification only once (5th Century AD) and the city's enclosure remained unchanged until the Eighteenth Century." Consequently, the inhabitants of Constantinople had plenty of time to soberly comprehend the evolution of their environment and finally conceive it as a piece of art in which they were living and which they were a part of. Adding to the above, Doxiadis cited Michelangelo who lived long in Florence, roaming its narrow alleys and searching for the most worthy location for his art to be placed. After Michelangelo finally set up his David in Piazza de la Signoria, citizens of Florence practiced a ritual-activity of approaching the statue during the night and placing on its foundation paper notes with personal critique. For Doxiadis, this established interaction between citizens and public artwork was a profound and sophisticated example of the slow metabolic process that happens in cities where art and architecture were placed, with wisdom and latent need, "functioning in a co-operative-systematic and mostly unconscious way."[16]

Back in the "Curvilinear City" by Dr. Shiber, after exposing his general compulsions on geography, topography, philosophy, and ecology, he narrows down to the actual facts and pathologies of Kuwait. The old settlements of the country such as Jahra (a former oasis), old Kuwait (originally called *Kout*, i.e. fortress or arsenal), Salmiya, Al-Fintas, Fahaheel, and many others, were built along the shore of the Arabian Gulf. Oil exploitation resulted in a new settlement located in the proximity of oil fields: the suburb of Ahmadi built by the British oil company as a garden city in the desert. For Dr. Shiber, Ahmadi was a good example of "a compact green simple and functional town."[17] However, as the article prescribes, this particular example was not the case in the broader region of Kuwait. Dr. Shiber witnessed the old city as "tampered with" and the surrounding desert as the base of an impulsive and careless development.[18] Instead of following the natural guideline of the seaside (as traditionally done by Kuwaitis) residential units were allowed to grow inwards towards the desert. Dr. Shiber argues that this was a fundamental mistake, and continues that by positioning the public facilities in the sectoral desert space, the latter would be centrally located in respect to the outlying curvilinear shape of the residential development on the coast.[19] Similar to Doxiadis, Dr. Shiber used in his rhetoric terminology from the anatomy of the human body in order to describe the conception of the Kuwaiti regional plan in a single phrase:

> While the curvilinear residential growth would be the spinal cord, the belly of the city should have been zoned to be the nerve system of transportation.[20]

What Doxiadis and Dr. Shiber had also shared was the belief that the new-built environment in the newly-developed regions had to be styleless and archaic in a contemporary sense and that this could only be achieved with a subjective and thorough study of the context. Coincidentally enough, in the book by Doxiadis entitled *Architecture in Transition* (1963), there is a chapter called "Laying the Foundations." He starts the chapter by stating:

> We have seen ourselves, so far, breasting a sea of architectural confusion, bewildered by problems and crises; we have defined the architect's role and responsibility, and have established what meager influence he in fact has over contemporary movements. Moreover, we have surveyed the new problems and sensed the new solutions that they require. Finally we have seen that we must move from the traditional to the contemporary, from the local to the universal, and that we are returning to an ecumenic architecture.[21]

Some years later, in 1968, Dr. Shiber died at the age of forty-five and left behind his catalogue for the city of Kuwait – a passionate work resembling the author's dream on how to urbanise the desert by respecting and utilising the principles of a broader but ancient non-Western culture. The osmosis of the correspondence and interaction between the two men came finally in 1975, less than a year after Doxiadis's death, when the Doxiadis Associates won the second prize in an international competition for the creation of a leisure area on a waterfront not far away from the city of Kuwait.

The time frame of the competition was notably short and the loss of the leader particularly big, as the project manager of the design team Constantinos Xanthopoulos recollects from memories back in the mid-seventies.[22] Despite the intense workload of the office, Doxiadis had organised it in such a way that he could obtain the maximum control upon every possible project. The Um Qasaba waterfront happened to be one of the first projects that did not have his supervision. According to Professor Xanthopoulos, Doxiadis' absence during this project is evident through the deficient stance of the grid. Um Qasaba was designated to be a weekend destination for the urban residents of Kuwait since the distance from the city was less than fifty km. Therefore the Touristic Enterprises Company held a competition that required the coastal area to be articulated in several land uses in order to provide facilities and circumstances for recreation. Moreover, the competition-brief required that the use of cars should be reduced and hidden from the residents' eyes albeit ensuring the environmental quality of the area. As far as possible, locally available materials were to be employed in the construction resembling the discourse between Fathy and Doxiadis about fifteen years ago.

> In order to lay the foundations for the architecture of the future and prepare the proper program of action, we have to start with a definition of our subject which can be generally accepted. We must, find out what architecture is and what it is trying to do. We must first remind ourselves that architecture is the discipline not of designing houses or buildings, much less of designing monuments, but of building the human habitat. As such it consists of a science, a technique and an art.[23]

9. Chalet cluster nucleus of Um Qasaba Waterfront, Doxiadis Associates, 1976. © Doxiadis Archive.

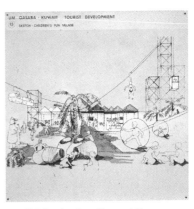

10. Children's play village at Um Qasaba Waterfront, Doxiadis Associates, 1976. © Doxiadis Archive.

20. Ibid.

21. Constantinos Doxiadis, *Architecture in Transition* (London: Hutchinson, 1963).

22.Interview with Constantinos Xanthopoulos in March 2015.

23. Doxiadis, *Architecture in Transition*, 173.

In the exact paradigm of its founder, the Doxiadis Associates study-team laid the foundations for the Um Qasaba waterfront by subdividing the region into five categories. The foremost guideline is the traditional affinity of Kuwaitis for the sea and the culture behind it. Residential chalets, active recreation areas, passive recreation areas, water-based recreation, and communal and technical facilities were arranged in a way that the access to and view of the sea were maximised.[24] The deficient stance of the grid mentioned above, is transformed into a matrix composed by triangulations on a north-south axis, starting from a point close to the high-water mark.

Doxiadis declared time as the absolute dimension of cities and considered space comparatively of minor importance, "a four dimensional complex serving the actual needs of the people in a dynamic, not static synthesis."[25] For him, a settlement was a continually evolving organism, at once biological and technological, thus, a resilient planning with phases was inevitable in every project of Doxiadis Associates. The recreational suburb of Kuwait City would be composed of a three-phase developmental plan. The first phase of the proposal provided approximately 700 chalets for 4.900 people all along 3,000m of the coastal zone. In a linear trajectory of development laterally to the sea shore after the three phases of the project, it would have a total of 2.500 chalets for 17.500 people.

Mark Wigley in his essay "Network Fever" provides insight for Doxiadis's attitude towards city growth: "If a city grows radially outwards, as it usually happens, pressure increases on the centre until the organism collapses. Surgery on its heart like feeding new arteries as highways into the core will speed up its death."[26] Wigley outlines accurately Doxiadis's insistence in most of his projects that the city should grow only in one direction and the core itself needs to move sideways and expand at the scale of the overall expansion. Such a city does not simply grow; it moves across the landscape. Growth becomes movement.[27] In Um Qasaba Waterfront three major community centres would be located gradually at the coastal zone with access to the main regional road network of Kuwait. The holistic idea of a networked city, therefore a well-connected world, is evident here. That being the case, Um Qasaba is definitely part of Doxiadis's interwoven world.

Seeding the Evolutionary Change

Throughout his lifetime, Doxiadis often predicted the emergence of a single city covering the whole Earth. As Wigley adds: "like a lava lamp network, a fluid biomorphic growth extending itself everywhere." Doxiadis in his book *Between Dystopia and Utopia* announces that people should accept the very big city as a concept because it is already a fact.[28] Nevertheless, he does not encourage decentralisation and sprawl. On the contrary, he advocates centralisation in static neighbourhoods-towns to be part of dynamic cities. In order to express this ideal condition, Doxiadis uses the term "Entopia to define the conceivable space between dream and reality, utopia and practice." By neglecting the chimera of utopia as something yet positively lacking rationale, albeit dodging a solid ground for progress, Doxiadis embraced Dionysios Solomos's lyric "with reason and dream" and Oscar Wilde's "even with our feet in the mud we look at the stars" to suggest with a certain degree of lyricism an ideal circumstance for living and working.[29]

24. "Kuwait: Um Qasaba Recreation Area," *DA Review*, v. 12, n. 96 (April 1976): 10.

25. Doxiadis, *Architecture in Transition*, 145.

26. Mark Wigley, "Network Fever," *Grey Room 4* (Summer 2001): 88.

27. Ibid.

28. Doxiadis, *Between Dystopia and Utopia*, 58.

29. Ibid.

For Jacqueline Tyrwhitt, consultant of Dioxiadis for landscape matters, Entopia is a garden community in the hillsides of Athens, on the steep rocks overlooking the plains with a glimpse of the Aegean Sea.[30] After she found her ideal location in 1963, with a self-financing scheme she managed to buy and sell all the adjacent properties. The agreement was that only a two-story house could be built in each orchard and no fences allowed so that the landscape could be preserved. A small community of like-minded garden enthusiasts was formed after a short amount of time. However, the substance of Tyrwhitt's idea for sustainable global future through local action goes further. During the summer months in the broader area of Athens, local flora turns yellow under the intense sunlight. Therefore, Tyrwhitt had to introduce non-native plants that would grow vigorously in the Mediterranean environment during summer. After experimenting with several species collected from botanical gardens around the world and enriching the soil, she ended up with an acclimatised environment which acted as the manifestation of her international technical assistance:

> Supplementing local material with imports suitable for adaptation to particular local circumstances, thereby adding to the vitality of the local ecosystem and seeding evolutionary change.[31]

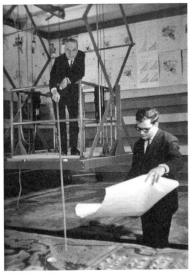

11. Constantinos Doxiadis standing on a platform, analysing a scale model, 1965. © Constantinos and Emma Doxiadis Foundation.

The same manipulation of the soil, though for a different purpose, was implemented also in Ahmadi, the suburb next to the designated area for the Um Qasaba Waterfront. The first British residents and employees of the British Oil Company introduced non-native plants in the harsh desert environment of Kuwait. The result was that Ahmadi ended up being a lush green city like a real oasis, with the very first tree planted in 1948.[32] The same intention from Doxiadis Associates is evident in the Um Qasaba's proposal with a prominent irregular green zone disposed centrally across the overall site and green "fingers" serving as the connectors between the different facilities of the public realm.[33] In other words, the idea of manipulating the natural ground and the local ecosystem of the desert in order to create the circumstances for comfortable living reveals again the evolutionary process of modernisation that Doxiadis endorsed. People, culture, and the human agglomerations are in permanent mutation, as well as the earth according to Doxiadis.

Doxiadis and his associates, during a lifetime endeavor, researched the evolution of every possible parameter that could affect the human shelter and attempted to design cities that eliminate traits gradually over time. They interpreted tradition solely as the tested experience of the past that evolves and benefits the formation of the contemporary identity. They attempted to predict the shape of the city's growth based on rationalised criteria and tried to set up a landscape in which nature acts as a fertile ground and not as a monstrous enemy. Doxiadis Associates paved the way to rephrase Modernity under the lens of a new Humanism, through science and knowledge that avoided piecemeal social engineering and used instead a holistic and unstoppable vision. •

30. Ellen Shoshkes, Jaqueline Tyrwhitt: A Transnational Life in Urban Planning and Design (Surrey: Ashgate, 2013), 227.

31. Ibid.

32. Reem Alissa, "The Oil Town of Ahmadi since 1946: From Colonial Town to Nostalgic City," Comparative Studies of South Asia, Africa and the Middle East, v. 33, n. 1 (2003): 46.

33. "Kuwait Um Qasaba Recreation Area," 10.

SELECTED BIBLIOGRAPHY

PUBLICATIONS

Ali, Evangelia Simos. *Kuwait Historical Preservation Study – Old Kuwait Town*, v. 1. Kuwait Municipality, Kuwait, 1988.

Al-Ghunaim, Abdullah Y.; Rais, Ali; Gholoum, Ali. eds. *Kuwait in Postcards*, Centre for Research and Studies on Kuwait, Kuwait, 2009.

Al-Mughni, Haya. *Women in Kuwait: The Politics of Gender*, Saqi Books, London, 2001.

Al-Mutawa, Subhi. *Kuwait City Parks: A Critical Review of Their Design, Facilities, Programs, and Management*, KPI, London, 1985.

Alsager, Noura, ed. *Acquiring Modernity*, National Council for Culture, Arts and Letters, Kuwait City, 2014.

Antonius, George. *The Arab Awakening: The Story of the Arab National Movement*, Capricorn Books, New York, 1939.

Bjorn, Malene. *The Light & Air. How it All Began in Sweden in 1945*, transl. Eva Lindstrom, Baltic Books, Växjö, 2013.

Burdett, Anita, ed. *Records of Kuwait 1961–1965: 1961* Archive Editions, Anthony Rowe, England, 1997.

Chadirji, Rifat. *Concepts and Influences: Towards a Regionalized International Architecture*, KPI, London and New York, 1986.

Colin Buchanan and Partners. *A Plan for Kuwait*, Kuwait Municipality, Kuwait City, 1972.

Collins, Peter. *Concrete: The Visions of a New Architecture*, McGill University Press, Montreal, 2004.

Connah, Roger. *Fantômas Fragments Fictions: An Architectural Journey through the Twentieth Century*, MIT Press, Cambridge, 1989.

Colquhoun, Alan. *Modern Architecture*, Oxford University Press, Oxford, 2002.

Crinson, Mark. *Modern Architecture and the End of Empire*, Ashgate Publishing Company, Aldershot, UK and Burlington, Vt., 2003.

Doxiadis, Constantinos. *Architecture in Transition*, Hutchinson, London, 1963.

Doxiadis, Constantinos. *Between Dystopia and Utopia*, Faber & Faber, London, 1968.

Elshestawy, Yasser. *The Evolving Arab City: Tradition, Modernity and Urban Development*, Routledge, New York, 2008.

El-Wakil, Leila. *Hassan Fathy dans son temps*, inFolio, Gollion and Paris, 2013.

Fabbri, Roberto; Soares, Sara Saragoça; Camacho, Ricardo. *Modern Architecture Kuwait 1949–1989*, Niggli Verlag, Zurich, 2016.

Foyle, Arthur M., ed. *Conference on tropical architecture 1953: a report on the proceedings of the conference held at University College*, London, March 1953, George Allen & Unwin, 1954.

Frisby, David. *Fragments of Modernity: Theories of Modernity in the Work of Simmel, Kracauer, and Benjamin*, MIT Press, Cambridge, 1986.

Frampton, Kenneth; Correa, Charles; Robson, David, eds. *Modernity and Community: Architecture in the Islamic World*, Thames and Hudson, London, 2001.

Gardiner, Stephen. *Kuwait, The Making of a City*, Addison Wesley Longman Ltd, Harlow, 1983.

Gilbert, Eva Franch I; Lawrence, Amanda Reeser; Milijacki, Ana; Schafer, Ashley, eds. *Office US: Agenda*, Lars Müller Publishers, Zurich, 2014.

Government of Kuwait. *Law Of Antiquities*, Kuwait Government Printing Press, Kuwait City, 1960.

Grathwol, Robert; M. Moorhus, Donita. *Bricks, Sand, and Marble: U.S. Army Corps of Engineers Construction in the Mediterranean and the Middle East 1947–1991*, Center of Military History and Corps of Engineers, United States Army, Washington, D.C., 2009.

Hall, Stuart, et al. *Modernity – An Introduction to Modern Societies*, The Open University, Blackwell Publishers, Oxford and Massachusetts, 1996.

Hourani, Albert. *Syria and Lebanon: A Political Essay*, Oxford University Press, Oxford, 1968.

Isenstadt, Sandy; Rizvi, Kishwar, eds. *Modern Architecture and the Middle East: architecture and politics in the twentieth century*, University of Washington Press, Seattle, 2008.

Jackson, Iain; Holland, Jessica. *The Architecture of Edwin Maxwell Fry and Jane Drew: Twentieth Century Architecture, Pioneer Modernism and the Tropics*, Ashgate, Surrey and Burlington, 2014.

Jankowski, James. *Nasser's Egypt, Arab Nationalism, and the United Arabic Republic*, Lynne Rienner Publishers, Boulder, 2002.

Joyce, Miriam. *Kuwait, 1945–1996: An Anglo-American Perspective*, Routledge, London, 1998.

Kassir, Samir. *Being Arab*, translated by Will Hobson, Verso Books, London, 2006.

Kultermann, Udo. *Contemporary Architecture in the Arab State: Renaissance of a Region*, McGraw-Hill, New York, 1999.

Khaldūn, Ibn. *The Muqaddimah: An Introduction to History*, translated by Franz Rosenthal, 3 vols., Princeton, New York, 1958.

King, Anthony D. *Urbanism, Colonialism, and the World's Economy: Cultural and Social Foundations of the World Urban System*, Routledge, New York, 1990.

Lang, Frederick W. *Housing Activities In Lebanon 1956–1958: A Summary of Operations,* USOM Housing Division, Beirut, 1958.

Larkham, P.J. *Conservation and the City*, Routledge, London, 1996.

Morris, A. E. J. *John R. Harris Architects*, Hurtwood, Westerham, 1984.

Mostafavi, Mohsen; Leatherbarrow, David. *On Weathering: The Life of Buildings in Time*, MIT Press, Cambridge, 1993.

Quantrill, Malcolm. *Reima Pietilä: Architecture, Context and Modernism*, Rizzoli, New York, 1985.

Ramady, Mohamed. *Political, Economic and Financial Country Risk: Analysis of the Gulf Cooperation Council*, London, Springer, 2014, 100.

Roth, Alfred. *Alfred Roth: Architekt der Kontinuität*, Waser Verlag für Kunst und Architektur, Zurich, 1985.

Said, Edward. *Orientalism*, Penguin, London and New York, 1978.

Sampson, Anthony. *The Seven Sisters: The Great Oil Companies and the World They Shaped*, Bantam Books, New York, 1975.

Schofield, Richard. *Territorial foundations of the Gulf States*, UCL Press, London, 1994.

Shair, Kamal. *Out of the Middle East: The Emergence of an Arab Global Business*, I.B.Tauris, London, 2006.

Shaw, Ralph. *Kuwait*, Macmillan London Limited, London and Basingstoke, 1976.

Shiber, Saba George. *The Kuwait Urbanization*, Kuwait Government Printing Press, Kuwait, 1964.

Shiber, Saba George. *Recent Arab City Growth*, Kuwait Government Printing Press, Kuwait, 1969.

Smithson, Alison and Peter. *The Charged Void: Urbanism*, The Monacelli Press, New York, 2005.

Smithson, Alison and Peter. *Without Rhetoric: An Architectural Aesthetic 1955–1972*, MIT Press, Cambridge, 1974.

Stephens, Robert. *The Arabs' New Frontier*, Westview Press, Boulder, 1976.

Sweet, Rod, ed. *SSH Design – The first 50 years*, Al-Khat Printing Press, Kuwait, 2011.

Trench, Richard, ed. *Arab Gulf Cities: Kuwait City*, Archive Editions, Oxford, 1994.

Vale, Lawrence. *Architecture, Power and National Identity*, Yale University Press, New Haven, 1992.

Watenpaugh, Keith David. *Being Modern in the Middle East: Revolution, Nationalism, Colonialism, and the Arab Middle Class*, Princeton University Press, Princeton, 2006.

Volait, Mercedes. *Architectes et architectures de l'Egypte moderne (1830–1950): genèse et essor d'une expertise locale*, Maisonneuve et Larose, Paris, 2005.

Volait, Mercedes; Nasr, Joe, eds. *Urbanism – Imported or Exported? Native Aspirations and Foreign Plans*, Wiley-Academy, Chichester, 2003.

THESES

Alissa, Reem. "Building for Oil: Corporate Colonialism, Nationalism and Urban Modernity in Ahmadi, 1946–1992." PhD diss., University of California, Berkeley, 2012.

Albaqshi, Muhannad. "The Social Production of Space: Kuwait's Spatial History." PhD diss., Illinois Institute of Technology, 2010.

Al-Jassar, Mohammad. "Constancy and Change in Contemporary Kuwait City: The Socio-Cultural Dimensions of the Kuwait Courtyard and Diwaniyya." PhD diss., The University of Wisconsin – Milawaukee, 2009.

Al-Mosully, Suhair. "Revitalizing Kuwait's Empty City Center." Master's thesis, Massachusetts Institute of Technology, 1992.

Al-Najjar, Ghanim. "Decision-Making Process in Kuwait: The Land Acquisition Policy as a Case Study." PhD diss., University of Exeter, 1984.

Al-Nakib, Farah. "Kuwait City: Urbanization, the Built Environment and the Urban Experience Before and After Oil (1716–1986)." PhD diss., School of Oriental and African Studies, 2011.

Al-Ragam, Asseel. "Towards a Critique of an Architectural Nahdha: A Kuwaiti Example." PhD diss., University of Pennsylvania, 2008.

Baki, Sami Abdul. "The New Palace of Baal in Ain-Baal Lebanon." Diploma's thesis, American University of Beirut, 1947.

Beshir, Tarek. "Architecture Beyond Cultural Politics: Western Practice in the Arabian Peninsula." Master's thesis, Massachusetts Institute of Technology, 1993.

Haddad, Charles. "A Development for Bedouin Settlement." Diploma's thesis, American University of Beirut, 1956.

Khatib, Mounir Tahir. "Model Village." Diploma's thesis, American University of Beirut, 1946.

Riad, Mahmoud. "The City of Cairo, Proposed Development Scheme for the Central Area." Diploma's thesis, Liverpool University, 1932.

Sadik, Rula Muhammad. "Nation-Building and Housing Policy: A Comparative Analysis of Urban Housing Development in Kuwait, Jordan, and Lebanon." PhD diss., University of California, Berkeley, 1996.

Soares, Sara Saragoça. "The Identity of Modern Heritage: Kuwait City." Master's thesis, Faculdade de Arquitectura da Universidade Técnica de Lisboa, 2012.

ARTICLES

Al-Bahar, Huda. "Kuwait's Post-War Reconstruction." *Mimar*, n. 40 (September 1991): 14–17.

Alissa, Reem. "The Oil Town of Ahmadi since 1946: From Colonial Town to Nostalgic City." *Comparative Studies of South Asia, Africa and the Middle East*, v. 33, n. 1 (2003): 41–58.

Al-Nakib, Farah. "Kuwait's Modern Spectacle: Oil Wealth and the Making of a New Capital City, 1950–90." *Comparative Studies of South Asia, Africa and the Middle East*, v. 33, n. 1 (2013): 7–25.

Al-Ragam, Asseel. "The Destruction of Modernist Heritage: The Myth of Al-Sawaber." *Journal of Architectural Education*, v. 67, n. 2 (2013): 243–252.

Al-Ragam, Asseel. "Critical Nostalgia: Kuwait Urban Modernity and Alison and Peter Smithson's Kuwait Urban Study and Mat-Building." *The Journal of Architecture*, v. 20, n. 1 (2015).

Al-Sayyad, Nezar. "Space in the Islamic City: Some Urban Design Patterns." *Journal of Architecture and Planning Research*, v. 4, n. 2 (June 1987): 108–119.

Anderson, Richard; Al-Bader, Jawaher. "Recent Kuwaiti Architecture: Regionalism vs. Globalisation." *Journal of Architectural and Planning Research,* v. 23, n. 2 (2006): 134–146.

Antoniou, Jim. "The Challenge of Islamic Architecture." *Middle East Construction*, n. 10 (1979): 16–17.

Amps, L.W. "Kuwait Town development," *Journal of the Royal Central Asian Society*, v. 40, n. 3–4 (1953): 234–240.

Banham, Reyner. "The New Brutalism." *Architectural Review* (December 1955): 355–361.

Banks, R. L. "Notes on a Visit to Kuwait." *Town Planning Review*, v. 26, n. 1 (1955): 48–50.

Barnett, Michael N. "Sovereignty, Nationalism, and Regional Order in the Arab States System." *International Organization*, v. 49, n. 3 (1995): 479–510.

Bates, Ülkü. "Two Ottoman Documents on Architects in Egypt." *Muqarnas*, n. 3 (1985): 121–27.

Colin Buchanan and Partners. "Kuwait." *The Architects' Journal*, v. 159, n. 21 (1974): 1131–32.

Dood, Stuart C. "The village welfare service in Lebanon, Syria and Palestine." *Journal of The Royal Central Asian Society*, v. 32, n. 1 (1945): 87–90.

Hoyt, Charles. "The Oil-Rich Mideast: The new frontier for professional services?" *Architectural Record* (June 1975): 101.

Jamal, Karim. "Destruction of the Middle East?" *The Architects' Journal,* v. 164, n. 30 (1976): 161–62.

Jamal, Karim. "Kuwait, a Salutary Tale." *The Architects' Journal,* v. 158, n. 50 (1973): 1452–57.

Karim, Sayyed. "1939–1949." *Al-Emara*, n. 1–2 (1949): 6.

Karim, Sayyed. "What Is Architecture?" *Al-Emara*, n. 1 (1939): 10–1.

Karim, Sayyed. "The Engineering Conference and the post-War Projects." *Al-Emara*, n. 2–3 (1945): 10.

MacFarlane, P.W. "Planning an Arab Town: Kuwait on the Persian Gulf." *Journal of the Town Planning Institute*, v. 40, n. 5 (1954): 110–13.

Morris, Tony. "Precast concrete's Middle East Future." *Middle East Architectural Design* (May/June 1979): 19–23.

Mortada, Sayyed. "The First Engineering Conference." *Al-Emara*, ns. 2–3 (1945): 7.

Moustapha, Ahmed Farid. "Islamic Values in Contemporary Urbanism (1)." *Albenaa*, v. 7, n. 41 (1988): 18–33.

Parkyn, Neil. "Kuwait Revisited." *Middle East Construction* (September 1983): 39–42.

"Proposals for Restructuring Kuwait." *Architectural Review* (September 1974): 178–190.

Pyla, Panayota. "Hassan Fathy Revisited: Postwar Discourses on Science, Development, and Vernacular Architecture." *Journal of Architectural Education*, v. 60, n. 3 (2007): 28–39.

Shuaib, Hamid. "Urban Development in Kuwait." *Alam Al-Bina*, n. 98 (1989): 4.

Soares, Sara Saragoça. "Man of Kuwait, Other Modernities." *Acquiring Modernity*, Noura Alsager ed., 17–9.

Squire, Raglan, ed. "Architecture in the Middle East." *Architectural Design* (March 1957): 72–108.

Stanek, Łukasz. "Mobilities of Architecture in the Global Cold War: From Socialist Poland to Kuwait and Back." *International Journal of Islamic Architecture*, v. 4, n. 2 (2015): 365–398.

Sultan, Ghazi. "Criteria for Design in the Arabian Gulf Region." *The Arabian Journal for Science and Engineering*, v. 7, n. 2 (1982): 165–171.

Sultan, Ghazi. "Kuwait." *The Architects' Journal*, v. 160, n. 40 (1974): 792.

COPYRIGHTS FOR ADDITIONAL IMAGES

CONTRIBUTORS

For additional biographies regarding other contributors, please see interviews.

ADEL ALBLOUSHI

Adel Albloushi (b. 1985) holds an M. Arch. from McGill University (2010), and a Master's in Advanced Studies in CAAD from ETH Zurich (2017). Currently, he researches new design methodologies while projecting and producing buildings and small-scale objects using a multi-disciplinary approach. Albloushi strongly believes in responsible social production of human environments, and that design creates hypothetical solutions to problems that resist thorough formal definition. Albloushi also pursues cultural projects. He is currently immersed in research new design methodologies, projecting and producing buildings and small-scale objects using a multi-disciplinary approach, and also cultural projects.

ASSEEL AL-RAGAM

Asseel Al-Ragam (b. 1977) is an architect and Assistant Professor at Kuwait University College of Architecture where she teaches modern architectural history, criticism, and design studio. Her 2008 PhD dissertation from the University of Pennsylvania (USA), entitled "Towards a Critique of an Architectural *Nahdha*: A Kuwaiti Example," focuses on mid-twentieth century Kuwaiti urban and architectural destruction and development, and draws links between societal transformation, modernity, and space. Her published papers, lectures, and teachings expand on themes of housing production and consumption, urban planning, preservation, and the adaptive reuse of modernist buildings, and challenge Eurocentric accounts of cultural modernity. She served as visiting researcher and guest lecturer at the *École Nationale Supérieure d'Architecture Paris–Malaquais* and at *Sciences Po*, France. She is a member of the Technical Advisory Committee for Architecture and Urban Planning at the Private University Council in Kuwait.

CLAUDIA CAGNESCHI

Claudia Cagneschi (b. 1973) is an architect and researcher. She graduated from the Università degli Studi di Firenze Facoltá di Architettura (2000, Italy) and earned her PhD from the Università di Bologna (2009, Italy). She alternates professional practice with theoretical studies and her research focuses on modern and contemporary architecture, particularly about school, home, and temporary buildings. She participated in international research programs, conferences, and seminars, and released a monograph about the work of Giuseppe Pagano and a study about Edoardo Gellner. She is adjunct professor at Università di Bologna, Scuola di Ingegneria since 2009. She currently runs CRoE architecture firm, firm that participates in international competitions and focuses particularly on school building design, interiors, and restorations.

DALAL M. ALSAYER

Dalal M. Alsayer (b. 1986) is currently pursuing a PhD in Architecture at PennDesign, University of Pennsylvania (USA), where her interests lie at the intersection of modernisation, development aid, and the environmental history of architecture in the context of the Middle East. Alsayer is the recipient of several awards and grants including the Kuwait University Master's and PhD Scholarship, three grants from Harvard University including: the Penny White Fund Grant, the Philippines Grant, and NRC Funds Grant, as well as the Will M. Mehlhorn Scholarship from PennDesign. She holds a professional Bachelor's of Architecture from Kuwait University (2008), a post-professional Master's of Science in Architecture and Urban Design from Columbia University (2010, USA), and a Master's in Design Studies with a concentration in Urbanism, Landscape, Ecology, from Harvard University (2015, USA).

ENRICO MAMBELLI

Enrico Mambelli (b. 1977) is an architect with a degree from the Università di Bologna, Scuola di Ingegneria e Architettura in Italy. His research interest focuses on the relationship between the urban form and human behaviour. He lectures on photography in relationship to the representation of the landscape and anthropic signs. As of 2010, he is Assistant Professor of History and Technique of Photography at Università di Bologna, Scuola di Ingegneria e Architettura. In 2010 he founded CRoE, an architectural firm that participates in international design competitions, interiors, and rehabilitations.

ISMAIL I. RIFAAT

Ismail Rifaat (b. 1936) holds a Bachelor's in Architecture from University of Alexandria, (1957, Egypt), and a Master's degree and PhD from ETH in Zurich (1965, Switzerland). He served as teaching assistant at the University of Alexandria and is a regular design critic at the University of Houston, Texas. Prior to his experience in Kuwait, he collaborated with Walter Thommen Architects in Switzerland and several other practices in Canada and the United States. In Kuwait, he worked with KISR, UNITEC, and SSH between 1980 and 1984, and later joined Kuwait Architectural Consultants. After 1986 he moved to North America where he still lives and practices.

ŁUKASZ STANEK

Łukasz Stanek (b. 1976) is Lecturer at the Manchester Architecture Research Centre, at The University of Manchester in the UK. He authored *Henri Lefebvre on Space: Architecture, Urban Research, and the Production of Theory* (2011), and edited Lefebvre's unpublished book about architecture, *Toward an Architecture of Enjoyment* (2014). Stanek also studies the Cold War transfer of architecture from socialist countries to West Africa and the Middle East; he published the book *Postmodernism Is Almost All Right: Polish Architecture After Socialist Globalization* (2012), and edited an issue of *The Journal of Architecture* (2012) on this topic. Stanek taught at the ETH Zurich, Switzerland, and at the Harvard Graduate School of Design in the United States.

MANAR MOURSI

Manar Moursi (b. 1983) is the founder of Studio Meem, an interdisciplinary design and research studio. Her design work has been widely published and awarded. She received the ThyssenKrupp Elevator Architecture Award, the ArcVision Award, as well as the Red Dot and Good Design Awards. Her portfolio includes built projects in Kuwait and Egypt. In addition to her design practice, Moursi publishes regularly, participates in art exhibitions, and teaches. Her writings on urban issues have appeared in *Domus*, *Thresholds*, *Lunch*, *Mada*, *Cairobserver*, *the Funambulist* and *Egypt Independent*. Her book *Sidewalk Salon: 1001 Street Chairs of Cairo* co-authored with David Puig was published by Onomatopee in 2015.

MARISA BAPTISTA

Marisa I. Rodrigues Baptista (b. 1979) received her M. Arch. from Faculdade de Arquitectura – Universidade Técnica de Lisboa (2004, Portugal), and a Master of Arts in Aural and Visual Cultures from the Visual Cultures department at Goldsmiths, University of London (2014, UK). Architectural professional collaborations include OFIS, 4+arquitectos, and CasaGranturismo. Since 2010, she collaborates with the artist Clemens von Wedemeyer as exhibition project manager and designer. Her theoretical and artistic practice and research delves into cultural and political participation, representation and perception, approached through film, music, architecture, and art. Her artistic projects with Nuno Barreiras, under the moniker *rewotwint*, involve among others, sound and video installations, film, and video-essays. She is also co-founder of *plataforma download,* a cultural association dedicated to urban reconquering and cultural activism in Portugal, where she acts as curator, programmer, designer and artist-educator.

MICHAEL KUBO

Michael Kubo (b. 1978) is the Wyeth Fellow at the Center for Advanced Study in the Visual Arts, National Gallery of Art. He is a PhD candidate in History, Theory, and Criticism of Architecture at the Massachusetts Institute of Technology in the United States, where his work focuses on the rise and international extension of the architectural corporation after 1945. He was Associate Curator for *OfficeUS*, the U.S. Pavilion at the 14th International Architecture Exhibition at la Biennale di Venezia, and is co-author of *OfficeUS Atlas* (2015). Kubo is a director of pinkcomma gallery in Boston and co-author of *Heroic: Concrete Architecture and the New Boston* (2015).

NAJI MOUJAES

Naji Moujaes (b. 1972) is the founder of PAD10 and an award-winning architect. Moujaes was awarded 'Architects of Healing' Presidential Citation by the AIA Board of Directors, for the design of the World Trade Center Memorial Museum in New York City, and the recipient of the Young Architects Forum and the Emerging Voices awards from The Architectural League of New York. Moujaes conducted a workshop in collaboration with National Council for Culture, Arts and Letters and Docomomo on Kuwait Modern Heritage and participated at the 15th International Architecture Exhibition at la Biennale di Venezia – Kuwait Pavilion's 'Between East and West: A Gulf. Moujaes holds a Bachelor's of architecture from American University in Beirut (1996, Lebanon) and a M. Arch. from Southern California Institute of Architecture (1999, USA).

THORSTEN BOTZ-BORNSTEIN

Thorsten Botz-Bornstein (b. 1964), did his undergraduate studies in Paris, and received a PhD in philosophy from Oxford University (1993, UK). As a postdoctoral researcher based in Finland, he undertook research for four years on Russian formalism in Russia and the Baltic countries. He received a 'habilitation' from the EHESS in Paris (2000, France). He has been researching for three years in Japan on the Kyoto School, worked for the Center of Cognition of Hangzhou University in China, and as well at Tuskegee University in Alabama, USA. He is now Associate Professor of Philosophy at Gulf University for Science and Technology in Kuwait.

YANNIS KITANIS

Yannis Kitanis (b. 1983) is an architect based in Athens, Greece. He studied architecture at the University of Patras (2006) and at Harvard Graduate School of Design (2009). Kitanis has collaborated with the climate engineering firm TRANSSOLAR in Stuttgart, and has worked as the assistant of the artist Warren Neidich in Berlin, Germany. He also practiced as a project architect with Deca Architecture in Athens for numerous housing, leisure, and landscape projects across Europe. In 2015 he launched his personal practice dealing with installations, research, and architectural projects. Kitanis is currently teaching Architectural and Urban Design Studio at the University of Patras, Greece.